The
Devil's Bastard

For Judy,

Enjoy the escape!

Charlie Russell

BLUE DOORS

150 YEARS OF JESUIT EDUCATION
AT CANISIUS HIGH SCHOOL, 1870-2020

Paul Cumbo

CANISIUS HIGH SCHOOL

BUFFALO, NY

Canisius High School

1180 Delaware Avenue

Buffalo, NY 14209

www.canisiushigh.org

Ordering Information:

Quantity sales. Special discounts are available on quantity purchases by corporations, associations, and others. For details, contact Canisius High School at the address above. This book is also available for purchase online.

A note about images: Several images in this book contain scanned impressions of old, archived paper documents. The author has made efforts to modify the formatting so as to enhance the text to be as legible as possible. However, depending on the available printing resolution, small text contained in some of these images may be difficult to read in print editions of *Blue Doors*.

Blue Doors – 150 Years of Jesuit Education at Canisius High School, 1870-2020 / Cumbo, Paul J. —1st ed.

ISBN 9781688249752

Contents

Dedication

This book is dedicated to two pillars of CHS: Mr. Nicholas H. Kessler '28 and Rev. Ronald W. Sams, S.J., '46. Both committed their lives to Jesuit education, and both were inducted into the Alumni Hall of Fame in recognition of their outstanding contributions to education and their community. In addition, each of these men took great efforts to chronicle the history of this institution; as such, it is fair to say their work laid the foundation for this work.

Nicholas H. Kessler '28
A disciplined scholar, consummate
teacher, and loving father.

Rev. Ronald Sams, S.J., '46
A teacher, leader, pastor, and
lifelong servant of God.

The Prayer for Generosity

"LORD,
TEACH US TO BE GENEROUS;
TO SERVE YOU AS YOU DESERVE;
TO GIVE AND NOT TO COUNT THE COST;
TO FIGHT AND NOT TO HEED THE WOUNDS;
TO TOIL AND NOT TO SEEK FOR REST;
TO LABOR AND NOT TO ASK FOR REWARD;
SAVE KNOWING THAT WE ARE DOING YOUR WILL.
AMEN."

SAINT IGNATIUS LOYOLA

"Canisius Alma Mater"

CANISIUS, ALMA MATER,
THE GLORY OF THY NAME,
THY WISDOM STRONG WE SING AS LONG
AS MEMORIES REMAIN.

THY VOICE IS MIGHTY,
LINKING OUR YEARS,
MIGHTY THY MEMORIES
THROUGH HOPES, JOYS, AND FEARS.

CANISIUS, MIGHTY POWER,
THY SONS KEEP TRUE AND BOLD
THEIR LOVE FOR THY HONOR,
CANISIUS, BLUE AND GOLD.

FROM ARENA 1949

Saint Peter Canisius
Canonized by
Pope Pius XI
May 21, 1925

Dedication page of the 1925 *Arena* commemorating the year St. Peter Canisius was canonized. Source: CHS Archives.

Author's Note

I will begin with an admission—an apology, really.

I can't do the story of Canisius High School any real justice. It's too long, and it's too big. It's an estate of immeasurable value. Those of us who have had the privilege to be a part of it are the inheritors of that estate; likewise, we in turn are the ones charged with its stewardship for the next generation.

This book is part of my labor of stewardship. It is my attempt to preserve and promote the stories of so many who have realized that dream—moreover, it's an imperfect attempt to repay some of my own debt of gratitude for all Canisius High School has given me, my brothers, and my friends.

It was a calculated risk to commission me to undertake this project. Before our President, Father David Ciancimino, S.J., approached me, he must have considered whether or not an alumnus—let alone an employee—could be objective enough.

On the other hand, he knew the book would be written from the heart. Of my forty years, twenty-five have been spent as a student, coach, and/or teacher at one of two Jesuit high schools. My four brothers are also alumni (Tom '91, John '93, Peter '94, and David '00), which means Canisius was a significant part of my family's life—a combined twenty student-years from 1987-2000.

Early in this process, I realized that the most significant challenge would be deciding what this book was supposed to be. I had to figure out which book about Canisius High School *I* could write; this meant acknowledging the many I couldn't. This last thing was the most intimidating. There are so many stories that I *won't* be able to tell. There is simply too much to include. Put more simply: I'm going to disappoint some of you.

This work is not a patronizing exercise in self-aggrandizing, blue and gold chest-thumping. But neither is it a journalistic exposé full of institutional dirt-digging. Anyone who has been here a while knows there have been moments of shortsightedness. There have been casualties and disappointments, as is the case in any company. Sometimes, over the years, things haven't been fair. I haven't gone purposely looking for the bad times. I've lived enough of them to know that they are only part of the journey. They pass. The school has survived the toughest times because of people's generosity and sacrifice. Because of people's belief in what this place stands for.

Saint Ignatius included in his *Spiritual Exercises* guidance on the "presupposition," encouraging us to be patient with others with whom we disagree or whose behavior troubles us. He does not urge us to be naïve in assuming good intentions; rather, he asks us to avoid pre-judging one another's intentions—in other words, to listen and understand before responding, and correcting if necessary, lovingly. I have no doubt that across my years as both a student and teacher in these halls, I have been the beneficiary of this patient disposition more often than I have practiced it myself. I have tried to bear this principle in mind as I encounter, recall, and attempt to portray our history.

Early on in this endeavor, I began on a tack that would have involved considerably more detail regarding athletics, dramatics, et cetera. However, as I got deeper into the project, I realized it would have been unsustainable. There was simply too much to include while giving equitable focus to the many athletic and extracurricular traditions. I decided to limit my treatment, generally, to only some of the most noteworthy events. Even this attempt, I fear, will fall far short of some expectations. I challenge someone among my fellow alumni, or among the many devoted friends of the school, to take on an athletic history of CHS. There is more than enough material for a lengthy volume—in fact, there are teams whose history could easily comprise their own books.

This is not an academic journal, or an extended exegesis on Ignatian philosophy and Jesuit pedagogy. Better ones already exist. This being said, it's nearly impossible for me to separate entirely my lived experience as a career Ignatian educator from my thoughts as they pertain to Canisius High School. I would like to think that is an asset to this history, rather than a liability. Ultimately, the mission of Jesuit education is at the core of all that CHS does. Or, at least, it should be. I've told my students many times that I consider them foot soldiers in the global war on hopelessness. One challenge we issue to Jesuit-educated men is to channel hope. To accomplish this, we must channel hope ourselves while those young men are in our care. I'd like to think that in these pages there's some tribute paid to those who've done this so well, for so many of us, for so many years.

Finally, and importantly: *this is not a book about our alumni.* I wish to be clear on this. I am aware that many readers will be looking for just this type of profile. But like an adequate athletic history, this would demand an encyclopedic work of its own, and I challenge someone else to take that on. My focus is the institution as it existed for its students—not upon the men they became. My limited focus on alumni should take nothing away from the nearly immeasurable impact so many of these men have had upon our school, our city, our nation, and our world.

Well, if this book isn't any of those things, then what *is* it? My answer is simple: It's the best narrative history of Canisius High School that *I* could write. In a way, this is the same humble task to which a teacher is called. We do not teach our students alone. Our course does not comprise the whole of their education. This book offers a look at the past, an appreciation of the present, and a hopeful anticipation of the future. It is my sincere hope that along with knowledge of history, it will bring the Canisius community—especially my fellow alumni and colleagues—joy, fond remembrances, and an even deeper respect for the school that patiently embraced and lovingly formed so many of us as boys—with our "hearts linked."

Paul J. Cumbo '97
Buffalo, New York
June 2019

Paul J. Cumbo

"...On the strength of one
link in the cable, dependeth
the might of the chain..."
-Adm. RA Hopwood, R.N.
Much appreciation to Dad, Mom,
Family, Brian, Scott, Pete, JH
Nate, BPC, TPF, GMK, DSC & CHS

"Canisius Marching Song"
from **Arena** *1948*

Canisius! Canisius!
When the battle rages strong,
We'll cheer, men! We'll fight, men!
Though the struggle's hard and long.

With shoulder to shoulder
As Crusaders stout and bold,
We will pledge ourselves to conquer,
For Canisius Blue and Gold.

So, sing, men, and swing, men,
'Til the bands no longer play!
With arms linked, and hearts linked,
In our old Canisius way.

Forever, forever,
'Til the dying sunset's flame,
'Til the last, faint glowing ember,
Sing the glory of her name.

CHAPTER 1

Introduction: 150 Years of Jesuit Education in Buffalo

ONE MIGHT UNDERSTAND why the young men who file through Alumni Hall into the Canisius High School auditorium generally take little note of the thousands of faces in the class portraits. The intensity of adolescence puts a premium on the present moment. Certainly, it is difficult for the very young to appreciate the fleeting nature of time, even as they navigate its relentless currents. A cascade of more pressing concerns consumes the attention of the Canisius student: the Latin test, unfinished homework, an essay, the weekend's baseball game, or perhaps the electric anticipation of his first date.

Nonetheless, with each passage through that narrow corridor, the eyes of the past bear witness to the inevitability of the future. Thus, even on the first day, as hopeful, nervous boys shuffle awkwardly to their seats, shoulder-to-shoulder with strangers, they are hurtling toward that commencement. Their time together within these "hallowed halls" has already begun to diminish. And while they have no sense of this—how could they, after all—one might imagine the collective sentiments bestowed upon them by those thousands of alumni:

"Do well, son."

"Be yourself."

"Don't be afraid."

"Be careful, kid."

"Take care of each other."

"Enjoy every minute."

"Pray."

When that commencement day arrives four years later, some of their rank will have departed their company, either by choice or circumstance—occasionally, in tragedy. But most will pass through this hall again. Their shoulders—broader, now—will bump up against each other with pride and affection as they stride toward an end and a beginning. Beneath their white tuxedo jackets, many will wear a cross—a symbol of the faith, struggle, and commitment to which they've been called. Their confident voices will echo, a full octave deeper, in warm recollection, musings, and the sort of surprising, insightful wisdom that surfaces in moments of such consequential change. Later that evening, when the celebration has ended and the commotion has passed, Alumni Hall will be plunged again into silent darkness. A space will be made on the wall, and the new class's portrait will join the others. The exuberance of their youth—with all their hopes, dreams, fears, and joys—will be captured for posterity.

And so it has continued for a century and a half. Boys arrive and young men leave. The transformation is remarkable, arguably among the most significant of their lives. Canisius High School has likewise transformed over the past one hundred and fifty years, while paradoxically remaining unchanged in the most important ways.

This Book's Approach to CHS History

This work's title is an obvious reference to the Consistory building's main entrance, a signature feature of the Delaware Avenue campus to which the school moved in the late 1940s.[*] Thus, the main focus of this history is upon the years since that move. Obviously, however, that was not the beginning of the CHS story by any means.

Mr. Nicholas H. Kessler '28 was a longtime teacher and is a member of the Alumni Hall of Fame. During his postgraduate studies at Canisius College, he composed a history of Canisius High School that began with the early origins of the Jesuit mission in Buffalo and ended with the school's move to the new campus. Because Mr. Kessler's work provides a detailed and well-informed portrait of this early period of the school's history, it is included herein as a posthumous publication (with the permission of his daughter, Gretchen) and comprises our principal focus on those earlier years.

Not only is Mr. Kessler's work of excellent quality, but it is, itself, arguably an important *piece* of Canisius High School history. Indeed, it has been cited countless times in school publications and provides some of the only known documentation of the institution's early years. Conveniently, Kessler's history—written in 1948—covers, almost to the year, the first half of our *alma mater's* lifetime to date.

Therefore, it bears emphasizing that this book and its grateful author both owe a great debt to Nick Kessler. Certainly, the later years (1948-2020, roughly the second half of the school's history to date) comprise the main focus, but it is upon the foundation of his work that this more recent historical narrative is built.

Another consideration: given that the vast majority of living alumni attended the school on Delaware Avenue, focusing on these later years, on the new campus, provides a "living history" for readers today.

---

[*] Though the Blue Doors weren't blue back then. (Considerably more on this later.)

Jesuit Education in the 21st Century

This is not a book about the history of the Jesuit order. Certainly, any such history would be eminently difficult to contain in a single book. It is essential, however, to begin a history of Canisius High School with an informed look at contemporary Jesuit education at the "macro" level. Without this broader contextual understanding, one would be deprived of an informed appreciation of the scope and influence of Jesuit education as a global phenomenon. The buildings at 1180 Delaware, for all their uniqueness and fascinating history, are only a small part of a larger whole—a single outpost in a worldwide enterprise. When a student graduates from Canisius High School—or rather, when he enrolls—he joins the ranks of a very large community, indeed.

Despite the diversity of this community—it comprises a multitude of languages, cultures, ethnicities, and a vast geographic range—it is grounded fundamentally in a clear, unified mission under the banner of the Roman Catholic Church's largest religious order.

A Global Community

As of the publication of the 2016-2017 *Directory*, there were 80 Jesuit secondary and pre-secondary schools in the Jesuit Schools Network (JSN) in the United States alone.[1] Across the globe, these numbers expand. The organization Educate Magis, a collaboration of more localized networks, recently published a comprehensive map that has been distributed to apostolates across the world (see next page, or view the map in more detail online at www.educatemagis.org).

This map locates 805 Jesuit schools (including presecondary, secondary, and postsecondary). These institutions enroll approximately 780,000 students and employ nearly 37,000 staff members.[2]

Global Network of Jesuit Schools courtesy of Educate Magis. Available in high resolution at www.educatemagis.org).

Grounded in The Ignatian Tradition

Anyone familiar with the life of St. Ignatius knows that his is a quintessential conversion story. Alan G. McDougall's *Thoughts of St. Ignatius for Every Day of the Year* is a translation of *Scintillae Ignatianae ("Ignatian Sparks")*, a collection of Ignatius's aphorisms first translated and assembled by Hungarian Jesuit Fr. Gabriel Hevenesi in 1712. Patrick J. Ryan, S.J., of Fordham University, in his introduction to McDougall's work, tells us that the founder of the Jesuits was baptized Iñigo Lopez de Loyola and that "Iñigo aspired to engage in bold knightly deeds of derring-do, apparently hoping thereby to win the notice and approval of a lady of the highest nobility...."[3] This was the young Ignatius, possessed of a fiery, ambitious desire to do great things.

This brash youth, despite his own powerful momentum, experienced a collision with fate in the form of a cannonball. By shattering his leg during a battle at Pamplona in 1521, this projectile sent Iñigo on a vastly different trajectory. With a dearth of the romance and hero stories he'd always enjoyed within reach during his convalescence, he was limited to several accounts of the lives of saints. As Ryan explains, "Diverted from thoughts of fair ladies and knights in shining armor, the disabled Iñigo started to compare the inner reactions he used to have to the typical romances that had so enthralled him...with the new inner reactions he was having to the life of Christ and the lives of the saints."[4]

Thus began his conversion journey. Though the "cannonball moment" is often cited as the conversion moment, this interpretation is lacking. Though this injury precipitated the conversion, it is not the injury itself that converted him. Arguably, it was rather the (literal) change of pace and inherent limitations of convalescence that set the stage for such a radical change in his heart. Pain—physical and existential—played no small role in his development.

Among the most important steps for Ignatius was the embrace of formal higher education with renewed purpose. It's worth considering that this was an act of not unsubstantial humility, since he found himself in his thirties among adolescent classmates. The journey continued in the years to come, with Ignatius taking on his priestly vocation, building his "least company" of brother priests, and eventually establishing a very different kind of religious order within the Church. As Father Ryan explains,

Ignatius and his companions...evolved from a devout company of educated clergymen recently ordained to becoming a new and very different religious order of men. Previously, such religious orders had been mainly monastic...Stability of location...had significantly marked their foundations. Ignatius and his companions had a diametrically different vision of what the religious order they were founding would entail...The companions of Jesus, as they came to call themselves, dispersed almost immediately throughout Europe on various missions...."[5]

The Jesuits were, from the beginning, a missionary order with a peripatetic nature. This was reinforced even more powerfully in the journeys of Francis Xavier to the far reaches of southeast Asia by the middle of the sixteenth century.

A certain paradoxical nature emerges, when one considers the origins and early history of the Jesuits. On one hand, the order was born, arguably, from one man's spiritual conversion to genuine humility before God. (Notably, the organization took root *before* he was a priest.) On the other hand, the ambition of the enterprise—indeed, the courageous conviction to be of service—is striking in its confident boldness. Among Ignatius' most frequent turns of phrase, "All for the greater glory of God" appears no fewer than 367 times in his *Constitutions*.[6] Moreover, Ignatius emphasizes *action* in no uncertain terms, declaring in his *Contemplation on the Love of God*, that love ought to be shown more in deeds than in words.[7] He urges us to recognize God's living, active role in the world—not only dwelling in creation, but also working, always, in and through all of creation.[8]

The Jesuit school, then, carries forth this complex call. It is charged simultaneously with several things, some of which might appear, on the surface, at odds with one another. It is charged with the spiritual formation of students, engendering their recognition of God's living presence in the world around them and even within them. Likewise, it calls them to the highest standards of academic and intellectual excellence, positing that excellence of effort is, in fact, a means of glorifying God. Concurrently, however, a Jesuit education must call the student to an authentic humility embodied in openness to growth, love of the other, and a relentless commitment to justice for the poor and marginalized. This is no small feat.

Such an intricate tapestry of mission is daunting, but Ignatius's *Spiritual Exercises* provide some wonderful tools to engage it. Not the least of these is a methodology of prayer and reflection that encourages authentic discernment. Along with this is an implicit encouragement to the Jesuit educator: Patience is key. Indeed, the nature of Ignatian discernment and reflection calls for a humble patience. The voice of God is often quiet (1 Kings 19:11-13), requiring a determined, open mind to hear it.

One engaged in the work of Jesuit secondary education might readily make the comparison between the young Ignatius and the adolescent student of today: both are full of youthful idealism, motivated in no small part, perhaps, by the natural sort of ego-driven aspirations native to the age. Over time, however, circumstance, experience, reflection, and the teachings of others engage this young person in a life-pilgrimage. One of the most important elements of the Jesuit approach to formative education is *cura personalis*, or "care of the individual person." It is a call to all those in this enterprise to be attentive to the needs, desires, strengths, weaknesses, and aspirations of each student as he or she travels the pilgrim path. Along this journey, any number of small, seemingly inconsequential moments—perhaps helped along by a few more obviously consequential ones—combine to form a potential conversion experience. If the brief span of years between a freshman's entry through the Blue Doors and the senior's departure at Commencement seems too finite a space for such conversion to take place, we might consider that conversion is not so finite—rather, it is an ongoing experience. A journey that begins at fourteen or fifteen does not end at seventeen or eighteen. It is, however, a pilgrimage that for many young men has begun at 1180 Delaware Avenue.

A Dynamic Body: Reading the "Signs of the Times"

An enterprise dedicated to the formation and development of young men must embrace change—and must, itself, be open to change. Thus the pilgrimage analogy might well apply to the institution of Canisius High School itself. Just as students emerge transformed by the experiences they confront between induction as freshmen and commencement as seniors, so too does the school change with them—and most often, because of them. This fluidity and adaptability are not indicative of instability; rather, they are arguably vital elements of a resilient institution. Indeed, a pedagogical maxim of Ignatian education is to "meet students where they are." This doesn't mean arbitrary standards or succumbing to every cultural fluctuation. What it does mean is that in order to provide *cura personalis,* the Jesuit educator (and the Jesuit institution) must be attuned to the realities of the present. Without an ongoing willingness to do this, the institution will be less able to "reach" the students of a given era. Of equal importance, of course, is the institution's ability to teach in the context of the present—that is, what's going on in the world in which the students live. The leadership of Jesuit institutions has always embraced this principle. One leader, Rev. Pedro Arrupe, S.J., expressed the importance of this dynamism with particular eloquence—and resonance.

Rev. Pedro Arrupe, S.J., served as the 28th Superior General of the Jesuit order from 1965 to 1983. On July 31, 1975, Father Arrupe addressed the Tenth International Congress of Jesuit Alumni of Europe in Valencia, Spain. Offered ten years into his tenure as head of the Jesuits, and on the Feast of St. Ignatius, his reflective, incisive remarks issued a clarion call to alumni of Jesuit schools across the globe. The address was both a critical acknowledgment of apostolic complacency and an optimistic look at the future. Perhaps the most famous element of this address was near the beginning, wherein Arrupe coined what has become, essentially, the universal motto of Jesuit education: "men for others."

Today our prime educational objective must be to form men-and-women-for-others; men and women who will live not for themselves but for God and his Christ - for the God-man who lived and died for all the world; men and women

9

who cannot even conceive of love of God which does not include love for the least of their neighbors; men and women completely convinced that love of God which does not issue in justice for others is a farce.[9]

Of course, this language has been updated for the 21st century audience more than once. Foremost, "Men for Others" has become widely adapted to "Men and Women for Others." This change is reflective of the more diverse body of students, staff, and alumni who comprise the community of Jesuit education across the globe. More recently, the language has been updated further. It is now common to see "Men and Women For and With Others" on the logos and letterhead of Jesuit schools. While this updated language has taken on a certain unwieldy nature from a purely stylistic perspective, it certainly expresses the ethos of the collective more fully and accurately. While one can reasonably assume that Father Arrupe's original language carried the intention of inclusivity, one associated with Jesuit education can also safely assume that he would have welcomed this adaptation of his language. The evidence for that argument lies within the context of the 1973 address itself, where Arrupe called for adaptability and openness to growth among those apostolically engaged in the mission:

...despite our historical limitations and failures, there is something which lies at the very center of the Ignatian spirit, and which enables us to renew ourselves ceaselessly and thus to adapt ourselves to new situations as they arise.

What is this something? It is the spirit of constantly seeking the will of God. It is that sensitiveness to the Spirit which enables us to recognize where, in what direction, Christ is calling us at different periods of history, and to respond to that call...

This is not to lay any prideful claim to superior insight or intelligence. It is simply our heritage from the Spiritual Exercises of Saint Ignatius. For these Exercises are essentially a method enabling us to make very concrete decisions in accordance with God's will. It is a method that does not limit us to any particular option, but spreads out before us the whole range of practicable options in any given situation; opens up for us a sweeping vision embracing many possibilities, to the end that God himself, in all his tremendous original-ity, may trace out our path for us.

It is this "indifference," in the sense of lack of differentiation, this not being tied down to anything except God's will, that gives to the Society and to the men and women it has been privileged to educate what we may call their multi-faceted potential, their readiness for anything, any service that may be demanded of them by the signs of the times.[10]

Another key phrase, rooted in thought emerging from Vatican II, can be found in this excerpt of Arrupe's talk. That phrase, "the signs of the times," by which he meant the realities of a changing world, has become a touchpoint of great importance among the leadership of Jesuit aposto-lates across the globe. It refers to a dynamic versatility with the resilience to endure change and adapt to it, all the while remaining true and faithful to foundational principles.

It is this commitment to mission that has seen Canisius High School through its most difficult struggles. Some of these have been of a financial nature; others have to do with maintaining, when necessary, a truly coun-tercultural stance in the face of changing social norms. Still others involve betrayals of trust, such as the embezzlement of school funds by a former employee. But some of the most troubling moments in the school's his-tory, though they occurred decades ago in the 1950s and 1960s, have come to light only recently. The CHS community learned in January 2019, through a report released by the Northeast Province Jesuits, of credible allegations against two Jesuits who were assigned to Canisius High School at one time.

These revelations have given rise to a challenging period for the global Roman Catholic community. As a Catholic institution, Canisius acknowledges that these terrible incidents in its past are part of this broader issue of sexual abuse and impropriety encountered by the Church (and other institutions, as well). Acknowledging the past is important. Thus, it is with humble awareness of these moments that the school focuses on the present and future.

The history of Canisius High School is an institutional pilgrimage that has spanned a century and a half. In the course of that journey, there have come to pass innumerable "signs of the times." It is a testament to the institution's endurance—and the commitment of its faculty, staff, alumni, and benefactors—that it remains a vibrant cornerstone of education in the City of Buffalo.

Notes

[1] *Directory.* 2017. Jesuit Schools Network (JSN). Web publication. Accessed from the Internet March 30, 2017. www.jesuitschoolsnetwork.org

[2] Educate Magis. 2017. Accessed from the internet March 30, 2017. www.educatemagis.org

[3] Ryan, Patrick, S.J., Introduction to *Thoughts of St. Ignatius for Every Day of the Year*, a translation of a translation of *Scintillae Ignatianae ("Ignatian Sparks")*, a collection of Ignatius's aphorisms first translated and assembled by Hungarian Jesuit Fr. Gabriel Hevenesi in 1712 2006. Fordham University Press.

[4] *Ibid.* p. 3.

[5] *Ibid.* p 10.

[6] *Ibid.* p 15.

[7] *The Spiritual Exercises of St. Ignatius.* [230]. Quoted in *What Makes a Jesuit School Jesuit? The Relationship Between Jesuit Schools and the Society of Jesus. Distinguishing Criteria for Verifying the Jesuit Nature of Contemporary Schools.* 2007. The Jesuit Conference.

[8] *Ibid.* [235].

[9] "Men for Others." 1973. Arrupe, Pedro, S.J., Accessed from the Internet March 31, 2017. http://onlineministries.creighton.edu/CollaborativeMinistry/men-for-others.html

[10] *Ibid.*

CHAPTER 2

Nick Kessler: "Mr. Chips" and His History of CHS

THE BUFFALO EVENING NEWS, on Friday, April 6, 1973, ran a story by Karen Brady headlined "Canisius Will Honor School's Living Legend." The focus was Mr. Nicholas Kessler (CHS Class of 1928), "a quiet, unassuming man with white hair and dancing eyes," Brady wrote. "Known fondly by his students as 'Mr. Chips,' Mr. Kessler is that rare combination of the very old-fashioned and quite up-to-date teacher."[1]

Not long after Ms. Brady's article, a testimonial dinner was held to honor both Nicholas Kessler and longtime physical education teacher and coach John Barnes. (A later section of this book will focus on Coach Barnes.) In the evening's program, which contained a wide array of accolades and recognitions, including on behalf of the Bishop, County Executive, and Governor, was a brief biography penned by Dr. Jerome J.

Glauber. It recalls Kessler's early childhood: the ninth child born to a large family in Springville, N.Y., his proficiency as a student at St. Aloysius' Parochial School, and his eventual daily commute by train from Springville to 651 Washington Street to attend Canisius High. After graduating in 1928, he attended Canisius College until graduating in 1932 and began teaching at CHS: "In 1934 he began the career that steadily endeared him to thousands of the Blue and Gold family.... Teaching primarily the incoming Freshman classes, he exerted a special influence on the new students. As a layman, he became the link between these young men and the Jesuit faculty...."[2] This particular observation of Dr. Glauber's is quite astute—at a time when lay faculty were a tiny minority among their collared colleagues, it is understandable that a young layman might seem accessible and relatable to a population of adolescent boys. For this author, this invites reflection on the important role of the "Jesuit-lay collaborative" that has emerged as a touchpoint of Ignatian education in the 21st Century. Certainly, Nick Kessler was an early indicator of the potential success and vitality of such collaboration for mission. Indeed, for this author and fellow in the ranks of the "lay collaborative," there is a sense of kindred spirits in learning about the life of Mr. Kessler.

Dr. Glauber's biography recalls the interruption of Nick Kessler's postgraduate studies (which he pursued concurrently with his very full teaching schedule, including variously "Latin, Algebra, Ancient History, English, Religion, and Social Studies") by the call to arms in 1942. Kessler served "a four-year tour of duty with the U.S. Air Corps, serving in Iceland, England and Sweden in intelligence and code work (his work in Sweden supplying a chapter in one of Col. Bernt Balchen's books)."[3]

Kessler was married in 1954 to Margaret (Peg) Harmon, a secretary at CHS, and had a daughter, Gretchen (who would go on to a long and devoted career in Jesuit education, first at CHS and eventually as the founding Principal of the Regis Jesuit High School Girls' Division in Aurora, Colorado).

Among the laudatory items addressed in the testimonial dinner was a personal congratulatory letter from the Superior General of the Society of Jesus at the time, Rev. Pedro Arrupe, S.J., The letter read as follows:

Dear Mr. Kessler:

On this significant testimonial occasion, allow me to add my personal congratulations to those of so many of your associates and students who have gathered to applaud your long years of service and dedication to them and to Canisius High School as teacher, librarian, and registrar.

To these positions you have brought a sense of professionalism and self-dedication of which Canisius High School can be justly proud.

To the master teacher of Latin for so many years I say with gratitude: "Macte virtute, comes, sic itur ad astra!!" [Editorial translation: "Those who excel, thus reach the stars."]

Sincerely in Christ,
PEDRO ARRUPE, S.J.,
General of the Society of Jesus[4]

Mr. Russ White, among the longest-serving members of the Canisius faculty, taught chemistry from 1969 until his recent retirement in 2016. He echoed these sentiments. When asked about his recollections of Mr. Kessler, White had this to say:

Nick Kessler is probably as close as we're ever going to come to Mr. Chips. When I started at Canisius, I lived in Cheektowaga, and he lived a few blocks away. As you can imagine, we didn't have too much in common. He taught Latin, and was much older. At some point, he was taking some medication that prevented him from driving. So his wife approached me and asked if I'd be willing to drive him to work. I said fine. So, I drove him for a few months, maybe. We got to be pretty good friends. I really respected the man.

I recall after he passed away, we were at Gambit, and his wife was helping...We were down on the aud floor, and she mentioned that her house needed painting. I said, "We'll paint it!" Meaning, the faculty. Then I thought, "Oh, what did I just say?" Anyway, we waited for some decent weather. I don't know who bought the paint... pretty much the whole faculty showed up. We painted in a day. It made the Buffalo News.

NICHOLAS HENRY KESSLER

K. B. S. 1, 2, 3, 4; Sodality 1, 2, 3, 4; Consultor 1, 2; Class Vice-president 1, 2; Debate 2; Class Medal 1; Arena Representative 1, 2; Business Manager Dramatics 3, 4; Book Store 1, 2, 3, 4.

It was just a quartet of short years ago that Springville sent its favorite son to blazon its fair name mid the walls of Canisius. He was then a shy and quiet, rural youth, but through the years, Canisius and its environments have made him a dashing, smiling, champion of fellowship.

But to say that he only lived the happy-go-lucky side of life, would not be fair to him. On the contrary, he seemed to have his days all scheduled, part for fun, and part for work. And work he did. For whenever a question in Homer arose, Nick's notebook was sought as a reference by all.

Too, the bookstore has much to be thankful for, since Nick was its student manager during the past four years. We will never forget the recreation periods spent there, teasing him, boycotting him, and then teasing him some more, but we never could force a disgruntled note from his lips.

Above: From 1928 Arena. Below, undated print. Source: CHS Archives.

Fr. Rich Zanoni, S.J., had similar praise and warm memories of Mr. Kessler. During an interview for this book, he commented as follows:

I will tell you the most important thing. It was the first time I met Nick. I've told this to [his daughter] Gretchen many, many times...

In February, 1969, we had received our assignments already to go to our schools for Regency. For the first time, we were expected to go and visit our schools before we went there to work...

I tried to do a little homework. I was meeting faculty members. I knew that Nick Kessler had been here for a long

NICHOLAS H. KESSLER

time. So when I finally met him, I introduced myself, and asked a typical question, even though I already knew. I asked, you know, 'What do you teach here, Mr. Kessler?' And without hesitation he said, "I teach students. I teach young men. And I happen to teach them algebra and Latin."

Well, that really floored me. I said, "This is what a school is about. It's about teaching people, not about teaching subjects." And that was very, very important for me at that very moment, and it's become kind of my creed throughout all of my teaching career. That's what we are about. I really value that moment, and I go back to it frequently.[5]

Mr. Joseph Lucenti '73, who would eventually become a counselor, Admissions Director, long-time Dean of Students, and Assistant Principal of Canisius High School, spoke of Mr. Kessler with similar affection:

Nick Kessler was my homeroom teacher, my Latin teacher, and my Algebra teacher. And I could not have asked for a better foundation than to have probably one of the most classic teachers ever have me for three different classes daily.[6]

Fond remembrances of Mr. Kessler abound in the archives of Canisius High School. In his interview for *The Buffalo News,* he revealed some of what must have endeared him so much to students and colleagues alike—a remarkable sense of empathy and care:

I have a deep sympathy for the boys I teach today. They have so many problems. They have them from their parents, their teachers, their clerics—be they ministers, rabbis, or priests. I admire them, though, for weathering the storms as well as they do.[7]

This level of inter-generational solidarity is all the more significant considering that Kessler, whose teaching career was interrupted by his Army service during World War II, was no stranger to troubled times. The "Assistant Principal's Diary," kept by Father Lorenzo Reed, S.J., lamented Mr. Kessler's departure from an already "much depleted faculty."

> *December 30*   *a much-depleted faculty was further weakened Wednesday. by the loss of Nicholas H. Kessler, who was today inducted into the Army through Selective Service. His draft board never answered Mr. Reed's appeal.*

December 30 [1943] Wednesday. A much-depleted faculty was further weakened by the loss of Nicholas H. Kessler, who was today inducted into the Army through Selective Service. His draft board never answered Fr. Reed's appeal.[8]

That experience equipped Mr. Kessler to understand well some of the challenges facing the young men he taught in the late 1960s and early 1970s. The 1976 *Arena* was dedicated to him, with the inscription: "*Arena 1976* dedicates itself to the man who dedicated himself to Canisius...Nick Kessler."[9] Indeed, according to his daughter, Gretchen Kessler, his own wartime experience only deepened and broadened his concern for and understanding of his students.

He never should have been in the Army. He was the sole caregiver of his mother, he had spots on his lung...he was a teacher. So he had all these reasons that he shouldn't have ever been in the military, but they got him anyway. He spent those four years intercepting and translating messages, because he spoke a number of languages. I think he had a very different experience in the war than many other people did, since he wasn't in direct combat, but I think what it did was really open his mind to that part of our culture...to understanding what service meant. And obviously having students in future years go into different wars...there was a great compassion for that. I know that he stayed in touch with a number of students who were in wars after WWII, and he prayed for them all the time. I think it brought a newer level of compassion than he even had before.[10]

At Mr. Kessler's funeral in 1975, Rev. Robert Cregan, S.J., President of Canisius High School, offered the homily:

Like any good teacher, he did not teach Latin or Mathematics; he taught boys, he taught living people...There is nothing distant about what a great teacher does. The persons before him and with him mean everything to him...there are two other Latin words which I must mention, for they were mentioned to me by his friends in the last two days. They are words learned from him and not forgotten.

Photo Courtesy Gretchen Kessler

The first is 'porta,' the modal noun of the first declension, proudly recited for me yesterday by one of Canisius' not-so-young alumni. It is an eminently appropriate word, 'the gate.' Nick opened the gates of knowledge to so many, shaped their habits, instilled in them a love of learning, of accurate thinking and expression. Many of you have said that he launched you on the road which led you to further success. In that freshman class, he introduced you to wisdom. And he was himself the gate through which you passed to higher learning.

The second word recalled was 'amo,' the modal verb of the first conjugation. 'I love.' It sums up the meaning and value of Nick's life, as it does the life of every Christian. Nick had wisdom, dedication, integrity—but as St. Paul says, I can have all things but without love I am nothing. Because Nick did have love, his life meant something, and will continue to mean something for us. Love is the real mark of the following of Christ, the love that points to God and points outward to others. He had that. He lived it.[11]

Of course, perhaps the most intimate portrait of Mr. Kessler was offered by his daughter, Gretchen. Miss Kessler also taught for many years at Canisius, eventually serving as Assistant Principal. She departed midway through the 2002-2003 school year and headed to Aurora, Colorado, where she took on the role of Founding Principal of the Regis Jesuit High School Girls Division—a new "co-institutional" model of school wherein separate Boys' and Girls' Divisions operate on adjacent campuses. She offered an interview for this book in August 2017.

Dad died when I was eighteen, so, unfortunately as a teenager, I don't think I listened to his stories as much as I should have. But there are a couple things that always struck me. No matter where I went with him, he always ran into someone he knew from Canisius. I was always impressed as a kid by everybody who knew him, by the stories they told about his classroom, and it's truly what drew me to Jesuit education, was listening to the stories about him. Even when he died, at the wake, it was story after story after story about how Nick changed their lives. That Nick gave them the basics. The things that still serve them to the present day.

It's funny, because Nick was actually an introvert...I think like many teachers, we gain our energy alone, but we're very much on stage when we're in our classroom. You could just see Dad light up whenever he would run into his former students.

He was one of the first lay teachers, which I think, we just kind of assumed that lay teachers just absorbed what Jesuit education was and what it meant. Nowadays, I think we're a lot more intentional about making sure people understand and buy into Jesuit education. Dad lived it.

He had ups and downs over the years. I remember him talking...It must have been the early seventies when the Principal wanted to knock out classroom walls and have open classrooms. Dad was just horrified. He didn't believe that was Jesuit education, or best for the kids. He struggled through those years, along with the financial ups and downs. A lot of things over the forty-something years he was there weighed heavily on him at times, especially when there was an administrator whom he didn't think understood the school. But the tough times were few and far between. The majority of the time, he was just there to teach the kids. To have a relationship with them. That's where his joy came from.

She [my mom] has a fascinating story. She moved from Detroit to Buffalo right before freshman year of high school and attended Holy Angels Academy. She went back to Detroit to Mary Grove College and was going to become a nun, but returned to Buffalo to take care of her mom after her father died. His dad was the head of the Chevy River Road plant, and she got a job after college there, and hated it. She went to St. Michael's Church and did the Novena of Grace. She prayed that she'd find another job that she could feel fulfilled in. She applied for a blind ad in the paper and it was for the secretary to the Principal of Canisius High School. So, she applied, was hired, and worked there for fourteen years. She left only when she was pregnant with me. She met my dad there.

He retired, and he and my mom went on a trip to Spain for a couple of weeks. It was a great time in his life, but it was very short. It was November when we took him to the emergency room. He'd had three days where he couldn't swallow. It turned out that he had stomach cancer, and that it had spread to his liver. He was in the hospital for six weeks, and then died on December 12 of 1975. So, he didn't get to live too long after he retired. But I will say those last few years he worked were when he and mom and I traveled a lot. We went to Mexico when I was in sixth grade, and we did a seven-countries-in twenty-one-days tour in eighth grade. We went to Europe a couple of times. We went to England and met the family he lived with during the war, and we went to Sweden and visited all the places he saw, too. I'm so glad we did those things, because had we waited until he retired, we never would have done that...The [travel] bug bit me, and that's part of my fascination with language, was going to all those different countries, and everyone speaking different languages.[12]

As the last chapter explained, Nick's 1948 Master's Thesis, entitled *The History of Canisius High School*, has long served as the "go-to" reference point for inquiries about the school's past. It has been an invaluable resource to this author, and it deserves to be incorporated into—rather than simply referenced—in this updated history. Thus, with the blessing and permission of his daughter, Mr. Kessler's history comprises the following three chapters. The work remains generally unchanged with the exception of a few minor corrections and the addition of some corresponding images.

Those alumni fortunate enough to have had Mr. Kessler in class at some point during his long tenure at Canisius High School will, no doubt, hear his kind, enthusiastic voice echoing herein.

Nick Kessler '28 with his daughter, Gretchen, in the CHS parking lot. Undated photo provided by Gretchen.

Notes

[1] Brady, Karen. "Canisius Will Honor School's Living Legend." *The Buffalo Evening News*. April 6, 1973.

[2] John Barnes and Nick Kessler Testimonial Dinner Program, May 8, 1973.

[3] *Ibid.*

[4] *Ibid.*

[5] Rev. Richard Zanoni, S.J., Interview with the author. January 27, 2017.

[6] Joseph Lucenti. Interview with the author. December 21, 2016.

[7] Brady, Karen. "Canisius Will Honor School's Living Legend." *The Buffalo Evening News*. April 6, 1973.

[8] "The Academic Diary of the Principal of Canisius High School, August 1941 – September 1943." Kept by Rev. Lorenzo Reed, S.J., Principal. CHS Archives.

[9] *Arena.*

[10] Interview with Gretchen Kessler. Regis Jesuit High School. Aurora, CO. August 22, 2017.

[11] Canisius High School Faculty *Book of Remembrance*. 1975 entry by Gretchen Kessler.

[12] Interview with Gretchen Kessler. Regis Jesuit High School. Aurora, CO. August 22, 2017.

CHAPTER 3

The Kessler History, Part I: The Buffalo Mission & The Founding of Canisius

The History of Canisius High School
June 1948
Nicholas H. Kessler

Table of Contents

Preface

List of Tables

Preface

Although Canisius College and Canisius High School are celebrating their seventy-eighth birthdays this year, a complete and detailed history of neither has ever been written. This work should under no circumstances be considered as such. It is rather a scratching of the surface, so to speak, of a formidable task yet to be done. Of necessity, the recounting of the history of the High School and College are one and the same up to the year 1912. Both were quartered in the same building until 1912, had the same faculty, and the same administrators. Beyond the period of 1912, no attempt is made in this brief work to continue the history of the College.

The author is deeply indebted to the Very Rev. James J. Redmond, S.J., present President of Canisius High School, for his many kindnesses and especially for his gracious permission to use the Woodstock Letters, a private publication of the Society of Jesus. Without this work, many of the facts listed in this history would not have been available.

I. Background: The Buffalo Mission

Long before the founding of the Diocese of Buffalo in 1847, Jesuit Missionaries had visited various sections of New York State. Well known to all are the labors of Isaac Jogues and his companions in this State, and their eventual martyrdom at the hands of the very Indians to whom they attempted to bring the word of God. Death has never deterred these intrepid soldiers of Ignatius from carrying out the Divine Mission to preach the gospel to all nations. Many followed in the footsteps of Isaac Jogues in bringing the word of God to the inhabitants of New York State. Many of them were German and French Catholics. Their needs had to be met, so at an early date we find Jesuit Missionaries in the Buffalo area.

"The diocese of Buffalo was established on 23 April 1847 by Pope Pius IX. Very Rev. John Timon, then Visitor of the Congregation of the Mission in this country, was named the first Bishop of Buffalo."[1] He was consecrated in New York City on 17 October 1847. Various histories of the Diocese record the innumerable problems that beset this esteemed Bishop. From a small hamlet, Buffalo had grown to a city of considerable size. Because of this rapid growth there was demand for more schools and churches. In 1848 two Jesuit Missionaries, the first members of the Society of Jesus since the founding of the Diocese, came to Buffalo at the request of Bishop Timon. These two priests, the Rev. Bernard Fritsch, S.J., and the Rev. J. Fruzzini, came from the Mission of Upper Canada, the land of Jesuit Apostles and Martyrs.[2] Shortly after their arrival they conducted a mission at St. Louis Church at the request of Bishop Timon in an attempt to restore the disrupted peace of that parish. The purpose of this mission, however, was not realized—but for this they were not to blame. A few months later we find these same Jesuit Fathers at Williamsville, where they made their headquarters for several years.[3] From there they ministered to the Catholic populace in the districts of Transit, Pendleton, Elysville, and Tonawanda.[4]

In 1851 Bishop Timon made another attempt to solve the difficulties of St. Louis Church. Another retreat and mission was given by the Jesuit Fathers but a satisfactory settlement was not reached. St. Louis Church was finally interdicted. In order to provide for the German element of the Church, we find the Jesuit Fathers in this very same year saying mass for them in the basement of St. Peter's Church, which was then located at the corner of Washington and Clinton Streets, now the site of the Buffalo Public Library.

Bishop Timon had purchased a part of what was then called "Squire's Lot," a piece of property then belonging to Mr. Miles P. Squire and located on Washington Street north of Chippewa. Here he had intended to build his cathedral. The fact that the Germans needed a parish impelled him to offer this site to the Jesuits for a nominal sum, on the condition that they should build there a college for the education of youth and a church for the Germans. Herein lies the origin of St. Michael's Church, first built in 1852, and rebuilt in 1861, and the origin of Canisius College and Canisius High School.[5] Part of the south wing of the old High School Building at 651 Washington Street and the present St. Michael's Church stand on that property.

From its inception, Buffalo had been a part of the New York-Canadian Mission of the Society of Jesus. At the same time this Mission was under the jurisdiction of the French Provincial. Many of the early Jesuit fathers stationed in Buffalo were sent from various stations in Canada and New York City. The fathers of the German Province had mentioned to the Very Rev. Ferdinand Coosemans, S.J., Provincial of the Missouri Province, while he was in Rome in the summer of 1867, the possibility of organizing a school in the United States. At the time, it failed to gain Father Coosemans' sympathy. However, upon his return to the United States, he discussed the matter with father James Perron, S.J., Superior of the New York-Canadian Mission. Father Perron favored it because his men were already overburdened with work in the big centers of population along the Atlantic seaboard. At the conclusion of the conference Father Coosemans resolved to lend his support to this project. As he saw the matter the Church had much to gain if the German Jesuits were enabled to open residences of their own in America, dependent on their own province of Germany. Upon his return to St. Louis he laid the matter before his consultors on November 19, 1867. They expressed their approval and decided that the territory of the projected mission should be, "The Lake Region from the City of Buffalo to the State of Wisconsin."[6] This decision was then communicated to the Very Rev. Peter Beckx, General of the Society in Rome. Upon reading this communication the General did not render a decision, but reserved it for more mature consideration.

Father Peter Spicher arrived in the United States on September 18, 1868. After a conference call with Father Perron, he headed for St. Louis to confer with Father Coosemans, from whom he received excellent cooperation and many suggestions. As a result of these conferences the Buffalo Mission was finally established in 1869, and within a year had opened residences in Buffalo and Toledo. However, it was not until midsummer of 1871 that the territorial limits were finally determined upon. Upon the advice of Father Beckx, the Jesuit General, that anything like an "imperium in imperio" was to be avoided, it was agreed to allow the Buffalo Mission, the Dioceses of Cleveland, Detroit, and also, if the Buffalo Mission desired, the whole State of Wisconsin. Finally, at a meeting at Woodstock College, Woodstock, Maryland on August 3, 1871, which was attended by the Provincials of Maryland and Missouri, and the ex-Provincials, Fathers Coosemans and Perron, the definite jurisdictional limits of the Buffalo Mission were agreed upon. It was determined that it would include the dioceses of Buffalo, Erie, Fort Wayne, Rochester, St. Paul, LaCrosse, Green Bay, and one station in Milwaukee, or else in Racine or Madison. This agreement of all the superiors present was later ratified by Father General Beckx.[7]

By 1888, eighteen years after its founding and eighteen years before its dissolution, the "Missio Germanica Americae Septentrionalis" consisted of the following: in New York State, the Churches of St. Ann's and St. Michael's in Buffalo, and Canisius College; in Ohio, the College of St. Ignatius in Cleveland and St. Mary's Church in Toledo; in Wisconsin, the College of the Sacred Heart, Prairie du Chien; in Iowa, St. John's Church, at Burlington; in Minnesota, the Church of St. Peter and Paul, at Mankota; in Dakota, the St. Francis Mission and the Mission of the Holy Rosary.[8]

This mission continued its glorious history until September 1, 1907, when it was dissolved by a decree of the Very Rev. Father Wernz, its territory and personnel being divided between the Provinces of Maryland-New York and Missouri.

To the reader all this matter pertaining to the establishment of the Buffalo Mission may seem irrelevant. It is, on the contrary, very important; for it has a great bearing on the understanding of Canisius in its formative years. The presence of compulsory German in the curriculum, the strict discipline, and the thoroughness of the training are a reflection of the German Fathers who made up the majority of the faculty from the years 1870 until 1907, the period when Buffalo was a mission of the German Province.[9] What is more Buffalo may never have seen such illustrious men of the Society as Fathers Henry Behrens, Martin Port, J. Ming, Anthony Guggenberger, Frederick Bunse, Francis Betten, and Ludwig Bonvin, who gave much to the sterling character of early Canisius students.

II. The Founding of Canisius College and Canisius High School

At the same time, Father Coosemans had written Father Roder, Provincial of the German Province, suggesting that he seek the General's approval to establish a mission in the United States. Father Roder acted on this advice without delay. Not long afterward he received the General's approval so he immediately dispatched Father Peter Spicher, as his personal representative, to go to the United States to organize the contemplated mission.

In the previous chapter we saw how the Jesuits residing in Buffalo were first under the jurisdiction of the New York-Canadian Mission, and how in 1869 it became a mission of the German Province. As a result the greater number of the Jesuits sent to Buffalo from 1869 were predominantly of German Extraction. These German Fathers were most intent

upon carrying out the wishes of the Rt. Rev. Bishop Timon to found a
school based upon the famous "Ratio Studiorum." Previous attempts were
made in this direction. In November of 1855 a class in Latin was started
at St. Michael's. It contained eight students, the names of six having been
recorded in the Jesuit diaries. They were Messers. Zimmerman, Rossbach,
Fleischmann, Peter Schmidt, and the two Fuell brothers. However, the
school did not prosper and was soon to be abandoned.[10]

We are told that in 1857 two young men, Messers. Chase and Bettinger, were taught philosophy by Father Charles Jannsen.[11] In April,
1857, Fr. Huss, S.J., Superior of the New York-Canadian Mission, came to
Buffalo for a short stay, his purpose being to draw up plans for a college
building. No definite action was taken, however, toward the construction,
either on this visit or on his second one in September when he was accompanied by Fr. Larkin of St. Francis Xavier's College, New York. Several conferences were held with Bishop Timon during both visits. The
matter was again taken up in October when Fr. Larkin had been sum-
moned from New York for a second consultation on the projected enterprise.[12]

During the following year, 1858, Fr. Lucas Caveng, the first pastor of
St. Michael's Church, had bought as a possible site for the new college a
large plot of land which at that time was on the outskirts of the city. This
too had to be abandoned. Instead, the large parish of St. Ann's was started
there.[13]

In 1863, Father Joseph Durthaller was made pastor of St. Michael's
Church. He had taught in the Society's schools in Europe. Numbered
among his students was the celebrated artist, Gustave Dore. The revolution of 1848 and its consequent expulsion of the Jesuits from France
drove him to America. He labored for a while in the Indian missions of
Canada. Poor health forced him to St. Francis Xavier's College in New
York. Eventually, he became President of the College, and while in that
office built the new College and secured its charter from the Board of Regents. While Pastor of St. Michael's Church he built the present edifice on
Washington Street.

In the summer of 1866 two young men, Nelson Baker and Daniel
Walsh, consulted him about entering the priesthood.[14] Always generous

with his time, Father Durthaller designated two evenings a week when he would be at their service. On each occasion, he spent fully two hours teaching them with all the ardor and skill one might use in addressing a large body of students. When his duties called him elsewhere Father Fritsch taught the boys Latin. According to the account of one of these men, Daniel Walsh, even at this time Father Durthaller was aware that Buffalo would become a large city and that at no distant date there would be a College under the shadow of St. Michael's Church, and that he and Nelson Baker would be its first students.[15] Both later became priests of the Diocese of Buffalo. Father Daniel Walsh became Rector of the Church of the Nativity while Father Nelson Baker built the famous institutions in Lackawanna which today bear his name and the beautiful Basilica of Our Lady of Victory. Later he became Vicar General of the Diocese.

In 1870 the supreme effort was made to establish a college. Though it met with very little sympathy on the part of the citizens of Buffalo and encountered difficulties of every description, the Jesuit Fathers resolved that it would be a success. With such determination such a project could not fail. Hence, the new school was opened on September 5, 1870. Your author has found many conflicting accounts of the day that Canisius opened. As a verification for this opening date an advertisement which appeared in the educational section of the *Buffalo Daily Courier* on September 1, 1870 is here quoted in full:

German – English
Canisius College of the Society of Jesus at St. Michael's Church, Buffalo, N.Y.

We beg leave to call your attention to our College which will be opened September 5th. With a view of satisfying a want long felt in this large city, it is our purpose to offer the advantages of a thorough Classical and Commercial education by establishing a Day-College into which boys who have passed through an ordinary elementary course will be admitted. Parents and guardians will readily appreciate the facilities thus afforded them, in giving their children an opportunity of fitting themselves to the pursuit of higher intellectual and business life without sending them away from home and incurring expenses beyond the means of a large and respectable portion of our

34

community. The College will, in proper time, acquire the privilege of confer-
ring degrees on those who graduate at the institution. The College will be con-
ducted by members of the Society of Jesus, and every care will be bestowed
upon the moral training of those committed to their charge, the system of ed-
ucation being firm, yet paternal and mild.

The College terms payable half yearly in advance are the following: Classical
Course, including the German language, $50; Commercial Course, including
the German Language, $50.

N.B. The latter course comprises too, all branches of a thorough English edu-
cation. Books and stationary the students will provide for themselves.

The opening of the yearly session will take place and end about commence-
ment of July with the usual holidays of Christmas and Easter.

Most respectfully,
E. A. Reiter, S.J., President[16]

The archives of Canisius College and High School reveal no information why the name Canisius was chosen by the early Jesuit Fathers.
Thus, it befalls your author to conjecture why that name was selected. At
the same time, he believes the reasons he gives do not fall very short of
being the correct ones. St. Peter Canisius was one of the pioneer Jesuits
having joined the order three years after its organization in 1540. He was
the first Jesuit writer, and completed the first book ever produced by any
member of the order. He founded six Colleges of the Society at Ingolstadt,
Prague, Munich, Innsbruck, Doellinger, and Frieburg. Many schools of a
lower level than College were started by him. He was a great figure in the
Council of Trent. He was the first German Jesuit and the first Provincial
of the Upper Rhine. At the time when Canisius was founded, Peter Canisius had been called Blessed by the Church and the cause was being advanced for his canonization. By this time, he had also gained the
appellation—the Second Apostle of Germany. Education was always his
greatest interest. Add to all these reasons the fact that Buffalo was the first

German Mission of the Society in America, under the supervision of a German Provincial, that most of the Fathers sent here were born in Germany, and had been educated or taught at schools founded by Canisius. With such compelling evidence the author considers it a fair conclusion that these are the reasons why the name Canisius was selected by the Jesuit Fathers for their new college in Buffalo.

As we saw from the advertisement appearing above, Father Ernest A. Reiter, S.J., was the first president of Canisius. Shortly after its opening he was succeeded in this capacity by the Rev. William Becker, S.J., who is listed in many of the Jesuit Archives as the first president and founder of Canisius. At any rate, it was due to the combined zeal of these two men that a small two-story building then occupied by Mrs. Haefner, standing on Ellicott Street on the site of the present St. Michael's School, was purchased and remodeled into a temporary college.[17] The first floor had been used as a store, in the rear of which was a workshop. Both places were changed into classrooms, the store to be occupied by the students of the Latin course, which was expected to be the larger, and the workshop by the Commercial Course. The Fathers were located in the rooms on the second floor.

CANISIUS 1870 - 1872

Line drawing of the Ellicott Street school by Robert Ziemer in the 1946 *Arena* Yearbook. Source: CHS Archives. (Image added; not in original Kessler history.)

In the second year, the Fathers had to surrender their rooms to the increasing number of Latin students who occupied the entire second floor, the Commercial students occupying the two rooms below. The rooms were very small, about 15 x 25 feet each, and badly heated. Records reveal that winter snows often blew through the seams and cracks of the windows because they were in such bad condition. During severe storms the writing on the blackboards was obliterated by the winter snows. However, the hardy students of those days didn't complain, for they were unspoiled as yet by our modern luxuries. On opening day, September 5, 1870, there were twenty day scholars and five boarders,[18] this number increasing to thirty-four during the first year. The five boarders were from Boston and came to Buffalo with Father Reiter. They were Messers. Joseph L. Ecker, John Berg, Alys Ochs, Henry Dirksmeier, and John Kormann. Later College records show that Mr. Ecker became organist and choir director of Trinity Church in Boston where he remained for twenty-five years.[19] The names of the first day-scholars have been preserved for us by Mr. Anthony Gerhard, S.J., the first teacher of the Commercial Course. Since no catalogue was published in those days, in fact until the year 1873-74, it is considered of great historical value that these names be listed here. They were: George Agler, Anthony Behringer, James Cronyn, Eugene Fredericks, Aloys Groell of Cheektowaga, John Hiple, Peter Jordin, John Knickenberg, Francis Metzen, William Mullenhoff, Joseph Ott, Maurice Vaughn, Anthony Vollmar of Elysville, Michael Wittmann, and Andrew Wutz, all of whom were students in the Latin Course. In the Commerical Course were Charles Bawl, Albert Bettinger, Edward Dreher, Francis Cebhard, Adam Glasser, Albert Kraus, Jacob Lang, Peter Messner, Alphonsus Meyer, Francis Rieman, John Schwartz, John Spies, William Bernard Vaugh, Albert Widrich, and Francis Zenner.[20] The first boy who entered the College on the day that it was opened was Mr. Jacob Lang, who was later to become an outstanding citizen of Buffalo. He was met at the door that morning by Brother Philip Schneider who had come to Buffalo in 1868. He it was who lent a helping hand in the building of St. Michael's Parochial School on Ellicott Street, and of the central portion of Canisius College on Washington Street.[21] Typical of the Jesuit system of education that the school year should start on a spiritual note the boys attended 8 o'clock Mass at St. Michael's Church. After Mass, they were brought back to the school by their future professor, Fr. Henry Knappmeyer. As an official opening of the school year Father Knappmeyer wrote on the blackboard the Jesuit Motto – A.M.D.G. Next, he wrote the 'Pater Noster' and the 'Ave Maria' in Latin on the board with the instruction to memorize them for the following day. Thus, we have the first home task ever given to a Canisius student.[22] Your author as a student sixty-six years later was given the same assignment his first day in school.

The boarders at Canisius during the first semester lived with various families in the city until Christmas, when they took up lodging in a house rented by the Jesuit Fathers on Ellicott Street. One of the Fathers lived with them as prefect. Finally, they moved to Goodell Street where the first music teacher at Canisius took charge of them.

During the first year Fr. Henry Knappmeyer was Professor of the Latin Class; Mr. Anthony Gernard, S.J., a scholastic from New York, taught the Commercial Class. Discipline was very severe under Fr. Knappmeyer, yet he was beloved by his pupils.

The boys were obliged even in their first year to make a three days' retreat, another characteristic religious practice at every Jesuit school. The boys religiously observed silence during these three days, at the end of which they were commended by Fr. Knappmeyer for their good behavior and awarded a free day.

The first commencement was held on June 30, 1871. Many outsiders were present besides the parents of the boys. Obviously, there were no graduates, the first commencement being only the awarding of honors for the first year of the school's existence. The audience seemed to get a good deal of entertainment out of the exercise and applauded the young participants very liberally. Immediately after the exercises Mr. Gerhard, S.J., left for New York City.[23]

Classes were resumed on September 4, 1871 with sixty boys in attendance, of whom eighteen were boarders. Father Knappmeyer and Father F.X. Delhez, S.J., were the teachers in the Latin Course, while the Commercial Classes were in charge of Mr. Benedict Gouldner, S.J., Mr.

Fitzgerald, who came to Canisius to pursue a course of Philosophy, was added to the teaching staff, on September 8, 1971.[24] Among the boarders of '71 was John I. Zahm, who was later to become President of the College. The accommodations of the boarders at Goodell Street became entirely insufficient during the course of the year and so room was made for them in the residence of the Father in the back of the old St. Michael's Church. Fr. Delhez became prefect of the boarders. To secure more space a basement was excavated in which Brother Schneider figured prominently. This basement was used for the Boys' dining room and parlors. Besides this extension, the room of one of the Fathers was changed into a study hall and the attic was transformed into a dormitory. But even these accommodations could only be temporary and it became necessary to make plans for a large separate structure for the use of the students.

III. The Years of Father Behrens and Father Port: 1872-1883

In April of 1872 a new Catholic paper in English started publication in Buffalo. It was entitled the *Catholic Union*. Others had preceded it, in fact the *Buffalo Catholic Sentinel* made its appearance shortly after the inception of the Diocese of Buffalo, but its existence was brief and few copies are now in existence. Your author was of the opinion that the *Catholic Union* would be an excellent source of information for these early years of Canisius but, after examining numerous copies, he was sorely disappointed. Possibly the German papers published at this period carried the news about Canisius.

In one copy of the *Catholic Union* for the month of August, 1872, there was a letter to the editor in which the President of the College included the following information:

At present the course at Canisius consists of a complete classical course (at present consisting of three classes), a study of German a necessity, and includes a complete commercial education in its curriculum. It commenced in September, 1870 with about a score of students, it received seventy last year and expects to more than double that in the coming academic year. The new college building is to be opened in September of this year. The staff of instructors consists, at present, of six professors with their assistants, and will be increased as occasion will require.

With completion of the new building the College will be able to afford construction to about 250 students, though not more than 40 or 50 boarders can be received.

The full course of study at this College embraces six years in the classical course and three years in the commercial and scientific courses. This ensures thoroughness whether it be in the department of arts, of philosophy, or of industrial pursuits.[25]

Although this letter was unsigned we may be sure that it was written by the Rev. William Becker, S.J., The Rev. Henry Behrens, S.J., who succeeded Father Becker as President, did not arrive in Buffalo until December 14, 1872, and was not appointed President of Canisius College until December 22, 1872.

To the Rev. William Becker goes the credit for having the courage to erect the first building of the new Canisius College. Plans were drawn up by John Wild and Florian Huss to occupy the site of the girls' play-room on Washington Street. Along the rest of the street was a number of lots, only a few of which belonged to the Jesuits. The Scheres, whose son was graduated from Canisius, became a priest, and later pastor of Our Lady Help of Christians at Cheektowaga, had their home in a lot now occupied by the central portion of the old building at 651 Washington Street.[26] Early in the winter of 1871 ground was broken along Washington Street for the new building. The first stones were brought in on February 11, 1872 and work was begun a few months later.[27] This was one school in which the boys demonstrated a keen interest. Stories are told of how they saved pieces of the building stones as souvenirs and some even mailed them home to their parents. In contrast to present day construction, the work progressed rapidly so that by May 5, 1872, everything was in readiness for the laying of the cornerstone.[28] In the absence of Bishop Ryan, the ceremony was performed by the Rev. Edward Kelly of the Cathedral staff. An immense crowd of people was present to witness the blessing. Various Catholic societies in the city sent delegations, while those of St. Michael and Blessed Canisius were present in a body. However, there was a scarcity of city officials, though they had been sent special invitations. A discourse in English was given by the Rev. Edward Quigley, while one in German was delivered by the Rev. William Becker, S.J., the President.

The red brick structure rose rapidly so that by the end of June it was covered by a French roof. The structure was 103 feet long, 50 feet wide, and 70 feet high. It consisted of four stories, the first and second being used for classrooms, the third was one large hall extending over the entire building and used as a study hall, while the fourth floor contained the dormitories for the boarders. The third-floor study hall later became Alumni Hall and at the present time houses the library. This edifice erected in 1872 forms the central portion of the present building at 651 Washington Street. It is little changed in appearance from that day. When vacation time arrived in the summer of 1872, many of the students joined the Jesuit lay brothers in finishing the interior of the building. Brother Schneider, who had greeted the first student to enter Canisius, supervised much of the work. John L. Schwartz, one of the first day scholars at Canisius, later Chairman of the building fund committee for the new Canisius College at Main and Jefferson, was the right-hand man of Brother Schneider. The students eagerly pitched into such tasks as scrubbing, painting, varnishing and moving furniture.

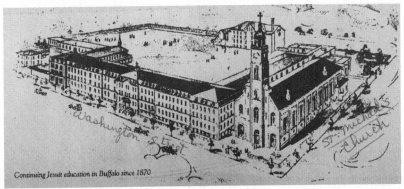

Continuing Jesuit education in Buffalo since 1870

Depiction of the Washington Street Campus and St. Michael's Church from CHS Archives. Original source unknown. Handwritten notes by

Rev. Ron Sams, S.J., '46. (Image added; did not appear in original Kessler History.)

When the new scholastic year began in the Fall of 1872, all the classes were transferred to the new building. On Thanksgiving Day of 1872, it was solemnly blessed by Bishop Ryan and, when the days of November had gone the last workingman had left the building. In the course of ten months the first building of the new Canisius College in Buffalo was completed.

For the third time within three years Canisius was to have a new President. Fr. William Becker, S.J., who had served only two years, returned to his native Germany. A few years later he returned to the United States, serving at Prairie du Chien, Wisconsin, Burlington, Toledo, and Cleveland, until he finally returned to Buffalo to end his days at St. Ann's Church on January 22, 1899. He was succeeded as President of Canisius by the Rev. Henry Behrens, S.J., whose life story reads much like that of a legendary hero. He was born on December 10, 1815 at Munstadt, Hanover, in the Diocese of Hildesheim. He was ordained a priest of the Society of Jesus on August 7, 1842. Up to 1847 he was a professor of mathematics and general Prefect at the College of Frieburg in Switzerland, which was founded by St. Peter Canisius in 1580. When the Sonderbund War against Catholics broke out in the year 1847, Father Behrens was spiritual father of the scholastics at the College. Since he was very influential in the life of Freiburg, he knew his life was in danger. Before the approach of the hostile troops, he had packed up in cases objects of value, such as chalices, church furnishings, rare volumes from the library, and had marked them for a definite destination. The scholastics he provided with civilian clothes. The enemy troops arrived sooner than expected so Father Behrens consumed the Sacred Hosts to save them from outrage. Soon the revolutionaries swarmed over the building, seizing and looting. Suddenly Father Behrens appeared, dressed in the uniform of a superior officer of the revolutionaries, and shouted orders to the looting soldiers to bring the cases to a spot where he deemed they would be safe. The ruse worked perfectly. For Father Behrens not only saved himself and the scholastics but also the most precious valuables of the college, amongst them many relics of St. Peter Canisius. Following this incident more than two hundred Jesuits were expelled from Switzerland.

In the following year the Provincial, Father Minoux, commissioned Father Behrens to escort a group of forty-two Jesuits, mostly scholastics, to America, and establish a house for them, where they might continue their studies. They crossed the Atlantic in a sailing vessel manned by a motley crew. The trip took forty-five days, during which the store of food was depleted, so that bean soup became the sole ration. Eventually they docked in New York, where they encountered considerable difficulties before they could disembark and pass through Customs. Furthermore, Father Behrens had no letter of introduction to any house of the Society in America. Finally, he got in touch with the Superior of the Maryland Province, the Very Rev. Father Broccard. After due consultation, the group split up, some of them being committed to the care of Father Broccard who sent them to Georgetown to continue their studies, and the rest were sent to the Missouri Province. Upon completion of this mission he returned to his native Europe.

In the year 1850, we find him in the German Province of Friedricksburg, a suburb of Muenster in Westphalia, where he founded the first novitiate of the Society there. Shortly afterwards he was appointed Rector of the House that he had founded. From 1856-59 he was Provincial of the German Province. Later he went to Paderborn, Germany to act as Superior and instructor of the Tertians.

During the Franco-Prussian War in 1870-1871 he was appointed Superior of all the Fathers, Scholastics, and Brothers who were sent out to labor among the sick and wounded on the battlefields and in the hospitals of France. The number of Jesuits chosen for this work was very large. He met untold opposition in all his endeavors from the Prussian High Command, for Prince Bismarck was very hostile to the Catholic cause. In spite of this he worked ceaselessly so that thousands of Catholic soldiers, German as well as French, received the last sacraments before death. For all his self-sacrificing endeavors, he was upon his return to Germany decorated with the "Iron Cross," a medal given in recognition of valiant deeds. He participated in the triumphal entry of the victorious army into Berlin, in fact rode on the same train with Prince Bismarck. Then, by irony of fate, he was expelled from Germany a few weeks later along with many of his Jesuit brethren as a menace to the German Empire. Germany's loss was Buffalo's gain, for thus it happened that this eminent man came to seek refuge and work among his brethren in America.

He arrived in Buffalo December 14, 1872, just before noon, in time to offer up the Holy Sacrifice of the Mass. What better way to start one's labors in a new field! On December 22, eight days after his arrival in Buffalo, he was proclaimed Superior of the German Mission and President of Canisius College. Many difficulties confronted him in his new job, but as always, he was equal to the task. Not the least of these was to master the English language. We are told that not only did he study it avidly but that he took every opportunity to listen to sermons in English, to write sermons in English and have them corrected, to give sermons many times before the final delivery in public and have his pronunciation criticized by those who knew the language well. He was a strict disciplinarian, strict with himself and strict with those who came under his charge. He labored ceaselessly for the College and the parishioners of St. Michael's Church. For many years, he was the advisor and confessor of Bishop Ryan, the second Bishop of Buffalo. His confessional at St. Michael's was always crowded. He was a very holy man, as both the Bishop and his fellow Jesuits knew. Upon his death Bishop Ryan said, "I have a saint in my Diocese, and his name is Father Behrens." The archives state that Bishop Ryan visited Father Behrens several times while he was very ill. Upon being informed of his death he wept.[29]

Father Behrens held the Presidency of Canisius College until 1876, when poor health forced him to relinquish his duties and seek rest. Father John B. Lessman held the position for a year when the Rev. Martin Port, S.J., was named his successor. During his term of office the College was enlarged. Sensing the inadequacy of the existing building and the need for a college chapel, he, in 1880, built the north wing of the College, which contained the music rooms, some classrooms, and another dormitory. Soon the hall, which later became the gymnasium, and a beautiful chapel were added.

The old St. Michael's Church, the residence of the Fathers, had become too small for the Jesuit community. In early 1881, it was torn down to make room for the south wing of the present building at 651 Washington Street. A new museum was also started. In a very short time an extensive collection of minerals, shells, animals, and rare specimens were gathered. Some of these items were contributed by Jesuits doing missionary work among the Indians in the West. Others were gifts of former students and friends of the College. Every issue of the College Catalogue contains acknowledgments of gifts to the museum. Mr. Thomas Ashton, professor of English and Commercial Law, from 1883 to 1892, aided the Rev. Martin Bischoff, S.J., professor of natural sciences, in collecting the specimens. Many of these items are today in the Horan-O'Donnel Science building of Canisius College. In his last year of office, upon the petition of Fathers F.X. Delhez, H. Knappmeyer, and Joseph Kreusch, Father Port obtained from the Regents of the University of the State of New York, the charter, which was later amended. Canisius College was "in January, 1883, incorporated by the Regents of the University of the State of New York with power to confer Degrees and Academical Honors."[30] At the 13th Annual Commencement held on June 26, 1883, the first degrees ever granted by Canisius College were conferred upon the following men: John Baxter, Olean, N.Y.; Wenceslaus Koudelka, Cleveland, Ohio; Frank Kowald, Buffalo, N.Y.; Joseph Poupeney, Louisville, Ohio; Frank Traeutlein, Buffalo, N.Y.; and Simon Yenn of Mishawaka, Indiana.[31]

The first catalogue published by Canisius College was in the year 1873-74, no copy of which now exists. In 1879, the first class of Philosophy was added to the Latin course. Father Port, a Jesuit of the old school, was a staunch advocate of a thorough course in Latin and Greek, mathematics and languages, history and religion, and ardently inimical to all superficiality. When he added the course of philosophy it was not compulsory. The Rev. John Ming, S.J., was the first professor of philosophy. He was an eminent philosopher, but apparently, a course in philosophy did not appeal to the average scholar in those days for it does not appear again in the curriculum until the Presidency of Rev. Theodore Van Rossum, S.J., Eventually the Philosophy course became necessary if one wished to obtain the A.B. degree.

From its very inception, the number of boarders had increased yearly at the College. The strict discipline under Father F. X. Delhez, S.J., had recommended the institution to many parents. Father Delhez had been Prefect in the Jesuit College at Feldkirch, Austria, before he came to

America where he introduced the same discipline that prevailed in the Jesuit Colleges of Europe. He enforced his strict discipline with an iron will and an iron hand. The rod was not spared. To give some idea of what the early Canisius discipline for the boarders was like, a few of the regulations are listed below.

- *Those whose parents reside in the city will be allowed to visit them once a month.*
- *No boarder shall be permitted to visit the city, unless for urgent reasons, at the special request of parents or guardians, and accompanied by them or by one of the faculty.*
- *The use of tobacco is strictly prohibited.*
- *The correspondence is subject to the inspection of the president.*
- *During Christmas vacation, leave of absence from the College will not be granted, unless for urgent reasons.*
- *Ordinary causes of dismissal are: continued inapplication and bad conduct.*[32]

Recreation was provided for the boarders at the Villa. This was a piece of property located at Main and Jefferson, where the present College now stands. It was purchased in 1875 by the Jesuit Fathers. The students did not have class two afternoons a week so they walked out to Villa, where they played ball, had lunch, and then walked back to the College.

Regulations for Day-scholars.

1. Day-scholars are required to be regular and punctual in their attendance.
2. In case of absence from College they should give prompt notice of the cause to the Prefect.
3. They are forbidden to bring anything to or from Boarders or to do any errand for them, or to associate with them more than is necessary in Class and Academic Exercises.
4. The weekly Reports should be returned on Monday, signed by the parents.
5. Bad conduct in or outside the College, insubordination, continued inapplication to studies, or irregularity in attendance, are causes of dismissal.
6. The introduction of intoxicating liquor into the Institution is prohibited under pain of expulsion. The chewing of tobacco is forbidden.
7. They are required to be present at Mass every day, to make the Annual Retreat and to receive the holy Sacraments at least once a month.
8. Silence is to be kept in the Study-Hall and in the Corridors.
9. The play-ground is free for the Day-scholars:
    every day till 9 o'cl. A. M.
    "   "   during Recess.
    "   "   from 12, 15 o'cl. P. M. to 1 o'cl. P. M.
   On School-days from 3, 15. P. M. " 4, " "
   On Tuesdays and Thursdays from 2, 30 o'cl. P. M. to 4 o'cl P. M.
   At other times the play-grounds are not accessible to day-scholars.
10. On Saturdays Confessions are heard at 3, 15 o'cl. P. M. in the Chapel.
11. Library will be open on Mondays, Wednesdays, Fridays, Saturdays from 1 P. M. – 1, 45 P. M. Without special permission no books can be taken home.
12. On School-days Mass begins at 8 o'cl. A. M. School begins in the afternoon at 1, 45 P. M. – No School on Tuesday and Thursday afternoon.
   Punctuality in attendance, — am. — Pm.

An undated parcel listing "Regulations for Day Scholars" makes clear that strictness of discipline applied to them as well as boarders. (Image added; not in original Kessler history.) Source: CHS Archives

An Addition - "The History of Boarding at Canisius"

At this point the author from the Class of 1997 respectfully interrupts the author from the Class of 1928 to insert a series of pages (pp. 28-31) from the 1908 Canisius High School Yearbook, which was entitled *Lest We Forget*. These pages, which contain "The History of Boarding at Canisius," provide a fascinating and informative look at the boarding era[1] of the school as it ended. This provides a context for the modern reader. The author of these pages is listed only as "J.C.S. '10," but it is likely to be J. Carlton Short, whose name appears in a few places in the publication, including as the recipient of oratorical contest recognition. Other possibilities with those initials include Joseph Slattery, Joseph Seitz, and John Schmitt. It is difficult to determine for sure, based on the limitations of these early publications—but this author is confident, based on a few telling clues throughout the 1908 issue, that J. Carlton Short wrote the piece.

There is present in the writing some considerable wit, and one is left to wonder to what extent the compliments extended certain Jesuit masters are, in fact, subtle ironic jabs. From the final paragraph, in which "J.C.S. '10" quotes *Hamlet*, one might infer either genuine nostalgia for the departing boarding program—or relief. Perhaps it was a combination of both. Mr. Kessler's history will, in the next section, address the closure of the boarding program in more detail.

The History of Boarding at Canisius
Excerpted from *Lest We Forget*, the 1908 Yearbook

Seldom has there been a proverb which, at some time or another, has not been verified, and Canisius, with its reputation as one of the leading

---

[1] While several Jesuit secondary schools maintained boarding programs for a time, there is only one remaining, Georgetown Preparatory School in North Bethesda, Maryland. Ironically, this last boarding holdout is also the veteran: "Founded in 1789, Georgetown Preparatory School is America's oldest Catholic boarding and day school for young men in grades 9 through 12, and the only Jesuit boarding school in the country." (Source: Georgetown Preparatory School website.)

educational colleges of the country, is a striking example of the well-known saying: "Labor Vincit Omnia."[2] One of the chief factors in giving Canisius its fame was its excellent boarding department and, now that this feature of Alma Mater is about to pass out of existence, we deem it but fair to give it a few words before we close the last volume of its history.

Canisius, like many other educational institutions, had a humble origin. In 1870, the Jesuits purchased a small two-story brick building on Ellicott Street, which stood on the present site of St. Michael's School, and converted it into a place of instruction. That year there were five boarders, all from Boston, including Messrs. Dicksmeyer, Ecker, Dorman, Ochs, and Berg. As no quarters were available in the improvised school, a house was rented on Ellicott Street, where students lived, until they removed to the home of Mr. Hartfuhr on Goodell Street. As the number of boarders had increased to eighteen during the second year, they moved to the parish house of St. Michael's towards the end of April. By this time, the new college was under way and, as a proof of the certainty of its advent, the boarders shipped fragments from the stone structure to their parents. Though not completed, the building was occupied in September, and the opening saw twenty-six boarders on hand. The college was solemnly blessed by the Bishop on Thanksgiving Day and the cornerstone was laid and blessed on the feast of Blessed Peter Canisius, April 27, 1872. On the very same day the Bishop blessed the college, Fr. Simeon, of happy memory, organized the college band which, upon making its debut on Christmas day, became very popular.

In '73-'74, the Jesuits purchased from the Sisters of St. Joseph the large tract of land at the corner of Main and Jefferson Streets, now known as Villa Park. As the Sisters could not use the grounds for their original purposes, they were not reluctant to make a sale. At that time, the only building on the premises was the brick structure, where the Sisters taught school. The new owners-built additions, reclaimed the land from the wilderness and metamorphosed the grounds to an extent that has made the property one of the most beautiful spots in the city.

Previous to the founding of Canisius, Fr. Dehlez had been General Prefect at the Jesuit College at Feldkirch, where he had attained the art most requisite

---

[2] "Work conquers all."

in a prefect of maintaining discipline. Accordingly, when the Canisius boarding department was in its incipiency and needed a strong hand to direct it
aright, Fr. Dehlez was the man chosen for the task. The boys arose at 5:30
and work was the program of the day. After supper, those who had finished
their tasks and were so inclined, could retire, while the others remained in the
study-hall, studying or reading books and—I had almost said magazines, but
in those pioneer days, the possession of newspapers or periodicals was considered a very serious breach of discipline, and culprits were severely dealt with.
Tobacco, in all its shapes and forms, was absolutely forbidden. The food was
plain, but substantial, and there was no lunch or dessert, except on Sunday.

For many years there was but one division of boarders. Vacation at Canisius, to say nothing of Easter, was an unknown quantity, and it was considered
a singular boon to be allowed to receive a box from home on Christmas Day.
Under this strict regime, which found favor with many parents, the boarders
waxed so numerous as to necessitate an addition to tbe building in 1879.

For nearly twenty-two years, Fr. Dehlez was at the helm and, though he
always made the performance of his duty a strict matter of conscience, he retired esteemed and loved by the boys who had come under his jurisdiction. In
the following year, under Fr. Leiter, military discipline was introduced by Mr.
Patrick O'Brien, U.S.A. For a few years, all went well, but drill finally became
so irksome to certain individuals and circumstances so unfavorable, that the
system was abandoned.

In 1894, Fr. Martin became General Prefect and held the office for two
years. Thus far the restrictive policy of Fr. Dehlez had been followed out, more
or less, by his successors, but when Fr. Heiermann stepped into the office in
1896, the boarding department was revolutionized. Privileges, formerly cur-
tailed, were granted with a lavish hand. Basketball was taken up enthusiastically and the representative team was allowed to play on other courts, even in
the evening. Life grew enjoyable, but the spell was broken in 1898, when the
mantle fell on Fr. Martin again, this time for three years. During this administration, privileges were annulled right and left; basketball was crushed, and
a general return to the radical policy of Fr. Dehlez was noticeable. In September, however, while the Pan-American Exposition was in progress, a change
was made and Fr. Theis came from Cleveland to assume his duties as General

Prefect. Precedents were again disregarded and deviated from, and the boys enjoyed the same good times as before.

Fr. Theis retired in June 1902, and was succeeded by Fr. Strerath. During the last six years great progress was made in many respects, and while the boys were not wholly unrestrained, several iron-bound, custom-worn regulations were successfully abrogated. Basketball was resumed, the villa days were lengthened, and in the year a whole free day was given in place of two half days.

As the College was conducted by an order whose origin dates back some three hundred years, a few time-honored customs took the firm root within its walls. For instance, every week the students were accustomed to walk to the villa, take dinner there, and enjoy themselves. The distribution of May cards to those who had signalized themselves by good behavior during the month of Mary, was always looked forward to with eagerness. The devotion of the Six Sundays of St. Aloysius was practiced by special services, which were held on six successive Saturdays and Sundays, terminating on the feast of the Patron of Youth.

The Sodalities, which were established during the first year of Canisius' existence, flourished to the very end. The boarders were represented by the Immaculate Conception Sodality in the Junior Division and the Sodality of the Annunciation among the Senior Boarders. Confinement to the precincts of the College proved irksome to many a boarder, but those whose parents or relatives lived in the city enjoyed the privilege of visiting them on the first Sunday of each month.

In the '90s, football was played, but its abolition soon followed, owing to the number of injuries sustained during the games. The winter season saw the yard converted into a skating pond and the Junior Boarders always had a toboggan. An excursion down the Niagara River or into the country was an annual affair as well as an Altar-boys' outing, both being enjoyed immensely. The Glee Club has always been a potent factor in making the boarder-life a happy one.

The faculty, in dispensing with the boarding, are prompted by the best of reasons. The College building has outgrown its usefulness and can no longer afford the requisite accommodations. In a word, boarding at Canisius has a record that spells glorious success. And considering the difficulties that had

to be surmounted in the beginning and the great progress that was made, we may be pardoned if we apply the words of Hamlet to the boarding department at our College: "Take it all in all, I shall not look upon its like again."
  -   *J.C.S. '10*

Two images from the boarding school. *Lest We Forget*, 1908.

(Here we return to Mr. Kessler's history.)

In those days, the college term extended from around the first of September to the last week of June. From the list of students in the catalogue, the name of Canisius had spread rapidly. Students were in attendance from the States of Ohio, Illinois, Pennsylvania, Michigan, Kentucky, Massachusetts, Missouri, Indiana, New Jersey, Iowa, and all parts of New York. Students from Canada are also listed in the catalogue.

Father Port had done much for Canisius in expanding its physical facilities. Europe had been his birthplace, but the Buffalo Mission was the field of most of his labors. While he was a student in Europe the famous Lord Acton was one of his classmates. Buffalo was the first scene of his labors in America and Florissant, Missouri his last, for there he died on October 9, 1914. He was succeeded by the Rev. Theodore Van Rossum, S.J..

Notes

[1] John Timon, *Missions in Western New York, and Church History of the Diocese of Buffalo*, Buffalo: Catholic Sentinel Print, 1862, p. 236.

[2] *Canisius Monthly*, Vol.II (1915-1916), p. 38.

[3] Henry W. Hill, ed., *Municipality of Buffalo, New York, a History 1720-1923*, New York: Lewis Historical Publishing Co., Inc., 1923, Vol II, pp. 531-532

[4] *Metropolitan Catholic Almanac and Laity's Directory For the Year of Our Lord 1851*. Baltimore: Fielding Lucas, Jr. p. 170.

[5] Rev. Thomas Donohue, *History of the Catholic Church in Western New York*. Buffalo: Catholic Historical Publishing Co., 1904, pp. 256-257.

[6] Gilbert J. Garraghan, *The Jesuits in the Middle United States*, New York: America Press, 1938, Vol. I, pp. 583-587.

[7] Garraghan, *op. cit.*, p. 586.

[8] *Catalogus Sociorum et Officiorum Dispersae Provinciae Germaniae Societatis Jesu*, ineunte anno MDCCCLXXXVIII. Gestel St. Michaelis, in Institutu Surdo-Mutorum, 1888, pp. 38-49.

[9] See Table A.

[10] *Woodstock Letters*, Vol. 48 (1919) pp. 330-340. Same: *Canisius Monthly*, Vol. 2 (1915-1916), p. 304.

[11] *Woodstock Letters*, Vol. 48 (1919), pp. 330-340.

[12] *Canisius Monthly*, Vol. 2, p. 325.

[13] *Lest We Forget*, June 1912. p. 60.

[14] *Canisius Monthly*, Vol. 1 (1914-1915) p. 293-295. This account about Father Durthaller was written by the Rev. Daniel Walsh mentioned in the above account.

[15] *Ibid.*, p. 294.

[16] *Buffalo Daily Courier*, September 1, 1870, p. 3. Same: *The Arena*, Vol. V. No. 9, March 12, 1920, p. 155.

[17] *Woodstock Letters*, Vol. 48 (1919), pp. 330-340.

[18] Records show that the intention that Canisius was to be a Day-School exclusively was not followed from the very first day of its inception.

[19] *Canisius Monthly*, Vol. 4 (1917-1918), pp. 43-44.

[20] *Woodstock Letters*, Vol. 48 (1919), pp. 330-340.

[21] *Ibid.*, Vol. 53 (1924), pp. 94-95

[22] *Lest We Forget*, June 1912, p. 61.

[23] *Woodstock Letters*, Vol. 48 (1919), pp. 330-340.

[24] *Ibid.*, pp. 330-340.

[25] *Catholic Union*, August 22, 1872. p.5

[26] *Woodstock Letters*, Vol. 48 (1919), pp. 330-340.

[27] *Ibid.*

[28] *Woodstock Letters*, Vol. 48 (1919), pp. 330-340.

[29] The information about Rev. Henry Behrens was obtained chiefly from *The Chronicler*, Vol. 2, No. 3, January, 1908, pp. 11 & 16. Same: *Canisius Monthly*, Vol. 3 (1916-17), pp. 149-153.

[30] *Canisius College Catalogue*, 1882-83, p. 3.

[31] *Ibid.*, pp. 26-27.

[32] *Canisius College Catalogue*, 1877-78, pp. 4-5.

CHAPTER 4

The Kessler History, Part II: CHS Comes into its Own

IV. Separation of Canisius College & CHS: 1883-1912

The story of Canisius continues with the appointment to the presidency of the Rev. Theodore Van Rossum, S.J., Under him the system of oral examinations was introduced at Canisius. For a student to graduate it was necessary to pass oral examinations in the evidences of Religion, Rhetoric, Latin, Greek, Mathematics, English, Poetry, History, Natural Philosophy, and Chemistry. Besides these oral examinations, there were written examinations in Latin, Greek, English, Evidences of Religion, Mathematics, Chemistry, and Natural Philosophy.

Beginning with the Fall semester of 1885, a student to obtain the Bachelor of Arts degree had to after completing the six-year Classical

55

Course, pass an examination in Mental and Moral Philosophy, Higher Mathematics, and Mechanics, which required either one or two years of further study. Gradually one can see the full Classical Course as outlined in the "Ratio Studiorum" taking shape. The policy, which had been in vogue since the founding of the school of awarding a certificate for the successful completion of the Commercial or Classical Course, was still continued.

The school year 1886-87 brought another innovation in to the school curriculum. Besides taking the course of Philosophy in Latin, the students had to defend the theses assigned, publicly before members of the Faculty in Latin at regularly assigned periods throughout the school year. At the close of the year certain theses were assigned from the various branches of philosophy, which every student had to defend publicly before members of the Faculty and invited guests. From the year 1886-1887, the number of theses was seven from Logic, seven from Ontology, and sixteen from Psychology. As the years went on the number of theses increased as well as the branches of Philosophy.

It was during the Presidency of Father Van Rossum that the first Master's Degree ever granted by Canisius College was conferred upon Frank Sindele, B.A. at the 17th Annual Commencement on June 21, 1887. His Lordship, Rt. Rev. S.V. Ryan, Bishop of Buffalo, presided.[1]

In the Fall of 1888 Father Von Rossum was succeeded by the Rev. J. Ulric Heinzle, S.J., as President. It was during his administration that the Classical Course was lengthened to seven years and made compulsory for all who wished to graduate from Canisius. From that year on no one could obtain a certificate for completion of six years of the Classical Course. Students had to prove their proficiency by written and oral examinations at the end of Rhetoric as well as at the end of Philosophy class to obtain the Bachelor of Arts Degree. It was also during his term that German became compulsory in all classes of the high school and college course. Even the Preparatory class had to take German as well as those students pursuing the Commercial Course.

The year 1891 brought a new President to Canisius College. He was the Rev. John Zahm, S.J., who was one of the early students of Canisius College. Under Father Zahm a radical change took place. In the year 1893 he secured a Mr. Patrick E. O'Brien, late of the United States Army, as a teacher of gymnastics and military tactics. The college is beginning to take on the appearance of a military school, although the catalogue does not classify it as such. However, evidence that it is, is given to us in the Outfit that the school demands each boarder have:

Each boarder shall be supplied with two suits of uniform clothing, one for every day wear, and a dress suit for Sundays and Holidays; six shirts, six collars, three night-shirts, six pairs of stockings, six handkerchiefs, six towels, six napkins, two or three pairs of boots or shoes, a pair of rubbers, and an overcoat. The full name, or the respective number must be marked on every article.[2]

At the same time there was a fee of one dollar charged for calisthenics and military drill. This, however, was limited to the boarders only. The year 1895 saw a further advance along the lines of a military school when all the students, both boarders and day scholars, had to wear the College uniform as it was termed. However, only boarders had to be outfitted with the dress uniform (pictured in Archive photo, below).

In 1896 a military organization was formed consisting of a band and five companies, in which there were three hundred and four men. Each Company consisted of a Captain, First Lieutenant, Second Lieutenant, non-commissioned officers, and privates. Mr. Patrick E. O'Brien, who had come to Canisius in the Fall Semester of 1893, was the instructor. Why the military organization was eventually abandoned, your author was unable to discover. At any rate the year 1900 saw the end of this organization at Canisius, for the year 1899-1900 is the last year anyone is listed as teaching military drill, and the year 1898-1899 is the last year of the listing of any military roster at Canisius.

Under Father Zahm the College Chapel was enlarged, giving Canisius an outstanding Chapel for a College its size. At the same time the playground was enlarged and improved. An adjacent residence, which was purchased some years before, was not utilized for college purposes.

The Old Washington Street School

Photo of Washington Street School. Undated Photo from CHS Archives, front matter of 1948 Arena Yearbook. (Image added; not included in Kessler history.)

The Silver Jubilee of Canisius was likewise celebrated under the presidency of Father Zahm. The exercises began in St. Michael's Church on the 30th of April, 1895, with the celebration of a solemn pontifical Mass. The celebrant of the Mass was the Rt. Rev. S.V. Ryan, Bishop of Buffalo.

The assistant priest was the Rev. William Becker, S.J., one of the founders of the College. All the other assisting clergy were Alumni of the College. The Rev. John Schaus of Williamsport, Pennsylvania preached a sermon entitled, "Blessed Canisius." Music for the Mass was furnished by the combined choirs of St. Ann's and St. Michael's Churches under the direction of Mr. Gregory Kiefer. Following the Mass, a dinner was served in the College to the visiting clergy, the faculty and the officers of the Alumni Association. Besides the Bishop, the Presidents of Georgetown University, St. Francis Xavier College, New York City, and St. Ignatius College, Cleveland, were present.[3]

At a meeting of the Alumni Association, the Rev. Father Nelson H. Baker of West Seneca, who took private lessons at Canisius before the formal establishment of the College, was elected as an honorary member. Father Baker is the first person thus honored by election to honorary membership.[4]

Washington Street Campus. Undated photo from CHS Archives. (Image added; not in original Kessler history.)

That same evening there was a banquet in the College Hall attended by about one hundred and fifty of the Alumni. Among the distinguished visitors who spoke was "the Rev. William Becker, S.J., who was sent to this country from Germany twenty-five years ago to found two Jesuit Colleges. The first was Canisius College and ten years later he founded another College at Prairie du Chien, Wisconsin."[5] Several other speakers appeared on the same program.

On the following day, May 1, 1895 the members of the Alumni Association and their friends took a carriage ride to various points of interest about the city. Twenty-five carriages and a tally-ho were used. On the trip a stop was made at the Villa, the site of the present College, where a lunch was eaten followed by entertainment. In the evening a very formal program was held at the Music Hall. The exercises consisted of music by the College Orchestra, three addresses, one by an alumnus and two by students, a tableau, and the closing address by Bishop Ryan. A march entitled, "The Jubilee March," written by the Rev. Ludwig Bonvin, S.J., music teacher at the College, brought the evening's program to a close.

The Silver Jubilee Commencement was held on June 21, 1895. At these exercises the first Honorary Degree ever granted by Canisius College, a Master of Arts Degree, was conferred upon James G. Smith.[6] At these same exercises Francis E. Fronczak received the Degree of Master of Arts. Later he was to become a well-known and highly respected Buffalo citizen and international figure. He was an intimate friend of the late Ignace Jan Paderewski, the great pianist, and one-time President of Poland. He was also a member of the Committee that drew up the Treaty of Versailles. For many years he held the post of Health Commissioner in the City of Buffalo.

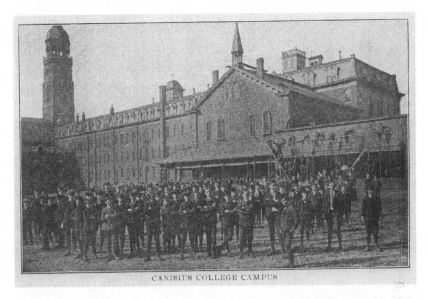

Image from *Lest We Forget, 1904-1905*. Addition; not in original Kessler history.

The Class of 1901 conducting field exercises on Washington Street. Source: CHS Archives. Addition; not in original Kessler history.

An Addition: The Relic of St. Peter Canisius

Here again, we interrupt Mr. Kessler's history to present another relic—literally—from the archives of Canisius High School. These annotated, typewritten documents included on the following three pages comprise an original record signed by Rev. F. J. Bunse, S.J., dated August 30 and 31, 1922, entitled "About the Authenticity of the Precious Relic of Bl.[3] Peter Canisius Preserved in the domestic Chapel of Canisius High School, Buffalo." The relic, pictured below, remains in the Chapel at 1180 Delaware Avenue.

---

[3] "Bl." Stands for Blessed. At the time of these documents, Peter Canisius had been beatified (1864) but not canonized. He was canonized in 1925 by Pope Pius XI and thus became Saint Peter Canisius.

About the Authenticity of the Precious Relic of Bl.Peter Canisius
Preserved in the Domestic Chapel of Canisius High School, Buffalo.

We have a large relic, a (part of a) rib, enclosed in a reliquary resemblin
a monstrance, and preserved in a niche made at the order of ReV.Rob.H.Johnson
S.J., Superior of Canisius High School, Buffalo,N.Y. in the wall(gospel side)
of the domestic chapel of Canisius High School.

This relic is, according to constant and immemorial tradition, a rib of our
Blessed Peter Canisius. No authentic of its genuineness has been found.

All we have been able to ascertain about it, are the following facts:
On August 28, 1864, relics -among them four ribs- were taken from the body of
blessed Canisius by Rev.Father Anderledy, Provincial of the German Jesuits,
and put into the Archives of the German Province. The authentic of these relic
is still kept in the German Archives. A copy is in Our Archives (of Can.H.Sch.

These four ribs are no longer in the German Archives: no one knows where
they are: no document pertaining to their disappearance has been discovered.
(See letter of Father Mundwiler, the German Archivist.)

Our Relic was exposed for veneration on April 27, 1898. (See Mittheilungen
aus der deutschen Provinz, Volume 1, page 345.)

Father john I. Zahm S.J., who became Rector of Can. College, which was in
the building that is now Can. High School, on Nov.5,1891,had the relic encased
in the present reliquary in the year 1894-1895. he wrote on Jan.20,1922: "The
photos you sent are those of the reliquary, which I had made (Cost $50.00)
and of the relic itself." The photographs mentioned and others were made by
Father Henry Wolff S.J. in Dec.1921 or Jan.1922. Copies of them are in our archives.

The relic was here in 1892. For Brother Joseph Stamen S.J. told me that
Father John Zahm promised in 1892 to have the relic encased if Father Kerckhoff should recover from a serious disease: Father Kerckhoff died, but - Broth
er Stamen says- Father Zahm had the relic encased anyway.

How the relic came to what was then Canisius College and is now Canisius
High School, is uncertain.
Father U. Heinzle S.J., Rector of C.C. till 1921, "remembered," as he said
on in Dec.1921. "nothing about it"; tho Father Zahm writes "he knew the relic
and was delighted when I showed him the case I had made."

Father Zahm S.J. writes Jan.20, 1921: "I was not in Buffalo when the relic arrived, and was never told how we got it, except that it was presented by
the German Provincial." *had been Rector of Can. Coll. since 9 July 1883, and*

Father Theodore van Rossum S.J., who became Superior of the Buffalo Mission
on July 7,1892, writes on Oct.10,1921: "As far as I remember, the precious
relic was sent to us by Rev. Father Lohmann, then Provincial. That a Provincial sent us such a treasure, was proof enough for its authenticity and genuineness..." Father Lohmann was Provincial from 1884-1888.

Neither the Historia Domus nor the Diary of the Minister gives any information about the source of the relic. Brother Stamen thought that Father Behrens
had obtained it for the College.

Together with the above remarks and statements I place the following documents in the archives of Canisius High School:
1. Report of Father John B. Mundwiler S.J., Archivist of the German Province,
sent to Rev. John Druding S.J., Socius of the German Province, by whom it was
sent to Father F.J. Bunse S.J., Buffalo, on Dec.13,1921.
2. Letter of Father Theodore van Rossum S.J.. to F.J.Bunse, Cleveland,Oct.12,
1921.
3. Letter of Father John I. Zahm S.J. to F.J. Bunse, from Toledo, O.,Oct.8,'21.
4. Letter of Father John I. Zahm S.J. to F.J. Bunse, from Toledo,O., Jan.20,'22
5. *Three large photographs of the reliquary, 2 of part of the reliquary, 2
of the relic itself. One of the photos shows the seal of J.V. Ryan, Bishop of Buffalo.*

Canisius High School, August 30, 1922.   *F.J. Bunse S.J.*

Testimony of Father Theodore van Rossum S.J.:
Brooklyn, O., Oct.12, 1921: "As far as I remember, the precious relic was
sent to us by R.F. Lohmann, then Provincial. That a Provincial sent us such
a treasure, was proof enough for its authenticity and genuineness. When Bl.
Canisius was beatified, the Provincial, R.F. Anderledy, opened the tomb and
took out a number of relics. Most likely some of them were preserved in the
Provincial's keeping, and from them Canisius College received its relic."

Testimony of Father John I. Zahm S.J.
Toledo, O., Oct.8,1921: "The relic in question is one of the lower ribs of
Bl. Peter Canisius. We never had an authentic of it. Fr, Rathgeb brought it
with him when he came over to visit the mission in the year 1891 and gave it
to Canisius College. He brought it from the archives of the German Province."
(Note: See the following testimony.) "I had the reliquary made in the year
1894-95, and when the relic was enclosed, asked Bishop (Stephen Vincent) Ryan
to seal it with his seal. He gave me the seal and told me I could write the
authentic myself, which I - for obvious reasons - never did. The relic is certainly authentic. ..."

Testimony of John I. Zahm S.J. (Second Testimony.)
Toledo, O., Jan.20,1922: "I was not in Buffalo when the relic arrived, and
was never told how we got it, except that it was presented by the German Provincial. Fr. Heinzle certainly knew about the relic, and was delighted when I
had the relic case made. I was under the impression that Father Rathgeb had
brought it over with him. But Fr. van Rossum told me, when I made my retreat
in Brooklyn last October and asked him about it, that Fr. Lohmann had presented it to the College.... The photos you sent are those of the reliquary which
I had made (cost $350.00) and of the relic itself."

Authentic of the Relics Preserved and - in part-
still being preserved in the German Archives.
Friburgi Helvetiae, 28. Augusti 1864: "Stephanus Marilley (Episcopus) .....
Universis et singulis praesentes Nostras litteras inspecturis fidem facimus
et attestamur, quod, ad maiorem Dei omnipotentis gloriam eiusque Sanctorum
venerationem, exhibitas Nobis sacras Reliquias ex Ossibus Venerabilis Servi
Dei Petri Canisii, Sacerdotis Professi Soc. Jesu, scilicet unam vertebram
fere integram, quatuor fragmenta costarum et tres phalangas manuum, pro com-
missi Nobis officii munere ex locis authenticis extractas opportunis documen-
tis recognovimus et posuimus in plico papyracee formae oblongae ac bene clau-
so et funiculo laneo coloris viridis colligato nostroque parvo in cera hispa-
nica rubra impresso sigillo pro earundem sacrarum Reliquiarum identitate qua-
ter signato atque munito, concessimus facultatem illas apud se retinendi, aliis donandi et post Beatificationis Romae celebranda solemnia in quacumque ec-
clesia, oratorio aut capella publicae fidelium venerationi exponendi. In quo-
rum fidem ..."

Testimony of Father John B. Mundwiler S.J.,
Archivist of the German Province.
Exaten, December 1921: "I have not been able to find any document or notice
referring to the relic preserved in Buffalo. Nothing can be found showing that
either Father Rathgeb or anyone X else presented the relic (the rib of Blessed Canisius) to Canisius College in Buffalo."

Testimony of Father Zahm (Third Testimony): *August 31, 1922.*
F. J. Bunse S.J.

On Oct.17,1924, Father Zahm, when at S. Ann's, in the presence of Fathers
Maeckel, Faber, Wolff, Munding and myself, said that Father Behrens, the former Superior of the Buffalo Mission, collected money for the reliquary bought
by Father Zahm for the relic of Bl. Canisius. Father Behrens would not have
done that, had he not been convinced of the genuineness of the relic.
S. Ann's, March 17, 1925.

F. J. Bunse SJ.

De Magna Beati Petri Canisii Reliquia
Quae in Sacello Scholae Canisianae Buffalensis
Domestico Asservatur.

Magnam Reliquiam - Costam aliquam paene totam Beati Petri Canisii,-
habemus in ostensorio pulchro pretiosoque inclusam inque aedicula e pa-
riete sacelli domestici excisa positam. Quam esse costam Beati Canisii
constat ex constanti ac bene fundata incolarum huius domus traditione,
quam a sua fere origine sequi possumus.

Etenim P. Theodorus van Rossum litteris die 12. Octobris 1921 ad me
datis testatur Provincialem aliquem Provinciae Germaniae Societatis Iesu Collegio Canisiano Buffalensi reliquiam illam dono dedisse, seque
putare Provincialem illum fuisse Patrem Lohmann. Huius autem administra-
tio Provinciae coepit anno 1884, uno fere anno postquam P. van Rossum
Rector Collegii B. Canisii factus erat.

Adfuisse vero reliquiam illam in nostra domo anno 1892 certum est.
Nam, ut Frater Coadiutor Iosephus Stamen mihi testatus est, eo anno
P. Ioannes Zahm, Rector Collegii Canisii, promisit se velle, gratia qua-
dam per intercessionem B. Canisii impetrata, reliquiam in ostensorio
includendam curare. Qui gratia non obtenta tamen reliquiam anno scholas-
tico 1894/5, ut ipse mihi scripsit, in ostensorio ad id pretio 350 dol-
larorum facto includendam curavit. Quod ostensorium sigillo Reverendis-
simi Domini Stephani Vincentii Ryan, Episcopi Buffalensis, obsignavit.

Die vero festo Beati Canisii, 27. Aprilis anni 1898, cum P. Iacobus
Rockliff esset Rector Collegii Canisiani, reliquia - secundum paginam
345 voluminis 1. commentariorum "Mittheilungen aus der deutschen Provinz" fidelibus exhibita est veneranda.

Postremo ante hos duos annos P. Robertus H. Johnson, Rector Scholae
Canisianae Buffalensis, quae easdem nunc aedes, quas antea Collegium
Canisianum, occupat, ut idoneo sacroque, quo digna esset, loco honora-
retur, reliquiam pretiosam nostram in aedicula supra memorata vitro bene occlusa servari iussit.

Quod autem huius reliquiae litterae authenticae neque umquam aderant
neque nunc adsunt, minime mirum videri debet. Nam testante Patre Ioanne
B. Mundwiler, archivista Provinciae Germaniae Societatis Iesu, nihil in
tabulis archivi eius Provinciae invenitur quo cognosci possit cuinam
aut ulla ex 4 illis costis aut ulla ex aliis reliquiis in litteris Re-
verendissimi Domini Murilley, Episcopi Friburgensis Helveticorum, memora-
tis donata sit: neque enim reliquias illas in archivo iam adesse neque
ulla re indicari quo pervenerint. Nostra autem reliquia una ex illis
4 costis fuit. *Non est dubium quin costae illae praeter nostram in minimas particu-
las divinae plurimasque dono-donatae sint. Inarum habeo unam cum authentica. F.I.B.*

Quo facilius autem quae dixi aliaque eandem rem attinentia pertenta-
ri atque perspici possent, quinas litteras (unas Patris van Rossum, Patris Mundwiler unas, trinas Patris Zahm) et septem picturas photographi-
cas (duas ipsius reliquiae, duas partis ostensorii, tres totius ostensorii) in archivo scholae nostrae ponendas curavi.

Ac nihil aliud maioris momenti de reliquia scribendum in mentem ve-
nit. *Die 29. Augusti 1923.*
In schola Canisiana Buffalensi.
F. I. Bunse S.I.

(We now return to Mr. Kessler's history.)

Under Father Zahm another great change took place in the curriculum. The Board of Trustees of Canisius decided to drop the Commercial Course. In a letter to the Provincial of the Maryland Province he said, "Last year we dropped the fourth Commercial Class (first year), and this year the Third Commercial. In the First and Second Commercial, there are 23 and 26 students respectively. Dropping of the Commercial Course has proved a decided gain in every respect."[7]

The year 1894 marked a further change in the Classical Curriculum at Canisius. The course of studies was broken up into eight years, four in the Academic Department and four in the Collegiate. A fourth year was added on the College level, which was called Senior Philosophy. With this addition the course as outlined in the *Ratio Studiorum* is now in full application in the Canisius curriculum. Along with this innovation a Post-graduate Class was added.

With the opening of the Fall semester in 1896, the Rev. James Rockliff, S.J., became the new President of Canisius. It was during his term that scholarships came into existence at Canisius. They were of two kinds: A course scholarship for the whole period of eight years, and annual scholarships offering free tuition for one year. At that time a course scholarship could be established by a donation of one thousand dollars. Twelve such scholarships were awarded in the month of August, 1896, to those students of Fourth Academic who passed the best examination on entering College. Annual scholarships were provided by a donation of forty dollars. For the school year 1897-98 five annual scholarships were competed for by students entering the Fourth Academic, and five in the Collegiate Department.

In the graduating class of 1897 was Theodore H. Revermann of Louisville, Kentucky, who received the degree of Bachelor of Arts. Later he became Bishop of Superior, Wisconsin. When Canisius celebrated its Golden Jubilee in 1920, Bishop Revermann returned to celebrate the pontifical High Mass opening the celebration. He along with William Jansen were the first graduates to win an A.B. Degree after a fourth year was added to the College Course, though it was still not a compulsory year.

In 1898 the Rev. John B. Theis, S.J., succeeded Father Rockliff to the Presidency. The following year there were no graduates from Canisius College because the fourth year of College, Senior Philosophy, was made compulsory for all to win the A.B. Degree. Hence, the twenty-ninth Annual Commencement might be termed the Commencement without any graduates. The exercises were held June 21, 1899 with honors only being awarded to the students of the three years of the college course and the four years of the academic course.

In the graduating class of 1900 was Robert T. Bapst, who is today the Superintendent of Schools in the City of Buffalo. He began his illustrious career in the field of education by first teaching at his *alma mater*. Later he entered the public school system in this city, where in a short time he became Principal of South Park High School.

The Fall Semester of 1901 marked the return of a former Canisius graduate as President of the College, in the person of the Rev. Aloysius J. Pfeil, S.J., His term ended in 1905 when he was succeeded by the Rev. Augustine A. Miller, S.J., During the presidency of Father Miller the charter of the College was amended so as to include the Academic Department. This took place during the year 1906. As a result, after the completion of the third year of the Academic Course, the law student certificate, and at the end of the fourth year, the medical student certificate could be obtained from the Regents on application to the President of the College.

It was also during Father Miller's term that one of the most important changes in the history of Canisius College took place. At a meeting of the Board of Trustees who convened on January 20, 1908, at the summons of the Very Rev. Joseph Hanselman, S.J., Provincial of the Maryland-New York Province, the fate of the Boarding Department of Canisius College was discussed. The final decision reached was that there were to be "no more boarders at Canisius after June 21, 1908."[8] The reason given for such a decision was that it was the only way to provide for the future growth of Canisius College. At the same time, it was decided to follow the suggestion of the Catholic Educational Association, viz., to separate the collegiate department entirely from the high school. Thus, the Fathers of

Canisius decided to select a suitable site somewhere in the city where they would erect a College.

As the reader will have noted, the above meeting was called by the Very Rev. Joseph Hanselman, S.J., Provincial of the Maryland-New York Province. Beginning with September 1, 1907, Canisius College was no longer a part of the German Province, but was annexed to the Maryland-New York Province. The decision to do this was reached at the general congregation of the Society held in Rome in September, 1906, there the reason for such a change was recognized:

It decided that the German Mission in North America, consisting of the Colleges in Buffalo, Cleveland, and Prairie du Chien, the residences in Buffalo and Mankota, together with the Indian Missions in Dakota, should be dissolved and amalgamated with the American provinces. After the necessary steps were taken the decree of amalgamation was publicly announced September 1, 1907.[9]

Fr. Hanselmann honored the College on that occasion with a visit and welcomed the new member of his Province in a hearty address. The Province was divided among the Missouri, Maryland-New York Province, and the missions of the Rocky Mountains and California.

This change affected the College in no way, neither in its legal relations, curriculum, or method of teaching; rather, it merely meant a change of jurisdiction within the Society.

What had been decided at the meeting of the Board of Trustees of Canisius College in 1908 was to start to bear fruit two years later. It had been decided that the property that the College owned at Main and Jefferson, which had been called the Villa, was to become the site of the new Canisius College. "July 2, 1910, saw the breaking of ground for the new College."[10] On June 18, 1911 took place the laying of the cornerstone and its blessing by the Rt. Rev. Charles Colton, Bishop of Buffalo, before many dignitaries and friends of the College. The completed structure was dedicated on December 30, 1912, and a few days later classes met for the first time in the new college building. At the same time Canisius was assigned a new President, the Rev. George J. Krim, S.J., Thus with the closing of the year 1912 Canisius College and Canisius High School became separate institutions, each with its own building, facilities, and faculty.

V. A High School in Its Own Home: 1913-48

Beginning with January, 1913 Canisius High School students acquired a distinction all their own. They now had their own faculty, although the President of the College was to continue as President of the High School. They were now in complete possession of the building at 651 Washington Street, together with its beautiful chapel, large library, gymnasium, and spacious playground behind the building on Ellicott Street.

The Washington Street entrance to Canisius High School. Undated photo from CHS archives.

Photo and drawing of the Washington Street Campus, from the 1934 *Arena* Yearbook, p. 10.

The Washington Street library. Undated photo from CHS archives.

The Washington Street Chapel. Undated photo from CHS archives.

Washington Street playing fields. Undated photo from CHS Archives.

No further expansion took place in the buildings at 651 Washington Street during the ensuing years, though many changes were made in the interior of the building from time to time. The curriculum met with few changes during the years. The Jesuit Fathers, through their many years of experience in teaching, knew the great value of the *Ratio Studiorum* in training leaders, and so were little influenced by the tides of the times in education. They shunned the superficialities of modern education, and even to this day do not permit much of the elective system to invade the high school curriculum.

In the year 1915, the *Arena*, a fortnightly publication, was started at Canisius High School. It boasts of being the first and only publication the High School ever had. Some years later it became a quarterly with a Thanksgiving, Christmas, and Easter number, the final issue being the Yearbook. The explanation for the title, the *Arena*, is that the editors would be proud to see the sons of Canisius hold an honorable place in the athletic world, but prouder still to see her sons crowned in the literary arena. These hopes and aspirations of the first editors have been met on numerous occasions, for ever since the magazine has been strictly a literary magazine; hardly a year has gone by in which some scholastic award was not given to the school for its literary work. Some of the awards have been local; many others have been national. Its crown is piled high with laurel wreaths.

The first catalogue published exclusively by the high school appeared in the year 1913. On its cover appeared the seal of the school. Just when it was adopted by both the College and High School, records do not reveal. At any rate the history of this shield is interesting and deserves a worthy place in the history of the school.

At the American Catholic Congress held in Baltimore, November 11 and 12, 1889, it was suggested by the Alumni Association of Jesuit Colleges that a button or badge, significant enough to indicate the wearer as a Jesuit student or alumnus, be adopted by all Jesuit colleges. The suggestion warmly advocated by Dr. Conde B. Pollen, the delegate for St. Louis University, was approved but no steps were taken to execute it. In the spring of 1895, St. Ignatius College of Chicago took up the matter again. Finally, "on the occasion of the Silver Jubilee of St. Ignatius College, Chicago, June 24, 1895, the badge was adopted as a formal design for the College."[11] The design selected was the seal of St. Ignatius, the founder of the Society of Jesus. The choice for this design was made by the Rev. James F.X. Hoeffer, S.J., Rector of St. Ignatius College. He did so with the general view that it would be adopted by all Jesuit Schools in the country, with slight variations to suit the needs of the local institutions.

Thus it happened that Canisius, being a Jesuit school, adopted the badge or seal of St. Ignatius for its own. The ancestry of St. Ignatius can be traced to at least the tenth century. He belonged to the noble Spanish family of Loyola. In 1261 the estate came into the hands of Lady Inez de Loyola, who married Don Lope de Onaz, of a family not less noble than that of his bride. After this, the armorial bearings of the two families were united on one shield, just as the names of both houses were preserved in the title of Onaz y Loyola. Hence, the seal of both Canisius High School and College conducted by members of the Society of Jesus, has the armorial bearings of the two Spanish Houses Onaz and Loyola.

The device of Onaz was originally seven red bars on a field of gold. These bars represented the seven heroes of the family who distinguished themselves in the famous battle of Beotibar, in 1321, where eight hundred Spaniards defeated seventy-thousand French, Navarres, and Gascons. It was a mark of honor bestowed upon the family by the King of Spain, that it was allowed thus to commemorate their ancestors' dauntless bravery.

On the other side of the seal are represented two gray wolves, with forepaws resting on the handles of a cauldron, suspended from black-pot hooks. The wolves and the cauldron answer to the name of the family of Loyola. *Lobo* is Spanish for wolf, while *olla* means a cauldron. These two words were united into Lobo y olla, (i.e., the wolf and the cauldron) and later contracted into Loyola. The design represents the boldless [sic] liberality of the Loyola family. In feudal times, when great lords made war upon one another with bands of armed followers whom they were obliged to sustain, the Loyola family so generously distributed food to their soldiers, that the wolves always found something in the cauldron to feed upon, after the men had been supplied.

Thus we have the meaning of the seal: The bars are the insignia of the Onaz family; the wolves and cauldron those of Loyola.[12]

An Addition: A Closer Look at the Canisius Seal

While Mr. Kessler's history presented what had become (and remains, in some circles) a traditional interpretation of the seal of the Loyola family, other scholars have since disagreed with this construal. According to Dr.

Charles A. Brady '29, Ph.D., a Harvard alumnus, author, and literary critic who served as Head of the English Department at Canisius College, the "lobo" and "olla" interpretation is incorrect.

Brady (1912-1995) was a highly regarded scholar whose poem "Keeper of the Western Gate" was awarded the 1968 Poetry Society of America's First Prize. According to *The Buffalo News*, "C.S. Lewis, the eminent British author, once called Brady's critique of his work the best published in Great Britain and the United States."[13] According to Brady, the imagery of the wolves and kettle, while evocative of both nobility and hospitality, does not warrant the etymological interpretation described above. Rather, recalling the 1956 work of Ignatius biographer James Broderick, he suggests a more mundane origin rooted in the Basque language:

Naturally enough, the original Canisius shield was that most omnipresent of Jesuit heraldic symbols, the coat of arms of the whole family of Loyola. It employs two familiar heraldic images: two wolves en rampant, on either side of...a hanging kettle...The Canisius predators, far from suggesting Milton's 'grim wolf with privy paw,' seem to be dancing...For a long time, the wolves-and-kettle motif set loose an ingenious but spurious etymology for the Basque name, Loyola, as a contraction for the Spanish words for wolves and kettle, lobos y olla. It was James Broderick's valuable St. Ignatius Loyola *which, in 1956, offered the English reader a probable rationalization of the Loyola cognizance as well as the true etymologization of the name:*[14]

> Some exploit or other...may account for the Loyola wolves which anyhow were an accepted emblem in the heraldry of the period. The boiling cauldron or pot symbolized hospitality, a virtue for which the Basques have always been justly celebrated...Loi is Basque for loam, ol again is a suffix meaning abundance or profusion, and a is the definite article, the abundance of loam. That is the lowly, earthy, unromantic derivation of a name as celebrated as any in history.[15]

Whatever the correct interpretation of the Loyola family coat of arms, it served, as Kessler explained, as the centerpiece of the Canisius seal. Today, the seal incorporates a circular enclosure with the elements of the Loyola crest, surrounded by an outer circle. The seven bars, representing the seven heroes of the Onaz family, are the narrower (and more distinct) of the bars.

Several modifications to the seal have been made. While small, they are significant. A look at a few examples from the last one hundred years will reveal this subtle evolution. One might be tempted to dismiss them, but it appears that periodically, significant efforts were taken to formalize and standardize the seal, with varying focus on location vs. legacy, and with varying levels of attention to its heraldic origins.

 This seal, from the cover of the 1925 *Arena*, reveals an important difference: at the bottom, in the outer circle, we read "Buffalo, N.Y." We can also see a disparity on the right side of the seal, wherein there are not seven bars, but rather eight (regardless of whether one is counting the "embossed" or "engraved" bars.) At the top of the interior pages of the same *Arena*, we see this apparent error replicated, although inconsistently—here we see ten light bars and nine dark ones. Moreover, the proportion of the wolves-and-cauldron image, as well as the typeface in the surrounding circle, are inconsistent, even  within the same publication. This is representative of the general inconsistency we see throughout the school's history with regard to the seal.

In 1990-1991, there appears to have been some attention given to the seal. The attentive reader will notice a significant shift that occurred by examining two editions of *The Citadel*. The image below, left appeared in the April 1990 issue. The image at right appeared in Fall 1991.

The Citadel, April 1990   *The Citadel*, Fall 1991

Here we see an intentional shift of the outer-circle text, from "Buffalo, N.Y." to "Established 1870." And again, noting the incorrect number of bars (and the disparate thickness), we see a return to the correct seven bars by 1991. As for the undulations on the outer-most border, we see 17 in 1990, and 11 in 1991. Prior to this, there are variations on this design, including a plain ring with no undulations (as in the 1925 *Arena*).

Between 2002 and 2003, yet another set of refinements was made, which brings us to the current standard for the seal. The undulation pattern of the outer ring was adjusted (now 10 undulations, with top-to-bottom symmetry, unlike before, where this varied). Perhaps more importantly, the design of the seven bars was fixed, making a clear distinction as to which bars represented the seven Onaz brothers represented in the Loyola seal. These narrower, distinct bars are plainly discernible from the thicker offset "blank" space. As for colors, the seal is portrayed using various school-approved color variations depending upon the use (silkscreen, letterhead, advertising, etc.), which range from navy and gold, to navy-and white only, to black-and-white-only.

2002 *Arena*   2003 *Arena*

Since 2003, the school has adopted this official seal (center, right). It is occasionally represented without the outer circle of text or outermost ring (center, left) such as on the lapel pins provided to juniors who opt not to purchase a class ring, and sometimes as a recognition to those enrolled into the National Honor Society. A new athletic logo with crossed swords and helmet was embraced in the late 2000s, roughly corresponding with the opening of the Stransky Athletic Complex and the Kennedy Field House (below, left). A more recent shield crest designed by Mark Venditti '17 has proved quite popular among students and was adopted widely in dress-code-approved polo shirts beginning in 2017-2018 (below, right).

Official CHS Seal, 2018.

(Here we return to the Kessler History.)

The year 1919 marked a new era in the history of Canisius High School. On July 20, 1919, the Rev. Robert H. Johnson was appointed to the first President of Canisius High School. Heretofore the preparatory department of Canisius College, though separated from the latter since December 30, 1912, has always been under the direction of the President of the College. From that day on the governing authority of the High School was distinct from that of the College.[16]

From the date of separation in 1912 up through the years the registration has gradually increased. In 1921 there were 705 students, and in the following year 736 students. These two years are singled out for these were years in which Canisius High School gained not only local, but also national recognition, because of its debating teams.

The High School Debating Society was organized in the Fall of 1914, and from the first year was simply called the Canisius High School Debating Society. In the following September, the members decided to name their flourishing society, and at the suggestion of the Rev. G.J. Krim, S.J., Principal, who wished to honor the memory of one who may truly be called the Father of Canisius College and High School, it was henceforth known as the Behrens Debating Society.[17]

From its very inception, this organization prospered at Canisius High School, and with the advent of the twenties carried the name of Canisius and Buffalo to all parts of the United States. Their first trip was in 1921 into the Midwest to explain that New York State's opposition to the St. Lawrence ship canal project was not selfish, sentimental, and provincial. This was the first appearance of any Buffalo team in the cities they visited, and according to the press reports, and quotations from Western officials, they were a tribute to the Buffalo schools. On this trip they visited Detroit, Chicago, and Cincinnati. The only match lost was in Detroit. Besides the very public debates they also spoke before many schools in the cities visited. Everywhere they went they were feted royally with theater parties, banquets, and sightseeing tours. Good will messages from the Governor of New York State, as well as many local officials, accompanied the debaters. Eminent men acted as moderators and judges in all the cities. "An offer was made to have the Canisius debaters tour the Southern States at the expense of an Ohio banker who heard the debate in Cincinnati."[18]

In 1922, they went on a three weeks' tour of Southern States. They left Buffalo with the endorsement and best wishes of Federal, State, and City officials. They visited seventeen states and debated in the most prominent Southern cities. The subject of this trip was, Resolved, the political solidarity of the South is still justified. The Canisius debaters always upheld the negative. On this trip they won every debate.[19]

The Southern Tour

The debating team returned from a three weeks' tour of the Southern States undefeated. They left Buffalo with the endorsement and best wishes of Federal, state and city officials. The local press published the letters sent to the school by United States Senators Calder and Wadsworth, Congressmen MacGregor, Dempsey, Mead, and S. D. Fess of Ohio, chairman of the Republican Congressional Committee, Senators Gibbs, Swift, Hill and Martin, Assemblymen Rowe and Beardesley, and from presidents of the local clubs. Mayor Schwab wrote in part: "As Mayor of Buffalo, I commend the tour of the Canisius Debaters. The fact that a team of Buffalo students will appear before prominent clubs in Southern cities cannot but bring our city and its educational standards to the attention of the South. This will be done in a way of which Buffalo can indeed be proud and thankful. . . . . May the debaters represent Buffalo in the South as I know they can." The Buffalo Chamber of Commerce wrote: "It is with extreme gratification that we learn that Canisius High School has ar-

Excerpt from the 1922 *Arena* Commencement Number, p.45, detailing the debate tour. Source: CHS Archives. (Image added; not part of original Kessler history.)

Again in 1923 they went on another tour using as their subject, Buffalo's advantages for development excelled those of each particular city they visited. They debated the leading schools in Cleveland, Toledo, Detroit, Chicago, Omaha, Denver, San Francisco, Los Angeles, Kansas City, St. Louis, Indianapolis, and Pittsburgh. Everywhere they debated they were greeted by jammed halls. Leading Buffalo business concerns contributed the money for the trip. The banks of Buffalo subscribed to a fund to pay for one half page notices in the newspapers of the cities visited. Seven of the decisions favored Canisius High School, four of which were unanimous, and three were defeats. Upon their return to Buffalo they were given a tremendous reception by the city. During the weeks following they spoke before most of the local clubs, and over the local radio stations. The present President of Canisius College, the Very Rev. Raymond Schouten, S.J., was a member of this team.

The curriculum of Canisius High has deviated little from the days of 1870. Possibly the greatest change came with the gradual development of science into the curriculum. In the early days science played little or no part in the curriculum. However, by the early twenties the curriculum was twofold, each course comprising the same subjects with this one exception, that on the completion of the first-year class, one course includes three years of Greek, while the other substitutes in place of Greek, three years of elementary science, viz., Biology, Physics, and Chemistry. The elective system has never had much of a place in the course of studies at Canisius High School.

On September 27, 1928, Canisius High School obtained a new charter from the Board of Regents. From then on it was independent of Canisius College, of which it was formerly the Academic Department. From this year on it bore the corporate title: "The Canisius High School of Buffalo, New York."

Since 1927 Canisius High School had been approved and accredited by the Association of Colleges and Secondary Schools of the Middle States and Maryland. It is also a member of the Jesuit Educational Association, the National Catholic Educational Association, and the National Council of Independent Schools.

In 1941 the Jesuit High Schools of what was then the Maryland-New York Province introduced a modified curriculum, which was to be put into effect over a period of years. In 1943-44 all four years were to follow the new program as outlined below. To give the reader an idea of the curriculum at Canisius High School, the full curriculum is given below:

Greek Course	*Science Course*
First Year Latin English Elementary Algebra Civics (one term) Economic Citizenship (one term) Health Library Science (one term)	*First Year* Same as the Greek Course
Second Year Latin English Geometry French or German	*Second Year* Same as the Greek Course *Third Year* Latin
Third Year Latin English French or German Intermediate Algebra (one term)* Trigonometry (one term)* Health Greek	English French or German Intermediate Algebra (one term) Trigonometry (one term) Chemistry* Health *Fourth Year* Latin
Fourth Year Latin English Greek American History Physics or Chemistry* Solid Geometry (one term)* Advanced Algebra (one term) Health	English Physics or Chemistry American History Advanced Algebra (one term)* Solid Geometry (one term)* Health

* Indicates the supplementary courses which may be taken with the approval of the Principal.

Religion, Physical Training, and Speech are taught in all years. All subjects are taught five periods per week except: Latin (8) in first year, 6 in second, third and fourth years; Algebra, 6 in first year; Religion and Physical Training 2; Speech, 1; Health, 1 in first year and 2 in third and fourth year. All periods are forty-five minutes in length. Sixteen units are required for graduation, while eighteen may be completed by qualified students.[20]

The year 1944 marked another great step forward in the history of Canisius High School. "On March 21, 1944, Canisius High School purchased from the City of Buffalo, the property formerly known as the Consistory. To this beautiful site at 1180 Delaware Ave., the entire school will be transferred as soon as conditions permit. On September 29, 1944 the new School was opened to a record enrollment of 342 first-year students."[21]

Since 1944 only first and second year have been at 1180 Delaware Ave., while third and fourth year have continued to use the old building at 651 Washington Street. [Editor's Note: A reminder to the reader that Mr. Kessler's history was published in June 1948.] In November of 1946, ground was broken at 1180 Delaware Ave., adjoining the Consistory building, for a new classroom wing. This new wing is four stories high, and contains 27 classrooms with the full basement being devoted to the cafeteria. The new wing is modern in every respect and will include the latest features of a good school building. When classes are resumed this

THE NEW CANISIUS-ON-DELAWARE

FRESHMAN CLASSES

Image from *Arena* 1945. Addition; not in original Kessler history.

Fall, all students will attend school at 1180 Delaware Avenue, while the old building at 651 Washington Street, which has echoed to the voices of young men since 1872, will be closed. St. Michael's Church, which has cast its shadow over Canisius High School for 76 years, and served as the gathering place for many of Canisius' religious functions, will remain to minister to the needs of the working population of downtown Buffalo.

New classroom wing. Image added; not in original Kessler history. Source: CHS Archives.

VI. The Curriculum

Since Canisius was founded by the Jesuits and has been maintained by them ever since, its curriculum is substantially that of the other schools conducted by the Society of Jesus in every part of the globe. Based on the *Ratio Studiorum Societatis Jesu*, a system originally outlined by the most prominent Jesuit educators in 1599, revised in 1832, and always attended with great success, it secures on the one hand that stability so essential to educational thoroughness, while on the other hand it makes liberal allowances for the varying needs of the times.

It gives prominence to the refinements embodied in the ancient classics through the vernacular; mathematics, history, and the natural sciences receive the attention of essential branches.

The study of Latin and Greek has ever been regarded as the best means of a uniform and perfect development of all the mental faculties, of training a youthful mind about all [things vital] to accurate and logical thinking. As we have seen in previous chapters the classics were the core of the curriculum when it opened in 1870, and even to this day a student desiring to graduate from Canisius High School must have four years of Latin, although he may substitute scientific subjects in place of Greek.

In the year 1870 there appeared in one of the local papers an advertisement, which stated that the purpose of Canisius College was, "to offer the advantages of a thorough Classical and Commercial education."[22] The diaries of the early Jesuit Fathers at Canisius testify that both of these courses were started the very first year. As we have already seen the first assignment given at Canisius was the memorization of the "Our Father" and "Hail Mary" in Latin. We can only surmise what the classical and commercial courses consisted of the first few years since no catalogue was published until the year 1873-74. Moreover, no copy of that exists today, with the result that we must rely upon early diaries and the newspapers for our information about the curriculum.

From an account in one of Buffalo's early Catholic newspapers we do know that the Classical Course embraced six years and the Commercial Course three years.[23] The exact year in which the Commercial Course was lengthened to four years is uncertain. Later catalogues would lead us to believe that it was always four years but, as was pointed out above, the advertisement in the newspaper listed it as three years. In the catalogue for 1879-80 for the first time it is mentioned that the Commercial Course embraces four years. The six years of the Classical Course would be comparable to our present four years of high school and the first two years of college.

In the first catalogue your author was able to find, the year 1874-1875, there appears this notice. "Preparatory course will be opened for the benefit of those students whose insufficient knowledge of the rudiments prevents them from following the regular course."[24] The entire curriculum is still not listed, although from the prizes awarded at the Fifth Annual Commencement, June 30, 1875, we can gain some knowledge of the courses offered. Honors were awarded to students in the following subjects: Christian Doctrine, Latin, Greek, English, German, French, Mathematics, Algebra, Geometry, Geography, History, and Bookkeeping.[25] In the following year United States History and Universal History were added. The first listing of the complete course of studies at Canisius is given in the catalogue for the year 1876-77. Because it is the first one it is quoted in full.

The whole course of instruction comprises three different departments: the Preparatory, the Classical, and the Commercial.

The Preparatory: This department is intended to receive such pupils as are not sufficiently prepared to enter the classical or commercial department, provided they know how to read and write.
- English: Reading, writing, and spelling
- Arithmetic: Rudiments, mental arithmetic
- Geography
- Penmanship
- Christian Doctrine

The Classical Department: This department consists of six classes:
- First Grammar Class: Latin, English, Arithmetic, Geography, Christian Doctrine, Penmanship.
- Second Grammar Class: Latin, English, Arithmetic, Geography, Ancient History, Christian Doctrine, Penmanship (optional).
- Third Grammar Class: Latin, Greek, English, Algebra, Roman History, Christian Doctrine, Bookkeeping (optional).
- Humanities: Latin, Greek, English, Algebra or Geometry, Modern History, Christian Doctrine, Bookkeeping.
- Poetry: Latin, Greek, English, Trigonometry, Modern History, Christian Doctrine, Natural Philosophy.
- Rhetoric: Latin, Greek, English, Trigonometry, United States History, Christian Doctrine, Natural Philosophy.

The Commercial Department: The studies in this department are regulated so as to fit a young man for the commercial pursuits. It embraces the following branches: English, Arithmetic, Geography, Bookkeeping, Penmanship, Natural Sciences, United States History, Christian Doctrine, Algebra and Geometry (optional).

A full course in German and French was open to all students in both the Classical and Commercial Departments.[26]

In the year 1879, a seventh year was added to the Classical Course, and was Philosophy. It consisted of Mental Philosophy, Moral Philosophy, Natural Philosophy, Mathematics, Astronomy, and Christian Instruction. This course was optional and the student could continue one or two years longer. After the College obtained its charter from the Board of Regents the seventh year became obligatory. Eventually the eighth year was added to the Classical Course and it became necessary to complete the eight years to obtain the Bachelor of Arts Degree.

Beginning with the Fall Semester of 1894, the first step in a definite separation of the high school and college curriculum was made. The course of instruction was divided into an Academic and Collegiate department. It embraced as obligatory branches Christian Doctrine; the English, Latin, and Greek Languages; English Literature, Rhetoric and Poetry; Elocution; Penmanship; History and Geography; Mathematics, Bookkeeping; Physics, Chemistry, Geology, and Astronomy; Logic, Metaphysics, and Ethics. The German language was obligatory for all in all departments.[27]

Besides the obligatory branches, instruction was given to those who desired it, in the French language, Drawing, Typewriting, and Instrumental Music. From these optional studies, however, pupils were excluded who did not give satisfaction in their obligatory studies.

The Preparatory class was still maintained. A further innovation was the establishment of a Post-graduate class in Philosophy, offered twice a week and open to graduates and professional men. At the same time the method whereby a Master of Arts Degree was obtained is listed. It was granted to those attending the Post-graduate Class, provided they passed satisfactory examinations in the subject matter of the lectures. It could also be attained by those graduates of the College who, although they did not attend the Post-graduate Class, successfully pursued some learned profession, two years after graduation.

The classes in the Collegiate Department were known as Senior Philosophy, Junior Philosophy, Rhetoric, and Poetry. In the Academic Department, the senior year was termed First Academic; the junior year, Second Academic; the sophomore year, Third Academic; and the first year, Fourth Academic.

With four years now equivalent to the high school course offered in other schools in the city, candidates applying for admission into Fourth Academic had to be well-grounded in the preliminary studies specified in the Syllabus of the University of the State of New York. These studies indicated were English, Arithmetic, and Geography.

Students seeking admission to the Collegiate Department had to meet certain specified requirements in the fields of English, Latin, Greek, History, Mathematics, and German. This indicates that students would now be accepted who were graduates of high schools other than Canisius.

Beginning with the Fall semester of 1894 the first year of the Commercial Course was dropped. By the year 1897 the Commercial Course ceased to exist in the curriculum of Canisius. Once this happened Canisius offered only one course and that was the Classical Course. For the next twenty-five years the Classical Course remained quite constant, with only minor changes being made. Early in the twenties we find science creeping into the High School curriculum. Eventually the Classical Course was divided so that in the second year instead of taking Greek, a boy could pursue three science subjects during the next three years. Other than these three science subjects, he followed the very same course as those students who were taking the Classical Course. Another modification took place in 1941 when the curriculum was divided into two courses, the Greek Course and the Science Course. The first and second years of these two courses are identical. In the third year, students who do not take up the study of Greek, may study two branches of science during the next two years. In other respects, the Science Course is the same as the Greek Course.

Thus, we see that over a period of 78 years the *Ratio Studiorum* of the Society of Jesus has been maintained pretty much in its original form. It has not fallen prey to so many of the modern trends in education, trends which the Jesuits contend are superficialities. Certainly, one can justly conclude that it has weathered many tests and still appears to be the best system yet devised for through training of the minds of the youths of all lands.

Notes

[1] *Canisius College Catalogue*, 1886-87.

[2] *Canisius College Catalogue*, 1894-95.

[3] *Buffalo Courier*, May 1, 1895.

[4] *Ibid.*

[5] *Buffalo Courier*, May 1, 1895.

[6] *Canisius College Catalogue*, 1894-1895, p. 62.

[7] *Woodstock Letters*, Volume 24 (1895), p. 496.

[8] *The Chronicler*, Vol. 2, No. 3, January, 1908, p. 9.

[9] *Lest We Forget*, June, 1912, p. 79.

[10] *Lest We Forget*, June, 1912, p. 79.

[11] *Woodstock Letters*, Vol. 29 (1900), p. 5.

[12] *Lest We Forget*, June, 1912, p. 7. Same: *Woodstock Letters* Vol. 29 (1900), pp. 120-122.

[13] "Charles A. Brady Dies; Canisius Prof, Author, Literary Critic for News was 83." May 6, 1995. Accessed from the Internet May 16, 2018.

[14] Brady, Charles A. '29. *The First Hundred Years: Canisius College 1870-1970*. Canisius College, Buffalo, NY. 1970, pp. 271-272.

[15] Broderick, James. *Saint Ignatius Loyola: The Pilgrim Years*. Ignatius Press, San Francisco, 1956, 1998, qtd. in Brady, Charles A. '29. *The First Hundred Years: Canisius College 1870-1970*. Canisius College, Buffalo, NY. 1970, pp. 271-272.

[16] *The Arena*, Vol. 5, No. 1, October 3, 1919.

[17] *The Arena*, Vol. 5, No. 7, February 6, 1920.

[18] *Woodstock Letters*, Vol. 50 (1921), p. 227.

[19] *Woodstock Letters*, Vol. 51 (1922), pp. 266-268.

[20] *Canisius High School Catalogue*, 1943-44, 1947-48.

[21] *Ibid.*, 1944-45.

[22] *Buffalo Daily Courier*, September 1, 1870.

[23] *Catholic Union*, August 22, 1872.

[24] *Canisius College Catalogue*, 1874-75.

[25] *Ibid.*, 1874-75.

[26] *Canisius College Catalogue*, 1876-1877, pp. 7-10.

[27] *Canisius College Catalogue*, 1894-95.

CHAPTER 5

The Kessler History, Part III:
Summary & Appendices

VII. Summary & Suggestions for Further Research

The History of Canisius begins about ten years after the arrival of the first Jesuit Fathers in Buffalo. However, it did not become a reality until after the Buffalo Mission of the German Province was founded in 1869. These German Fathers, sent as missionaries to Buffalo, realized the desires of Bishop Timon, when on September 5, 1870, they opened Canisius College in a small structure on Ellicott Street, which had formerly been used as a store. Two years later a new school building was opened on Washington Street. This building formed the central portion of the building when the north and south wings were added in the eighties.

In 1883 Canisius College obtained its charter from the Board of Regents, granting it authority to confer honors and degrees. By 1894, there appears for the first time a definite separation of the curriculum into the Collegiate and Academic departments, along the lines set up in the *Ratio Studiorum Societatis Jesu*. In the year 1906, the charter of the College was amended so as to include the academic department.

Because of the gradual increase in enrollment, crowded conditions necessitated the abandonment of the boarding department at Canisius College in 1908. At the same time, the decision was made to select a site for a new college building. In 1910, ground was broken at Main and Jefferson Avenues for the new building. The end of the year 1912 saw the completion of this new building. When the New Year dawned, the college students were moved into this building and the high school students were in complete possession of the old building at 651 Washington Street. The President of Canisius College continued as President of Canisius High School also until 1919, when the Rev. Robert Johnson, S.J., became the first President exclusively of Canisius High School.

In 1928 Canisius High School secured its own charter from the Board of Regents. Its course of studies still was patterned after the *Ratio Studiorum Societatis Jesu*, and remains that way today. Severely tested and not found wanting, it has yielded little to the trends of the times in education. Of all the modern trends, science alone has made a small inroad into the classical curriculum of Canisius High School.

This year [1948] the old building at 651 Washington Street, Canisius' home for 76 years, will be closed. During the summer the move will be completed so that the Consistory building at 1180 Delaware Avenue, purchased in 1944, together with the new wing started in 1946 and now nearly completed, will be the new home of Canisius High School.

During the research work done on this history many subjects were discovered in which needed research can be done. An urgent need exists for a History of the Diocese of Buffalo. At present two exist, but both are woefully inadequate and contain many inaccuracies. In the case of the Bishops of Buffalo it is the same story. Extensive work could be done these men.

In regard to Canisius the field is practically untouched. There is need for a thorough and detailed History of Canisius. The story of the Buffalo Mission of the German Province would be an excellent topic, although it would require a thorough knowledge of German and Latin. A detailed survey of the Alumni of Canisius would be of inestimable worth. The development of the *Ratio Studiorum* in the Canisius curriculum would make an interesting study. If these few were done, they would lead to many more, which would be of great historical value to the Society of Jesus, to the College and High School, and to the City of Buffalo.

Appendix

General Order of Class Days for Boarders

5:30 A.M. Rising
5:50	Morning Prayers, Study
7:10	Breakfast
7:30	Recreation
8:00	Mass
8:30	Class
10:15	Recreation
10:30	Class
11:55	Study
12:15 P.M.	Dinner
12:45	Recreation
1:45	Class
3:15	Study
4:00	Recreation
5:00	Study
7:15	Supper
7:30	Night Prayers, Spiritual Reading, Free Study
9:15	Dormitory

Tuesday and Thursday afternoons, no school.

Sunday's Order

6:00 A.M. Rising
6:30	Morning Prayers, Study, or Mass and Communion
7:15	Breakfast
8:30	Mass and Sermon
9:30	Recreation
10:30	Study
12:00 P.M.	Dinner
12:30	Recreation
2:00	Benediction
2:30	Study
3:30	Recreation
5:00	Study, etc., etc., as above.

Student Organizations at Canisius

1870	Immaculate Conception Sodality
1875	Canisius Literary Society
1878	Palestrina Society
1880	Dramatic Association
1880	Caecilian Band
1880	Canisius Silver Cornet Band
1881	Sodality of the Annunciation
1883	Euphonia Orchestra
1886	Canisius Caecilia Choir
1886	St. Thomas Philosophical Society
1889	Sodality of the Immaculate Heart of Mary
1893	Canisius Commercial Literary Debating Society
1895	Canisius Day Scholars' Association
1895	Columbian Dramatic Association
1896	Canisius Alumni Sodality
1896	Sodality of the Purification
1896	Canisius Military Organization
1896	St. John Berchmans Society
1898	Apostleship of Prayer, League of the Sacred Heart
1901	Canisius Glee Club and Dramatic Association
1902	Kappa Delta Sigma
1907	The Palestra
1908	Literary and Dramatic Society
1909	Academic Literary Society
1914	Behrens Debating Society

Mr. Kessler's Bibliography

Canisius Archives

The Arena. Volumes 1 (1915) through 33 (1948). The literary magazine of Canisius High School, edited by the students and published quarterly.

Canisius College Catalogue. 1874 to 1913. A yearly issue of the college.

Canisius Monthly. Volumes 1 (1914) through 5 (1919). The literary magazine of Canisius College, edited by the students.

Catalogue Sociorum et Officiorum Dispersae Provinciae Germaniae Societatis Jesu, ineunte anno MDCCCLXXXVIII. Gestel St. Michaelis, in institu Surdo-Mutorum. 1888.

The Chronicler. Volumes 1 and 2. (1906-1907). A monthly news and literary magazine published by the Canisius College Glee Club and Dramatic Association.

Canisius High School Catalogue. 1913-1947. Issued yearly by the High School.

Lest We Forget. 1908 through 1914. Issued yearly and edited by the students of Canisius College. A yearbook combined with literary works.

Silver Jubilee Program of Canisius College, 1895.

Woodstock Letters. Volumes 1 (1872) through 63 (1935). A private publication of the Society of Jesus. Published at Woodstock College, Woodstock, Maryland.

General Works

Donohue, Thomas. *History of the Catholic Church in Western New York.* Buffalo: Catholic Historical Publishing Co., 1904.

Garraghan, Gilbert J. *The Jesuits in the Middle United States.* New York: America Press. 1938. Volumes 1 and 3.

Harney, Martin P., S.J., *The Jesuits in History: The Society of Jesus through Four Centuries.* New York: The America Press, 1941.

Hill, Henry W., Editor. *Municipality of Buffalo, New York, a History 1720-1923.* New York: Lewis Historical Publishing Co., 1923. Volume 2.

Larned, J.N. *A History of Buffalo, New York.* New York: Progress of the Empire State Co. 1911. Volume 2.

McGucken, William J., S.J., *The Jesuits and Education.* New York: Bruce Publishing Co. 1932.

Metropolitan Catholic Almanac and Laity's Directory for the Year of Our Lord 1851. Baltimore: Fielding Lucas, Jr., 1851.

Timon, John. *Missions in Western New York and Church History of the Diocese of Buffalo by the Bishop of Buffalo* (John Timon). Buffalo: Catholic Sentinel Print. 1862.

White, Truman C., Editor. *Our Country and its People: A Descriptive Work on Erie County, New York.* The Boston History Co. 1895. Volume 1.

Wilner, Merton M. *Niagara Frontier: A Narrative and Documentary History.* Chicago: S.J., Clarke Publishing Co. 1931.

Newspapers

Buffalo Daily Courier   September 1, 1870, May 1, 1895, June 22, 1895.
Catholic Union   August 22, 1872.

CHAPTER 6

The Rand Mansion and The Buffalo Consistory

AS MR. KESSLER'S HISTORY made clear, the transition throughout the mid-to-late 1940s from the Washington Street Campus to the new "Canisius-on-Delaware" represented a major step in the school's evolution. The current campus is among the most remarkable among Jesuit high schools because of its unique architectural characteristics and fascinating backstory. One element of that story is the fortuitous series of events that brought Father James Redmond, S.J., and George "Chicky" Evans '18 to 1180 Delaware Avenue—and the school itself soon thereafter. Father Ron Sams S.J., '46 shared the story in an interview for this book:

We bought the building in March of 1944 for $95,000. And that was a steal. What had happened was, we had some money in the bank at the time because beginning in January 1944, we had a fundraising raffle. The idea was to build a swimming pool in the old school. There was no thought of moving. Now, how we could have done that [build a pool], I have no idea, because the buildings were just not set up for it. [For example,] would you believe...that in the gymnasium of the old school,  Rev. Ron Sams, S.J., '46 *there were pillars. Two pillars in the basketball court! So when we would play schools there, they'd always say we had seven men on our team!*[4]

Anyway, we didn't buy it from the Masons. We bought it from the City of Buffalo. The City of Buffalo used it as a municipal auditorium until Kleinhan's [Music Hall] was built. The Masons lost it in the early 1930s. This place was empty, and that's why R.O.T.C. was able to use it. [Editor's Note: More on this later.]

This fellow, Chicky Evans '18, was a member of the Buffalo Common Council. He knew about this building being empty.... He was a very good personal friend of Fr. Jim Redmond, who was Principal, President of Canisius High School, and Pastor of St. Michael's, all together, for years. Chicky Evans finds out that this building is available. He says, "Father, why do you want to renovate that old building down on Washington Street. There's a beautiful building right on Delaware. It's a good location, the facilities are terrific, and it has a swimming pool! Father, let me show you this building." They got the keys, and went through it, and Father Redmond was taken. He was all for it. And so, within a matter of a few weeks, this thing went through the Common

---

[4] As Mark Russell '50 explained during an August 2017 interview for this book, the truth about the pillars is hilarious: "For decades, they had to dribble around the pillars. And when they tore the building down, it turned out the things were only decorative. Turns out they supported nothing."

Council...and there was opposition because it went so fast, and because it was only $95,000.... I think we paid it off within two years.[1]

This author asked Fr. Sams, "Would it be safe to say that we're here on this campus because of Chicky Evans?" His response: "Absolutely."

George "Chicky" Evans '18

George Evans, Jr., shared a typewritten biography of his father, George "Chicky" Evans, Sr., '18, with Father Sams. According to this biography, Chicky Evans, Sr., was born in Buffalo on July 14th, 1901. He attended St. Brigid's Parochial School and then Canisius, enrolling in the fall of 1915. Following his graduation from Canisius, he attended Canisius College, graduated with a B.A. in 1922, and then progressed to the University of Buffalo School of Law. After a year, illness required him to withdraw from law school, but he returned to finish school, eventually earning admission to the Bar in 1929.

George "Chicky" Evans Sr.,
Class of '18 Image: CHS Archives

Following four years of employment at the Merchants Mutual Casualty Company, he entered private practice in association with former Surrogate Charles T. Yeager in the Ellicott Square Building. The biography describes his rise in the local political arena:

When he first began practicing law he entered into the political field as a committeeman for the Republican Party, and later as General Chairman of the Fourth Ward. In 1943 he was chosen to run for Councilman-at-Large and was successful in his campaign. He was elected President Pro Tem of the Council, which position he held for the full four-year term.[2]

It was at this time, as Evans was preparing to take his seat on the Council, that Rev. James Redmond, S.J., became President of Canisius High School in 1942. Redmond and Evans had been friends from childhood.

Evans, Jr.'s biography of his father goes on to describe the events that Father Sams retold, above. It was at a homecoming party held at the Statler Hotel, at which Evans served as Toastmaster, that the drive to raise money for the aforementioned swimming pool envisioned for the Washington Street campus began. The drive succeeded in gathering $25,000 for the pool.

It was at this time that the federal government, having leased the Rand Mansion on Delaware from the City of Buffalo for $1.00 per year, ended the lease, thus returning the property to the City's ownership. (During the federal government lease, the property was used as an Army ROTC barracks and training facility.)

According to the Evans biography, Evans and Father Redmond met with Charles Wick (CHS '28) of the Niagara Mohawk Power Corporation and Louis Perrone, a former newspaperman, on three occasions to map out a plan of action to secure the property. The initial step was to make an offer to the City, and Evans submitted an offer of $95,000. Apparently, the speed with which the bid was approved took Evans and the others somewhat by surprise. Despite having submitted a cash bid, the only monies immediately on hand were the $25,000 raised during the recent swimming pool drive. As such, the original offer had to be modified to involve a $25,000 down payment and a $70,000, two-year mortgage. A second drive quickly raised this amount and enabled payoff of the balance. It is worth noting the tremendously favorable nature of this purchase for Canisius High School. According to *The Buffalo Courier Express*, the property was valued at $2 million.[3]

Evans—along with his classmate Walter Koessler '18 (who graduated from Canisius College in 1922 and for whom the College's athletic complex is named[4]) —worked closely with Father Redmond to initiate the process of acquiring adjacent property for the new campus, including grounds that would eventually contain the new classroom wing.[5]

The Common Council Proceedings Related to 1180 Delaware

A perusal of the City of Buffalo Common Council Proceedings from late 1943 into 1944 offers an interesting chronicle of these events leading to the acquisition of the new campus property.

December 17, 1943: "The City Board of Canvassers having canvassed the whole number of votes cast for all candidates for the office of Councilman-at-Large...hereby certify that the following named persons received the votes set opposite their names...." George J. Evans, Republican, is listed as having received 86,015 votes, the highest among the six candidates and the total votes of 304,798.[6]

January 3, 1944: The Proceedings name "President Pro Tempore GEORGE J. EVANS Councilman at Large."[7]

February 29, 1944: The Proceedings mention item "No. 110—Canisius High School –Offer to purchase premises known as No. 1180 Delaware Avenue. Referred to the Committee on Finance and the Comptroller."[8]

March 14, 1944: "FROM THE COMPTROLLER [Frank M. Davis] No. 4, Buffalo, March 6, 1944. Offer of Canisius High School to Purchase No. 1180 Delaware Avenue. (C.C.P., No. 110, February 29, 1944.)

Your Honorable Body has referred to Finance Committee and to me the above offer of Canisius High School to purchase these premises, acquired by foreclosure, and formerly occupied by Buffalo Consistory.

The question of disposition of this magnificent property is peculiarly one of policy, to be determined by the Common Council, and I am therefore of the opinion that a recommendation from me would be inappropriate.

I wish to report that there is at this time no other offer before me. At the time Canisius College took over the building for cadet-training purposes at the request of the War Department, the Congress on Industrial Organization was negotiating for a lease with the option to purchase. I learn through the Press that the War Department has recently addressed to the City Clerk an inquiry as to whether the premises will be available from time to time for induction purposes at the rate of $35.00 for each day of such use.

I deem it my duty to add that it would cost over $25,000.00 per year merely to maintain this property if no purchaser or tenant is secured when Canisius College surrenders possession under its current lease. This figure does not cover operating the building but merely preserving it from damage by the elements and by vandalism. The only alternative would be demolition of the building which would certainly cost upwards of $100,000.00, and would involve ruining a monumental building the equal of which can scarcely be found in this City of beautiful buildings."[9]

Later in the same record of Proceedings for March 14, 1944, the details of the Recommendation by the Committee on Finance, chaired by Anthony R. Lombardo, to pass the resolution paving the way for Canisius High School to secure the property. The content of those Proceedings describes, in exhaustive detail, the particulars of the property's dimensions and boundaries, along with the deed history.

Part of the recommendation included the financial arrangement for purchase:

...That the Comptroller be, and he hereby is, authorized to deliver to the said Board of Trustees of Canisius High School a deed to the premises upon receipt within sixty (60) days from the effective date of this resolution, of the sum of $25,000.00 in cash and a bond secured by a purchase money mortgage covering the premises, in the sum of $70,000.00, payable as follows: The whole of said principal sum of $70,000 to be due and payable on or before July 1, 1946, together with interest thereon at the rate of four per cent (4%) per annum on all of the principal sums remaining...[10]

It was 1944. Canisius had found a new home.

Delaware & West Ferry: a "History of Misfortune"

The Jesuits were arguably quite lucky, by financial measures, to have secured such a magnificent property for such a relatively low cost. Certainly, it was fortuitous that Chicky Evans Sr. '18 was able to learn about the opportunity, convey it to Father Redmond, and thus set into motion an unlikely and serendipitous series of events that landed Canisius High School in possession of its current site.

This being said, it is also known to longtime faculty members and administrators that whenever the school struggles with hard times, there are inevitably (only half-joking) whispers among the old guard of a "curse" that lies on the property. Some attribute it to the Masons, upset that their property fell into Jesuit hands—others consider it an older dynamic rooted in earlier years. Because certainly, well before the tragedies that would befall George F. Rand and his family, the corner of West Ferry and Delaware Avenue was the site of a far more infamous tragedy.

Death of a President

Where the current Montante Academic Wing stands, at the corner of Delaware Avenue and West Ferry Street, once stood the Milburn Mansion. More specifically, the building's foundation lay partially in what is now a nondescript parking lot used by faculty and some upperclassmen with permits. One can assume that as teachers or boys get in their cars to

Postcard depicting the Milburn Mansion. Image from CHS Archives.

go home each day, it is unlikely they stop to consider that their parking space may well be within yards of—or perhaps even be on the exact spot—where a United States President died.

As Erik Brady wrote in his 1979 *Buffalo Courier Express* article, "History in the Hallways," the home took on great significance in the hours and days following the shooting of President McKinley during Buffalo's Pan American Exposition in 1901:

The flower-decked Milburn home was converted into a makeshift heart of the nation: it was the Capitol, the Cabinet meeting place, a diplomat's headquarters, the guest house, the hospital, the news bureau—and, finally, the place where William McKinley died. For eight days he lay hovering between life and death on a brass bed trimmed with gold. Huge cakes of ice were placed beneath giant fans to cool the air when a heat wave set in. Traffic was blocked off to ensure the patient's rest. Servants approached on foot, and prominent visitors arrived in rubber-tired carriages. After a slow turn for the better, McKinley took a sudden turn for the worse, and at 2 a.m. Sept. 14, he died. Simple funeral services were held in the Milburn house, and the body lay in state at City Hall for a day (Abraham Lincoln is the only other president to have lain in state in Buffalo). Theodore Roosevelt was inaugurated further

down Delaware at the Wilcox Mansion. Then McKinley's body and the focus of the world were transported to Washington.[11]

The Milburn House was demolished in the late 1950s; all that remains to commemorate the site is a metal plaque. Where students and faculty begin and end their days—undoubtedly with myriad responsibilities on their minds—they tread where our nation's history took a consequential turn.

The Tragic History of the Rand Mansion

Not far from the site of the Milburn House still stands the Rand Mansion, now known as the Koessler Academic Center, home of what Canisius long ago designated Berchmans Hall.

George F. Rand, Sr., was the President and Chairman of the Marine Trust Co. and was key to the development of New York State's first consolidated banking system, Marine Midland Corporation. The 29-floor Rand Building on Lafayette Square, named for George, Sr., was the tallest building in Buffalo when it opened in 1929.[12]

H. Katherine Smith's article in *The Buffalo Courier-Express* dated Sunday, March 16, 1952, is headlined "School Site Has History of Misfortune." The headline was apt, for 1180 Delaware Avenue was, indeed, the address of great sadness for the George F. Rand family. Smith describes how the site went from dream home to unintended memorial in a relatively short span of years:

The mansion was planned for the late George F. Rand, Sr., Chairman of the board of the Marine Trust Co. and one of Buffalo's foremost bankers and financiers. Mr. Rand worked with the architects to create a home in which he, his wife and their two sons and two daughters could live luxuriously and entertain their many friends. Hardly had construction been started when Mrs. Rand died. The following summer, 1919, Mr. Rand made a combined business and pleasure trip to Europe. In Paris, he visited Clemenceau, then premier of France, and made him a gift of $500,000 for a memorial to the heroic *battalion of the 136ᵗʰ French Infantry, buried alive in the trenches during the historic Battle of Verdun. Mr. Rand was a passenger on a plane flying from Paris to London. The plane crashed over England and all aboard lost their lives.*[13]

The Rand children, including George Jr., Calvin, Gretchen, and Evelyn, moved into the mansion following its completion in 1921. Designed by architects Franklyn J. and William A. Kidd in the Jacobean and Tudor Revival styles,[14] the home provided a beautiful but emotionally uncomfortable home for the Rand children. H. Katherine Smith: "The move was not a happy occasion. The shadow of the tragedy of the father's sudden death seemed to linger on the home in which he'd planned to live. During the few years the four young people lived in the mansion, they were saddened by the recurring thought that neither of their parents had enjoyed the home intended for them.... As members of the Rand family married, none of them wished to continue to live in the mansion. In 1925, it was sold to the Masons and converted into the Buffalo Consistory."[15]

Entrance to the Rand Mansion. Note the "R" formed in the metal-work. Photo: CHS Archives. Photo undated.

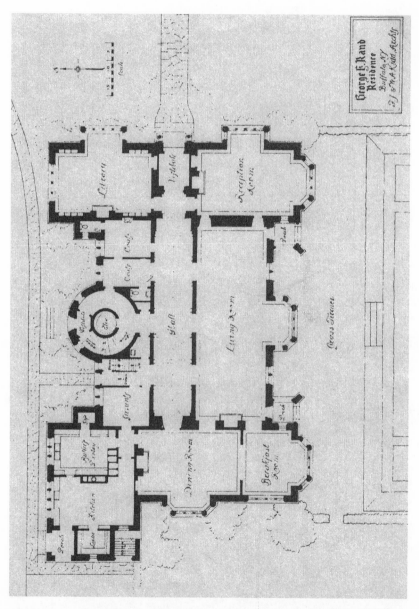

Floorplan as depicted in The American Architect--The Architectural Review. October 10, 1923. Image Source: CHS Archives.

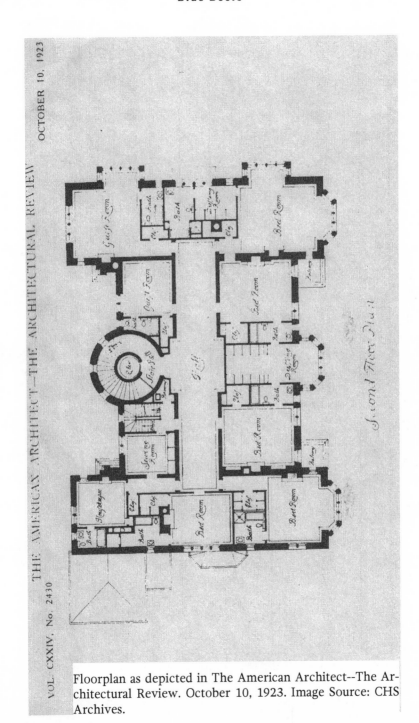

OCTOBER 10, 1923

THE AMERICAN ARCHITECT—THE ARCHITECTURAL REVIEW

VOL. CXXIV, No. 2430

Floorplan as depicted in The American Architect--The Architectural Review. October 10, 1923. Image Source: CHS Archives.

The Buffalo Consistory - A Masonic Triumph

If the tragedy associated with the Rand family cast a desolate shade upon 1180 Delaware, the Masons ushered in the dawn of a new era for the property—symbolized brilliantly in the well-recognized stained-glass sun that looms large upon the auditorium ceiling. However, the informed reader will bear in mind that despite the architectural glories of the Consistory building, and the prestige of prominent concert performances that took place there, this was a short-lived era lasting no more than about twenty years. Erik Brady offers a succinct introduction to the transition:

The stone mansion with the English Tudor architecture lent itself readily to the purposes of a fraternal organization. To that end the Masons erected the huge auditorium in the back, complete with swimming pool; Johnny Weissmuller [the Olympic swimmer and actor who portrayed Tarzan] swam in it as part of the gala opening ceremonies. The auditorium is still filled with ancient Masonic designs, and the ceiling scene of the sun and the constellations reputedly serves as the building's cornerstone—an astrologer could look at the configurations and determine the exact day of the aud's dedication.[16]

Commemorative Pamphlet offers a Narrative Tour

A pamphlet distributed by the Ancient and Accepted Scottish Right of Freemasonry (A.A.S.R.) upon the opening of the Buffalo Consistory Temple provides fascinating insights into the architectural features of this historic complex. Its introduction reads:

The Contractors of Buffalo, employed in the construction and equipment of the new Buffalo Consistory Temple A.A.S.R., take pleasure in presenting to Consistory members this souvenir booklet, a booklet including pictorial presentations—commemorating the completion of the finest Consistory Temple in the country. They share with you a mutual pride in such a magnificent structure, and are happy to have had a part in making it a reality.[17]

The pamphlet offers a narrative tour of the original Consistory. Excerpts shall be included here with images interspersed.

The main entrance is at the side, parallel to the automobile road, and has large oaken doors embellished with Masonic carvings and wrought iron. Just beyond the vestibule is the grand lobby, from which lead the principal staircases and promenades, adhering closely to Greek simplicity. The floor and wainscot are of black and gold marble, the walls of gold and the ceiling polychrome, supported by huge monolithic Doric columns of black and gold marble to match the surrounding colors. The furniture includes dull green carpets and davenports, chairs and tables of walnut and color, bronze torchers and other interesting features...[18]

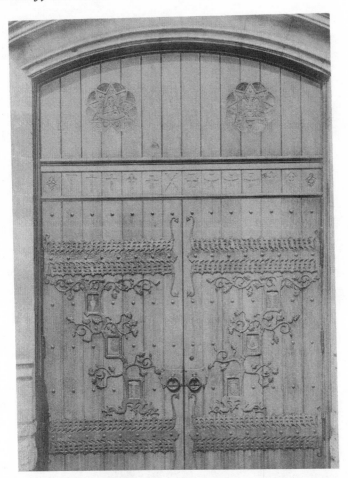

Image of "The Blue Doors" in their original form, before they were blue. Source: CHS Archives.

The "Grand Lobby," now known formally as Higgins Hall, named in memory of CHS President Rev. James P. Higgins, S.J., '77. More commonly known simply as "The Foyer," this expansive room also contained the ticket office. Images: CHS Archives.

On entering the auditorium, one is suddenly awed by the orderly spaciousness of the huge room. Ten columns of the Corinthian order support the ornate cornice. The proscenium arch is surmounted by the Consistory double eagle. Above the double eagle and radiating from it is a great sun whose rays extend across the entire ceiling representing the open sky. Contrary to usual auditorium procedure the organ has been housed above the back of the room. In this way all the organ tones come from one expanse of grille, the entire width of the room, which gives the Consistory one of the most perfect installations. The stage is complete in every detail, having drops, sides, and props telling the story of Masonic history from its early beginning to the present day...[19]

The sunburst above the double eagle over the auditorium stage. Image: CHS Archives.

Interior of the auditorium. Images: CHS Archives.

Free-masonry pursues the oldest method of instruction in the world—Symbolism. So with great care and study a certain amount of Masonic symbolism has been introduced into the architecture of the Temple. In the Auditorium frieze are the symbols of all the Consistory degrees from the 4th to the 32nd. In the promenades, various characters and symbols have been painted upon the wall frieze. Symbolism of color—blue, yellow, and red—is the keynote of the lighting scheme.[20]

Ballard Crooker and Townsend S.M. Carpenter, themselves 32nd degree masons, were the general contractors...To these contractors is due the credit of incorporating such fine workmanship into its construction.[21]

The pediment is the dominating feature of the entire room [the auditorium], and portrays the principal masonic steps to the 33rd degree with their respective insignia. Supporting this pediment are ten columns, five on each side, each column molded and cast in two separate pieces—the seams running full length of the shaft. All column and ornamental model work for the entire building was executed in the studio of the contractor.[22]

The auditorium, including the balcony, has a seating capacity of approximately 2500...and is 175 ft. long, 115 ft. wide and towers to a height of 50 ft. to the sunburst in the ceiling. The opera chairs are the product of the American Seating Co., the largest manufacturers of high-grade opera chairs in the world. The castings are finished in brown and the upholstering in genuine blue leather, with hinges of the famous ball-bearing type.[23] Without question the ballroom is the most beautiful of the entire scheme. It is an oblong room with a side aisle, broken by arches whose groins pierce the ceiling. The room is a rich fantasy of color harmoniously blended from the golden tinted walls and ceiling. Beautiful transparent French crystal chandeliers, bronze grilles and carvings with old mythology as their theme, flashing mirrors, brocaded draperies and a few sumptuous bits of old furniture all add to its beauty.[24]

The Consistory's Ball Room is a glorious ensemble of colorful decorative motifs, made dramatic by a pageant of figures telling the story of the dance from the dawn of time, and by huge French crystal chandeliers in gold with cut pendalogues, hanging from the ceiling. Side wall brackets of antique gold complete the lighting effect. Sparkling mirrors and rich brocaded draperies emphasize the luxury of the room. Chandeliers and lighting furniture were furnished and installed by the H.I. Sackett Electric Company.[25]

The Consistory ballroom, now the CHS Library. Image: CHS Archives.

In the basement are the gymnasium, kitchens, eight bowling alleys, guard room, a swimming pool, Turkish baths, exercising rooms, etc. Here, also, is the apparatus which filters and sterilizes the water for the plunge. Here is the heating and ventilating plant. The fuel oil system has completely proven itself. Here are fans for all purposes, house pumps, vacuum pumps, and all the apparatus of a perfect installation.

The Consistory swimming pool. Image: CHS Archives.

The Canisius High School pool, which has changed little since the Consistory days, had a moment of fame on Saturday, October 22, 1927, when Olympian Johnny Weissmuller of Chicago set a new world's record for a 300-yard swim in a meet held there.[26] Other accounts indicate that the pool was christened by Weissmuller. Agnes Geraghty, US Olympic medalist who was inducted in 2003 into the Metropolitan Swimming Hall of Fame, set the world record for the 300-meter breast stroke in the Consistory pool.[27]

The Consistory Bowling Alley, in the location of the current CHS weight training facility. Image: CHS Archives.

High Society and Memorable Events

The Consistory, between the time of its construction and its transfer of ownership to the Jesuits, was home to a wide variety of notable performances and events. This catalogue of activity is worthy of its own history, but a few highlights shall be included here.

The CHS archives hold a printed copy of a web article, source listed as the website of the New York Scottish Rite Masons, accessed from the Internet on February 14, 2010. The URL is no longer active, but according to this printed article:

In 1927 the Consistory was a site of national [sic] convention of the American Bar Association with many dignitaries present, including Chief Justice William H. Taft. This was the beginning of a widespread use of the Consistory

Cathedral* and facilities for major events and activities in the City. Indeed, the Consistory became the Social and Cultural Center for the City, which function existed until the construction of Kleinhans Music Hall. The Consistory auditorium was the scene of concerns, plays, operas, and a variety of events including balls and dances.²⁸

A partial list of performances and events at the Buffalo Consistory held over the years includes:
29

- Fritz Kreisler, "the supreme master of the violin," performed on November 27, 1929 and November 17, 1931.[30] Kreisler was featured on the February 2, 1925 cover of *Time*.[31]

A 1929 program cover for the Buffalo Symphony Orchestra and the 1937 concert program for John McCormack. Source: CHS Archives.

- The famed American vocalist John Francis McCormack (1884-1945) performed his last concert in the United States at the Consistory on March 16, 1937.[32]
- The Consistory hosted the Buffalo Philharmonic Orchestra, and became its regular home following the demolition of the Elmwood Music Hall in 1938 and prior to the opening of Kleinhans in 1940.

- The State University at Buffalo's Ninety-Third Commencement Exercises were held at the Consistory on June 14, 1939, including an address by Dr. James Rowland Angell, President Emeritus of Yale University.[33]

---

* The Masonic term for the facility

The Departure of the Masons

The article referenced above, published by the website of the New York Scottish Rite Masons, indicates that "in June of 1942, the City of Buffalo took over the property at 1180 Delaware for back taxes."[34]

This dispels the common misconception that the Jesuits purchased the Consistory building from the Masons. In fact, given the historical animosity between the Roman Catholic Church and the Freemasons, the Masons would likely be reluctant to see their facility in Jesuit hands. This very long history is not the subject of this book, but the informed reader should know that this antipathy is no small matter, and the antagonism is centuries old. The Inquisition saw anti-Masonic efforts, and the 1917 *Code of Canon Law* declared that membership in the Freemasons would earn automatic excommunication from the Church. While a 1983 revision saw the removal of the explicit rule for excommunication, the fundamental incompatibility between Roman Catholicism and the Freemasons remained implicit.[35]

On some occasions, the Jesuits have made efforts to diminish the Masonic imagery in the aud. For example, one of the double-headed eagle's heads was meticulously painted over for just this purpose. According to Rev. Ron Sams, S.J., '46, it was the first maintenance director of the Delaware Avenue facility, Brother William Vogelsang, S.J., who undertook this project. "He was upset by all the Masonic symbols in this now-Catholic school. When he saw the double-headed eagle all around, he said, 'Well, this is obviously a Masonic symbol, but it could be canonized as the Holy Spirit!' So he blacked out one of the heads, to make it look more like the Holy Spirit."[36]

Wartime Duty...for the Duration

Since the Consistory was now under the ownership of the City of Buffalo, having been relinquished by the Masons for back taxes, the City sought a use for the facility. This didn't take long, given the need for wartime training space. It became a barracks and training ground for Army Air Cadets and ROTC programs. The March 5, 1943 issue of *The Griffin*, the Canisius College newspaper, ran with the headline "AIR CADETS TO

BEGIN CLASSES. CADETS ACQUIRE CONSISTORY; BUILDING TRANSFORMED INTO EFFICIENT ARMY BARRACKS." A few interesting details point to how the facility was utilized for military purposes.

The transformation worked on the consistory is nothing short of miraculous. The huge main ballroom**, once the glamourous setting for many of Buffalo's social events, is now the "bunk house" quarters. Double-decked type, wooden bunks, are lined in regular rows right through the ballroom. The two huge, pendulum chandeliers are all that is left of its former grandiose fittings. One of these massive, glass fixtures, hangs directly over one of the upper bunks, and so low is it that its occupant can reach up and touch it. Here most of the cadets will lie wrapped in the arms of Morpheus at night where once whirling figures danced to the strain of ballroom music and soft lights.

Underneath the Auditorium proper are many recreational facilities. There is a modern swimming pool, billiard tables, eight bowling alleys, badminton and handball courts, steam baths, and rubbing rooms.

In the front part of the huge building is the great dining room** or, as it is now termed, the "mess hall." A large kitchen runs directly off the dining room.

The individual, smaller rooms on the second floor have been converted into quarters for the officers of the unit.

All is in readiness. The stripped and streamlined Consistory lies cleaned and glistening, aptly readied for its wartime duties, of the duration.[37]

Certainly, today's students fight different battles on the playing fields, in the swimming pool, and in the weight room. The coach's whistle echoes now instead of cadence calls. If a boy is sleeping in the library, it's with his head down on a desk, not in a bunk. His daily wanderings through and

---

** The current Canisius High School Library

** Based on the author's best interpretation of available information, this refers to the current location of Higgins Hall, aka "The Foyer," along with the current Principal's Office suite.

across the Canisius High School campus map out a path through a fascinating historical terrain, where the scenes of history have played out: the death of a President, a family's tragedy, Olympic records, performances by famous musicians and composers, and the rigorous training of thousands of young men before them—training for everything from the gridiron to the battlefield, from war to peace and all parts of life.

The Consistory building is an unforgettable landmark in the memory of every Canisius student. From the first day of freshman orientation to Commencement, the imposing columns and ornate detail loom overhead—constant reminders of the fraternal legacy of which they will forever remain a part. And while the ranks of the Freemasons may be long departed from the echoing, lofty heights of the auditorium, the most visible inscription upon its walls remains utterly resonant for every young man within:

"HE THAT DWELLETH WITH YOU SHALL BE UNTO YOU AS ONE BORN AMONG YOU & THOU SHALT LOVE HIM AS THYSELF."

Notes

[1] Interview with Rev. Ron Sams, S.J., '46. October 3, 2016.

[2] Evans, George, Jr. Typewritten Biography of George Evans Sr. provided to Rev. Ron Sams, S.J..

[3] Brady, Erik. "History in the Hallways." *The Buffalo Courier Express.* December 9, 1979.

[4] Canisius College Website describing Walter Koessler's membership in the Canisius College Athletic Hall of Fame http://www.gogriffs.com/ViewArticle.dbml?DB_OEM_ID=20500&ATCLID=204846005

[5] Evans, George, Jr. Typewritten Biography of George Evans Sr. provided to Rev. Ron Sams, S.J..

[6] City of Buffalo Common Council Proceedings, December 17, 1943

[7] City of Buffalo Common Council Proceedings, January 3, 1944.

[8] City of Buffalo Common Council Proceedings, February 29, 1944.

[9] City of Buffalo Common Council Proceedings, March 14, 1944.

[10] *Ibid*

[11] Chuck LaChusia, Buffalo Architectural History.com http://www.buffaloah.com/h/milb/ Accessed from the Internet June 8, 2017.

[12] Chuck LaChusia, Buffalo Architectural History.com http://www.buffaloah.com/a/del/1180/index.html Accessed from the Internet May 31, 2017.

[13] Smith, H. Katherine. "School Site Has History of Misfortune." *The Buffalo Courier Express.* Sunday, March 16, 1952.

[14] Chuck LaChusia, Buffalo Architectural History.com http://www.buffaloah.com/a/del/1180/index.html Accessed from the Internet May 31, 2017.

[15] Smith, H. Katherine. "School Site Has History of Misfortune." *The Buffalo Courier Express.* Sunday, March 16, 1952.

[16] Brady, Erik. "History in the Hallways." *The Buffalo Courier Express.* December 9, 1979.

[17] Commemorative Buffalo Consistory Temple pamphlet, distributed by the Buffalo Consistory A.A.S.R. upon completion of the facility. Page 1. Copy of original pamphlet in CHS archives.

[18] *Ibid*, pg. 3.

[19] *Ibid*, pg. 3-5.

[20] *Ibid*, pg. 5.

[21] *Ibid*, pg. 7.

[22] *Ibid*, pg. 8.

[23] *Ibid*, pg. 9.

[24] *Ibid*, pg. 5.

[25] *Ibid*, pg. 11.

[26] Page 21 *The Pittsburgh Press* Pittsburgh, PA, Monday, October 24, 1927. Accessed from the Internet June 17, 2017.

[27] *Time Magazine.* "Sport: New World's Records: March 3, 1924" http://content.time.com/time/magazine/article/0,9171,717879,00.html Accessed June 11, 2017.

[28] "A Historical Sketch of the Valley of Buffalo"
http://www.nyscottishritemasons.org/vob/history.htm Pg. 8-9. Accessed from
the Internet 2/14/10; printed copy of article in CHS Archives. (URL no longer
active at time of research.)

[29] Image from CHS Archives.

[30] "Fritz Kreisler in Buffalo" http://www.music.buffalo.edu/bpo/kreisler.htm
Accessed from the Internet 2/14/10; printed copy of article in CHS Archives.
(URL no longer active at time of research.)

[31] http://content.time.com/time/covers/0,16641,19250202,00.html

[32] "John McCormack Biography, Chapter 4"
http://www.mccormacksociety.co.uk

[33] University at Buffalo Archives.
http://ublib.buffalo.edu/archives/tudents/events.htm Accessed from the
Internet 2/14/10; printed copy of article in CHS Archives. (URL no longer active
at time of research.)

[34] *Ibid.* Pg 9.

[35] Catholic.com "What Does the Church say about Freemasonry?"
https://www.catholic.com/qa/what-does-the-church-say-about-freemasonry
Accessed June 13, 2017.

[36] Interview with Rev. Ron Sams, S.J., '46. October 3, 2016.

[37] *The Griffin – The Canisius College Newspaper.* Volume X. No. 10. March 5,
1943.

CHAPTER 7

The 1940s: Decade of Transition

THIS HISTORY IS FOCUSED on the school since its move to Delaware Avenue, and thus the later part of the 1940s. However, we backtrack at this point in order first to consider the wartime years at Canisius—an era generally untreated in Mr. Kessler's history (and perhaps understandably so, as he was drafted in 1943).

Father Lorenzo Reed, S.J.,* Principal from 1940-1948, kept an "Academic Diary of the Principal of Canisius High School." This meticulous, handwritten chronicle provides fascinating insights to the daily workings

---

* Father Reed founded McQuaid Jesuit in Rochester and went on to several leadership roles associated with Jesuit high schools.

of the institution, from the most mundane details of personnel management to incisive (and sometimes quite witty) commentary on student antics. Such "Diaries" were kept for many years by various school leaders. This author begins this focus on the 1940s by highlighting a conspicuous and, perhaps, telling gap in this otherwise consistent record. Despite careful attention to detail and great consistency, there is an interesting aberration visible on page 26 of the "Diary" volume covering August 1941 to September 1943.[1]

Page 26 of Father Lorenzo Reed, S.J.,'s "Academic Diary of the Principal of Canisius High School, August 1941-September 1943"

The reader will notice that there is no entry for December 7, 1941—the day the U.S. Navy base at Pearl Harbor was bombed. We can only speculate as to why no entry was made. Perhaps Father Reed, understandably preoccupied with the day's events, had no time to attend to the Diary. Perhaps, on the other hand, he simply had no words for such a day.

No matter the reason, however, it is telling also that on the following day, December 8, the entry is entirely mundane: "Holy Day. Immaculate Conception. In the evening the Sodality held a very successful skating party at Scott's rink. Over $100 will be realized."[2]

This apparent irony demonstrates the somewhat paradoxical nature of wartime life at Canisius High School, as expressed by Father Ron Sams, S.J., during his interview for this book, less than a year before his passing:

"The only thing the war affected us by was rationing. For example, certain foods—bananas were a treat.... It was hard to get cigars and cigarettes because they were all going to the military. Gasoline was rationed. The cars had letters – A, B, and O depending what category you were in for getting gasoline, and you had a booklet of coupons from the government...depending on your occupation and your situation."[3]

Interestingly, the young Ronald W. Sams '46, as a graduating senior and Salutatorian for the Class of 1946, penned the Salutatory Address with a focus on the wartime experience of his class at CHS. It is included here in its entirety as it lends some insight into the perspective of the young men of that era:

"A World at One"
Salutatory Address of 1946
Ronald W. Sams '46

Tonight, the graduating class of 1946 of Canisius High School welcomes you to its commencement exercises. Tonight, we have taken another great step toward life's education. The first important step towards that goal was our completion of grammar school. The second, the step which we took haltingly as children, we are completing with trust and confidence—with trust in the principles of truth and religion that we have been taught here at Canisius, and with confidence, that, under our leadership, the world will again come to love and respect the laws and principles of God.

Today, Canisius is proud to be housed in a beautiful building. We graduates did not have the privilege and opportunity of attending class in the new Canisius. But we were present in the old building when the new Canisius began to take form. We had the opportunity of seeing that change take place—from old to new—from Washington Street to Delaware Avenue. But it was not the material change that we noticed so much as the spirit and feeling of security with which this change developed. For something sound and stable, something profound and enduring, was being transmitted amid the disorder and uncertainty of a world deplorably at odds.

The world itself was changing. It passed from a happy, peaceful place in which to live, to a burning, blazing arena of global strife, sparing no nation or individual from its ravages. But this transition, unlike the confident and stabilized transfer from the old to the new Canisius, was carried out in fear, confusion, bloodshed, and war. Men seemed to have lost their true sense of value. Too many heiled Hitler, and too few fell on their knees and prayed the "Our Father." Yes, the world was changing and Canisius was changing. But the transition in the world was uncertain and confused. The transition of Canisius was marked by certainty, security, and order.

Today, the United States is at peace—alas, not the true and genuine peace everyone hoped for, but at least the peace that follows the cessation of hostilities. When first we entered the old, red-brick building on Washington Street in the Autumn of 1942, the war was not one year old. With the cry of Pearl Harbor still ringing in our ears, we began our new life behind the tradition-laden walls of Canisius High School. In the carefree days of Freshman year, we paid but passing attention to the war news. We heard about our soldiers landing at Casablanca, on Sicily and on Salerno. We read about and saw pictures of the devastating effects of our bombing raids on Hamburg, Bremen, and Berlin. But we did not realize at the time just what it all meant—what effect it would have on our individual lives. Gradually, however, as month after month of class went by, and we began to distinguish our goal more clearly, we saw that all this death and destruction had a purpose. There were ideals of freedom and security behind this awful holocaust of war. As we advanced in learning, this realization became clearer. But we, as high school students, did not yet realize that these ideals were ours to put into effect. Accordingly, we forgot about the Four Freedoms* and endeavored to solve the more immediate problems of Caesar and Cicero, while we went about our ordinary high school life and activity.

As the picture grew brighter and the lance of power in that great world conflict shifted in our favor, we were developing into manhood. We were no

---

* A reference to President Franklin D. Roosevelt's January 6, 1941 State of the Union Address, in which he spoke of "four freedoms" to which all people were entitled: freedom of expression, freedom of religion, freedom from want, and freedom from fear.

longer children, but young men, who realized that if we were to become anything worthwhile in this world, we must be well educated. In order to endure
for any length of time, we knew our education must have a firm foundation,
based on the principles of God's law. That foundation we felt growing day by
day more firm, more secure.

Senior year came up on us swiftly. The war had ended. The world was presumably at peace. Everyone thought that normality would soon return to
soothe his shattered nerves. But we in America were living in a Paradise, compared to the wretched condition of life existing in the countries of Europe and
Asia. Famine and death lurked behind every pile of rubble. Families were still
separated—many never again to be reunited. The cities of Berlin, Essen, and
Munich were masses of ruin. The haggard, ragged children of Europe
stretched out tiny, feeble hands, pleading for bread. Europe, once the center
of culture and civilization, of learning and art, was now a helpless wreck.

We in America had our shortages, but we were not starving. Our buildings
were still erect, our families still united. Hopefully we looked for peace following the cessation of hostilities and now, after nearly one full year we are still
seeking that peace. Confusion, dissension, and mistrust continually block all
attempts at real peace. Until men become unselfish and have respect for the
rights of their fellow men, until their lives are directed, as ours have been, by
eternal principles, true peace will be only a goal on an ever-distant horizon.
During our school years, we have noticed the unmistakable contrast between
this turmoil and confusion existing in the outside world, and the order and
concord prevailing in our own lives while at school. The outside world seemed
to be following divergent aims, with mistrust among nations and individuals
continually choking all hope of advancement towards a common goal. Hardly
were men living as children of the same Father. In our lives, however, we were
conscious of order, harmony, and unity; we had come to the realization that
this order, this harmony, and peace must flow from following a definite set of
principles and from seeking a definite goal. We, more than any other individuals in the world, had received the best in education because it was Christian
education. We have the responsibility, not only to ourselves but to all of our
fellow men, of leading them along the path pointed out to us during our four

years here at Canisius. We are leaving school as soldiers leave their training camps, prepared for life's battle for the salvation of our immortal souls. We have been trained and taught the difference between right and wrong—we have come to realize the respect due to the rights of our fellow men. And we have learned to love truth and to despise what is not true. We are leaving Canisius with confidence, hope, and trust in the future. Ours are the assurance and faith that are necessary to make a world at odds, a world at one.[4]

Ronald W. Hams

42 Durham Ave.
Buffalo, N. Y.
Sodality 1, 2, 3, 4; Secretary 4;
Duces 1, 2, 3, 4; K.B.S. 1, 2, 3, 4;
Student Council 1, 3, 4; Arena Yearbook 4; Dramatics 3; Debating
2, 3, 4; Glee Club 2, 4; Class Officer
1, 3, 4; Class Honors, Gold Medal
1, 2; Silver Medal 3; Football Dance
Committee 4; Football 3, 4; Intramurals 1, 2, 3, 4

Father Reed's "Principal's Diary" entry for December 11th, when the United States declared war upon Germany, is similarly paradoxical. Father Reed notes that the official office Christmas card has been ordered. In the following sentence, however, he notes that he has been "asked to serve as sector warden in the air-raid setup of the Civilian Defense. He will be responsible for people and buildings in the two blocks bounded by Washington, Chippewa, Ellicott, and Tupper Streets."[5]

Rev. Lorenzo Reed, S.J., Image from the 1945 *Arena* yearbook.

Indeed, the day-to-day life for Canisius students appears, by all accounts in the *Arena* yearbook and *Citadel* newspaper during the war, to have been relatively untroubled by the war. Nonetheless, the dedication of these yearbooks, a series of which were penned by school president and Rector Father James Redmond, S.J., convey the magnitude of the era's challenges. His address at the 1942 Mass of the Holy Ghost, which Father Reed's "Diary" tells us took place on September 11, underscores the existential menace facing the generation. Here is the text of his notes:

Purpose of meeting today – invoke the blessing of H.G. [Holy Ghost] dedicate year to Him.

We forget that the H.G. is our Friend and trusted helper – Step + realize – who He is who actually resides in us – bestows His blessings + graces – light + strength. First coming of H.G. results – fire – set world on fire – Apostles in Jerusalem + thru world.

Youth eager – full of ambition – great deeds to do – but alas, all is done! No it isn't. World has forgotten Christ – abroad – savagery of conflict. At home – doubt + uncertainty – greed – worldliness – materialism. Abroad – totalitarianism which puts a man in place of God. At home – a democracy which has forgotten God – tries to build a utopia – brotherhood of man without Fatherhood of God.

If tyranny wins – we shall have to live Christ like lives to win civilization back for God. If tyranny fails, our last chance to put Christ's principles into practice + to bring His Kingdom – real Utopia – to realization. Reconstruction for Christ. We may be called upon for great sacrifices – will we be ready – depends on what we do now.

We are Christ's soldiers. How can we fight? By preparing now – we serve Him now in what he wants. By living now as He wants. By preparing ourselves for our place in His plan. Don't wait for big things which never come. Do little things well – daily duties[6]

Rev. James J. Redmond, S.J., Image from the 1945 *Arena* yearbook.

While the seriousness of Father Redmond's address evoked the existential threat of wartime life, it was Father Reed's assembly three days later, on September 14th, that perhaps put more fear of God into the boys at Canisius High School. His notes for the day:

Fr. Reed held an assembly at 9:20 for the purpose of explaining school routine and disciplinary regulations. He prefaced his explanation by stating that under war emergency conditions we could not permit any fooling or wasting time, etc. and that the regulations were to be observed strictly...

General: no loitering smoking within two blocks of the school in any direction. No going to windows, hanging out of windows, throwing paper, etc. out of windows, no eating, running, shouting, whistling, anywhere in the building. Silence after leaving assembly, on corridors, stairs, classrooms. If no assembly, upon reaching 1ˢᵗ floor after recess or lunch. Talking permitted after dismissal bells, recess, lunch, end of day... ⁷

If transported back in time, today's CHS student would find himself in unfamiliar territory with regard to some of these 1940s-era disciplinary rules. In terms of others, he would likely find little has changed!

A Prominent Sodality

The most prominent student organization (at least based upon its prominence in the yearbooks of that era) was the Sodality of Our Lady. *Arena 1945* describes how central this organization was to the life of the school:

This is our most honored organization. Its purpose is to honor our Queen, the Mother of God and to serve her other children, those with whom we live...To serve her children we have our Mite Box drives during Lent and Advent; stamps are collected to help her sons and daughters in distant corners of the world; Christmas comes and our Food Baskets go to her chosen ones, the poor...June comes and the year of service is done.

The Sodality of Our Lady

While today's students are likely unfamiliar even with the word "Sodality," they would no doubt be familiar with the service-oriented activities like those described above. Perhaps the high participation in the Sodality during this time was connected to the troubles of a war-torn era.

Hoping for Peace

The 1945 *Arena* yearbook leaves no question that the war was a defining aspect of life for the young men of this class. The very first item on the very first page is an image of the invading troops at Normandy, with the caption, "Armies win a peace." This is followed immediately by another photo, of the Yalta Conference (February 4, 1945), with the caption "Statesmen plan a peace...but...." When the page is turned, the following text continues: "The concept of a life of peace as we see it is an enduring, lifelong pattern woven together from the following materials. Inspiration – Leadership. The Other Man's View point. Competition – Friendly Rivalry. Fusing the Elements of Peace. Achievement – Man of Peace."[8]

In Father Redmond's *Rector's Letter* in the 1945 *Arena*, the dark pall of war still weighs heavily upon the sober message:

The close of your four years at Canisius is almost simultaneous with the end of bloodshed and cruelty all over the world. It will be for you to then rebuild the society that we were not wise enough to build well. Yours is the opportunity and necessity to find successfully the formula that will enable all of us to live together as peaceful people.

The mistakes of our generation need not be your mistakes. The lessons that we learned at the bitter price of global war you may profit by. The blunders in understanding and cooperation that we made you can correct. The failures that were ours you should never repeat.

Peace is built by the individual in his dealings with others. Here you have learned for four years, on the ball field, in the classroom, in debate and club room the value of getting along with your fellows. Your most cherished memories will always be the times you spent working or playing with your friends. Those memories are the seeds of peace in your own lives and in the life of the world. Keep those memories. Join to them the ideals you have learned here. Add the spirit of prayer and hard, cooperative work and you have the beginnings of that formula for peace that we were too blind to see. God bless you and give courage to your hearts for the task that lies ahead of you.

Sincerely in Christ, James J. Redmond, S.J.[9]

It is with this tempered optimism, and the impending end of the war, that the "new era" of Canisius High School began. 1945 is the first year that saw students at the Delaware Avenue campus.

The Transition to Delaware

Line drawings by Robert George Zeimer '45, one of the Art Editors of the 1944 *Arena*, offer a visual portrayal of the evolution of the Canisius High School Campus, from its earliest days on Ellicott Street to its impending move to Delaware Avenue.

CANISIUS 1870 - 1872

CANISIUS 1880 - 1944

CANISIUS, 1944

It was a relatively short timeframe, then, in which Canisius made the transition from its Washington Street Campus to the dedication of the new wing at 1180 Delaware. Arguably, this process began with George Evans' appointment to the Common Council and thus his becoming aware of the opportunity to secure the property and ended with the dedication of the new classroom wing in August 1948. See timeline below:

- January 3, 1944: Evans named President Pro Temp of Buffalo Common Council
- February 29, 1944: Canisius' offer to purchase 1180 Delaware Avenue is recorded in the Common Council minutes
- March 14, 1944: The Common Council Committee on Finance passes the resolution to accept the CHS offer (CHS buys the property)
- 1944-1945 Academic Year: Freshmen (only) begin classes at 1180; upperclassmen remain at Washington Street
- 1945-1946 Academic Year: Freshmen and sophomores attend 1180; juniors and seniors attend Washington Street
- 1946-1947 Academic Year: Freshmen and sophomores attend 1180; juniors and seniors attend Washington Street
- November, 1946: Groundbreaking for classroom wing at 1180
- 1947-1948 Academic Year: Freshmen and sophomores attend 1180; juniors and seniors attend Washington Street
- 1948-1949 Academic Year: All classes attend 1180 Delaware

	Washington Street Campus	Delaware Avenue Campus
1944-1945	[Class of '45] [Class of '46] [Class of '47]	[Class of '48]
1945-1946	[Class of '46] [Class of '47]	[Class of '48] [Class of '49]
1946-1947	[Class of '47] [Class of '48]	[Class of '49] [Class of '50]
1947-1948	[Class of '48] [Class of '49]	[Class of '50] [Class of '51]
1948-1949	n/a	[Class of '49] [Class of '50] [Class of '51] [Class of '52]
1949-1950	n/a	[Class of '50] [Class of '51] [Class of '52] [Class of '53]

(CHS Class of 1950 was first to attend all four years at 1180.)

Transformation: From Consistory to School

Notes in the CHS Archives of the "Consultors' Minutes" recall that on "June 10, 1944—Sat—A meeting was held today to determine ways and means of making the Delaware Ave. property available for the fall term. It was decided to use the new building for the first-year high students, so that we could raise the tuition from $120 to $150. Even at this early date, the prospects for an overwhelming registration look great."[10] Months later, the Minutes include: "August 7, 1944—Mon—On Saturday last, high school registration for 1st year went over 300 mark. This is probably a record. The Prefect of Studies plans to start a waiting list."[11]

A typewritten summary of the plans for campus development, which this author discovered buried in the archives, is undated with no author indicated. Despite attempts to determine the original source, he was unsuccessful. Given the similarity in style to the aforementioned "Consultors Minutes," it is this author's best guess that this summary was generated from those Minutes, perhaps derived from an architectural plan. Because of the detailed insights it offers about the formulation of plans for the campus (and the apparent genesis for some elements still in use today), it is offered here in its entirety, despite its considerable length. No doubt it will prove interesting to alumni readers, since the descriptions will evoke memories of the campus design. To be clear, the "New Classroom Wing" described here refers to the Beecher Classroom Wing, which was dedicated as such in the early 1970s.

Description of the Plans for the New Classroom Wing of Canisius High School, 1180 Delaware Avenue, Buffalo, New York

General

On the south side of the property at 1180 Delaware Avenue, formerly the Masonic Consistory, a classroom wing is planned. This addition will provide classroom space for between 800 and 900 students.

The wing will be 166 feet long and 61 feet wide. Its nearest end will be about 40 feet away from the present building, to allow daylight to enter into the present building. The wing will contain three floors and a basement. It will be connected to the present building by a two-story walk-over, which will enter the present building at the west end of the present terrace on the south side. Attached to this walk-over on the west side on both floors will be a projection to provide double offices, on the first floor for the Prefect of Discipline, and on the second floor for the Student Counselor.

The new wing will run north and south, parallel to Delaware Avenue, and at right angles to the present building. This will allow east and west exposure in the classrooms.

The appearance of the exterior stone, but not the texture, will match the present building. The style of architecture will not sacrifice schoolroom utility to appearance. Thus, the windows will be much larger than those in the present building. The style will be simple.

Corridors

The corridors will be 12 feet wide, with five classrooms on each side, except for the west side of the top floor, which will have two science rooms and two classrooms. All ceilings are to be 11 feet high.

Lockers will be built in recesses in the walls on both sides of the corridors on each floor. Between the top of the lockers and the ceiling on each side of the corridor long glass panels will be inserted in the walls, to allow light to enter the corridor from the classrooms.

Recessed in the walls on each corridor will be drinking fonts and fire extinguishers. Provision will be made on each floor for electric wiring to control program bells and manual fire alarms. Electric outlets in the baseboard will be provided at convenient intervals for cleaning machines.

The lower part of the walls will be covered with wainscot of glazed brick in the spaces not occupied by lockers. Above the wainscot the walls will be finished in smooth plaster. A bright, cheerful color combination will be used.

The ceiling material will be acoustical tile, a material which can be painted repeatedly without losing its acoustical properties. The floor will be made of terrazzo, or possibly asphalt tile cemented to concrete. All floors will be joined to the walls by cove bases, to make cleaning easier and more efficient.

Classrooms

Classrooms will measure 22 feet wide and 30 feet long and 11 feet high. Science rooms, which will be combination lecture and laboratory, will be 22 feet wide and 45 feet long.

The sub floor will be composed of cinder blocks set in concrete ribs, reinforced. The floor covering will be battleship linoleum cemented to the concrete slab.

The ceiling, formed by the reinforced concrete of the floor above, will have a large recessed panel covered with acoustical tile. This will break the flatness of the ceiling and improve the acoustics.

The upper walls will be finished with smooth plaster. Slate blackboards will be provided across the front of the room and along two-thirds of one side. The other third of this continuous space will be covered with cork board for displays. A wainscot of glazed brick will cover the portion of the wall below the blackboard.* Recessed heating units of the convector type will provide the heat. They will be centrally controlled from the boiler room.

Windows will be of the architectural projection type, with double glass panes set in non-corrosive metal frames. The doors will open out into the corridors.

Color combinations will be used which are proper for each exposure and which will make the classrooms bright and cheerful.

Lighting fixtures will be of the incandescent type, with simple, practical globes in two rows of three each. Each row can be turned off and on separately. Thirty-foot candles** of light will be provided at each desk.

IV Toilets

A boys' toilet will be located on each corridor at the north end, east side, opposite the north stairs.

---

* Author's Note: All of these architectural details remain in place as of this book's publication, with the exception of the "smooth plaster" with which the upper walls were to be finished. They never were; they remain unfinished cinderblock above the glazed brick wainscot.

** A "foot-candle" is (basically) a measure of light output.

The toilet will have a separate entrance and exit. Between these two doors on the inside a janitor's closet will project. On the exposed side of the closet four wash bowls and a continuous mirror will be hung. On one side of the room four toilet compartments will be placed, and on the other side seven full-length, stall-type urinals. The window and the heating unit will occupy the east wall.

All toilet fixtures will be of vitreous china, and will have separate, hand-operated valves. All except the urinals will be of the wall-hung type.

The walls will be of glazed-brick wainscot with smooth plaster above the wainscot. The floor will be laid with small vitreous tiles. Walls and floor will be white with light green trim. The ceiling will be of smooth plaster.

Cafeteria

The entire basement will be used for the cafeteria. Most of the area of the wing itself will be used for the dining room, except that in the north-east corner a dishwashing room will be enclosed. The kitchen will be formed by excavating the space between the new wing and the present building and covering this one story with a flat concrete roof, upon which the lawn will be replaced. The kitchen area will be connected by a tunnel with the basement of the present building.

A storeroom will be conveniently placed at the north-east end of the kitchen. Regular kitchen equipment, such as ranges, ovens, sinks, tables, etc. will be provided. Much of our present equipment can be used.

The cafeteria serving counter will occupy the south side of the kitchen. There will be no wall separating the kitchen from the serving counter, but both will be separated from the dining room by a wall open at both ends and in the middle. This will enable us to serve two lines of boys simultaneously without loss of time. The upper part of the dividing wall will be made of glass brick to admit more light into the kitchen.

In the dining room daylight will be admitted through nine windows. Since half of the space of each window will be above, and half below the ground line, the ground will be dug out around the windows and areaways provided to admit more daylight.

The floor will be either an asphalt mastic composition or asphalt tile cemented to a concrete base. Upper walls will be of smooth plaster, wainscot of glazed brick. *Acoustical tile will be used in the ceiling. Simple, practical light-ing fixtures of incandescent type will be used. Pleasant color combinations will be employed to make the room bright and attractive.*

The floor of the kitchen, dishwashing room, and storeroom will be of red quarry tile. The upper walls will be of smooth plaster, and the wainscots of glazed brick. Ceilings of these rooms will probably be of perforated steel pan-eling filled with acoustical material.

Stairways and Exits

Two stairways from basement to third floor will be provided. One will be located in the south end of the wing, the other on the west side of the north end. All stairways will be of fireproof construction, eliminating the need for fire escapes. Wainscots will be of glazed brick, and upper walls of smooth plaster, matching the corridors. Frames will be of reinforced concrete or steel, with anti-slip abrasive nosing. Handrails will be installed on both sides. Large window areas of glass block without openings will admit daylight onto the stairs.

At the foot of each stairway a vestibule will be provided. The inside wall of which will be glass block. Both vestibule doors and outside exits will be wide double doors, opening out. Heating units will be provided in the vestibules.

Roof

The roof will be a flat deck roof with no parapet. It will be insulated with a layer of foam glass, imbedded in pitch and laid on concrete. The foam glass will be covered with five layers of built-up roofing paper and pitch, covered with asphalt—a 20-year bonded roof. If outside conductors are used, conduc-tor heads will be large enough to carry off water easily without overflowing down the outside walls, and will be made accessible for cleaning. If inside con-ductors are used, an auxiliary outside carry-off will be provided.

Facilities Available in Present Building

Community rooms, such as the Chapel, Dining Room, Recreation Room, and Library, can be arranged on the first floor of the present building, and can be separated from parts of the building used for the school. Likewise, about eight living rooms can be provided on the second floor front of the present building. *The remaining living rooms can be made available in the building at 1168 Delaware Avenue. Extra chapels can be provided in both buildings.*

Students' Chapel: The former grand ballroom will be converted into a large and beautiful chapel for the students. It will accommodate about 400 students at one time. *

Students' Library: The present dining room will be converted into a very beautiful library for the school. **

Auditorium: A large and beautiful auditorium is already being used. At present it lacks fixed seats and stage equipment. No remodeling will be necessary.

Office of the Prefect of Studies: The original offices of the Consistory can be adapted very easily to the requirements of the Prefect's Office. These are located conveniently for both School and public, just off the large foyer and beside the entrance to the walk-over. A vault for the records is included.

Teachers' Room: Just above the Prefect's Office, on the second floor, a work room and a rest room will be provided for the teachers. These will be equipped with desks, lockers, showers, and toilet facilities. They are conveniently located at the entrance to the walk-over on the second floor. ***

Jesuit Correspondence: An Inside Look at the 1940s

Certainly, the student opinions and spirit expressed in publications like *The Citadel* and the *Arena* Yearbook provide excellent insight into the life of the school. However, a more complete understanding of the challenges that faced its leaders requires a different perspective. Amidst the CHS archives are excerpts from various forms of correspondence between and among the Jesuits that offer an "insider's" perspective on the school's progress. With discretion and sensitivity, excerpts of these correspondences are included here. They provide a partial narrative of the decade that complements well the other aspects and elements presented in this book.

A reader of these excerpts will notice a continuous theme: financial struggle. There is no doubt that CHS has, for all of its recorded history,

---

* This plan called for the present library (the former "Grand Ballroom") to become a large Student Chapel. This was not realized, according to multiple sources.

** Likewise, this plan called for the current Chapel to become the student library. These plans were, eventually, reversed.

*** This is a reference to the current Guidance Center.

Rev. Timothy Coughlin, S.J., President. *Arena* 1941

struggled to reconcile its financial burdens with its daily mission and obligation. The beauty of this struggle, if one will forgive the concept, is that it has distilled the tremendous commitment of so many teachers, administrators, benefactors, and tuition-paying parents for so many years. While the minutia of debt-service obligations and enrollment trends does not make for fascinating reading (and so is abbreviated here), it does compel the reader—particularly the alumnus—to appreciate the generosity of so many who have kept Canisius High School going over the years. Without this insider's perspective, and with only a look at the "shinier stuff" of blue and gold lore, one might reasonably fail to appreciate the degree to which CHS has demanded the sacrifice of so many.

To begin this exploration, it is best to jump back a few years, to the very beginning of the 1940s. On February 27, 1940, in a letter to Rev. Timothy Coughlin, S.J., Rector and President of Canisius High School, the Rev. Zacheus J. Maher, S.J., Assistant for North America, cautions against the dangers of debt for a tuition-driven institution:

Wisely you have decided not to build until you have the needed money in hand. Canisius is now out of debt. Keep it so! Let it be your firm resolve not to go into debt. After all, there is no particular achievement in floating a loan, putting up a building and leaving it to one's successor to struggle and strangle in the effort to carry the load. Not he who borrows and builds, but he who secures the money and pays is the true builder. Put into concrete what you would have to put into interest and watch the building grow.[12]

This admonishment was timely, and the theme of indebtedness would go on to challenge the leadership of CHS for many years to come (and arguably, as a tuition-dependent institution, always will.) This underscores an important realization for the reader: an independent school, even more so than a government-funded public school, is in very many senses a business enterprise that demands careful fiscal management. Certainly, such correspondence (which will be included in subsequent chapters for the coming decades of the mid-20th century) makes clear that fiduciary stress was a near constant for the leadership of Canisius High School.

Jumping ahead to 1944, Father Maher repeats this admonition to Father Redmond, now Rector and President:

Father Provincial has already intimated your thought on the subject of the new high school. I am sure that you and your house consultors will give it a careful study....

Only do not go into debt. It is not the man who borrows and builds who is the real "builder." Such as these often leave a huge burden to their successors to struggle under for years. The man who pays for what he builds, he truly merits the name of "builder."[13]

In response to Father Redmond's enthusiastic report about burgeoning applications, Father Maher again urges caution in early 1945, nearly a year after the purchase of the Delaware Avenue property. "Your great problem will be man power. Do not take more boys than you can properly educate, for this would do irreparable harm to the school, nor is it just that we do so."[14] Likewise, he encourages efforts to sell the Washington Street property: "May I suggest that you turn to prayer so that you may find a sale for the old property. Delaware can never really be what it ought to be until you are in residence there. Keep in mind, too, the need of building a suitable faculty building along traditional Jesuit lines, with abundance of rooms for the community and for visitors."[15]

By 1946, with plans for the new classroom wing well underway, permission was granted by the Superior General to Father Redmond to proceed with taking out a nearly half-million-dollar loan. This green

Rev. James J. Redmond, S.J., President. Source: *Arena* 1943.

light was accompanied, however, by yet another word of caution, echoing the urging of Father Maher to proceed carefully:

By this time, you will have received through Rev. Fr. Provincial the permission to borrow the sum requested for the erection of the classrooms. It is my sincere hope that the enrollment will continue satisfactory during the years to come, so that it will be possible to pay off the loan within the time that you believe will suffice....

Your school has indeed grown in numbers, but I would advise you to be careful not to accept more students than can be given a solid training nor such as are not likely to do satisfactory work. The Society has neither the men and money nor the obligation to teach every applicant for enrollment in our schools....[16]

It was in the summer of 1948 that Rev. James R. Barnett, S.J., now Rector and President of CHS, began his series of letters comprising the regular reports to Rome on the progress of the school. In August, Father Barnett offered some insight as to the exciting completion of the school wing, the beginnings of the longstanding generosity of the Frauenheim family (who would figure very prominently over the next two decades), and the relationship between the "New Canisius High School" and the Jesuits' connections to Washington Street—both St. Michael's Church and the old school property.

We hope to have all ready by August 29 when His Excellency, the Bishop of Buffalo, will officiate at the blessing of the new Canisius High School. The heavy debt of five hundred thousand dollars will be a more constant problem.... I have asked Father Provincial to request a delay in the separation of the community that will take care of St. Michaels' Church from the high school...that the church may continue to enjoy the reputation of an abundance of ministerial services and that the high school may continue to obtain the revenue consequent upon such services.... A careful account will be kept of the separate establishments' expenses and income.... In addition, the sale of the former high school would be the source of considerable relief in our financial problems. Hence, have asked Father Provincial to request permission to sell the Washington Street property.

One month ago, the Frauenheim Foundation, which had been incorporated to furnish Canisius High School with a memorial to Mr. and Mrs. Edward Frauenheim, Sr., by their sons, acquired title to the house and land that are next to the Delaware Avenue School. There are two more pieces of property that adjoin ours which we hope to secure...which will eventually give us sufficient land for a recreation field for our students.

We expect to have a total of nine hundred and fifty in the high school, two hundred and eighty of whom will be in first year.[17]

Nearly a year later, at the end of July 1949, Father Barnett reported on the move of the Jesuit community to Delaware Avenue and the continued acquisition of adjacent property by the Frauenheim family for the benefit of the school:

Rev. James R. Barnett, S.J., President. Source: *Arena* 1949.

On August 20, 1948, we completed the move of the high school community to our new quarters in 1168 and 1180 Delaware Avenue. Sixteen priests, eleven scholastics, and three brothers have rooms in the 1168 residence and five priests have the rooms in the 1180 residence.... Most Rev. John F. O'Hara, C.S.C., the Bishop of Buffalo...blessed our new classroom building...on August 29, 1948. We began the school year with 923 students and fourteen laymen...."

In January last, the Frauenheim Foundation purchased a second piece of property that adjoins our school. In time these two properties may be converted into a recreation field...As yet we have not been able to sell the old high school property on Washington Street and our financial problem continues to be difficult....[18]

By the close of the decade, the transition to Delaware Avenue was nearly complete. However, financial struggle related to the still-substantial debt would continue to weigh upon Father Barnett and the trustees of Canisius. In the following excerpts, a few things emerge: the impact upon enrollment from the opening of other schools (ostensibly Bishop Timon and the new campus of Saint Joseph's Collegiate Institute, although he doesn't mention them by name), the continued struggle to sell the Washington Street property, and the ongoing support of the Frauenheim brothers:

While our total registration did decrease from 923 to 847, we were forced to hire another layman as teacher. This continued drop in the number of our students was caused, in my opinion, by a new diocesan high school for boys in the southern section of the city where there is a large percentage of Catholics and by the anticipated opening of a new school operated by the Christian Brothers, who are transferring from an old location to a suburb just north of the city, Kenmore, and finally, by rising cost of living.... The decrease is not an unmixed evil, for we were able to contain all our classes in the new classroom building and eliminate three rooms in the old building. We have redesigned these with little trouble as a study hall, a debating hall, and a remedial reading room....

We are dependent almost entirely on current income and an absolutely necessary part of that income is derived from the stipends and perquisites of priestly ministries. To date we do not have any serious prospect of selling the old high school property, the sale of which would considerably relieve our financial pains. However, we have been able to meet all our obligations and we have reduced our capital indebtedness during the past six months by $5,132.52. The Fathers' Club has undertaken to pay for the cost of purchase, installation, and re-upholstering of the seats for the auditorium.... Much of the success of this new organization is due to the efforts of Father Dolan, the moderator....

The most remarkable event during the last six months was the reception of the relic of St. Francis Xavier, which was in the diocese October 24 to 27.... About four hundred automobiles accompanied the relic from the airport...to the cathedral....

The Frauenheim Foundation has leased the two houses which it purchased and which adjoin our high school for a period of three years. This rental will carry the various costs of the properties and also pay current interest and amortization of the mortgages on these properties. Since we are not in a position to use the properties, I thought it best to agree to this arrangement. At a meeting of the trustees of this Foundation a few months ago, Mr. George Frauenheim advised me that his plan is to put seven thousand dollars per year into the fund....

St. Michaels' parochial school was closed this past fall by direction of His Excellency [the Bishop]. There was some criticism of this action by the parishioners.... However, this decision might help us in the sale of the property, since the high school owns the land on which the parochial school is situated....[19]

Correspondence from the end of 1950 brought into even sharper focus the prominent role of the Frauenheim family in the life of the "new" Canisius High School. The purchase of the Gratwick home at 22 Cleveland Avenue, as well as the establishment of the "Founders Club" during a dinner hosted by Mr. George Frauenheim, Jr., set in real motion the plan that would both provide CHS with a fitting residence for its faculty and help it to emerge from its significant debt. In a letter to Bishop O'Hara dated November 25, 1950, Father Barnett announced the acquisition of 22 Cleveland:

"Our Reverend Father Provincial has granted me permission to invest some community funds in the purchase of the Gratwick property, 22 Cleveland Avenue, which adjoins the high school on the northwest. While I should have preferred to put off this purchase until our debt had been further reduced, the possibility of a sale to another buyer made it imperative that we purchase the property now. Eventually, this property will be the site of a faculty residence,

probably a long time after my departure from Canisius. For the present, we plan on renting it."[20]

Then, on December 5, the first minutes of the new Founders Club, recorded by Secretary George J. Lenahan, marked the establishment of this core group of financial supporters who would be so crucial to the school in the coming years:

On December 5, 1950, a formal dinner was given by Mr. George Frauenheim at his home on Pomeroy Park, in honor of the Very Rev. James R. Barnett, S.J. During the evening, Father Barnett discussed the need for a Founders Club and it was immediately recognized as an important and worthwhile function by those present. Thus, the Association of the Founders of the New Canisius High School was germinated and originated...Its aims, purposes, and regulations were explained by the Rev. Barnett.... Elections were then held and the following officers were elected...President: George M. Frauenheim; Treasurer: Raymond A. O'Connor; Secretary: George J. Lenahan.... Credentials and keys were then presented.... Atty. Charles Wick was asked by President Frauenheim to draw up a Constitution and arrange for Incorporation papers....[21]

This correspondence, although certainly only a small glimpse at a complex institution, offers a unique look at the behind-the-scenes realities faced by its leaders and benefactors.

Community Life at CHS

Student Perspectives

We might consider that for the class years affected by this period of flux and transition, the change no doubt had a significant impact upon their experience. This is not to say it was necessarily a negative impact; rather, it was a notable aspect of their Canisius experience that differs from that of the great majority of students who attended before and after them. Consider, for example, the Class of 1949, which was the first to graduate from the new campus. Rev. William O'Malley S.J., '49, (of *The Exorcist* fame), composed the "Senior Class History" in the 1949 *Arena*. It offers some insight into this peripatetic journey from the new campus, to the old, and then back to the new again:

[From "Sophomore Year: 1946-1947"] "We were requested (If we valued our lives!) on the performance of any misdeed, to wear out the marble floors of the foyer. It didn't exactly build up the feet either! Jug! It was here to stay...."
"We ruled the Swimming Team, probably because of our undisputed possession of the important factor, the pool...."

[From "Junior Year: 1947-1948"] "Our triumphal return to Canisius was made not to the Delaware school, but to the old school on Washington Street. The building might have been somewhat dusty and crumbling but to us there was more of Canisius in those musty halls than anywhere else. There tradition reigned supreme. We were infected by the spirit of the school...."

[From "Senior Year: 1948-1949"] "We were seniors! We were to be the first class to graduate from the new school! And what a school it was. To its sparkling halls we were as green as the shiest freshman but that didn't last too long."[22]

United in "The Citadel"

We focus, then, on this 1948-1949 academic year, the first in which the entire community was united within the walls of the "citadel" on Delaware Avenue. This new era was marked by the initiation of a new school publication: *The Citadel*. Volume I, No. 1. is dated October 11, 1948, and is headlined with a fitting story (see image following page).

ʃE CITADEL

CANISIUS HIGH SCHOOL, BUFFALO, N. Y.   OCTOBER 11, 1948

CANISIUS MARKS NEW ERA IN HISTORY

New Wing Unites Four Years; Dedicated at Ceremony

Looking Ahead —

Oct. 15—Football—De Sales.
Oct. 19—Closing of marks.
Oct. 24—Football—Ryan.
Oct. 25—Reading of marks.

When venerable Seniors have that same look of confused wonder as the greenest Freshman, that is news! But it is only natural when a school begins a new chapter in its history, as Canisius does this fall, *Anno Domini*, 1948.

MODERNITY

For the first time since June, 1945, one building houses every classroom from 4A to 1H. The new wing, with its fluorescent lighting, acoustic ceilings, green glass "blackboards" and asphalt tile floors, surpasses the fondest imaginings of returning Canisius men.

DEDICATION

What, three years ago, was but the hopeful dream of Rev. James J. Redmond, S. J., then rector of Canisius, and Rev. Lorenzo K. Reed. S. J., then principal of the High School, was dedicated by Most Rev. John F. O'Hara, C.S.C., D. D., on Sunday afternoon, August 29. The impressive ceremonies were attended by more than 1,000 friends, old and new, among whom were Very Rev. John J. McMahon, S. J., Provin-

Cont'd on Page 3, Col. 1)

Bishop Dedicates New Wing

Top—View of new classroom building. Bottom—A few glimpses of dedication ceremonies.

Behren's to Meet St. Michael's

On or about the 15th of this month the Behrens Debating Society will parry argument for argument with St. Michael's College of Toronto. Michael McNulty, Bernard Kennedy and Richard Romanowski have been chosen to

A sidebar on page two introduces the new publication to students (see image on following page).

Albert Gunther '49, Editor, and Edmund Judd '49, Business Manager of the 1949 *Arena* offered a telling narrative of the transition in their editorial remarks for the yearbook:

We have departed from the dark corridors and the creaking stairs of the Washington Street school and stepped into the spacious, glistening halls of Canisius-on-Delaware. The venerable red brick of seventy-five years' standing has been transformed into the rough-hewn Gothic stone of our new "Citadel." It has been our privilege to enjoy for this one year, an all too brief span of time, and to hand down to our successors the grander surroundings, the advantages of progress and improvement, the benefits of better planning and modern equipment that personify the new Canisius.

Canisius—that name down the years has been another name for fair-play, loyalty, truth. Over the course of four years that spirit has grown strong and is now vibrant

JUST IN CASE . . .

"Just in case you're wondering who I am, and where I came from, let me introduce myself. I am the symbol of the new Canisius. I am THE CITADEL. Down from my parapets I look upon CRUSADERS, gallantly riding forth over the drawbridge on quests of honor and glory for their liege Lord. Off in the distance I see them struggling in sporting jousts. Near at hand I peer through the many-windowed story to see them laying plans for their future conquests over ignorance and doubt.

"And lest these noble deeds, inspired by lofty and knightly ideals, either be overlooked by our contemporaries or be forgotten by our posterity, I, THE CITADEL, shall clarion forth these gallant feats of CANISIUS CRUSADERS.

An introduction to the new school newspaper, *The Citadel*, established in 1948.

within us. It is that spirit that we now pass on to those who follow. It is that spirit that gives us renewed courage to meet the future with clear, bright vision, firm in our principles, strong in our faith. Let the light of that same faith glow through the shining rooms of the new Canisius! Carry on in your beautiful new Alma Mater, with truth, loyalty, fair play as your watchwords. Let us both find our strength in our Stella Matutina, our Morning Star, Mary, the clear beacon in the dawn of our new era. She it is who has kept the spirit of Canisius strong in all these years, she it is who will keep it burning in the years to come, she it is who will bless us and watch over us in this, our Second Spring.[23]

Several students offered their impressions on the new campus in the first edition of *The Citadel*. They were asked, "What impresses you most about the new school?" Some responses included:

Tom Boland, 3C: *The first impression of the new school I got was as I was looking at it from the outside, and with the sun shining on the windows there, it seemed to me that there was more window than wall.*
Bernard Kennedy, 4A: *After coming from Washington St., it's quite a change to be able to see out of the windows.*
Frank Sullivan, 4C: *Impressed isn't the word for the way I felt when I saw the "new look" of the lay teachers. Pretty stylish in those black gowns!*
Dan Roche, 1F: *My first day in school the trophy cases on the first corridor caught my eye. It impressed me that Canisius had won so many awards in so many different fields.* [24]

Student organizations had a prominent place in the newly unified school, including the Sodality of Our Lady, the Student Council, the Arena Quarterly and Arena Yearbook, the Dramatic Society (featuring future famed Jesuit priest, author, and actor William O'Malley, S.J., '49 as Cassius in *Julius Caesar*), and the Behrens Debating Society (under the leadership of president Bernard Kennedy '49).

Publications, likewise, demonstrated excellence. The *Buffalo Courier Express* reported on the results of the St. Bonaventure Press Contest in June, 1949. "The *Arena* was judged the best single publication entered in the contest, and the infant *Citadel* took second place in the school newspaper letterpress category."[25] The February 10, 1950, issue of *The Citadel* describes the success of the *Arena* yearbook: "Last Saturday, Feb. 4, the Buffalo Evening News, sponsors of the W.N.Y. Interscholastic Press Association, awarded a first place to the 1949 *Arena* Yearbook.... Quite a commotion was caused in the audience when it was announced that Canisius and St. Joe's were tied for honors, each receiving 850 out of a possible 1000 points."[26]

Athletics in the Mid-to-Late 1940s

In the athletic arena, Canisius had prominence in the mid-1940s. The 1945 *Arena*'s introduction to the athletics section is certainly evocative of the wartime era:[27]

Exercise To Build Toughness

To stand the long hours of marching in tropical heat, or driving rain, to withstand the screaming of shells and the roar of motors, the human body must be at the peak of its form: For this men train, for this they exercise. And existence is dependent on physical fitness.

Competition To Foster Cooperation

The field of sport is miles from the field of battle but only a short distance from the field of life. Here boys learn to work as a team, to admire a hard fighting opponent. To beat a team, to win a game, to clinch a title, all these require the ability to work together as a unit, to cooperate. And this necessity of working with others to obtain a common goal is aimed at the heart of the future when we must, again and in a bigger sense, work together to insure the peace that is to come.

Notably, the students of today (and for many years back) may be surprised to learn that in 1945, there's evidence that CHS was known commonly, at least in the athletics press, by the moniker "Canisius Prep" and the school's teams were referred to frequently as "the Knights" as well as the Crusaders. (See image below.) This appears to be a short-lived tendency, as no references to "the Knights" appear after 1945. We see only occasional uses of "Canisius Prep."

Clarification on all of this can be found buried on Page 4 of the June 4, 1968 *Citadel*, which included an explanation from Coach John Barnes as to how he arrived at the Crusader mascot. (See "The Story Behind 'The Crusader'" on the following page.)

The Story Behind "The Crusader"

Many times the sports pages of the *Citadel* have publicized the names Mackmen, hoopsters, cindermen, to mention but a few. But the title which is used most often as a synonym for Canisius High School is "Crusader," a nickname which has been with the school since the early 1940's.

"Jog and run anywhere."

FROM COACH BARNES

If your summer training program has consisted of "running down your friends, jumping to conclusions, side-stepping your responsibility, and pushing your luck," it is time you thought about something a little more constructive by preparing yourself to win a football championship. We lost a championship last year by seven points. Do you think that with a little more effort we might have reversed that score?

Not many present-day students or athletes know the background of this name or how it became identified with Canisius.

For a number of years the Canisius Teams were known as "Prepsters," due no doubt to a close association with Canisius College. These were the years when Canisius High School was still located on Washington Street. The value of the name diminished, however, when Canisius High lost its image as a "Prep" school. This was because many of the graduates began going to non-local colleges.

Coach John Barnes decided to update this vanishing image by running a contest to find a new name for the Canisius Teams. With a five dollar reward for the winner, the name of "Knight" was selected. Around this same time however, Kensington High School was founded and it also took up the name of "Knights." For a time the newspapers used the name Knights for both schools.

Realizing the confusion, he looked for another name. The problem was that Canisius had purchased a number of articles with the emblem of a "Knight." So he had to come up with something which would fit the symbol of a Knight. The nearest thing to a Knight was a "Crusader" so Mr. Barnes conveniently changed the name from Knights to "Crusaders." This christened a name which will be with Canisius High School as long as it fields athletic teams.

We learn the origins of the "Crusader" mascot--introduced by Coach John Barnes--in The Citadel, June 4, 1968, p.4. Notably, the Knight is the mascot of McQuaid Jesuit in Rochester.

While the resolution of this publication makes it difficult to read, it is plain to see that a collage of newspaper clippings in the 1945 *Arena* Yearbook, page 33, shows frequent use of "Canisius Prep" and "the Knights."

According to alumni of the era, it was the 1948 victory over Saint Joe's that defined the athletic spirit of the time. Because the contests had been suspended for several years due to the war, the resumption of competition marked a particularly resonant note for a generation attempting to return to some normalcy. For CHS, this first contest after a long hiatus was met with resounding victory.

Blue Doors

VOL. I, No. 3   9   CANISIUS HIGH SCHOOL, BUFFALO, N. Y.

Peppy Lungsters Loosen Rafters

Kmiec's Graphic catches Crusaders singing their war chants before moving in on Civic Stadium the night of October 29.

Strategy Upsets St. Joe's On the Night of Knights

10,559 yelling, anxious fans watched the smart, alert and powerful Crusaders down the Maroon and White of St. Joe's—once upon a time—unbeaten, and unscored upon.

Canisius received the kick-off. The genius of Johnny Barnes' plays caught the Maroon Marauders completely by surprise. In three end sweeps, Dick Griffin's 24 yard pass to Ed Jurewicz, a loss, and Earl Scheelar's crossbuck between left guard and tackle, it was a score and PAT by Don Diebold before many had even reached their seats.

All the practice of three months held the Crusaders in good stead as such stalwarts as Art Gross, Hank Adema and Scheelar stemmed the tide time after time. The men of the Institute seemed to have developed the discouraging disease of "fumbleitis" as they were so afflicted twelve times during the contest. This fact, combined with an alert Blue and Gold line, contributed the most to their loss.

Neither team seemed to be able to capitalize on the other's
(Continued on Page 3, Col. 1)

PIGSKIN FLING NO. 2 FOR DAISY

The holiday spirit will be very much in evidence over the Thanksgiving weekend this year. Canisius throws its annual Football Fling November 26th.

That your fellows may keep peace with the distaff side, let it be known and observed that this will be a "sports dance." Therefore, all such formalities as corsages are not 'de rigeur.'

Making the rounds for the next few weeks will be the Varsity football team. Collar one of them and get your ducat from him. Dancing from 8:30 till midnight.

The Citadel November 19, 1948 captured the spirit of victory over SJCI in the first game after a long hiatus.

157

Three men stand out prominently in the athletic context of the late 1940s: Coaches John Barnes, Connie "Mack" McGillicuddy '39, and Coach Paul Lamb.

Coach John Barnes

According to long-time Phys. Ed. teacher Jeff Gemmer, whose first year was John Barnes' last year, the 42-year veteran, who originally hailed from Shreveport, Louisiana, had a profound impact upon many students and a powerful reputation.

"He always took care of his athletes," Gemmer remarked. "His biggest thing was doing all he could for his athletes. He spent most of his time typing letters...for every senior he had, he would type letters and send them out to colleges...he was a very well-respected coach at that time."[28]

Athletic news in the third issue of *The Citadel*, dated November 19, 1948, offers insight into the esteem with which Canisius athletes held Coach Barnes. "Strategy Upsets St. Joe's On the Night of Knights," reads the headline. The article begins, "10,559 yelling, anxious fans watched the smart, alert and powerful Crusaders down the Maroon and White of St. Joe's—once upon a time—unbeaten, and unscored upon." Another article from the same issue captures the revered coach's aura, evoked in his halftime locker-room speech. (See "Pregame Peeks—One Reason Why We Won.")

NOVEMBER 19, 1948

Pregame Peeks— One Reason Why We Won

In a green-walled dressing room, high in the rear of Civic Stadium stands, 33 men in Blue and Gold huddled together and spoke in low, almost inaudible tones of the pigskin panorama that was to unfold in just a minute or so—the long-awaited St. Joe's game.

Comments came forth in firm, determined voices. Willie Johnson, the man who never has enough, said: "We're going to win tonight for those seventeen teams that haven't had a crack at them," echoing Marty Breen's sentiments at the rally that afternoon. Al Ryan looked up slowly and said, "We've waited a long time for this one." Ed Jurewicz chimed in with: "We're not only going to beat 'em; we're going to knock the stuffing out of 'em." Then Tom Cleary: "All I can say is that we're goin' to win."

As Coach Johnny Barnes rose to speak a hush fell over the players. The talk he gave was the most moving one your reporter has ever heard. It was an amazing sight to see the Coach so pent up with emotion that his words stuck in his throat. "Seventeen years—fellows . . . that's a long time to wait; it's your chance to prove something . . . that's been in question for a long time." Then he turned and left the room.

"Do you see who just walked out that door?" The next voice belonged to Al Petrella, the Assistant Coach. "That was one of the best coaches in the country and a terrific guy. A guy that's treated you fellows right and gone out of his way for you! Now let's see you do something for him. Win this one for him!"

And do something they did.

158

Sounding Off!

By DICK McGRATH

Every team that takes the field in any sport has one extra man who never gets in the game. This unsung hero, although he never plays, has just as much to do with the outcome as the rest of the team. Canisius is lucky in that we have a man like Johnny Barnes for our unsung hero. Coach Barnes doesn't score any T.D.'s or hit any home-runs but he makes all these possible.

When Mr. Barnes fields a team in any sport you can bet your boots they're good. They have to be. Any of the guys on the varsity teams will tell you that the coach works them pretty hard. He doesn't do this for fun, but so that every team sporting the Canisius Blue and Gold will be worthy of her colors.

Coach Barnes begins 19th year at Canisius.

Who do you think worries the most before a game? Whatever you do, don't ask Mrs. Barnes. The coach is not at rest until the Blue and Gold is hoisted high over the rival school.

Never before has Canisius had a coach with a record like Johnny Barnes. In nineteen years of coaching at Canisius never has Coach Barnes let down the confidence of the student body. Oh yes, we lose—now and then, but never until Johnny Barnes has done everything in his power to win. For nearly two decades now the name "Barnes" has been linked with the "Canisius tradition" of championship teams.

From *The Citadel* Oct. 7, 1949, page 5. Source: CHS Archives.

Barnes, whose teaching and coaching career at CHS began in 1930 and lasted until his retirement in 1972 (with a considerable period of years afterward working in support services and alumni initiatives), influenced thousands of students. He is best known as a football coach, but he also coached varsity basketball and baseball.

Coach Connie McGillicuddy

According to Jeff Gemmer during his interview with the author, "Connie was Coach Barnes' protégé. Coach Barnes was very much a mentor to him." Gemmer continued his praise: "He [McGillicuddy] was a class act. He taught Latin or whatever the school needed. He was upfront, and he loved to talk. But whereas Johnny Barnes was really intense, he was very soft-spoken. Not a real rah-rah; very soft-spoken."

CORNELIUS V. McGILLICUDDY
A.B.
Latin, Algebra

The following pages contain two profiles of Mr. Mack. The first was offered in the December 1984 issue of *The Citadel* marking 40 years of service to CHS; the second, published in March 1988, marks his reception of the Golden Diamond award.

Coach, Teacher, Gentleman

Every student at Canisius knows who Mr. Mack is — teacher, coach, and Canisius Athletic Director. However, few people know *who* Mr. Cornelius V. McGillicuddy is.

Born the third youngest of eight brothers and sisters in Buffalo, he attended Canisius on Washington Street. There were only sixty-three graduates in the small school body of three hundred. Mr. Mack played

baseball, football and basketball there, and went to Holy Cross College in Worcester, Massachusetts, where he played basketball. He graduated in 1943 and returned to C.H.S. to start his teaching and coaching career.

In 1944, Mr. McGillicuddy began teaching algebra and helping out with the baseball team; by the mid-1940's he was coaching the baseball and basketball teams. Because Mr. Mack was so active in the athletics at Canisius, he was appointed Athletic Director in 1959. In that year, as Mr. William Grotke said, Mr. Mack brought true dedication to Canisius High School. Mr. Grotke also added that he spends more time for the school than people realize. Mr. McGillicuddy works out schedules and keeps the athletics organized.

Mr. James Skipper, Cross-Country

Mike Sweeney/CITADEL

coach, noted that Mr. Mack has a strong memory of his career. Mr. Mack said, "When you've been teaching and coaching as long as I have been doing it, it isn't that you count the number of students or the number of wins and losses or the number of championships or things like that. I think you think of the outstanding students you've had or the outstanding events that have taken place. You think of the students that have gone on to fame and fortune."

People Mr. Mack noted were Larry Felser, *Buffalo News* Sports Editor, and comedian Mark Russell. Athletes he coached

and taught were Peter Grimm, Cincinnati Reds pitcher, and Phil McKonkey, New York Giants wide receiver.

Mr. Skipper also stated that Mr. Mack has a strong dedication and concern for the school, the students, and the Athletic League. Mr. Grotke said he teaches and coaches with a supportive attitude. Every practice is a learning session, where a player's weak spot is ironed out in an uncritical manner. Mr. Grotke commented that Mr. Mack "maintains a clear image of what his goals are, and keeps them realistic" and works towards those goals with a gentle,

caring attitude. He said Mr. Mack's main objective is to teach, test, reteach, retest.

Mr. Skipper remarked he works toward the tradition of the school, and Mr. Grotke observed that Mr. McGillicuddy drives for the image of C.H.S. and gives 100% to the academics and administration. These are the reasons why over 300 C.H.S. alumni, teachers, coaches and friends recently honored Mr. McGillicuddy. Mr. Skipper finished, "He stands out for and practices what he believes."

— *John Fisher*

A Lifetime of Service

When reflecting on society today, it can be said that people have a tendency to regard the contributions of man in terms of political power or financial genius. The newspapers, television and even history books emphasize such contributions. Consequently, a president, a county political chairman or the head of a banking empire are recognized as the lone builders of civilization. There are others though, whose quiet and patient work in building character cannot be seen or measured, but whose effectiveness is marked in the hearts and minds of the thousands of young persons trained, in their families, in their careers and occupations which they eventually adopt, and the outer reaches of their spheres of influence. Such a quiet builder

...udly accepted the Golden Diamond before students and media.

Mr. Mack *(cont'd from front page)*

was recognized two months ago when the United States Baseball Foundation honored Cornelius "Connie" MacGillicuddy for his years of dedication to youth baseball.

For approximately thirty years, MacGillicuddy has been the varsity baseball coach at Canisius. He has also coached teams in the Triple Amateur Baseball Association (ABA) for over twenty years. In addition to these accomplishments, MacGillicuddy has coached teams in the Buffalo Murry League and the Kensington Post American League, which is nationally known.

But by no means does MacGillicuddy's accomplishments stop at coaching. He was a co-founder of the Buffalo Evening News BEN-Pal Baseball League, and remained commissioner until last year.

In recognition of his efforts, the U.S. Baseball Federation awarded MacGillicuddy the 1987 Golden Diamond Volunteer Baseball Coach of the Year Award for New York State. This award is presented to an individual in each state for his exceptional contribution to the development of amateur baseball in his community.

MacGillicuddy was also given a Service Award, one of five throughout the country, for his dedication to amateur baseball.

William Grotke, a man who has coached along with MacGillicuddy, spoke of his dedication to teamwork and his devotion to sportsmanship. "Connie leads by example," Grotke said, "He loves baseball, its players, and what it can do for individual growth."

Father Zanoni, also a coach, praised MacGillicuddy's overwhelming knowledge of baseball and his humility. "Connie is a very fine man," Zanoni said, "and I am glad he got the award because he is humble."

— *Max Latona*

THE CITADEL

School Spirit Here to Stay

Says Dick Griffin

The Canisius Crusader has known bitter days, and sometimes has even been dispirited. But from defeat he has risen with a new courage born of the lofty crenelated walls of the citadel where he has dwelt.

This is the Canisius Crusader, greater than all of us, yet of all of us, because he is the personification of the manhood of a school which so challenges the world that the world gives to it, not the symbol of a beast or a bird, but the name of the flower of history's chivalry.

Hail to the Canisius Crusader, who rides a white charger, and casts across all the battlefields he invades the gracious shadow of his stainless shield!

With these words Mr. McGillicuddy struck the keynote of Canisius school spirit at the rally before the St. Joe game last month. The school spirit, which has been displayed at Canisius during the past football season, has assured old-timers that the old traditional "Washington St. spirit" has moved lock, stock and barrel up to Delaware Ave.

School spirit, however, isn't just enthusiasm displayed on the gridiron or the loudest rooting during a basketball game. It goes much deeper than that. School spirit is that indefinable something, which manifests itself in understanding between teacher and student in the classroom, in sincere, manly devotion in the Chapel, in all the sacrifices, big and small, made for a common cause—the glory of Canisius.

We of the class of '50 are proud to be the first graduating class to complete four years at the new Canisius-on-Delaware, and proud, too, to take the lead in transplanting a 75-year old Canisius spirit to the new building.

The Dec. 9, 1949 *Citadel* recounted Mr. McGillicuddy's inspirational words on school spirit.

Coach Paul Lamb

The June 4, 1968 issue of *The Citadel* contained a memorial column written by Tom Fontana '69. In it, Fontana includes the words offered by Fr. Robert Burns, S.J., Rector:

> *From the first day that Mr. Lamb came to Canisius as swimming coach and physical educational instructor until his lamented death, the boys at Canisius and the prestige of the school were of principal concern to him.*
>
> *His closest contacts, of course, were with the members of the swimming team, and both their reverence for him as well as the bond of affection between them were clearly evident.*
>
> *All at Canisius, however, teachers and students alike, gained a great deal of inspiration from their associations with him, for he truly gave an example of what a Christian gentleman should be and what a Canisius man should be.*[29]

Fontana's article reminded the CHS community that as a teenager, Mr. Lamb had been confined to a wheelchair as the result of arthritis—but that through his perseverance, he utilized water training to regain his ability

to walk. Likewise, Fontana's memorial tells us that, "According to Mr. James Palisano, a long-time friend and colleague, 'Mr. Lamb had tremendous determination, drive, and great faith in whatever he was doing. And he did his very best to instill this driving determination in all his students....'"[30]

Coach Lamb from the 1949 *Arena*.

Coach John Barnes said, "Mr. Lamb was one of the most conscientious teachers that I have ever worked with....[He] will be hard to replace."[31] Coach Lamb worked at CHS from 1946 until his death at age 57 in 1968.

New and Returning Sports at CHS

The creation of the CHS rowing team dates to 1949. The March 18 issue of *The Citadel* from that year announces the team's establishment.

The February 10, 1950, issue describes the emergence of two new teams at Canisius—that is, one new (hockey) and one returning (tennis). See images, below.

ROWING TEAM ORGANIZED

If you see a few tired stalwarts dragging themselves about the school corridors, please don't stare at their sorry state. They are probably members of the newly organized Rowing Team. These mighty men, under the direction of Father Burns, hope to whip themselves into shape, so that they might engage in keen competition with Lafayette, Technical and other schools.

At the present this "whipping" is being done at the West Side Rowing Club a site familiar to lovers of the sport. As of now, the members of the team include the Johnsons, Bill and Ed, Jack Weimer, Bill Wende, Tom Jakiel, Bob Nicaise, Bill McNally, Jerry Glasser, Jack Zahm, Ed Jurewicz and Bob Gillen.

Tennis Team Back By Popular Demand

By Kevin MacNaughton

In answer to many urgent petitions of fans last year, tennis has again taken its place among the interscholastic sports at Canisius. Although there is no official league, some excellent netmen, coached by Mr. Novak, S. J., will take the field against rival teams.

Canisius' last tennis team was coached by Mr. Mayer until 1942 and by Mr. Franchois in 1943, when it had to be disbanded because of the war, and has not been reorganized since.

13 Seniors show the greatest promise of forming the nucleus of this Spring's team. They are Vinnie Doyle, Jack Frysiak, Bill Gortzig, John Helminiak, Bill Joyce, Carl Leitten, Mike Marfino, Tom Mullen, Ray Naber, Ray Schreck, Tom Shanahan, Ray Sullivan and Al Kraus. Last fall underclassmen showed up in great numbers and assured Canisius a top-seeded team for the next few years.

Coach Enters Canisius In New Hockey League

By John Rodgers

The newly-formed International Scholastic Hockey League includes Niagara Frontier high schools, Timon, Lackawanna High, Fort Erie High and Canisius. Canisius was the last team to enter the tournament for which a trophy will be donated by the Buffalo Hockey Club.

The Canisius hockey team was formed about a month ago only after a great deal of controversy as to whether there was a sufficient popular demand for a team, where the team was to practice, who was to be coach, etc. When the smoke of controversy cleared, Mr. Joyce, S.J. had taken over the coaching job and issued the call for candidates.

Canisius-on-Delaware: Then and Now

The Canisius of 1948-1949, despite now having a central campus location, bore only some similarities to the school we know today. It's worth taking a look at the two side by side in the context of some statistics.

Enrollment was slightly larger, for example, but ultimately similar. Based on analysis of the 1949 yearbook, it stood at 898, with 178 in the graduating class, 209 in the junior class (1950), 234 in the sophomore class (1951), and 277 in the freshman class (1952).

One of two particularly notable differences in the school community is the lack of any female faculty members and the high percentage of Jesuits relative to lay faculty.[32]

	1949 *Arena*	2017 *Arena*
Teaching & Administrative Staff	46	108
Jesuits	32 (70%)	3 (3%)
Lay	14 (30%)	105 (97%)
Male	46 (100%)	55 (52%)
Female	0 (0%)	50 (48%)

The other highly conspicuous difference between CHS in 1948-1949 and today lies in the context of racial diversity. As of 1949, Canisius had not yet graduated an African American student, and the ranks of the class photos are almost exclusively white. The only exception, in fact, was Clarence R. Kregg of the Class of 1950, who enrolled in the fall of 1946 as a freshman. He would go on to be the first African American student to graduate from CHS. In an interview with the author, Mr. Kregg offered the following insights about being the first student of color at the school:

As far as the school was concerned, I was a student who happened to be black. My color didn't enter into it. There just weren't a lot of black families who were Catholic back then, you understand?

I played football. There was one guy who didn't like me, a year ahead of me, but that's it. I made varsity my sophomore year, so we played together for two years. That was the only racial thing. I remember Father Flood. He was kind of a mentor. I got in a fight one time, and he told me, 'The spoken word is mightier than the fist.' I've always remembered that.

Kevin Flood, S.J., in the 1947 Arena Yearbook. Source: CHS Archives.

I played for Coach Barnes for three years. I wasn't first string. My brothers were better than I was. I played right halfback. But one memory I have that's real clear is I played the Saint Joe's game. I was on defense, and this guy came running at me. I was all set to tackle him, and he ran right past me. It was caught on film, and they played it on television later. It was so embarrassing! But we won. We were champions that year.

Clarence R. Kregg '50

I remember I learned to bowl there, in the bowling alley in the basement. My next two brothers started, but they didn't finish. My fourth brother, Kenneth, finished. He was class of 1958.[33]

Mark Russell, a classmate of Clarence from the Class of 1950, shared a recollection about him during an interview for this book:

Clarence was our only African American student. We graduated one week before the Korean War started. And we heard a couple of years later that Clarence Kregg had been killed in Korea. So every time we'd get together for a reunion, fifth, tenth, fifteenth, we would mourn poor Clarence Kregg, killed in Korea. Finally, our fiftieth reunion, down at the Saturn Club, in walks Clarence Kregg. Wow! So we flock over to him, and we're like, oh my God! Clarence!? And he said, "Gees. I didn't think you guys would remember me!"[34]

Academics in the Late 1940s

The February 11, 1949 issue of *The Citadel* featured a lengthy article entitled "The Philosophy of Education at Canisius High School." It draws principally from the Philosophy of Education put forth by the Jesuits for all American schools. It provides some good insights as to the academic program of the school in this postwar era.

Education is not a haphazard affair. It is not a period of our lives spent in wandering aimlessly through the labyrinths of knowledge. Rather, it is a "vocation," a calling, something very definite. It implies a three-fold obligation— an obligation on the teacher, on the parent, and last but by no means the least, on the student himself. Should we lose sight of this truth, education will become a storehouse of INFORMATION instead of an intensive training in FORMATION. Hence, it is well that we pause to "take our bearings," to make certain that we have not allowed ourselves to "wander from the course," to realize more fully what we are doing here at Canisius High School. For this purpose, we have deemed it wise to reprint a statement on the Philosophy of Education in our Jesuit Schools. It is our firm belief that a study of this statement on the part of teachers, parents, and students will do much to make the period of education a serious one.

In many ways, the detailed contents of this "Philosophy," (not included here due to prohibitive length and detail) are the precursors to what more recent alumni will recognize as the Traits of the Jesuit High School Graduate at Graduation ("Grad at Grad" traits) as articulated by the Jesuit Secondary Education Association, or JSEA (now the Jesuit Schools Network, or JSN), later in the century.

The Annual Catalogue for 1949-1950 included a Course of Studies, as depicted on the following page.

THE COURSE OF STUDIES

In the first year all students take the same subjects. In second year eligible students may choose either the Greek or the Science Course. Other students must take the Basic Course. The Basic Course of sixteen units is required for graduation, while nineteen units may be completed by qualified students.

GREEK COURSE	SCIENCE COURSE	BASIC COURSE
First Year	*First Year*	*First Year*
Latin	Latin	Latin
English	English	English
Elementary Algebra	Elementary Algebra	Elementary Algebra
Our Economic World	Our Economic World	Our Economic World
Health	Health	Health
Library Science	Library Science	Library Science
Second Year	*Second Year*	*Second Year*
Latin	Latin	Latin
English	English	English
Geometry	Geometry	Geometry
American History	American History	American History
Greek	German	
Third Year	*Third Year*	*Third Year*
Latin	Latin	Latin
English	English	English
French or German	German	French or German
Intermediate Algebra (one term)	Intermediate Algebra (one term)	Intermediate Algebra (one term)
Trigonometry (one term)	Trigonometry (one term)	Trigonometry (one term)
Greek	Chemistry	
Fourth Year	*Fourth Year*	*Fourth Year*
Latin	Latin	Latin
English	English	English
French or German	German	French or German
Physics or Chemistry	Physics	Physics or Chemistry
Greek	Solid Geometry (one term)	
	Advanced Algebra (one term)	

Religion and Physical Training are taught in all years; Speech in the first three years.

All subjects are taught five periods a week, except: Latin, 8 in first year; 6 in second, third and fourth years; Algebra, 6 in first year; Sciences, 4 Lecture and 2 Laboratory; Religion, 2; Health, 2; Physical Training, Speech, Library Science, 1 each. All periods are 45 minutes in length.

From the *Annual Catalogue, 1949-1950*

The CHS Class of 1950: Recollections

Members of the CHS Class of 1950 who gathered for a retrospective, left to right: Joseph Basil, Donald Seitz, Jack Quinn, Richard Griffin, Joseph Scully, Mark Russell

This book is entitled *Blue Doors*. Fittingly, then, because they were the first class to attend all four years behind the Blue Doors* of "Canisius-on-Delaware," this author took the opportunity to meet with a small group of class representatives so that they could provide some recollections and reflections. Assembled by Joe Scully '50 (to whom this author is very grateful), their perspectives were wide ranging and presented here in no particular order.

From Mark Russell**, regarding retreats:
The senior retreat was on a different level than the others. The junior was hellfire and brimstone. But by the senior, it was not anyone on the faculty [leading]. It was somebody from New York or whatever. He was terrific. You left on a high note.

During some of the retreat experiences, some of us would go down to the bur-lesque theater. They had strippers and a comedian. Everyone would kid me and I'd say I was just going to see the comedians. The retreat leader would

---

* It is important to note that technically speaking, during the time these young men attended CHS, the Blue Doors were not yet blue. They were referred to, rather, as "the wooden doors." See details re: The Blue Doors in the chapter on the 1960s.

** For context on Mr. Russell's career, see *The Citadel* interview in the 1970s Gallery at the end of Chapter 10.

mention that "The Palace Theater" is an occasion of sin! Buck Leahy would ask, what about the guys who say they only go there for the comedians?" He got me cornered on that one.

From Joe Basil: On Richard Grimm and Balcony Water Bombs:

A number of us were friends with a Richard Grimm. He became a well-respected attorney. We used to sit at the same lunch table. Me, Leo Kane, Tommy Boland, and Grimm. Everybody brown bagged it. And every once in a while, Grimm would say, "I'll get those for ya. I'll do pick up." So I watch him. So the first couple times I'm not paying attention. But then I start watching him. He goes over to the bag, empties another one, and he puts the bags in his coat pocket. Now that happened to be a day when somebody got water bombed. Now those of us who sat with him, asked him, "How the hell did you get away with it?" He went up in the library. He would ask Ellie Houlihan for a special book. And he'd sit in front of where the altar was, near the doors to the library. So he'd sit there with the book open. And when no one was watching, he'd disappear onto the balcony. He'd discovered that the water fountains were still working there. So he had five bags, one inside the other, and he'd fill them with water. He'd walk along the top of the balcony while the intramurals were going on, and decide who he was gonna drop the water bomb on. And then he'd run back quick and sit and be reading his book. Nobody could figure it out. But Father Kirsch was the prefect of discipline. He was just about beside himself. But nobody that knew ever squealed on him. But one day he hit a priest. And it created a splash pattern, so a lot of guys got wet.

From Mark Russell, on Three Particularly Memorable Jesuits:

Father Dolan. He taught theater. He had this majestic theatrical voice. He walked in and said, "We're going to be studying Shelley. Percy Bysshe Shelley. That's a family name. So you might say he was a son-of-a-Bysshe." Wow. We were blown away that he was using language like that. He later had a nationwide radio show.

Father Raymundo. His English was not that great, so his line at confessional was the longest. Every Thursday we had confession, and everyone had the idea *that he didn't really have a firm understanding of the nature of the sins. So, he'd be like, "Eh, yeah, umm, three Our Fathers."*

Father Braun was our homeroom teacher. He lost his glass eye in the pool. There was a retrieval mission. Bernie Lyons found it. He was a champion swimmer. Braun was an okay guy, but I wouldn't want to go hunting with him.

From Mark Russell, on Getting Old and Staying in Touch:
"I get the Buffalo paper in Chautauqua. I look at the obituaries. And if I'm not in them, I eat breakfast."

From Mark Russell, on Deceptive Floral Practices to Impress Girls:
We had this senior prom, and there was a very high-class florist on Delaware Avenue. Hodge's Florist. So we went down and bought flowers at the Chippewa Market and went to Hodge's and asked if they had any empty boxes. And the girls would think we were all very high class.

From Mark Russell, on Marine Boot Camp Relative to CHS:
After Canisius High School, Marine Boot Camp was a piece of cake.

From Mark Russell, on Jesuits, Beer, and Milk:
You could look out the window of the new classroom wing on the driveway of the Millburn Mansion. Every morning the Iroquois Beer Truck would pull up and leave two or three cases of beer. And a few minutes later the milkman would show up and leave a little bottle of cream. Because they had a cat.

From Jack Quinn, on Just How Emotional Coach Barnes Would Get Because He Cared So Much:
In football, at halftime of every game, Barnes—whether it was a twenty-minute break or whatever it was at the time—Barnes never said a word until there were two minutes left. Then he'd try to speak with two minutes left. And he'd cry. Every single game. Whether you were winning by four touchdowns or down by one, it made no difference. He'd cry. He could barely get it out.

From Joe Basil, on Father Muenzen, S.J.

Father Muenzen, S.J., with the Bunsen. He was the chemistry teacher. He had a storage locker in the front of the classroom. He'd give us an assignment and then he'd disappear in there. I don't know if he was smoking or whatever. All the sudden some guys in the class would let out cat calls. And he'd stick his head out and say, "Who did that?" He could never find out. So he had this "list of the prescribed." He put certain people he thought were doing it on the list of prescribed. If you were on the list, anytime this happened, you would write twenty pages of the chemistry book. I happened to get picked. I don't know why. This was not very good. So it came to January exams, and he went around the room, and he would say, "Yeah, Griffin, you're okay, Seitz, you're okay, etc." He came to me and said, "Basil, if you pass, I'll stand on my head in the middle of Delaware." So this was January exams. I thought, that's not very nice. Long story short, I aced it, okay? So, when the marks came out, he didn't have much to say about anything. When I would come into the classroom, I was waiting for him to say something, but he wouldn't say anything. I'd say to him, "Father is today the day?" He'd say, "Go to your seat." Couple days later, I'd say "It's a nice day today, Father." The next time I said it I was put in my place and learned to keep my mouth shut. He never did it. He was a nice guy.

From Mark Russell, On His Short and Unglorious Timpani Career

I played the piano until a freshman came along who was a lot better. So no more piano for me. They put me on the kettle drums. So graduation day, the orchestra's down here, and you had to go up on stage to get your diploma. So when I went up to get my diploma, the other guys unscrewed all the screws on the kettle drum. So I come down. It was an ancient thing. Probably went back to WWI. So it was the National Anthem. So I'm ready, and I hit it, and the mallet went right through it, and that was the end of my timpani career.

From Jim Seitz, on the Importance of Math in the Korean War:

"When I got into the service, I was an artillery officer.... People coming in from the southern states didn't know an angle from a straight line. I ended up teaching remedial mathematics, probably because of my time here at CHS."

<u>From Dick Griffin, on Two Exemplary Priests from the Class of '50:</u>
"Two of our classmates were two of the most famous priests in the history of Buffalo. John Weimer and Joe Bissonette. Weimer was the best preacher in town, and Bissonette was the most devoted person to people of little means."

<u>From Mark Russell, on the Importance of Latin:</u>
"The four years of Latin has served me well. Because as a political satirist, the expressions nolo contendere[5] *and* quid pro quo[6] *came in handy."*

<u>Jack Quinn, on the Alumni Network in Buffalo:</u>
"In practicing law in downtown Buffalo, it was just a pleasure that every week you'd run into a classmate from Canisius High School or someone who graduated ahead or behind us."

<u>Joe Basil, on the Foundation Provided by His Canisius Education</u>
The foundation of my career and my education was right here.... There were so many things I was learning that I didn't know I was learning at the time, as a kid.... I had discipline that I learned here. I didn't know I was learning it. It all stemmed right from here.... When I got into these [business] opportunities, I didn't have any problem taking advantage of them. I never went into a job or a business that we bought thinking of failure or wondering how I was gonna make this happen. I just knew I could do it. This place taught me integrity. When you're trying to do business, when you're buying another man's business, and he is getting out of something he built and you are making promises to him, integrity counts.... Integrity is the most important attribute because when you have integrity, everything else comes easy.

1940s - Conclusion

While every lived era of school life—whether the four-year period for student or perhaps a thirty-year career of a teacher—presents significant transition and transformation, some eras are more transformational to the

---

[5] "I do not wish to contend." A plea of no contest, legally.
[6] "Something for something." An exchange of goods and services, with the transfer of one contingent upon the transfer of the other.

institution than others. Arguably, the decade of the 1940s saw the most visible transformation of Canisius High School, marked principally by its relocation to Delaware Avenue. Indeed, the widespread use of the names, "Canisius-on-Delaware" and "The New Canisius High School" make clear the dividing line between the old and new.

We might pause here to appreciate the significant courage and faith involved in this fundamental transformation. It was a courageous move to take the risks that led to securing the Consistory property—especially considering the narrow time window and the obvious pressure under which Father Redmond and the school's leadership had to make their decisions. Furthermore, there was courage and faith exhibited in the bold initiative to borrow such a substantial sum to construct the classroom wing. As the next chapter will make clear, this indebtedness created no small challenge for the Jesuits. What should we take from this? Arguably, a clear lesson in faith. The leaders and stewards of the school blended fiduciary discretion with bold risk-taking—a delicate and tenuous balance achieved and maintained, no doubt, only by diligence, perseverance, and faith.

And, in no small measure, the great generosity of many who believed so powerfully in the mission of Jesuit education in Buffalo. This set the stage for a decade of campus expansion in the 1950s that would solidify the "New Canisius High School" as a fixture at 1180 Delaware Avenue, where it remains today.

Gallery: Late 1940s

The images contained herein comprise an interesting gallery portrait of student life, from academics and activities to athletics.

THE SPORTSCOPE

In their wins over St. Mary's and St. Francis the Crusaders have proved their mettle. Nobody is surprised that local sport-writers rate Canisius as a more than likely contender for the Notre Dame Cup. This is no team of a star or two. Our victories have been the work of a score of men. Here are some of them—

At half-back we find **Earl Scheeler**, the shifty ball-carrier, who averaged 25 yards a crack in the St. Mary's game, and who had a big hand in setting up each touchdown.

The lad, who calls the plays, was almost unknown to the Crusaders' sport gallery till this year. He's short, crew-cut, and handles a

Canisius Halts St. Francis, 7-6

1500 fans left Lackawanna Stadium Friday night, September 24, with hearts still beating high, after witnessing the closest struggle of the Catholic H. S. League thus far. The Crusaders eeked out a meagre 7-6 victory over a strong, deceptive squad from St. Francis of Athol Springs

THE SCARE

Four times St Francis marched down the field to within Canisius' own 10-yard line, and four times our seven blocks of granite refused to budge. The fourth goal

UNDER THE ARCS AT LACKAWANNA STADIUM

Sports news from The Citadel, October 11, 1948.

Canitds by Harig, '50

Upper left—Weimer and Koch smother ball carrier. Upper right—Donius Plunges through center. Lower left—Donius skirts end. Lower right—Adema breaks through.

football as though it were a third hand. That's right, it's George Zenger. His handoffs to Jack Weimer, hardest runner on the squad, have written some of the longest gains charted this year. Jack tallied against St. Mary's.

Marty Veere has been playing consistently steady ball from the other halfback slot. The St. Mary's game convinced everyone that he is a handy man to have around in a tight spot.

We can't forget that line of ours. Those dogged stands with their backs to the wall in that fierce Lackawanna tussle proved that the linesmen have staying power as well as icy nerve. They have rounded into form early in the season.

Captain **Russ Rosati** patrols one end of the line; **Ed Jurewicz** looks after the other. Both are tall, rangy, smart ball-players. Russ (Continued on Page 4, Col. 2)

line stand was made in the last minute of play with grim defea staring the Crusaders right in th face. Kaczor, halfback for St Francis, squirmed off tackle from the 7, but was stopped dead in his tracks on the 3 by Big Tom Cleary, as the final gun was fired.

THE SCORE

Both teams played through a scoreless first quarter. Early in the second stanza, St. Francis' sustained drive, which featured (Cont'd on Page 4, Col. 1)

THE CITADEL

SHAKESPEARE REVIVAL PLANNED FOR DECEMBER

Early in December, for the first time in 20 years, Canisius will present a Shakespearean play. The custom of the annual play is being revived this year with the production of Shakespeare's great trady, *"Julius Caesar."*

Father Charles Dolan, S. J., who is himself an exceptionally capable Shakespearean actor, will direct the production. He has planned to use the Orson Wells version of the play, but has rejected the use of modern dress, a practice popularized by Wells in the '30's.

Canisius' "Julius Caesar" will have a cast of more than a hundred students, dressed in the tunics and togas of Ancient Rome, and acting before very realistic scenery. Such a large cast is demanded to recreate the atmosphere of the mob scenes, which dominate the earlier part of the action.

Tryouts for the many principal parts of the play were held the last week of September, so that at least a tentative cast could be drawn up and rehearsals begun.

Father Walter Stokes, S. J., Assistant Director of Dramatics, is making plans of seating arrangements in the auditorium, where the play will be presented on the evnings of December 2nd and 3rd. There will also be matinee performances for the religious of the diocese and school children.

Above: Announcement about the production of Julius Caesar in The Citadel, October 11, 1948. The play would cast Bill O'Malley '49 as Cassius. He would go on to become a Jesuit priest, author, and actor most famous for his role in The Exorcist. Below: A note regarding the "senior smoking lounge," a facility that has long departed CHS. *The Citadel*, Oct. 7, 1949.

The Lyon's Pen—The smoke screen in the senior lounge is being given an opportunity to clear. A few members of the senior class didn't seem quite accurate in aiming for the ash trays and there was evidence that some one or two people mistook the smoker for the cafeteria. Let's go boys! Keep it clean and keep it open. . . . Jack Carney scored a mild sensation in the

An Open Letter to the Timon Tigers

The Citadel

Canisius High School, Buffalo, N. Y.

Dear Herb,

All Canisius shouts three cheers to you, Captain Herb Hillery, and your Timon Tigers baseball team. We at Canisius congratulate you on your splendid record in Legion ball and consider you the State Champions of 1949.

We followed your success during the summer months and were high in praise of your team as it came off tops in elimination after elimination.

We also feel that you were victims of a so-called "raw deal" when your team was disqualified on "paper technicalities," which were never called to your attention during the whole season, and when the team you beat was installed as champions.

Another thing—we liked the sportsmanlike way you took it on the chin and will always be proud of keeping up a keen, but friendly, rivalry with Timon men of such calibre on the field of sport.

Sincerely,

DICK GRIFFIN.

Citadel Sports Staff

'Keep the Banner High' Battle Cry of Orators

By TONY PODLECKI

During the past years, Canisius High School has maintained a standard for one of the best oratorical societies in the City of Buffalo. Father Paone, moderator, hopes that the orators of 1949-50 will stand among the best that Canisius has ever had.

Under Father Paone, Canisius orators have reached great heights. Last year Ronald Becht, a Junior at Canisius, took third place in the Oratorical Contest sponsored by the American Legion. The prize-winning speech, "The Care of Our Constitution," won for him two other awards: the gold medal in the Senior Division of the annual Oratorical Contest, and first place in the Erie County finals last February.

This year, as in the past, Canisius will have representatives in the American Legion and the Knights of Columbus oratorical contests. There is also a possibility that we will enter the contest sponsored by the American Forensic League.

In the past, Canisius High School has had excellent representation in the various oratorical contests, both local and national. It is hoped that the 1949-50 school year will produce its share of fine oratory.

Top: A witty note to the Timon Tigers by Dick Griffin '50 in *The Citadel*, October 7, 1949. Bottom: An article about the always-successful Behrens Debate Society. *Citadel* October 7, 1949.

The Citadel

Vol. II, No. 3   16   CANISIUS HIGH SCHOOL, BUFFALO, N. Y.   November 18, 1949

1949 Yearbook Wins Columbia Press Award

In its 15th annual yearbook contest, the Columbia Scholastic Press Association awarded 1st place to the 1949 Arena Yearbook. The judges were particularly impressed by the way the book was designed around its theme, "Second Spring," in commemoration of the final transfer of students from the old Washington Street building to the new school. They were pleased with the analogy drawn between the rebirth of Catholicism in England, as celebrated in Cardinal Newman's famous sermon, and the rebirth of Canisius in Buffalo, as described by the yearbook staff.

The coloration employed throughout the book also received high praise from the critics. Still another reason for such a high rating was the adequate photographic and editorial coverage given to all our school organizations and athletics.

Congratulations to the staff that worked tirelessly to pro-

City Champ

This past month Ronald Becht took first place in "Voice of Democracy" oratory in the Buffalo area, was given the lead in "Macbeth," and received the Degree of Honor from the National Forensic League.

duce so outstanding an annual! Their success is a challenge to us to make the 1950 Arena even better.

Becht and Zolkiewicz Share Lead In December's Shakespearean Play

By Joe Bennett

The Canisius Dramatic Society announced last week its cast for the forthcoming presentation of Shakespeare's "Macbeth." Ronnie Becht, who has distinguished himself last year and this in the field of oratory, will handle the difficult role of Macbeth. This will be Ronnie's first appearance in Canisius dramatics.

Sophomore Ted Zolkiewicz will share the lead as Lady Macbeth, the strongest and most commanding of all of Shakespeare's feminine characters. Jerry Leahy will portray Duncan, King of Scotland; Bill Joyce, Banquo; John Campbell, Malcolm, Duncan's son; and Tom Daley, Macduff.

Bob Racicot, Joe Rice and Jerry Schabel will be seen as the elemental avengers, the three witches. These and many others in the cast have begun the reading of the play and the memorizing of their lines, so that by the time December 9th

Pigskin Prom

Just one week to go! Next Friday evening, Bill Johnson, chairman, informs us, the Canisius Starlight Room will be the scene of the Annual Football Dance. Bobby Meyers and his Revelers will provide the very tasteful musical setting. If you haven't got your ducat or your date, better take care of both real soon.

Students Venerate Relic

The Nov. 18, 1949 *Citadel* captures the school's success in oratory, dramatics, debate, and publications (above). Below (L) "Locker Rumors" explores the swim team's culture; Below (R) some witty remarks about JUG.

Locker Rumors

By Bill Johnson

We decided to journey down into the depths of the school and sneak into swimming practice. I was sitting leisurely at the bottom of the pool passing completely unnoticed when two dancing bubbles came down and struck up an interesting conversation. I couldn't help but overhear them.

"Winfred," said the larger of the two, "this fellow Regan moves faster than blue pike on Friday."

"Yea man, but this guy Buchheit isn't any poke either, an' how 'bout Wilson and Schwarz, too."

"And don't forget Kippel," I blurted out.

The two noticed me for the first time and in five minutes we were friends for life.

From what I gathered the two had been roaming the depths since the pool was opened in 1943. They told me that Mike Regan was the fastest thing they'd seen in any waters and, with Rudy Buchheit, Chuck Wilson, Henry Kippel, and Ken Schwarz, Canisius would have a good team.

After listening to them for more than an hour I heard the five o'clock warning bell and said I really must be on my way.

They gave me a word of warning though, as I ascended. "Unless some diver shows up here some day after school Canisius will lose valuable points," was their gurgling warning.

The Quiz Kid Asks

"What do you think is the quickest and surest way to get jug?"

Father Kirsch, Prefect of Discipline: "If some of 'my boys' like me enough to stay around my office, all they have to do is skip jug."

Norm Wild, 2F: "Although I have never had jug, I think that being a wise guy is as nice a way to get jug as any."

Charles Horlak, 3E, says: "Put slugs in the candy machine and wait for the results, jug and a candy bar."

Tony Podlecki, 1A: "Why, that's easy! Just ask Father Kirsch for a light or offer him a cigarette."

Robert Lascola, 2A: "Try to fool around in the library. I know from past experience that you will be pacing the floor that night."

Joe Mania, 2C: "Try throwing candy wrappers around in Father Kirsch's office; that is a national insult."

179

"This I Remember"

By Dick Griffin

FRESHMAN YEAR ('46-'47)

It was a chilly, blustering October afternoon, way back in '46, when 40 Canisius freshmen gridiron huskies returned home in step with a victory chant. They had just beaten Nichols J.V. 26-6, the first of the many colorful victories that were to mark the high school career of the Class of '50, soon to join the ranks of distinguished alumni.

Freshman basketball that winter produced two standout quintets, the Minims and Acrions. All will remember the shots of Acrions Jack Quinn and Pete Gugliuzza, and the stellar floor-play of Minim "Moon" Maier.

Spring saw two championship baseball teams in action. Again under the names of Minim and Acrion, the Freshman class made Legion fame. The Minims won Naval Post Championship with 12 victories. Al Donius, hard-hitting catcher, Pat Byrnes, fleet outfielder, and Jack Siebold, Captain-shortstop, looked like excellent varsity prospects.

SOPHOMORE YEAR ('47-'48)

As Fall of '47 rolled around, Canisius fans saw five ruggedly constructed Sophomore playing first string varsity football, Ronnie Koch, heading for All-Catholic fame in '48 and '49, Jim Denny, Jack Weimer, Dick Griffin and Bill Johnson.

Al Wukovits was the sole Soph on the varsity five that year, but "Moon" Maier and Bob Rodgers were first string J.V. men. A rough and ready all-Sophomore J.V.-B team had Hank Adema, Joe Bissonette and "Trigger" Tryjankowski as high scorers.

Jack Siebold was first string second baseman on the varsity, while Tom Boland and Ron Koch sparked the J.V. Crusaders to a good season in the South Buffalo Legion circuit.

JUNIOR YEAR ('48-'49)

Heading into stormy Junior year, the Class of '50 showed amazing versatility, winning niches in the Canisius Hall of Fame in ten different sports. Jerry Moga came back to school that fall after winning the National Amateur Archery Championship. Don Braun was one of the best high school bowlers in Buffalo.

Sixteen Juniors helped bring the new W.N.Y. Catholic League Co-Championship to Canisius. George Zenger came into the limelight as All-Catholic quarterback. Ed Jurewicz and Ron Koch took over end and guard positions respectively on the same mythical eleven. Gus Taglienti proved to be one of the best defensive backs in the league.

Bud Keppel and Ken Schwarz were top point-getters in swimming circles. Seven Juniors played with the League's Co-Championship basketball squad. Tex Williams, George Zenger and Noel Bartlo led the J.V. to Championship in their own hardwood league.

Three out of five varsity twirlers that Spring were Joe Bissonette, Dick Griffin and Don Lisowski. Jack Siebold turned in many a sterling performance at short.

This Spring, too, crew and golf teams made their first appearances. Jerry Glasser, strokeman, led the crew to a photo finish against Bennett High. Al Donius and Dan Webster were top men on the links.

SENIOR YEAR ('49-'50)

Then the big year came and the once pint-size Frosh were determined to make their weight felt in all sports circles. Captain Bill Johnson led the Blue and Gold on to the gridiron in quest of another Championship, but injuries and Duffy High played havoc with their fond hopes.

Al Donius, Ron Koch and Jack Weimer received All-Catholic recognition at the season's end, marred by losses to Duffy and St. Francis. St. Joe's fell Canisius' victim the second year in a row. Herb Hezel was the man of the hour, when he replaced the injured Hank Adema, center, in the Civic Stadium.

Dick Griffin '50's "This I Remember" feature, published in the May 24, 1950 *Citadel*, provides a nice review of the Class of 1950s athletic memories.

Arena Dedications: 1941-1950

The *Arena* Yearbook has been, in all but a few cases, dedicated annually to a member of the faculty or administration. Ostensibly, this is a person whom the students held in high esteem and who made a considerable impact upon the institution. As such, a listing of these dedications will be included for each decade from the 1940s to the time of this book's publication. Taken together, this compilation will serve as a tapestry of generosity, influence, and commitment among the CHS community.

1941 - Rev. Lorenzo K. Reed, S.J., Prefect of Studies; Rev. Stanley E. Curtin, S.J., Prefect of Discipline; and Rev. William A. Riordan, S.J., Class Teacher of Senior A

"How well Father Curtin has fulfilled his position.... In a class by itself is his boundless patience...never once has he deviated from his policy of directing the misguided and pointing out to the misinformed the road heavenward.... For only one year have we known Father Riordan, yet as is characteristic of the wholly likeable, we feel as if we have always known him...kind, genial, an excellent teacher and a master of discipline.... We welcomed Father Reed to the tedious and difficult task of governing and guiding the student body. He never betrayed our trust in him...always was the quiet, refined voice tempered with that of unconquerable will power...."[35]

Reverend William A. Riordan, S.J.
Class Teacher of Senior A

Reverend Stanley E. Curtin, S.J.
Prefect of Discipline

Reverend Lorenzo K. Reed, S.J.
Prefect of Studies

1942 - Rev. Stanley E. Curtin, S.J., Prefect of Discipline

"His energy, kindness, and boundless patience, his firm but considerate enforcement of discipline...above all shall we remember his concern and anxiety over our spiritual welfare...."[36]

1943 - Mr. Ryrie E. MacTaggart, M.A., History & Civics

"The seniors of Canisius High have come to know and respect him, not only as an excellent teacher, but as a man of sound judgment and character.... His occasional humorous remarks, inserted when the going was hardest, coupled with just the right amount of discipline, helped immeasurably...."[37]

1944 - Rev. Ralph A. Sturtzer, S.J., Student Counselor

"Throughout our four years at Canisius the office of the Student Counselor has ever been open to us all, and there has he been ready to give spiritual aid or temporal advice in our moments of difficulty or to talk in his friendly manner.... Under his wise and understanding guidance we have come to respect him as an advisor and a friend...."[38]

1945 - Rev. Francis P. Rowley, S.J., Prefect of Discipline

"To the man who disciplines us we have dedicated our yearbook, not in token of fear, but of respect for a man who knew his job and did it fairly, impartially and always firmly. From him we have learned the better qualities that discipline may engender: gentlemanliness, honesty, and a real sense of fair play...for his cheerfulness, his interest in our activities, his concern with our problems.... That he may remember the esteem in which we held him...."[39]

1946 - Mr. Ryrie E. MacTaggart, M.A.

"To a man who taught us more than the history and chronicles of men, who gave us inspiration, courage, and an ideal of manhood. To a man who convinced us that we, too, make a more significant history in our love of God than the wars of men...."[40] (See photo from 1943 dedication.)

1947 - Rev. Thomas M. Harvey, S.J., Assistant Principal

"'School Spirit' is perhaps the most abused phrase in school life. Yet for us 'School Spirit' has come to mean loyal attendance at all school functions, gentlemanliness and a regard for all the tenets of good sportsmanship. To the man who taught and made a living example of this code we cordially and thankfully dedicate the 1947 *Arena*."[41]

1948 - Thomas D. McMahon, S.J., Latin, English, French

"Alexander Pope tells us that 'the proper study of mankind is man.' In Father McMahon we have not only a gifted teacher but an ideal subject for study.... His presence is a living force. Like that Divine Teacher, he has given to us an example.... Fr. McMahon's big Gaelic grin and cheering wit.... He knows and likes the stuff of which we are made."[42]

1949 - Rev. Gerald A. Quinn, S.J., Class Teacher of Senior B, Assistant Administrator, Prefect of Discipline - Canisius-on-Washington

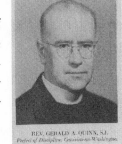

"The popularity he won last year as the prefect of discipline and teacher of Latin in third year at the Washington Street school has made a lasting impression.... His firm but genial nature, his ready wit, his infectious smile have won him many friends among our number...."[43]

1950 - Rev. Harry A. Boyle, S.J., Class Teacher of Senior C, Physics

FATHER HARRY A. BOYLE

"There comes a time during these days of high school training when some teacher ranks supreme in the eyes of his students...that teacher is Father Boyle.... It has been our good fortune to have known Father Boyle not only as an excellent teacher but also as an inspiring Jesuit. We will cherish his friendship and remember his example for many years to come...."[44]

Notes

[1] "The Academic Diary of the Principal of Canisius High School, August 1941 – September 1943." Kept by Rev. Lorenzo Reed, S.J., Principal. CHS Archives.

[2] *Ibid.*

[3] Interview with Rev. Ron Sams, S.J., '46. October 3, 2016.

[4] "A World at One – Salutatory Address of 1946. Ronald W. Sams '46. *The Arena Quarterly*, Fall 1946-1947, pg. 22.

[5] "The Academic Diary of the Principal of Canisius High School, August 1941 – September 1943." Kept by Rev. Lorenzo Reed, S.J., Principal. CHS Archives.

[6] Handwritten notes for Mass of the Holy Ghost, September 11, 1943, Father James Redmond, S.J., CHS archives.

[7] "The Academic Diary of the Principal of Canisius High School, August 1941 – September 1943." Kept by Rev. Lorenzo Reed, S.J., Principal. CHS Archives.

[8] *Arena,* The Canisius High School Yearbook, 1945, p.1

[9] *Arena,* The Canisius High School Yearbook, 1945, p.6

[10] CHS Archives. Consultor's Notes, 1944.

[11] *Ibid.*

[12] Correspondence from Zacheus J. Maher, S.J., to Timothy J. Coughlin, S.J., dated Feb. 27, 1940. Source: CHS Archives.

[13] Correspondence from Zacheus J. Maher, S.J., to James J. Redmond, S.J., dated Feb. 8, 1944. Source: CHS Archives.

[14] Correspondence from Zacheus J. Maher, S.J., to James J. Redmond, S.J., dated Jan. 29, 1945. Source: CHS Archives.

[15] Correspondence from Zacheus J. Maher, S.J., to James J. Redmond, S.J., dated Aug. 12, 1945. Source: CHS Archives.

[16] Correspondence from Very Rev. Father Vicar, N. de Boynes, S.J., to Rev. James J. Redmond, S.J., dated Mar. 14, 1946. Source: CHS Archives.

[17] Correspondence from Rev. James J. Redmond, S.J., to Very Rev. Father John B. Janssens, S.J., Father General, dated Aug. 6, 1948. Source: CHS Archives.

[18] Correspondence from Rev. James J. Redmond, S.J., to Very Rev. Father John B. Janssens, S.J., Father General, dated Jul. 30, 1949. Source: CHS Archives.

[19] Correspondence from Rev. James J. Redmond, S.J., to Very Rev. Father John B. Janssens, S.J., Father General, dated Jan. 26, 1950. Source: CHS Archives.

[20] Correspondence from Rev. James J. Redmond, S.J., to Most Rev. John F. O'Hara, C.S.C., Bishop of Buffalo, dated Nov. 25, 1950. Source: CHS Archives.

[21] Minutes of The Founder's Club, first meeting, as recorded by George J. Lenahan, Secretary, dated Dec. 5, 1950.

[22] *Arena,* The Canisius High School Yearbook, 1949, p.80-87.

[23] *Arena,* The Canisius High School Yearbook, 1949, pg. 5

[24] *The Citadel.* Volume I, No. 1. October 11, 1948. Pg. 2.

[25] *The Citadel.* Volume II, No. 1. October 7, 1949. Pg. 1.

[26] *The Citadel.* Volume II, No. 6. February 10, 1950.

[27] *Arena,* The Canisius High School Yearbook, 1945

[28] Interview with Jeff Gemmer. January 11, 2017.

[29] Memorial by Tom Fontana, *The Citadel,* June 4, 1968, p.1.

[30] *Ibid.*

[31] *Ibid.*

[32] *Arena,* The Canisius High School Yearbook, 1949

[33] Interview with Clarence R. Kregg '50. June 13, 2017.

[34] Interview with Mark Russell '50. Aug 2, 2017.

[35] *Arena,* The Canisius High School Yearbook, 1941.

[36] *Arena,* The Canisius High School Yearbook, 1942.

[37] *Arena,* The Canisius High School Yearbook, 1943.

[38] *Arena,* The Canisius High School Yearbook, 1944.

[39] *Arena,* The Canisius High School Yearbook, 1945.

[40] *Arena,* The Canisius High School Yearbook, 1946.

[41] *Arena,* The Canisius High School Yearbook, 1947.

[42] *Arena,* The Canisius High School Yearbook, 1948.

[43] *Arena,* The Canisius High School Yearbook, 1949.

[44] *Arena,* The Canisius High School Yearbook, 1950.

CHAPTER 8

The 1950s

"GRANT, O LORD, PEACE TO OUR DAYS." Thus begins the
introduction to the 1950 *Arena*, which continues to usher in the decade
ahead with a theme of peace: "After four years at Canisius, the vista of our
future opens before us.... We face it not with fear, but with fortitude, for
we know in Whom we believe, we look up to Him Who has told us to
have courage.... It is significant, then, that we enter upon this road of life
in this, the year of Jubilee. It sets a keynote of confident, realistic optimism. We look back with gratitude to the four fruitful years behind us
and forward with hope to the horizon ahead...."[1]

This message of hopeful confidence is a fitting entre to the 1950s at Canisius, at least from a student's perspective. Following the turmoil that marked the 1940s on the world stage, and the simultaneous ongoing changes to the school that would see it shift (rather unexpectedly) to a new campus, the new decade was an opportunity for a sort of institutional "settling in." The dedication of the 1959 *Arena* (to Very Rev. Gerald Quinn, S.J.,) lauds the Jesuits for having brought about "a new Canisius, time-tested in tradition, modern in facility."[2]

Despite the country's embroilment in the Korean War at its beginning, there is a certain sense of stability that permeates the student publications of the decade. Even the staffing of the school indicates stability. Thirty-three Jesuits and sixteen laymen comprised the faculty and administration of CHS in the 1949-1950 academic year (67% and 33%, respectively), and two-hundred-twelve seniors graduated in 1950.[3] By the end of the decade, this had barely changed. Likewise, two-hundred-twelve seniors graduated in 1960, and thirty-five Jesuits and sixteen laymen staffed the school in 1959-1960.[4] Despite this bird's-eye appearance of stability, Jesuit correspondence from the time will reveal ongoing fiscal challenges.

Nevertheless, throughout the *Citadels* and *Arenas* of the decade, a consistent sort of optimism and regularity permeates: success in athletics, drama, and debate parallels traditional adherence to classical curricula. Also very apparent throughout the school's published media of the decade is a conspicuous focus on its Catholic identity—seemingly more explicit than in the published works of the earlier past. Two *Arenas* are dedicated to Jesus Christ Himself, and one to Saint Ignatius Loyola. The school's tradition of performing a Passion Play at the end of Lent took center stage during the 1950s and garnered a fair amount of press.

It is within the context of this relative institutional stability that Canisius was able to make significant developments to its campus, including the demolition of several homes on its periphery. Amidst this "creative destruction" lay the opportunity for the school to secure its foothold in its still relatively new home on Delaware Avenue. The two images on the next page demonstrate this very tangible change to the campus. (It is worth noting at this point that, despite these considerable developments and in light of the title of this book, "the Blue Doors" still remained un-painted until the 1960s.)

Aerial view of campus from the 1952 Arena Yearbook. Note the Milburn Mansion, homes along West Ferry, and future site of Frauenheim Hall.

By contrast, this image from the 1958 Arena depicts Frauenheim Hall, the playing field, the site of the demolished Milburn House, and the absence of several buildings along West Ferry Street. (Photo by Edward W. Chester for the 1958 Arena.)

The Catalogue Review 1951-1960

Educating the Whole Man

The *1950-1951 Annual Catalogue* offers a compelling portrayal of the Jesuits' approach to providing a "well-rounded" education: "The Jesuit system is based on the principle that education consists in the compete formation of the whole individual by the progressive and harmonious development of all his powers, intellectual, moral, and physical.... The right view of education regards formation as more important than information."[5]

Similarly, the same *Catalogue* underscores the spiritual (and religious) identity of the school and its mission. Today's students or recent alumni will note the considerably more structured integration of religious practice in the daily life of the school: "It is in vain to pretend to give moral training without religion. Religion alone can purify the heart and guide and strengthen the will. Accordingly, the spirit of religion pervades the entire system of education at Canisius. Religious knowledge is imparted, religious principles are inculcated, religious ideals are inspired.... The practice of religion is carefully cultivated by the School.... Catechism lessons are heard daily, and these lessons are supplemented by a weekly lecture on Christian Doctrine. Catholic students are required to participate in the annual Spiritual Retreat...All Catholic students are expected to confess at least once a month...."[6]

Discipline and the Daily Schedule

Today's current students or recent alumni will note both some differences and similarities in the academic tempo of the days and years at CHS. In 1950-1951, the *Catalogue* tells us that classes "begin precisely at 9:00 A.M., [and] all pupils must report for assembly not later than 8:45 A.M." As has been the mantra for many years, it was likewise emphasized back then that "parents and guardians are urgently requested to insist that their charges devote three hours a day to study at home."

Academics

As for grades, there are likewise similarities and differences. There is a distinction noted between "passing marks" (65%) and "certificating marks" (75%); namely, "the school recommends for admission to college without examination only those students who have earned a year's average of 75 per cent in each subject." An honors system existed, in which gold seals (95% or higher in every course), blue seals (85% or higher in every course), and Honorable Mention (85% average, with no course below 80%) were awarded.

The Course of Studies underwent significant transition in the middle of the decade. By the 1955-1956 academic year, the school had abandoned the "Greek Course" in favor of an "Honors Course." Moreover, the "Basic Course" was renamed the "Regular Course." The changes continued, however. In the following year (1956-1957), the academic track was modified yet again. This iteration presented a uniform First Year, with three options—Course I, Course II, and Course III—each offering an increasingly challenging curriculum. By some measures, this appears to be on some levels a simple reorganization of the previous scheme. For example, Course II includes the addition of Greek, but not additional sciences—reminiscent of the previous Greek Course—while Course III includes the addition of sciences and advanced math (along with German) but not Greek—similar to the previous Science Course. (See images, next three pages.)

This last iteration, according to the *Annual Catalogues*, remained intact through the remainder of the decade.

Jesuit Correspondence: An Inside Look at the 1950s

As with the 1940s, a selection of correspondence among the Jesuits provides an important perspective on the inner workings of Canisius throughout this decade. Again, while these details are not the most exciting elements of the school's history, they do comprise a narrative thread that illustrates the ongoing challenges that beset its leaders. Despite the post-war optimism of the "Nifty Fifties," there was indeed a perpetual battle waged by the stewards of Canisius—a financial one. While the contributions of many made possible the continued development of the

Delaware Avenue campus, and indeed the overall solvency of the school, correspondence at the highest levels of school leadership makes abundantly clear the integral role of one family of donors in particular during this era: the Frauenheim brothers.

In early 1951, a letter from Rev. Gerald A. Quinn, S.J., House Consultor, to the Provincial expresses serious concern about various elements of instability, most specifically the impending temporary relocation of Father Barnett for an out-of-town assignment. It lends an ominous tone to the beginning of the decade:

Canisius High School is in a rather precarious position and needs an unusually competent rector. In 1941 the province procurator, Fr. Phillips, visited here to decide whether or not to close the school. Before Fr. Barnett's arrival there were a couple of years when we were not able to pay the province tax. Our registration has taken a serious drop in the past two years. Fr. Barnett has tackled these problems with energy and judgment. For years there was an air of hopelessness about the place.... Father Barnett has done a great deal to change that.... The old air of hopeless [sic] and defeatism will return, summed up by the not very humorous question: "What did you do to get sent to Canisius?" We feel now we are sweating blood to make a go of it, and with the present rector we can. With someone else, I doubt if we can.... [7]

One month later, in the winter edition of the twice-annual report from the Rector (and President) to the Father General, Father Barnett offers a more detailed (and arguably more optimistic) appraisal of things, without dismissing the challenges:

Our registration suffered a large drop, from 858 in September, 1949, to 746 in September, 1950.... The consequent serious drop in income from tuition made me feel it was necessary to develop new sources of income. We have been blessed.... A raffle held in November, under the direction of Father Bauer, was twice as successful as I had anticipated. The local Council of the Knights of Columbus answered my appeal by a gift of five thousand dollars. We have begun a new association.... "The Founders of the New Canisius High School" and who subscribe one hundred dollars per year for the single purpose *of amortizing the present debt.... Hence, despite our decreased enrollment, we are in better financial condition than we were a year ago and we have a net balance almost twenty thousand dollars more than on January 1, 1950. We have continued to pay off our indebtedness and in the past six months we reduced our principal by $5,288.*

We received permission to invest some of our funds in the purchase of an adjoining residence on the north side of the schools. The people who have lived there for forty years were moving and it was necessary to purchase to protect our future plans for a faculty residence.... We have already rented the property and the rental will pay us a four per cent interest on our investment....

Our major improvement projects during the past six months were a large-scale roof repair, the remodeling of the students' dressing and shower rooms and the change of the faculty kitchen from the basement to the scullery next to the faculty refectory. Most of this work was done by our own workmen and our excellent Brothers.[8]

A report from the Board of Trustees dated June 20, 1951, as recorded by Father Quinn, highlights the decision to demolish the Washington Street property to be leased as a parking lot. Father Quinn, who by then was serving as acting President and Vice-Rector, took over Father Barnett's correspondence. (He would, following Father Barnett's relocation, serve as Rector from 1953-1959.) His letter to Father General, dated July 1, 1951, conveys his continued concerns.

Our financial situation is still somewhat precarious. We are able to meet the regular payments on our loan. We paid $7,132 in interest and $5,367 on the principal, leaving our debt at $471,445. As regards the Washington St. building it becomes clear after three years of trying, that we will not be able to rent or sell the buildings as they are. There is however a very good hope that we could by removing the buildings realize a regular income by renting out the space to a firm for the parking of automobiles. In addition to the advantage of realizing an income, which we need so badly, there is also a possibility that *once the buildings are cleared the large size of the property may attract a buyer....⁹*

Father Quinn's report from early 1952 offers some optimism about enrollment and school life in general:

The registration in first year increased by about 45 boys, which was very encouraging. However, the total registration of the whole school is actually a few less than last year. The new diocesan high schools have had an effect upon our registration, though of course they are a fine thing for the diocese and Catholic education. Next year another high school will open in South Buffalo, a section of the city that is strongly Catholic...."

REV. GERALD A. QUINN, S.J.

Our finances remain in about the same condition. We are just about able to make ends meet. However, we are steadily but slowly reducing the debt. The property of the old school on Washington Street is now being leased as a parking lot for autos....I am rather hopeful...."

The school has been successful in many undertakings. Approximately 25 boys won scholarships to college and we placed second in the province exams. However, it is a struggle to make the boys study. Television is a definite handicap to the students and apparently, many of the other schools require little or no homework. One of the things that militate against large numbers coming here is that we have the reputation of being a hard school—in the sense that the boys have to study. Of course, this is as it should be and we have no intention of lowering our standards.¹⁰

By the end of the 1951-1952 school year, Father Quinn's July letter offers continued cautious optimism. He notes the school's new principal and a substantial rise in enrollment, due apparently to a recruiting initiative of the Mother's Club. He also underscores the importance of an increasingly robust athletics program as key to attracting more students. His financial concerns are again expressed, and he highlights the recommendation that the school and St. Michael's parish be separated on administrative levels:

Fr. Donald Kirsch has succeeded Fr. Costello as principal and has done an excellent piece of work. He is very efficient and very devoted to his work, spending long hours in his office.... Fr. Charles Dolan produced a superb Passion Play which was witnessed by about ten thousand school children and two thousand adults...."

At present our registration for the first-year class that will enter in September is above what it was...260 as against 199. However, if the steel strike continues we may have some cancellations...Last year we received favorable publicity for the school's success in studies, in winning scholarships, in oratory and in sports. A surprisingly large number of parents allow the boy to pick his school and so a program of sports is necessary to appeal to the boy. Another factor that helped was the enrollment committee of the Mother's Club. A group of mothers of our students visited the parents of the eighth-grade boys and explained to them the advantages that Canisius had to offer. This was very effective...

Our financial picture remains about the same. We now owe $460,465.79 on the school building and we are whittling this away. As you know, the old school building was removed and the land rented out as a parking lot. So far this has not done very much business. However, I am hoping it will improve...

Following the advice of the consultors I have submitted to Very Reverend Fr. Provincial our recommendations that Canisius High School and St. Michael's Church be separated....[11]

A year later, in July 1953, Father Quinn voiced increasing optimism at the improved enrollment and the school's fine reputation in Buffalo. It is important to note his emphasis on the school's commitment to financial aid; moreover, we see his commitment to establishing a retirement plan for the increasing proportion of lay faculty members.

The registration this year has increased and is most encouraging. We suffered for a few years because of the new diocesan schools but now it seems as though that period has passed. The school enjoys a very good reputation. With the larger numbers applying for admission we can select the better students. Among our applicants there are boys of poorer financial resources who ask for reductions. Each of these cases is carefully considered and no worthy boy is ever turned away.

Our financial situation is...a little improved this year. We still have a huge debt of $449,000 and are paying it off at a rate of $11,000 a year. With the help of benefactors and the return from the parking lot we are able to get by. This year I hope to put in a retirement plan for the teachers. It is something that should be done but it will take a good deal of the surplus that we have. Mr. Frauenheim, our benefactor, has given a scholarship last year and another this year; eventually he hopes to establish many of these....[12]

Midway through the '53-'54 academic year, Father Quinn reports on the meager but consistent income from the parking lot, as well as another initiative by the Frauenheim Foundation to expand the campus:

Our financial situation remains the same. After our February payment on our loan we will owe $439,942. The parking lot on the site of the old school should bring us about $11,000 for the past calendar year. It is necessary to seek new means of increasing our income as our expenses are rising every year. The Frauenheim Foundation, organized by two benefactors of ours, has purchased a piece of property adjoining the school. This will be used for a playing field for the students.[13]

Quinn's letter of July 1954, continues the optimistic tone, and reports on the slow-but-sure reduction in debt. It mentions the positive influence of several particular Jesuits, notably the new Prefect of Discipline, Father Sturm, as well as Fathers Dolan and Kinn, whose impact on the spiritual life of the student body was apparently quite substantial. The letter likewise includes news of the demolition of the house at the corner of Delaware and West Ferry, which would allow for a playing field:

The school has the reputation of being the best in the city. Fr. Kirsch has worked very hard at his post of Principal and Fr. Sturm has done an excellent job as Prefect of Discipline. Fr. Kinn has been outstanding as procurator and spiritual father.... I must mention Fr. Dolan who produced a magnificent Passion Play and Fr. Fullam whose sodality could well be a model for all our schools....

Our financial position is slowly improving. This was due to several factors: the increase in the tuition and in registration, the Founders...and the revenue from the parking lot.... We still owe $435,192. We razed the house on the adjoining property, which was secured through the Frauenheim Foundation, and the grounds will be used for recreation for the students.... [14]

Progress in 1955, according to Father Quinn, included the context of vocations among students and alumni: "We are trying to foster and help vocations and there is some sign of an increase among the seniors and juniors. The excellent sodalities should be a factor in this...." Also, he notes that "a number of improvements were put into the school this year, thanks chiefly to Br. Vogelsang, a very devoted and competent Brother...." His letter also makes clear that "Mr. George and [Mr.] Edward Frauenheim, who started the Frauenheim Foundation for the school, are both anxious to erect a faculty house.... The matter is under study now." [15]

A series of further correspondence, the details of which are too cumbersome to include here, details Father Quinn's request to the Provincial, Very Reverend Thomas E. Henneberry, S.J., for the Province to take out a loan from Mr. Edward O'Toole in the amount of $250,000, for the purpose of constructing a Jesuit residence. The correspondence indicates that the Frauenheim Foundation would provide an initial $75,000 gift in cash; the Foundation would also, over time, bear the responsibility of the $250,000 loan—thus covering the cost of the residence completely. Father Quinn's letter offers some justification for this further debt, insofar as it would, in the end, not actually fall upon the school to repay:

The benefactors feel inasmuch as the faculty house is needed now and inasmuch as it is not timely to liquidate the foundation's investments now, the financing offered by Mr. O'Toole should be accepted especially as it is most timely and most favorable in its interest and its terms.

Finally, as a further protection for the province, Canisius High School owns the former high school property on Washington St. This is assessed for $129,000. Sometime ago an offer of $200,000 was made for this property. Since then, property values have increased and hence if it were necessary to sell the property to meet the loan, a sum in the neighborhood of $200,000 could be realized. In view of all these factors I beg your reverence's approval on the proposed loan....[16]

Further correspondence of December 1st indicates that the request was approved at the Province level, pending approval from Rome. By mid-summer 1956, Father Quinn was able to report further progress in his letter to Rome. He cites improved revenue and the initiative to raise lay teachers' salaries to achieve parity with the public sector. Likewise, he reports on the acquisition of an additional adjacent property (along West Ferry Street) to continue development of athletic fields:

We had a very large increase in the number of boys who wish to attend Canisius this year.... This year too saw a great increase in vocations—9 for the Society, 5 for the diocese, and 2 for other congregations....

As regards finances we are making headway slowly in reducing the debt.... It is now $382,282. We have raised the salaries of our lay teachers for next year, since we expect more revenue from the increased tuition. With Rev. Fr. Provincial's permission we have started a fund which I hope will grow until we are able to use it to raise the teachers' salaries to a level of the public school teachers...

Our faculty house is underway.... When we applied for a building permit our neighbors objected and there was some delay.... Fr. Dolan saw these people and managed to satisfy most of their objections.... At the same time we are converting an adjoining piece of property to a playing field for the boys. This property was also purchased by the Frauenheims.[17]

Father Quinn's report one year later, dated July 12, 1957, offers another upbeat assessment, noting happy news in the context of school life, admissions, vocations, debt service, and construction of Frauenheim Hall:

There has been a very marked improvement in the school this year. This is due to the hard work of Fr. Kirsch, the principal, and the teachers. It has also been due to the larger number of boys who are seeking entrance, thus enabling us to be more selective. Even discipline, which under Fr. Sturm was always good, has improved...

This year again there were a good number of boys applying for the Society—7 from the school and 1 who graduated four years ago...

In finances we are making slow but study progress. The school debt is now $368,598.31. The faculty building is scheduled for completion by Oct. 1st and this will be a blessing.[18]

The positive tone continues a year later in July 1958. Also included here is mention of a new initiative, a summer day camp. This appears to be a precursor to the Higher Achievement Program (HAP) program that emerged later in the century and continues to play a prominent role in providing a first exposure to Jesuit education for many boys in Western New York. From Father Quinn's letter of July 14, 1958:

The debt is now $334,348.63. I have started a special fund that we hope can grow and this we will use to raise the teachers' salaries. The public schools have all been raising their salaries and it is difficult to attract new men unless our scale is raised. We have had various improvements around the school such as new classroom chairs and a new playing field...

This year we started a day camp on the school premises for boys from 6 to 14. We have four priests and four laymen working in it. There was no such

Catholic Day Camp around here and the parents sent their boys to the Y.M.C.A. or Episcopalian schools. We offer the boys a variety of games. We start each day with a visit to the Blessed Sacrament, and on Fridays we have confessions for them. About 42 boys came for the first session and we expect 56 for the second....

By January 1960, Rev. Donald L. Kirsch succeeded Father Quinn as Rector and President. In his mid-year letter to Father General in Rome, Kirsch reported on the continued struggle with debt. He also alluded to the increasing proportion of lay teachers—a challenge that he would continue to realize and focus upon in the coming decade:

Rev. Donald L. Kirsch, S.J., Source: *Arena* 1960

Father Edward Dolan, our new principal, appears to be handling his new office competently...

Financially, we have many problems but...I do not feel we are in a hopeless position. The debt has been reduced to under $300,000. We raised the yearly tuition to $280...This increase in tuition income is a blessing to meet the continual increase in lay-teachers and their salaries. More lay-teachers have and will be needed; at present we have four less Jesuit teachers this year than last and the prospects for next year are not encouraging....[19]

On September 8, 1960, George M. Frauenheim wrote to Father Kirsch, clarifying the terms of the Frauenheim Foundation's commitment to servicing the debt associated with the new Jesuit residence. As the school continued to struggle with the burden of its sizeable debt from the new classroom wing construction, this reassurance no doubt made for some sighs of relief on the part of its leaders. From Mr. Frauenheim's letter:

We are gratified at the financial progress being made. The Foundation is practically on a self-liquidating basis, so there is no undue burden on us.... Just to refresh the record, the original assurance by the Foundation to the High

School was to make available $325,00, of which $75,000 has been paid in cash, and $250,000 is being financed through "Loan A." Because of increasing costs, another $125,000 was required, and this was financed through the High School through "Loans B & C." Not as a legal commitment, but as an assurance, the Foundation has indicated that, just as soon as "Loan A" is liquidated, "Loan B" will be taken care of, and then "Loan C." Fortunately, there are sufficient assets in the Foundation to do this on an orderly basis. We appreciate the remembrances of the Jesuit Fathers....[20]

These correspondences make clear the tremendous commitment of so many to facilitate the growth of Canisius High School through the 1950s.

From Washington Street to Snyder

Rev. Ron Sams '46 recorded a story in the CHS archives that tells of how bricks from the demolished Washington Street campus, which was relinquished in the late 1950s, made their way to the home of a Canisius family in nearby Snyder. From Fr. Sams' typed notes: *

169 Berryman Drive. Photo dated Mar 27, 1999. Courtesy of Ron Sams, S.J.

But those bricks did not all get lost and buried! Many of them were carried away by a building contractor and used to build a private home in Snyder. Today[7] that is the home of a CHS alumnus, Gerry Schneggenburger, who graduated in the Class of 1963. Gerry himself never knew the "venerable old building on Washington Street." But his father did—Gerry Schneggenburger of the Class of 1922. Gerry the elder will celebrate his 96th birthday this year—one of our oldest alumni! We congratulate him and his family and especially his son who keeps the CHS legend alive, surrounded by the bricks of past years that saw his own father long ago in his high school days on Washington Street. Now, if only those bricks could talk![21]

---

* While Father Sams' typewritten account is undated, the accompanying photos that he took are time-stamped March 27, 1999. Thus it is safe to assume the account was recorded and added to the archives on or around that date.

November 7, 1955: Bill Haley and the Comets Play at CHS

The *Buffalo Courier-Express*, on Saturday, November 5, 1955, ran an article entitled "Haley to Give 'Rock, Roll' Concert Here." It announced a concert to be given at Canisius High School on Monday evening (November 7) at 8:15 P.M.

There was, apparently, skepticism about the concert. The article quotes an unnamed faculty member saying, "'It may seem unusual for a Catholic school to sponsor a concert of this music, but we are convinced the trouble has been with some off-color lyrics and not with the music.'" In response, the article says, Haley offered the school an assurance: "Some critics have said that subjecting teenagers to rhythm and blues music is like feeding them dope. It's a pity that the work of a few misguided writers has given the music this reputation. I'm going to continue my campaign to clean up this situation.... The solution is so simple...just writing decent, acceptable lyrics."[22]

Image: CHS Archives

A *Buffalo Evening News* article, published November 8, 1955, recalls the previous evening's event: "The effects of rock-and-roll music are soon to be felt in some remote sections of the Orient. Monday evening, 1600 Canisius High School pupils and their girlfriends packed the school auditorium for a concert by Bill Haley and his Comets. Proceeds from the successful event, sponsored by the school's Father's Club, will be used for the Jesuit missions in Japan.... The concert will long be remembered by both students and by the Comets...."[23]

(Oddly, there is no record of the concert in the subsequent issues of *The Citadel*, and no feature concerning the concert in the 1955-1956 *Arena* Yearbook, either.)

Campus Expansion: Fr. Quinn & the Frauenheim Brothers

Strategic Plan for Expansion

By the mid-1950s, with Canisius well established on its new campus, there was a growing need for additional operating facilities. Certainly, relative to the limitations of the Washington Street Campus, the Buffalo Consistory complex provided some excellent athletic facilities, such as the pool, locker rooms, showers, and bowling alley. The expansive classroom wing represented a new frontier in teaching space. Nonetheless, two significant needs emerged: accommodations for the largely Jesuit faculty—at the time, they were housed (mostly) in the Milburn Mansion—and playing fields for the students.

New Canisius Field Planned At Ferry-Delaware Corner

The air around 1160 Delaware is being shattered these days by the noise of demolition as the rooming house there is being torn down for progress' sake. However, when September comes, the site will resound with another noise: that of CHS gridiron grunters practicing their blocks, tackles, and plays for the Fall season. This new field is only one of a long-range series of improvements and expanded facilities at Canisius High.

Backing

The purchase of the building was financed by the Frauenheim Foundation, administered by George and Edward Fraunheim, Canisius alumni, who are vitally interested in the progress of their Alma Mater.

Wrecking work is scheduled for completion by early June. When Canisius opens its doors again in the Fall, the grounds will have undergone quite a face-lifting, authorities report.

From *The Citadel* June 11, 1954

The Very Rev. Gerald A. Quinn, S.J., previously Vice-Rector, was named Rector of Canisius High School in the 1953-54 academic year. Quinn was also a trustee of the Frauenheim Foundation, which was started in the mid 1940s by George M. and Edward E. Frauenheim in honor of their parents, Mr. and Mrs. Edward E. Frauenheim. The two brothers, alumni from the Classes of 1930 and 1932, respectively, made a major and generous contribution to the school during Father Quinn's term as Rector. George Frauenheim was president of Mayer Malt & Grain; Edward was vice-president.

Paul Cumbo

'DOZERS CLEAR PRACTICE FIELD

Things are busting out all over. Since last year, C.H.S. has begun two construction projects. The first, the Jesuit Faculty Residence, is progressing quite rapidly as we all can see. But we are concerned mostly with the new student playing field.

News Briefs

● Messrs. Flynn, McNeill and Meenan, S.J., late of the Canisius faculty, are back on the other side of the benches now, studying theology at Woodstock College, Maryland. Mr. Brzoska, donning chaps and spurs, has gone West to study theology at Alma College in California.

● Fr. Muldoon, Canisius' own C.B. DeMille, will be inducted into Uncle Sam's khaki-clad ranks sometime during October.

● Under the inspiration and direction of Fr. Joyce, the once-famous Canisius Glee Club will be re-formed.

● The Behrens Debating Society will travel to Cortland for a tournament on October 12-13.

● Last year's man-about-music-and-math, Mr. Smith, S.J., is now studying for his Ph.D in mathematics at the Catholic University of America in Washington, D. C.

The new field, which runs perpendicular to Ferry St., will contain an athlete's dream.

The predominant feature of the field will be, of course, the football field. Being of regulation size it will measure 100 yards with a girth of 160 feet. It will be used principally as a practice field and for the recreational use of the students.

Surrounding the field will be an oval track for our harriers to keep in shape.

For the more avid, long-legged members of the above-mentioned team, a pole vault, a high jump, and broad-jumping pits will be inaugurated.

This property, together with the corner field already is use, was purchased for Canisius by the Frauenheim Foundation. It is to our generous benefactors, Mr. George Frauenheim and Mr. Edward Frauenheim, that we owe these new and very welcome facilities. Our grateful prayers should be with them for their kindness and generosity.

From *The Citadel*, Oct. 5, 1955

Frauenheim Hall Plans Announced

A press release from February 1956 reported on the announcement that "construction will start this Summer on a new $325,000 residence for the Jesuit faculty of Canisius High School." Also noted in the release is a mention of the $30,000 playing field installation plans. Moreover, it announced the plans to demolish "the present faculty home at 1168 Delaware," which was the Milburn Mansion. "This yellow-brick landmark is nearly 100 years old and is the building in which President William McKinley died." Additional demolition plans were detailed: "Canisius High School also will tear down two other buildings it owns at 806 and 810 West Ferry St. about June 1.* Both are now nursing homes. This area will be a playing field." According to the release, the whole of the campus development project was "made possible by the Frauenheim Foundation." Notably, Father Quinn served as a Trustee of the foundation.[24]

The spring 1957 *Arena* quarterly (not to be confused with the *Arena* yearbook) included an article by student Joseph Papaj '57, which describes the project in considerable detail (and with some enjoyable witty remarks that illuminate the author's friendly disposition toward his Jesuit teachers). It also offers insights as to significant changes that affected the campus in other ways, including the establishment of the current student chapel and repurposing of the upper floors of the Rand Mansion (i.e., Berchmans Hall). Because of the quality of detail provided, the article is presented here in its entirety:

We are about to bring you a special announcement. After much work on the part of the Quarterly's investigators, Father Rector's office has released the top-secret information we are now going to publish. Here, with Father Quinn's gracious assistance, and for the first time anywhere are the facts concerning the building which perhaps a few might have noticed as they passed 1180 Delaware Avenue.

---

* This would also include demolition of the Gratwick home at 22 Cleveland Ave, which was acquired by the school for $29,000 to facilitate construction of Frauenheim Hall. Source: CHS Archives.

Planning for the building first began about two years ago. If the contractors maintain their schedule, as Wagner & Sons promise they will, this dream shall become a reality on July 15th.

The faculty residence will be of red brick in an "L-shape." It will have a total of 49 living rooms and also a large chapel, library, community rooms, dining room, and storage room.

The chapel will have, besides the main altar, five altars on each side. A venetian blind effect will separate the altars from the body of the chapel. Father Quinn confirmed the report that the Students' Chapel will be moved to the present faculty dining room. *The capacity of the new chapel will be 179.*

After the faculty move, six rooms in the Rand Building will be made available. They will be used as activity rooms and classrooms. The present faculty chapel and the remedial reading room will be converted into a classroom and others may later be converted to classrooms.

Another change will be the relocation of the switchboard in the residence, but nevertheless it will be accessible to the students. The connection of the school and residence will be through the present Health Room and this entrance will lead to the switchboard. The switchboard, three parlors, and a waiting room opposite it will be the only parts of the building not cloistered.

The old residence, the Milburn Mansion, can be considered a historic shrine, for in 1901 President McKinley died in it from gunshot wounds received at the Pan American Exposition in Delaware Park. When asked what would be done with the building, Father Quinn answered: "It will be torn down—that is, if it doesn't fall down first. After all it is 100 years old." (Father Dolan, if you are reading this, please control yourself, and even though you know where the one brick that supports the whole building is located, don't pull it out for a little while yet.)

What will be done with the front landscape after the building is torn down is still under discussion. These are the two major possibilities: black-top the area and use it as a parking space, or keep it as part of the front campus. *

---

* This is a reference to the current student chapel at the juncture of the Rand Mansion and Higgins Hall (i.e., "the foyer"), which has been in use since.

* The space would become the student parking lot for many years, and remains partially so today. This has been the source of grumbling among various preservationists in Buffalo, as all that remains to commemorate the Milburn Mansion is an inconspicuous plaque.

Unseen to public eyes is an area behind the new residence that is to be used as a garden. However, contrary to popular opinion, Jesuits are not farmers and so only grass will be grown.

Also in the rear of the building is a cornerstone dated 1880. This cornerstone is from the old Canisius High School on Washington Street. The main cornerstone in front of the building will be dated 1957 and will contain a copy of the Arena Quarterly, *the* Citadel, *and the* Yearbook.

The new residence will be known as Frauenheim Hall. Finances for the property of the residence and the two playing fields were realized by a foundation set up by two alumni, George M. Frauenheim and his brother, Edward E. Frauenheim, Jr., in honor of their parents. Mr. Edward Frauenheim, Sr., graduated from Canisius in 1906.

And this ends the story of how a building comes to life and how its neighboring surroundings will be effected. Once again the Jesuits will have a roof over their heads—another step in the making of a complete Canisius.[25]

Farewell to the Milburn Mansion

Peter Dixon '58, in the December 20, 1957 *Citadel*, penned an article that marks the occasion of the Milburn Mansion's demolition. Like the previous article focused on the campus expansion, Mr. Dixon's is included here both for its detail and its subtle insights into CHS culture.

"Site of the Milburn House", reads the sign in front of the classroom wing. And the site, indeed, is all that remains; the last traces of the Milburn house itself have almost completely vanished.

But there has been no mourning at its passing. Any sentimental attachment towards it which its former residents may have felt is overshadowed by the memory of its windowless, airless inside rooms, its dark, twisting corridors, and its dilapidated condition.

The poor condition of the Milburn has been a joke of some standing around the school for years. Tradition has long held that almost anyone could poke his hand through the paper-thin walls; your reporter counted this a gross exaggeration until he tried it himself, and found his fist stupidly sticking through the wall into the next room.

The Milburn has been regarded as so structurally unsound that one member of the ubiquitous Stage Crew remarked, "They ought to give us all fire axes, and we'd have the place down in two days, and save the school a lot of money." (Not that this casts aspersion on the building's soundness. The entire stage crew, armed with axes, could probably level Civic Stadium in two days.) And one anonymous Jesuit, apparently eager to save both the school's money and the stage crew's energy, claimed to know the location of the one brick which, if removed, would cause the whole building to collapse.

The school administration, however, evidently determined not to avail itself of the services of either stage crew or anonymous Jesuit, and so professional workmen under the banner of the Cuyahoga Wrecking Company moved in, bringing with them their heavy machinery.

It seems to be an almost inborn trait of twentieth-century man that he is fascinated by the actions of such machines as bulldozers, ditchers, steam shovels, and the like. Our CHS students are no exceptions. During all the time the destruction was in progress, the teachers in classrooms within sight of the Milburn fought a losing battle for attention against the distraction outside.

The technique employed to tear down the building was undeniably spectacular from a spectator's viewpoint, but actually the most efficient way: grab hold of a part of the building with a clam bucket, pull till it comes off, and drop it into a waiting truck. Such tactics were used on almost all of the building except where there was danger of breaking classroom windows.

The machinery is gone now, and a casual glance from Delaware Avenue would scarcely reveal that there had ever been a building there. The Milburn is gone, but—thanks not only to that little sign in front of the classroom wing, but also to its long history as an integral part of Canisius—not forgotten.[26]

Gratitude to the Frauenheim Brothers

Yearbook portraits of George '30 (left) and Edward '32 (right) Frauenheim.

The 1958 *Arena* Yearbook, which was dedicated to the Frauenheim brothers, offers some perspective on their commitment to the school, describing them as "dreamers."

In the golden autumn dawn of October 20, 1957, the sun rose to greet a new Canisius. The dedication of the new faculty residence, Frauenheim Hall, marked completion, after fourteen years of praying and planning, of the campus at Canisius-on-Delaware. It was the end of an old and the beginning of a new era in the history of Canisius High School; it was the fulfillment of a dream.

What was the dream? Who were the dreamers? The dream was that of a new Canisius, boasting a beautiful campus, complete with a fine classroom building, adequate accommodations for the many and varied facets of its wide-ranged sports program, and a fit residence for its Jesuit faculty to take the place of the ancient and inconvenient Milburn mansion. The dream itself belonged to many men—to the Father Rectors who had governed Canisius since it moved to Delaware Avenue, to the many Jesuits who have toiled here during the past fourteen years, to each member of the student body. But above all, the dream belonged to two of our most distinguished and devoted alumni, George M. and Edward E. Frauenheim, Jr.

[Their] dream...began to approach a practical reality with their contribution to the new Canisius of the practice field which now stands on the corner of Ferry and Delaware. This was only the beginning. The next great step forward was taken when the properties on Ferry Street, west of the school wing, were purchased by these same two far-seeing men and connected to the high school campus. The buildings which had stood on these properties were razed, and an impressive athletic field for football, baseball, and track was built that is comparable to the best in the area.

But the most lasting and significant contribution...was yet to come. In the spring of 1956 they began the construction of a new residence...Today Frauenheim Hall stands, complete in every detail, a lasting monument to the two generous and selfless benefactors who made it possible. What had been the dream of so many men for so long was now a magnificent reality due, in no small part, to the foresight, planning, and charity of two loyal Canisius alumni.[27]

During the 86th Commencement Exercises, after presenting Coach John Barnes with the Pro Bene Merenti award for twenty-five years of service to the school, Father Quinn presented the Frauenheim brothers with the St. Peter Canisius plaque in appreciation for their outstanding contributions.

The following pages contain images of the Frauenheim Hall construction and dedication events.

Frauenheim Hall under construction, 1956. Image: CHS Archives.

Laying of Cornerstone, May 29,1957. Edward E. Frauenheim, Jr.,
Fr. G.A.Quinn (Rector) George M. Frauenheim, Bishop Leo Smith,
Fr. James J. Redmond and Fr. James R. Barnett (former rectors).

Image: CHS Archives.

Above: Frauenheim Hall, completed. Image: CHS Archives.

Image: CHS Archives.

Fr. McConnell and Mr. Edden

The new residence afforded the many Jesuits on the CHS faculty much needed space.

Scholastics rec room: Messers Sweeney,Noonan,Simeone, Sippel, Barth and Roslovich

Athletics in the 1950s

Braving Hurricane Hazel - Victory in Speed

The bigger news story might be that the 1955 football team won the Catholic League Championship. Among alumni from this era, however, there is an athletic contest that stands out because of its unique circumstances—and because of the unorthodox strategy that Coach Barnes used to lead the team to victory. The story is told in the November 18, 1954 issue of *The Citadel*:

Canisius Splashes Timon in Hard-Fought Triumph

The football team, clad in mud-soaked shorts and pads, after the Timon game. From *Arena* 1955.

With sodden cheers echoing through the rain-swept Civic Stadium, Canisius hardy backers braved Hurricane Hazel to watch the Crusaders don shorts in the second half of a gridiron fray that was more like a water polo match and defeat Timon, 26-14.

Leading 13-7 at halftime, the Canisius backs came out for the second half in shorts over their hip pads. The move got fast results as Kenny Hohl and Don Testa added two quick touchdowns.

Once again Coach Johnny Barnes had been a step ahead of his rivals. By halftime, the players were weighted down by the wet uniforms. But with just the light shorts, the Crusader backs swept for long gains past the Timon defenders.[28]

Revisiting School Spirit - Another Tribute to "Mr. Mack" and the 1957 Basketball Champions

An editorial in *The Citadel*, dated March 1, 1959, echoes a previous tribute to Mr. Cornelius McGillicuddy (included in the last chapter). Citing his words celebrated in that tribute, the editorial proclaims:

With these inspiring words, written on the occasion of a football rally eight years ago, Connie, "Mr. Mack" McGillicuddy has done the near impossible, defined a Canisius Crusader. We'd like to offer this editorial as a tribute to Mr. Mack and to the champions he coaches—members of the first-place team in the Burke division of the Catholic High School Basketball League. This year's Canisius contingent has shown the people of Western New York the kind of play for which our school is famous—the best. In every sport, in every academic endeavor, Canisius High School is known, wondered at, feared and respected for consistently producing the best.

And yet, during the last three years, our basketball fortunes suffered a slight decline. We were still good, to be sure, still in the playoffs, still able to put in their place any team that thought it could beat us. But we were not in the place where we were accustomed to be, on top. This year we are in our accustomed place.

For the team and their coach, then, who are responsible for this, most of whom have been working and waiting for this moment not for a single year, but for the last four years—heartiest congratulations. We are proud of you and you have every right to be proud of yourselves. Truly you deserve the title: Canisius Crusaders, Champions.[29]

A Congressman Recalls Canisius

The Honorable John J. LaFalce '57, upon his retirement after twenty-eight years of service in the United States House of Representatives, offered an interview with Matt Kubus '04 in the February 10, 2003 *Citadel*. Some excerpts from Kubus's article covering that interview are provided here:

"First of all, I am grateful that I even went to Canisius High school. I almost didn't." *These were the first words that came out of former Representative LaFalce's mouth when he was asked what his fondest memory of CHS is. Why did he almost not attend Canisius? "I didn't think that I could afford to go...."* *He then proceeded to explain what steps he needed to take to attend the high school that was, in his mind, "the best school that he could...."*

Growing up in Holy Angels Parish in Buffalo, Mr. LaFalce always presumed that he would attend Bishop Fallon High School, which was run by the Oblate Fathers. His eighth-grade teacher, Mildred Donavan, however, had other plans. She wrote a letter to his mother, saying that young John should attend the best high school in the area—Canisius. Also, Donovan knew that Mr. LaFalce could not afford to attend CHS, but insisted that, if it was kept a secret, she would pay his way through high school. Young LaFalce realized that if his teacher felt that strongly about his attending Canisius, he probably should. He decided that Donovan would not pay for him; rather, he would work his way through high school. He made arrangements with the treasurer of Canisius to pay a little amount each week. For the first three years, Mr. LaFalce had a paper route, which earned him $5-10.

"When you pay your way through yourself, I think your education means a lot more to you than if your parents are paying your way through," said LaFalce. After his freshman year, in fact, he was offered a scholarship but declined. He though it would be more beneficial to work his way through high school.

While at Canisius, Mr. LaFalce was very active in the Debating Society and the theater. Some of his fondest memories were achieved while participating in these activities. In fact, he gave a speech that was directed toward the general rights of men and women. "There's absolutely no question that that began the foundations for my political philosophy, because it has been steeped within the social teachings of the Church and the rights of men and women," Mr. LaFalce avowed....

The Honorable John LaFalce has faithfully served the Western New York Community for 32 years, 28 of them in the United States Congress. He truly believes that without his education at Canisius, he may not have begun his journey through public service....

"Develop your mind and your body. Open your mind to all the experiences that you can while you're going to Canisius High School. Some individuals go through their four years and are exposed to a million and one different things, but are not open to it; therefore, gain nothing from it. Open yourself up.... Don't just develop your body or your mind. Don't just be a jock or an academic nerd. Try to be both, if you will. I think this is the Jesuit ideal, too: the development of the whole person...."[30]

Hon. John J. LaFalce '57. Portrait from *The Citadel.* Feb 10, 2003.

Gallery: 1950s

The images contained herein comprise an interesting gallery portrait of student life, from academics and activities to athletics. Images are presented in roughly chronological order.

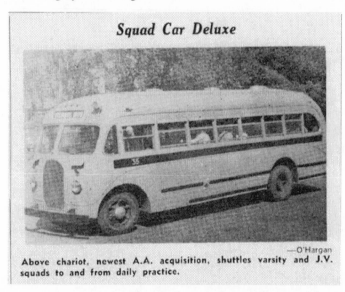

Squad Car Deluxe

—O'Hargan

Above chariot, newest A.A. acquisition, shuttles varsity and J.V. squads to and from daily practice.

The Citadel, Oct 5, 1950 (Above and below)

October 5, 1950   THE CITADEL   Page Five

Oarsmen Win Catholic Championship; Edged by St. Kit's in Summer Regattas

By Jerry Gibbons

First place, four second places, and one third in its six races—a golden record for a green crew. Canisius' rowing team finished its season on last September 14th with this fine overall record.

For its first test of the season, the crew journeyed to Cornell University, and amid all the splendor of its annual "Spring Weekend," lost to Cornell's 150-lb. Freshman Varsity and the 150-lb. J.V.

Full of hopes after their showing at Cornell against crews of a much higher calibre, the team traveled to Ecorse, Mich., a suburb of Detroit, to take part in the Middle States High School Regatta. Preliminary heats were held and the first two in each raced the next

Keglers Finish 31st In National Tourney

By Paul Schumacher

Before the closing of school last year Fr. Persich entered four teams in the American Legion-sponsored handicap tournament. The team of Bogart, Moliterno, Schmidt, Wagner and Tom Dzielski finished 31st in the nation out of 573 teams. They were second in the city and missed the state championship finals by only 20 pins.

School competition last year ended in a dead heat between Don Bogart's team and Joe

Crew-saders Catholic Champs

—Courtesy of Roy Ruehl

Victors over St. Joe's and Timon and runners-up for City crew title are (usual order) Nicaise (stroke), Gibbons, Jakiel, Glasser, Frank, Pauly, Conboy, Sawyer, Drapanas (coxy).

Canisius Helps Solve City's Parking Problem

To lessen the serious off-street parking situation in the downtown area, Canisius High School on Washington Street is being razed to make way for the construction of a 500 car parking lot.

The work, which began September 17, is expected to be completed in about 3 months. This parking lot will be operated by a private corporation with headquarters in New York City.

Canisius High School opened its doors on Washington Street on September 5, 1870, when 34 pupils came to be tutored by the Rev. Henry Behrens, S.J. These first classes were held in the back of a renovated store back of the present property. The corner stone of the Main Building was laid April 27, 1872; the north wing being added in 1880; the south wing in 1883.

In 1944 Canisius purchased the Buffalo Consistory property on Delaware Ave. and the freshman and sophomore classes were moved there that year. In 1948 the new wing was completed and the entire student body moved there.

The Voice of Canisius

Attention all classes! Seniors will no longer have to trudge up and down three flights of stairs to assembly. Freshmen will no longer sit in the peanut gallery when notices are read. From now on everyone can enjoy a ring-side seat at morning announcements without the inconvenience of climbing stairs to class.

Thanks to the Mothers' Club, you are now listening to our new Rauland Communication System. Part of the expense will be met by proceeds from the Mothers' Club Fashion Show to be held here the twenty-sixth of this month.

With forty-five speakers, located strategically throughout the building and in every classroom, it is very easy for the Principal to reach any student in the school without leaving his own office, where the master control board is located.

Besides enabling each student to hear his Headmaster's voice, it also permits the Headmaster to hear each student's voice—not an unmixed blessing, especially during unproctored study periods.

We pause now for station identification—WCHS, the Voice of Canisius, in Buffalo.

Senior Retreat Proves Great Success

Deeply impressed by Rev. Robert F. Grewen, S.J., as retreat-master, the senior class of Canisius made a very successful retreat.

December 22, 1952   T H E   C I

O Mighty Caesar, Dost Thou Lie So Low?

Antony (Bill Jacobs) bends over the corpse of Caesar (Chuck Wilson) as the assassins look on.

Two Performances of "Julius Caesar" Acclaimed by Enthusiastic Audiences

Under Father Dolan's expert direction, The Canisius Dramatic Society has added JULIUS CAESAR to its impressive list of hit productions. During the two-night run of the play about 1400 people witnessed Caesar's murder, Mark Antony's speech and many more of Shakespeare's impressive scenes.

John Campbell did a near professional job as Cassius especially in the tenth scene which was the high point of the entire play.

Jim Milne, as Brutus, gave an excellent portrayal of the tragic hero of the play.

Comic relief was very adequately provided by Ed Manning as Casca. Ed did a very convincing job in a difficult role.

Charles Wilson played Caesar convincingly in his first dramatic appearance for Canisius High School.

Mark Antony was portrayed by Bill Jacobs. James Ryan and Joseph Lukitsch played the roles of Portia and Calpurnia,

Behrens Toll-Taking At Clinton Spurs New Out-of-Town Debates

A flood of feminine tears marked the entrance of the Behrens Debating Society into the world of statewide debate contests at the Hamilton College Debate Tournament held in Clinton, N. Y., on November 21st. The tears came when Canisius defeated the girls from Jeffersonville, N. Y., to break the tie for first place between Jeffersonville and Jamestown. Although the Behrens team finished about halfway down the list of contestants, it was their influence on the final decision that brought them notoriety.

CHS Participants

French Circle Stands Divided

From reliable sources word comes that just around the holiday hub another active semester waits for Cercle

The Citadel Dec 23, 1953

Father Sturm turns on his welcoming smile for Jug Addicts.

Jug Addicts

The Citadel,
May 29, 1953

By Dave Karnath

After four years of jug-dodging he was an expert and was talking on his favorite subject.

"It takes a lots of imagination," he said, "a lot of imagination. But it helps if you have poor teeth."

I failed to see the connection. "Poor what?"

"Teeth! All you have to do is prove conclusively to the Prefect of Discipline, Father Sturm, that you have a dentist appointment. 'Course when you run out of teeth, you're out of excuses, but it works for a while."

He tipped back his chair. "Sure, there's plenty of excuses to get out of jug." Letting his chair come back to the floor with a crack, he put his elbows on the table and his chin in his hands. "But none of them work, of course," he added thoughtfully and almost regretfully.

* * * * *

Father Sturm, S.J. admits that most of his clientele are steady customers like our friend, but claims that he shares Father Flannigan of Boys' Town's feeling that there are really no bad boys and really hopes to straighten them out. (Jug assignments usually seem tough enough not only to straighten them out, but to lay them out besides.)

There has to be an explanation for the fact that certain people return to jug again and again. It is only too obvious that there are steady visitors; a one-timer walks in, sees that he is right at home, and gets a tourist feeling. He seems to find a strange fascination in it, not unlike the detached ecstasy of be-boppers.

Father Sturm says that perhaps it is the lure of the inner sanctum of the school, where the students imbibe with intellectual gulps the richer and more fragrant love of the school and its regulations. For this reason, the welcome mat is always out for any student who wishes to perpetuate the glorious tradition of jug. (Father insists he never jugs anyone. The student sentences himself by infractions of school discipline. Father merely executes the sentence.)

* * * * *

My friend had a different reason for jug's lure.

"You learn things about yourself," he said. "For instance, before I started jug, I never knew I had such strong convictions on things like 'The social disadvantages of being a pelican.' At least, I never looked at it from the pelican's viewpoint before."

Maybe that explains jug's lasting popularity. In fact, it has been the most popular extra-curricular activity since Canisius was founded. Like the classics, it has withstood the test of time in its present form and Father Sturm reports that he is pleased with the present form and does not want to change it. "The students never had it so good."

Why Canisius Men Carry So Many Books

Reporters Litz and Koch.

"Well," said the editor, "from whom did we borrow this question? Brooklyn Prep again?" "Certainly not," replied the indignant moderator, "this one is taken from Gonzaga High in Washington."

And so, ever-striving for originality, if only by varying the schools from which it bor- *rows ideas, the CITADEL'S nosy . . . er . . . inquiring reporters, Tom Litz and Arthur Koch, put the following question to the student body: "Why do Canisius students carry so many books?"*

Joe Custodi, 2F: "For the thrill of it."

‡ 彡 ⬧ ⌗ ⎯ ⬥

John Battig, 4A: "To study, of course." (Ed.'s comment: Do you want a punch in the nose?)

Frank Pellegrine, 3E: "A book is a legal weapon on the East Side."

Peter Noble, 2F: "Now that you mention it, I don't know, so I think I'll stop."

Pete Mancuso, 2C: "Because girls I know prefer the scholarly type."

Sean Hill, 4A: "Yes, I agree heartily." (Ed.'s comment: Oh?)

Norb Ostrozny, 2B: "We don't have an iron at home, so I use them to press my pants."

Earl Daigler, 3D: "Ha ha ha ha . . . ha ha ha ha ha . . . ha ha ha ha." (Ed.'s comment: God bless you, Earl.)

Stan Kwieciak, 2A: "Because I'm a bookie."

Martin Heavy, 1B: "I take them home to study that first declension. Wow, it's rough! Three hours every night, I hope there isn't much more to Latin. (Ed.'s note: No, not much, son!)

Mike Schnitter, 4A: "One of my arms is shorter than the other, and I'm trying to get it back in shape."

Tom Krug, 3A: "Unless I take three books home every night, I can't reach the cookie jar."

LETTERS to the EDITOR

The Citadel Nov. 19, 1956 (Above) and Nov 27, 1957 (Below).

Colleges Collect 85% of Graduates

by John Foran

Working on the assumption that there is someone here at CHS who does care what happened to the members of the class of '57, the Citadel has gone to the trouble of digging through the Principal's private files of facts and figures and has come up with a lot of interesting information. But the records show that Canisius grads have been accepted into (or at least have crashed) some of the top schools this side of the Mississippi.

Seventy-eight of the grads became so attached to the Jesuits, and to school itself, that they are right back where they were four years ago—freshmen at Canisius.

All in all, most of last year's alumni are now working for their Ph.D.'s, some have donned the black cassock in God's service, and the rest are either working or taking it easy with a full-time job toting a gun.

Best of luck to all last year's seniors, knowing they'll find success in all their undertakings.

Jesuit Novitiates	7
Other Seminaries	2
Canisius College	78
University of Buffalo	12
Notre Dame	7
LeMoyne	5
Erie County Technical Institute	5
Fordham	4
St. Bonaventure	4
Military Service	4
Working	18

Campus Summer Camp To Open on June 23rd

by John Thornton

Do you remember away back, and I mean away back, when you were a "kid"? Well, if you do, you must remember what fun it was to sit around and twiddle your thumbs all summer in the city. If you could, you went to summer camp; and this summer, CHS is having the next best thing — a day camp here at the high school for "kiddies" from 6-14 (the pre-switchblade set).

Father Sturm to Direct

Yes sir, once more, you can hear the buzzz-clank of the milk machine echoeing through the usually dormant cafeteria, while healthy little children hustle down the cookie-line. The "Camp on the Campus" will be headed by our beloved Prefect of Discipline, Fr. Sturm, who will be ably assisted by Fr. Barry, Fr. Fernandez, and Fr. Pfeiffer. Pitching in as Activities Director will be Mr. Ralph Duquin, and the Swimming Director's position will be held down by Mr. Lamb.

The camper's day begins with his arrival about 9:00 at the school by car pool or bus, to be greeted by the smiling counselors. Once in school, the boys will be able to take part in swimming, softball, basketball, volleyball, track, bowling, ping-pong, ham-radio, badminton, table games (whatever those are), handicrafts, and (PANT! PANT!) touch football, until 4:00 P.M. Of course, there will be a break for lunch, after which there follows a rest period. Whom the rest period is for isn't specified.

Certainly every well-run camp must have organization (for example, the neat, orderly files of young men en route to Friday breakfast). Canisius' summer camp is no exception. The requirements for membership are: (1) a check-up by a doctor (the check part of it is: $60 for a 3 week session, $110 for the full 6 week camp); (2) the boys need no uniforms, although specially emblemed shirts may be purchased.

If you have any little brothers whom you want to get rid of for the summer, run home now and tell your parents all about this camp, remembering the slogan, "Your boy deserves a super-safe summer — and then there's you!"

A CRUSADER SAYS:

"WHAT— ME WORRY?"
I'M GOING TO THE CHS
SUMMER DAY CAMP!

The Citadel Apr. 25, 1958

Passion Play Makes TV Debut; Neville Show Scene of Drama

On Good Friday afternoon, the Canisius High School Dramatic Society stepped onto the sound stage of the WGR-TV studios, to make its debut for the year on the highly-commercialized medium of television. In a half-hour telecast, the Canisius actors brought to Western New York viewers the religious significance and atmosphere of the most holy commemoration of Good Friday, through the medium of Fr. Charles Dolan's dramatization of the Passion of Jesus Christ.

The studios of WGR were filled with the clamor of dressing actors, the make-up room was filled to five times its capacity; then the moment came, and the airways were filled with the words of Our Lord, His words in prophecy of His Passion. Then the scene switched to the High Priests of the Sanhedrin and their vicious plotting against Christ. The TV appearance was then climaxed with the beautiful reproduction of the Last Supper.

Background of the Production

Between scenes, Mr. Barth explained to television viewers the background of our annual Passion Play and its development and reception the years.

Their appearance at the TV studios not only added to their acting experience, but it also forced upon them a very interesting realization. It was the fact that television is a much more artificial medium than the stage itself. Cameras, booms, microphones, and other odd pieces of equipment are continually swooping down upon the unsuspecting actors. As a result it is very difficult to present an involved or intricate dramatization. But these difficulties proved no obstacle to

WGR-TV's Director, Reg Reed, places Canisius actors in proper camera range.

the high caliber of acting which is born and nurtured at 1180.

The Audience

In the past the Passion Play has been viewed by a total of 80,000 people. But the television showing was performed before a potential audience of 600,000. If only a fraction of this number saw the performance, that in itself is an accomplishment. For the stirring portrayal moved many, not to mention the influence exerted upon the many non-Catholics who tuned in.

It is a very reasonable assumption that those Catholics who saw even those few televised scenes caught something of the mood of the Paschal season and of the Passion, and were, no doubt, just a little better prepared for the Resurrection of Christ on Easter morning.

THE CITADEL   December 23, 1958

Senior Retreat Called A Valuable Experience

by Chuck LaChiusa

One of the small joys afforded to fourth year teachers is the annual senior retreat. For not only does the teacher get a break from daily routine, but he realizes how much of a better person each senior will be after the retreat. One might ask why the senior retreat is so appreciated by the seniors themselves.

First of all, the senior's retreat is a closed one. That is to say that every class forgets the disappointments of life for an entire three-day period, and home becomes the retreat house at Derby, New York.

The retreat center itself is one of those mansions on the lake that everyone dreams of, but never owns. It's almost as huge as it is beautiful. But its outstanding characteristic is the absolute peace and quiet: peace of mind and peace of soul, as well as quiet from the hustling of the busy routine of daily life.

The retreat day is governed by bells. Bells announce the day's commencement: 7 A.M. The day starts with Mass and Communion, then breakfast. After this, the conferences begin; each followed by a meditation and a reading period.

Peace and Quiet Prevails

After a long day with lunch, a recreation period, stations of the cross, supper, and benediction, intermingled between the frequent conferences, the bed is a welcome sight for the contented retreatants. Concerning one of the chief functions of the day, Jim Nash of 4F says that the food was "good and plenty" and that he especially "enjoyed the turkey dinner on Wednesday."

But of course the real purpose of the retreat is to get to know "me." Jerry Strempka of 4A fame remarked that he did some serious thinking about himself for the first time.

Many fellows say that their life's purpose has been rediscovered by them; for others, the retreat brought forth a new life. Senior Al Indelicato uses the words "a more virtuous life."

The entire retreat is amply summed up by our student president, John Costello: "Its impression will never leave me."

The retreats were given by a fine group of retreat masters, including Fathers Thomas Burke, Arthur McGratty, Jerome Kleber, Vincent McCorrey, and Vincent Mooney, all of the Society of Jesus. They certainly deserve credit and will be remembered for many years to come by the seniors who have received tremendous benefits under their spiritual direction.

Senior Jack Molloy chats with Fr. Arthur McGratty, S.J., during the 4F retreat at St. Columban's Retreat House at Derby-on-the-Lake, New York.

News Briefs

• Word has recently arrived that

Paul Cumbo

Faculty Coaches Express Their Favoritism for Sport's Program

Many leading educators have gone on record that sports are not an important part of the school curriculum. Many colleges have openly de-emphasized sports, while others stopped granting college sports scholarships. The coaches here at Canisius were asked what was the place of athletics in developing the high school student.

All-around Canisius athlete Paul Smaldone prepares to pour in two points during the Canisius-Ryan tilt.

Mr. Doogan, S.J., replied that sports develop a boy's sense of responsibility, teaching him that others depend upon him just as a team does. Mr. Bischoff, S.J., feels that the individual is developed by becoming a part of a greater social unit. The boy also learns from sports to have a competitive spirit while maintaining consideration for the concerns of others.

Mr. Lamb said that through sports the student learns to work, play, and earn the respect of his fellow student through fair play and sportsmanship. When this is applied with the knowledge acquired in the classroom, the individual is better prepared for meeting future obstacles.

Mr. Barnes' Views

Mr. Barnes pointed out that St. Ignatius Loyola, the founder of the Jesuit order, had recommended vigorous physical exercise as a form of relaxation from studies. Mr. Barnes said that sports develop many qualities in the individual, including initiative, perseverance, courage, self-control, responsibility, leadership, loyalty, sportsmanship, and honesty.

Mr. McGillicuddy stated that competitive sports supply three main needs of the high school student. These are: Self discipline due to the fact that he must follow training regulations and the directions of his coach; a sense of responsibility since the school's team's, coaches, and his own reputation rest on his shoulders; and teamwork and sportsmanship, because the proper respect for others is necessary for success in any endeavor.

Through these remarks, we can see what each coach is trying to instill in his players through sports. Certainly, with these aims, no one will be any worse for having participated in sports.

Students Voice Attitudes Toward Value for Sports

by Mike Ryan

In order to find out the student's opinion of sports a Citadel reporter asked the following question to random passersby in C.H.S. corridors—"What is your opinion of the value of sports?" The answers were varied and touched on some interesting points.

Frank Clark of 3D feels that sports gives a school prestige. That is, a school with winning teams attracts grammar school students and influences their selection of a high school.

Many students looked at sports from a spectator's viewpoint.

and Jim Van Wie of 1B, feel that sports have a certain value inasmuch as they develop the body and offer an outlet to the students. But these fellows also feel that sports should be put in their proper place and that the body should not be considered more important than the brain.

226

CHS Heavy Four Becomes New National Champions

by Phil Wychodzki

Canisius High School's crew won the senior fours title in the National Scholastic Rowing Regatta on Lake Carnegie, near Princeton, New Jersey. The crew was comprised of Mike Peck, bowman; Bill Schmitt, No. 2; Kevan Green, No. 3; Paul Salm, stroke, and Jack Frauenheim, c o x s w a i n. Charley Fontana coached them for their May 26 victory. They reached the finish in 5:37 minutes, with their closest contender five lengths behind.

Ice Foes

During the season, due to the Lake's late thaw, the crew lost three valuable weeks of practice because Black Rock Canal was clogged with drifting ice. The crew attempted to row during this period on Ellicott Creek, but found it to be a poor substitute for the Canal.

Canadian Regatta

Despite a loss to St. Catharine's in the Schoolboy Regatta trials, the varsity eight crew, composed of Dave Raab, Jim Crotty, Mike Peck, Joe Militello, Kevan Green, Bill Schmitt, John Frawley, Paul Salm, and coxswain Mike Shurgot, are confident they can defeat St. Catharine's crew in the Canadian Schoolboy Regatta held at Port Delousie, Ontario. Last year our crew placed a close second. However, the 1960 t e a m is stronger than last year's, and the recent victory at Princeton has strengthened their spirit and confidence.

Shell Talk

Many at the West Side Rowing Club are of the opinion that Canisius will again take the All-High Varsity-Eight and Heavy Cox Four races, as they did last year in the Buffalo Regatta. Some also believe our crew will capture first place in the All Catholic Varsity-Eight race.

Beyond a doubt, we have a truly superior crew this year, and all are looking forward to an undefeated season.

The Citadel June 1960

Arena Dedications: 1951-1960

*1951 - Mr. Thomas J. Jones, A.B.**

"We, the Senior Class of 1951, take this opportunity to thank and congratulate Mr. Jones on his
25th anniversary as a member of the faculty at
Canisius. We thank him for the help, both spiritual and intellectual, he has given us, promise to
remember him in our prayers, and extend the sincere wish that he have 25 more years at Canisius."

Mr. Thomas J. Jones, A.B.

1952 - No specific dedication

While the 1952 *Arena* lacks a specific dedication, the intention of the seniors seems to have been to express gratitude for the faculty, staff, and administration. Accompanying various faculty photos, including first Rev.
James Barnett, S.J., and Rev. Gerald Quinn, S.J., the text reads, "With their
prayers and leadership we begin the year.... Scholastically, financially, and
spiritually, they guide Canisius...on the path to success training us for our
future as Catholic Gentlemen....."

1953 - No specific dedication

As in 1952, the 1953 *Arena* lacks a specific dedication, with similar opening commentary accompanying the faculty and administration portraits.

1954 - "Jesus Christ, the King"

Surely not with the intention of diminishing previous and
future dedications, the Class of 1954 dedicated their
Arena Yearbook to God. "The 1954 is reverently dedicated to Christ, the King by His Knights to be...Since our
training during these years has been dedicated to the service of Our Lord it is fitting that the account of these

Christus Rex

---

* Actually, the page labeled "Dedication" is devoted to Pope Pius XII; however, in
keeping with the spirit of previous *Arena* issues, it is this author's interpretation that
the "Tribute" to Mr. Jones is a continuation of the dedications in previous issues.

years recorded here in the pages of the *Arena* should likewise be dedicated to Christ, the King."

1955 - In Memoriam - Rev. William J. Bauer, S.J.

Continuing the trend of the previous years' *Arenas*, 1955 has no specific dedication. However, there is, on page 19, a memorial to Father Bauer. "Father had come to Canisius early in his priestly life and he spent three years as our energetic student counselor from 1950 to 1953. At the time of his death Fr. Bauer was principal at St. Peter's High School, Jersey City. Father made many great and lasting contributions to Canisius by which he earned our unending gratitude."

1956 - Saint Ignatius Loyola

The 1956 *Arena*'s dedication page reads: "This is the Ignatian year, the four hundredth anniversary of the death of St. Ignatius.... As students at a Jesuit high school, part of the vast Jesuit educational system that spans the world, we naturally join in this salute to the founder...and extend our congratulations to those Jesuits whom we know best of all, our teachers here at Canisius.... It is most fitting that we reverently dedicate this book as a tribute to the man who formulated the challenge most vividly and who answered it most fully."

1957 - Jesus Christ

"To Him then who is the Eternal Logos, Jesus Christ, Son of God, Our Savior, we dedicate this book as a symbol of the total dedication of our own lives. May He who is the Beginning and the End, the Alpha and the Omega always be for us the be all and end all of our existence, that as we have begun our lives through Him, and with Him, and in Him, we may so conclude them—at the evening of life."

1958 George M. Frauenheim '30 & Edward E. Frauenheim, Jr. '32

"...As a small token of our appreciation and devotion for all they have done to make Canisius the great school it is today, we, the graduating class of 1958, fondly dedicate the 1958 *Arena* to George M. Frauenheim ['30] and Edward E. Frauenheim, Jr. ['32]."

1959 - Very Rev. Gerald A. Quinn, S.J.

"For the past twelve fruitful years, you have devoted all of your energy to the improvement of Canisius. Today, the result of your long years of tireless effort stands before you – a new Canisius, time-tested in tradition, modern in facility...Although it has always been your wish to remain behind the scenes and accomplish good in your own quiet way, we would now like to make known our appreciation...and so it is to you, our father and our friend, we, the senior class of 1959, gratefully dedicate this, our *Arena* yearbook."

1960 - Very Rev. Donald L. Kirsch, S.J.

"As Assistant Principal in charge of Canisius-on-Delaware from 1944-48, Prefect of Discipline from 1948-1952, and Principal from 1952-59, he saw the new school increase from its small initial holding to the present block-long rectangle.... His was the task of expanding the curriculum to meet the demands of a modern world. Sacrificing none of the essentials of a justly renowned system of education, he introduced new courses and facilities so that Canisius would continue to impart to each student the best possible education."

Notes

[1] *Arena*, the Yearbook of Canisius High School. 1950. Pgs. 4-5.

[2] *Arena*, the Yearbook of Canisius High School. 1959.

[3] *Arena*, the Yearbook of Canisius High School. 1950.

[4] *Arena*, the Yearbook of Canisius High School. 1959.

[5] Canisius High School *Annual Catalogue 1950-1951*. Pg. 9.

[6] *Ibid.*, pg. 10.

[7] Correspondence to Father Provincial from Rev. Gerald A. Quinn, S.J., dated January 24, 1951.

[8] Correspondence from Rev. James R. Barnett, S.J., to Very Rev. John B. Janssens, S.J., Father General, Rome. Dated Feb. 22, 1951.

[9] Correspondence from Rev. Gerald A. Quinn, S.J., to Very Rev. John B. Janssens, S.J., Father General, Rome. Dated Jul. 1, 1951.

[10] Correspondence from Rev. Gerald A. Quinn, S.J., to Very Rev. John B. Janssens, S.J., Father General, Rome. Dated Jan. 31, 1952.

[11] Correspondence from Rev. Gerald A. Quinn, S.J., to Very Rev. John B. Janssens, S.J., Father General, Rome. Dated Jul. 7, 1952.

[12] Correspondence from Rev. Gerald A. Quinn, S.J., to Very Rev. John B. Janssens, S.J., Father General, Rome. Dated Jul. 19, 1953.

[13] Correspondence from Rev. Gerald A. Quinn, S.J., to Very Rev. John B. Janssens, S.J., Father General, Rome. Dated Jan. 4, 1954.

[14] Correspondence from Rev. Gerald A. Quinn, S.J., to Very Rev. John B. Janssens, S.J., Father General, Rome. Dated Jul. 19, 1954.

[15] Correspondence from Rev. Gerald A. Quinn, S.J., to Very Rev. John B. Janssens, S.J., Father General, Rome. Dated Jan. 5, 1955.

[16] Correspondence from Rev. Gerald A. Quinn, S.J., to Very Rev. Thomas E. Henneberry, S.J., Provincial. Dated Nov. 5, 1955.

[17] Correspondence from Rev. Gerald A. Quinn, S.J., to Very Rev. John B. Janssens, S.J., Father General, Rome. Dated Jul. 19, 1956.

[18] Correspondence from Rev. Gerald A. Quinn, S.J., to Very Rev. John B. Janssens, S.J., Father General, Rome. Dated Jul. 12, 1957.

[19] Correspondence from Rev. Donald L. Kirsch, S.J., to Very Rev. John B. Janssens, S.J., Father General, Rome. Dated Jul. 12, 1957.

[20] Correspondence from George M. Frauenheim to Rev. Donald L. Kirsch, S.J., dated Sep. 8, 1960.

[21] Sams, Rev. Ron, S.J., Typewritten account with accompanying photos (photos dated Mar 27, 1999). CHS Archives.

[22] *The Buffalo Courier-Express*. Saturday, November 5, 1955. Pg. 6.

[23] *The Buffalo Evening News*. Tuesday, November 8, 1955.

[24] *The Buffalo Evening News*. February, 1956.

[25] Papaj, Joseph '57. "A Home for the Jesuits." *Arena Quarterly*, Spring Edition, 1956-1957. Pg. 5.

[26] *The Citadel*. Volume 10, No. 3. December 20, 1957.

[27] *Arena*, the Yearbook of Canisius High School. 1958. Pg. 8.

[28] *The Citadel*. Volume 7, No. 2. Nov. 18, 1954. Pg. 3

[29] *The Citadel*. Volume 9, No. 4. March 1, 1957. Pg. 2.

[30] Kubus, Matt '04. "Canisius Alumnus Retires from Congress After 28 Years of Faithful Service." *The Citadel*. Volume 43, Issue 3. February 10, 2003.

CHAPTER 9

The 1960s

THE 1960s saw the tipping point of what is arguably among the most consequential transformations the school has undergone. It is the same transition experienced by many fellow Jesuit institutions in the middle and later part of the 20th century: the emergence of a faculty and staff composed by a majority of laypeople.

Though this may seem, upon initial reflection, a simple matter of personnel and human resources, it is a change that had (and continues to have) massive implications for a school founded by a religious order. While the move from Washington Street to the Delaware campus in the late 1940s obviously marked a major change on many levels, it is a fair assertion that even this represented a less transformational dynamic than did the shift from a mostly-Jesuit to mostly-lay institution. One was a physical change in location; the other would have a fundamental impact on the business elements of the school and usher in a new kind of Jesuit-lay collaborative.

The nature of the change is radically different, as was its duration. When Chicky Evans '18 suggested that Father Redmond take a look at 1180 Delaware, it would be only a matter of a few years before students began taking classes there. And, by the time the Class of 1950 graduated, they had spent all four years on the new campus. It was a radical change and it was a quick one.

The gradual transition to a lay-majority faculty, on the other hand, was a steady creep, with no single year-to-year leap particularly notable for wildly tipping the scales. Institutional correspondence throughout the postwar period contains occasional references to the growing proportion of lay faculty members; certainly, it is usually with regard to fiscal challenges posed by paying them. At times, there is a tinge of alarm; at others, there is some calm institutional reflection about the trend and its implications for the future. By the end of the 1960s, however, the 50% threshold was passed, and instructional salaries became a matter altogether different than they had been for the first half of the school's existence. Lay faculty—often with spouses, children, mortgages, and other expenses—required a paradigm shift in thinking, planning, and fiduciary decision-making for school leadership. Moreover, it became increasingly necessary to share the formation aspect of Jesuit education with lay "partners in mission."

It is impossible to ignore the turbulence of the decade when considering the life of a school for young men. The nation wrestled with so many things: the intensity of the Civil Rights Movement, the assassinations of Dr. Martin Luther King, Jr., President John F. Kennedy, and Senator Robert F. Kennedy, and the escalating war in Vietnam. The students of Canisius faced an uncertain future. As the nation struggled in the throes of its own social transformation, so too did CHS continue its mission through the decade in a constant state of flux.

Social Transformation - An Alumnus Recalls

At the time of this writing, Mr. Robert Reger '66[8] was serving in his fifth year as the Chairman of the Canisius High School Board of Trustees. In an interview for this book, Mr. Reger provided some insights about his own student days in the 1960s. His commentary offers meaningful perspective on the school during this transformative period of American history.

I have to put Canisius in the context of the effects of Vatican II. For many of us, it called into question a lot of the traditions that we assumed were unalterable. Certainly, grammar school didn't put you in a good position to be able to able to evaluate what's alterable and unalterable. But the point is, that all the sudden, all these expectations about what it meant to be a Catholic going forward were up for grabs. In the culture at large, we were experiencing music that was irreverent, music that targets traditional institutional knowledge, and since we're all reasonably intelligent students and we're picking this up, you know, things became, at least intellectually, challenged. There was an uncertainty, a confusion. I saw this in my classrooms there.

So, we come in as this wet-behind-the-ears freshman class, and the fundamental operative was discipline. It was routine. It was doing your homework. Presenting the papers when they were due. Not talking in class. All the stuff that you associate with an organization that was almost martial. And sure, there were unique teachers, and there was a sense of humor, and a time to laugh, et cetera. But the bottom line was that the expectations were very high and the standards were very high, and if you didn't meet these standards, you're going to get kicked out. Nobody's going to make any apologies. You're gonna get kicked out. And so that's something to be avoided especially if you're going to explain it to your parents who are paying the bills. So that was freshman year.

There was the disciplinarian of all disciplinarians, Father Sturm, who was beloved by many, and not so beloved by others. In my opinion, as a student, you

---

[8] Mr. Reger was the recipient of the 1966 "Mr. Canisius" Award.

couldn't have a rational conversation with him. It was his way or the highway. I learned very quickly that challenging Father Sturm was a very stupid idea, and I didn't want to spend my entire life in JUG. So that was freshman year, and sophomore year was more or less more of the same.

We'd just had the assassination of John F. Kennedy in 1963. We were all here. We were in a gymnasium for an assembly. And Father Bartlett, who was going to be talking to us about something, turns on the radio, and we had to listen to this report from Dallas...I have to tell you, it didn't make a difference [whether you were a Democrat or Republican] I mean the President had been assassinated. It just totally jumbled the decks. I mean, this just could not happen here in this country. So, I mean, now, there's a vulnerability that we're feeling as students, and we're certainly feeling as Americans. And you're injecting that into a vulnerability that's related to Vatican II, and the changes in the culture, and it starts to become turbulent. When we got into junior year, we were reading Catcher in the Rye. *And boy, that was kind of eye-opening. And then there's the stuff going on in the church, and the music is changing...*

By the time we were seniors, there was still plenty of discipline, you were still answerable for the same sorts of things we were as freshmen, but there is an undercurrent of...let's say, for lack of a better word, sassiness. You're beginning to see classmates, as their intellects are maturing, and their feeling constricted by the emphasis on discipline, talking back. And they're talking back in the form of asking questions in response to the lectures teachers are presenting in class. They were introducing topics and approaches to issues that the professors were simply not prepared to address. So instead of saying let me think about this and get back to you, there was a collision. So, by the time we graduated, you could say Canisius was, to some degree, the victim of cross-currents in the culture, and in the church, that undermined some of the basic tenets of the Jesuit approach to education. And then you see from '66 on, you begin to see the effects of that.

As for Vietnam, to be honest, I don't know how aware of the draft and the war we were. The war didn't really ratchet up until well into the Lyndon Johnson administration. I don't remember for a minute thinking about the war while I was at Canisius or worrying about getting drafted. We had to get our draft cards, but we knew going to college got us a deferment. I think a lot of us ended up going to law school when they turned to the lottery. The lottery either took the issue away or made it very immediate.

Yes, I think Canisius and the old models at work there served us well in that turbulent time. I probably would have been a lot more frivolous as a person and a personality but for the education and experience I received here at Canisius. And that's with full acknowledgement of the imperfections of the education. I don't think Canisius was a perfect place...but I want to say that it wasn't just the students who were experiencing the turbulence. It was the professors as well. And it had to have impacted them more, because they had been guided by this ethic for a hell of a lot longer than the students had. And to have all of that in play must have been hard for them.

The Blue Doors - Origins and Transformations

"The Big Blue Doors" have become a central symbol of the Canisius experience. Perhaps no other physical feature of the campus figures so prominently as the principal portal through which multiple generations have entered the building. They are entryway, rallying point, and common navigational reference. On the first day of freshman year, entry through them marks the "alpha" of the Canisius years, while on the day of commencement, the exit through the front doors of the Rand Mansion marks the "omega."

On the first day of freshman year, timid freshmen stand before their hulking, oaken mass, looking up at the threshold of this intimidating citadel. It takes effort—both physical strength and fortitude—to heave them open. In time, for most boys, the doors take on a purely utilitarian role— perhaps the fascination has, understandably, faded for the worldly-wise sophomore or sleep-deprived junior. For many seniors, however, a resurgent fondness for the Blue Doors grows with the steady countdown of months, then days, until graduation. As they walk through them for the final time as CHS students—dressed in white tuxedo jackets, swinging them open more ably, this time—there will be a nostalgic pause for many.

In the commencement addresses that follow, there will usually be at least one mention of them.

And so, it is understandable that in the mythology of Canisius High School—that blend of fact, fiction, fable, and lore—the Blue Doors have always existed. Alumni from as far back as the WWII era sometimes refer fondly to the Blue Doors of their own memory. However, the hard reality is this: in the grand scope of the school's 150-year history, the Blue Doors are "relatively" new. Rev. William O'Malley, S.J., of the Class of 1949, referred to them as "...the heavy brown oaken doors" in his 1949 *Arena* retrospective.[1]

The doors themselves date from 1924-1925. According to notes from an April 2010 interview between one Mr. Joseph Pisoni of Dunkirk, New York and the CHS library staff, the doors were crafted by Mr. Pisoni's grandfather, Mr. Ottone "Tony" Pisoni. The elder Pisoni was a blacksmith who worked for Wendell August Forge. "Wendell August Forge is America's oldest and largest forge, producing hand-wrought ornamental metalware and elegant giftware in aluminum and other metals since 1923," proclaims the company's website.[2] The younger Mr. Pisoni shared his story with the CHS library staff, who summarized it in the archive notes:

He searched and ultimately found the doors his grandfather had made for a "Cathedral" in Buffalo, NY. The younger Pisoni had a photograph of the doors from a book and had spent years trying to locate the cathedral they were in. Having looked at every cathedral he could think of in the city of Buffalo, Joe turned to the archivist for the Diocese of Buffalo, Sr. Ann Louise Hentges, SSMN, who through research and various conversations helped Joe to make the connection that Wendell August was a Mason and that the 'cathedral' was in fact the Buffalo Masonic Consistory that is now CHS.[3]

In an attempt to track down the truth—to distinguish history from mythology—this author turned to the obvious authority. To anyone familiar with the school in the past two generations, there is one name that comes to mind as soon as "paint" and "Canisius" are mentioned in the same sentence: Rev. Richard Zanoni, S.J., whose meticulous detail work has been a lasting gift to the Delaware campus.

Fr. Z. offered his rationale: "The ironic thing about our school was that no one ever entered by the front door; they entered by the side door. So as far as the students were concerned, this was the front door of the school. I felt that that doors should be welcoming doors. Not just doors you go through...so that's why I wanted to paint them the school colors and highlight the artwork."[4]

While Father Zanoni was able to offer some insight—as well as an amusing anecdote—he was, unfortunately, unable to solve the riddle. According to Father Zanoni, "I don't remember them being blue when I was a scholastic [1969-1972]. I'm sure, when I was a scholastic, they were brown.[5]

Unfortunately, there is evidence that raises questions about Father Z.'s recollections. A color photo in the 1964 *Arena* Yearbook, a period well before his scholastic years, clearly shows the doors painted a light, paler-than-sky-blue—one might call it a shade of bluish light gray.

The left image is in color in the 1964 Arena and clearly depicts a sky-blue color on the doors. The one on the right, from Arena 1963—though black and white—appears to be the same color.

Going back further still, a black and white photo in *Arena* 1963 (page 166) clearly shows a painted door. It appears almost white in the black and white photo—though no wood grain is visible—which indicates that it was the same light blue as in the 1964 *Arena* color photo, just mentioned. Going back one year, to the 1962 *Arena*, we locate a photo that *appears* to be the same color as the one in 1963. While it's hard to tell, readers will note that the ENTRANCE sign isn't visible in this photo, as is the case in the '63 and '64 images. Going back further still, to a photo in the November 17, 1961 issue of *The Citadel*, we see doors that appear to be painted as such. However, jumping back to 1956, the *Arena* makes it abundantly clear that the doors were unpainted oak at that time. There is no ambiguity there, and this is reinforced again in the 1958 *Arena*.

From Arena 1962 (left) and Citadel November 1961 (right).

1956 (left) and 1958 (right) Arena images reveal that the doors remained unpainted oak as of the end of the 1958 school year.

Thus, it can reasonably be concluded that the painting occurred after the conclusion of the 1958 school year but before the beginning of 1961. Unfortunately, coinciding with this window was a one-year pause in the long-running tradition of *The Citadel*. Volume XII ends in June, 1960; Volume XIII does not pick up again until the fall of 1961. (The first issue of Volume XIII begins with an inaugural editorial entitled "Hello Again!"). Sadly, then, the very timeframe which apparently saw the first painting of the doors was also the one without a regular student news publication. This only compounds the difficulty in obtaining a definitive answer to the question. Moving on, however, a color image from the 1969 *Arena* clearly depicts light blue, which suggests the doors remained so through the 1960s. Another image from *Arena* 1971, though black and white, appears the same. However, a 1975 color photo proves that the doors are a brighter blue.

Arena 1971 (left) and 1975 (right). The 1975 image is in color and (when viewed in color) is definitively a darker shade of blue than previous years.

This supports Father Z.'s recollection that:

...the first time I painted them was that blue that's in the stairwell. * *I'm pretty sure they weren't blue, but maybe they were! I know I painted them with that light blue and that God-awful yellow...Now, I painted them at least three*

---

* The "light blue" to which Father Zanoni referred is the same royal blue that covered the lockers until they were replaced in 2012. The "God-awful" yellow is the bright, pastel shade that has been officially shunned in favor of various shades, ranging from a light, beige-like "Vegas Gold" to a more traditional, darker yellow-gold. Periodically, students have managed to secure various spirit wear in shades of blue and gold not officially endorsed by the school. In particular, there was (and remains) considerable debate among the alumni community concerning "Vegas gold," which has received widespread criticism for being too pale, with many alumni favoring a darker, more traditional yellow-gold.

times. I remember one of the times vividly because I did it on a Friday. It was the end of my work; I'd just finished some of the yellow up at the top. I was on a ladder. I was interrupted by an alumnus, and we took a walk around the campus. We both forgot about the ladder and we spilled yellow paint all over the doors and all over the concrete.... It took me until 9:00 that night—thank God it was water based—to clean that up. This is when I did it in the 80s.... I remember it because I didn't use one curse word. I was amazed." [6]

Jesuit Correspondence: An Inside Look at the 1960s

In keeping with the previous two decades, a selection of correspondence among the Jesuits offers a telling view of the school's development during this time. Through these excerpts, the reader will see that while the school's financial struggles continued, it was a time of relative stability in this regard—even as enrollment faced the ongoing challenges posed by competing independent and diocesan schools. This paved the way for curricular innovation, both in the classroom and in other areas of student life, such as religious formation, service programs, and retreats.

In January 1961, Father Kirsch, in his correspondence with Very Rev. John B. Janssens, S.J., Father General of the Jesuits, wrote of the high number of priestly vocations:

Last year we had eleven vocations to the priesthood: two to the Society, seven to the diocese, and two to other religious orders... [7]

Likewise, he offered a report on the continued importance of the "Founders" and their impact upon reducing the school's debt:

Financially, even with our debts, we are in a sound condition at present. We are blessed with the assistance of about two hundred laymen who donate one hundred dollars a year as 'Founders of the New Canisius High School.' They make it possible for us yearly to reduce our debt of just under $300.000. [8]

We see here documented evidence of the school's commitment to financial aid, even in the face of stiff competition for enrollment:

Registration in the school is presently at capacity. However, next September two more diocesan high schools are opening [and] the diocesan schools with nominal tuition charges are always a threat to our enrollment. May I mention here, however, that we give reductions in tuition to boys in financial need; in the spirit of our Institute, one in every ten boys is assisted in this manner to the amount of over $10,000 yearly.[9]

One year later, in February 1962, Father Kirsch's letter implies concern in two areas. First off, he reports on the steady increase in the proportion of lay faculty (and its associated higher cost); secondly, he mentions a considerable decline in the number of applications, reflective of his concerns about competing schools expressed the previous year:

Five of our graduates entered the Society immediately from high school [and] the prospects of vocations for the coming year look as good or even better.... In the school there has been notable improvement in scholastic tone and achievement.... Each recent year we have had to add to the teaching staff one or two lay teachers, thus increasing the expense of operation; and at the same time, we have progressively and substantially increased the individual salaries of all lay teachers.... The present registration in the school is satisfactory. The prospects for next year, however, are not as encouraging. There are 90 less applicants for next September than there were last year.[10]

In September 1962, at the beginning of the 1962-1963 academic year, Father Kirsch was able to relay several items of an encouraging nature. College acceptances and vocations remained strong, the new Jesuit retreat house in Clarence, N.Y., was home to a successful three-day senior retreat, and, perhaps most notably, the imminent liquidation of a substantial portion of the school's debt:

Last June we graduated 203 boys of whom 119 won scholarships to colleges of an estimated worth of $325,000...Six of our graduates entered the Society *immediately from high school, and one from the class of 1958. Five entered diocesan seminaries.*

All senior students last year made a three-day closed retreat in groups of about 35 to the new Jesuit retreat house. This was a very satisfactory proce-dure and makes a very deep impression on the boys.

Financially the school is in generally good condition.... Particularly to be noted is the immediate prospect of the liquidation of our debt on the building of the community residence. Our most generous benefactors, George and Edward Frauenheim, have sold their business. This puts the Foundation, which they established in honor of their parents to provide us with a residence, in a posi-tion completely to clear up the debt incurred. The Foundation itself may pos-sibly continue in our favor* with the remaining assets.[11]

Father Kirsch's letter to Rome in January, 1963 tells of the school's successful first "Open House," a tradition that has remained in place con-sistently to this day. It also praises the teaching acumen of the faculty, and indicates that just under half of the teachers were laymen—very close to the majority tipping point. Finally, the letter confirms the good financial news connected with the Frauenheim Foundation and liquidation of the debt:

Over 300 boys have applied for admission for next September. The 'Open House' held for prospective students was praised by those who attended...

As for instruction, the impression is that the teachers are serious about their work.... The caliber of their teaching is high. It is interesting to note that about 48% of the instructional staff are laymen.

---

* A review of accompanying notes in the Archives, along with references in further correspondence not reprinted here for purposes of confidentiality, reliably suggests that the total contribution of the Frauenheims to Canisius High School, as of February 28, 1962, was just over $615,000.00 across all applications and projects. Considering the correlation of this generosity to the figures associated with the school's endeavors over the previous two decades, it should be plainly obvious just how vital was the Founda-tion's beneficence to the development of Canisius High School in the mid-20th century.

Financially, the school is in good status. We have announced...tuition will be increased next year by $40 to $320 per year. Our debt which was incurred fifteen years ago for $500,000 to build the classroom addition is reduced to $202,000 and will be renegotiated next month... The 'Founders' contributes [sic] annually about $19,000 toward taking care of this indebtedness.

As predicted in my last letter, the Frauenheim brothers...last week completely cleared up the entire indebtedness on our residence with a check for $210,000. May God reward them for their devoted charity.[12]

By the end of that school year, in July 1963, reports tell of continued curricular development and a particularly strong number of incoming freshmen for 1963-1964. Father Kirsch likewise alludes to the projected continued increase in expenses, including those related to the increasing proportion of lay teachers to Jesuits. On a hopeful note, however, he explains how the school's mortgage was refinanced (or, as he wrote, "renegotiated," to be precise), which apparently reduced the overall indebtedness of the school to the lowest possible six-figure sum.

Another successful year is completed with the graduation of 186 students. Of these five have been accepted as candidates to the Society.

...As a result of conferences among our college and high school faculties...additional changes in curriculum requirements are contemplated to meet the needs of college preparatory students in the present day.

The financial indebtedness of the school was reduced to $100,000 last February when our fifteen-year mortgage was renegotiated. In this respect, the school is on a sound basis, but the costs of running the school, including lay teachers' salaries and needed improvements, are continually increasing. It is becoming clearer that plans for a dependable annual income apart from tuition must be formulated for the future if we are to maintain our standards in competition with other schools.

The increase in tuition...has not affected the number of students entering next September. We have accepted a class of 245 boys of promising potential.[13]

The 1963-64 year saw the installation of a new Principal, Rev. Louis Mounteer, S.J., Father Kirsch offers positive remarks about the school's new academic leader; likewise, he notes the emphasis given to expanding the spiritual formation initiatives. In these efforts, along with continued good press for the senior retreat program in the decade's student publications, we see the groundwork for the increasingly important role such initiatives would come to play in the coming decades. While there was no formal office called "Campus Ministry" at the time, one might recognize its origins in these efforts to focus on spiritual formation.

The school, under the direction of Father Louis Mounteer, our new principal, is running smoothly.... We have had several meetings of the faculty focused on the religious, spiritual, and moral formation of the students. A small advisory committee of Jesuits and lay faculty members has been formed, [the] "Spiritual Action Committee...a concerted and detailed effort has and is being made to make religion more meaningful in the life of the school and its students.... With the pressures and emphasis on scholastic excellence, we might be taking our primary purpose complacently and took much for granted.... More than the usual number of applicants have applied for financial assistance, and we are...doing all we can to make it possible for deserving boys to attend our school...about one in ten boys has attended with some reduction in tuition.[14]

Amidst the correspondence later that summer, in August 1964, is an important observation. 1964 was the tipping point year when the number of lay faculty first exceeded Jesuits.*

---

* There is some ambiguity in this, however, and it is not entirely clear precisely where the line between "teaching faculty" and non-teaching personnel was drawn. Perusal of three *Arena* Yearbooks (1962-63, 1963-64, and 1964-65) reveals the following: In 1962-1963 there were 30 total Jesuit staff (teaching and non-teaching) to 20 laypersons; in 1963-1964 it was 32 Jesuit to 19 lay; and by 1964-1965 the ratio was 32 Jesuits to 30 lay employees. Applying the filter of specifically *teaching* staff, however, the ratio is, in fact 50:50 in that year. There were 23 teaching Jesuits and 23 teaching lay faculty. Again, there is some ambiguity depending on whether one considers a student

...As much as one responsible for the excellence of a school tries not to become preoccupied with its finances, it is a hard fact to be faced. The expansion of our curriculum this year necessitating additional lay teachers and the cost in salaries for qualified men is continually rising. At present over fifty percent of our teaching faculty is laymen...Fortunately, our student registration will be at capacity next September...[15]

Father Robert Burns, S.J., took over as Rector and President in 1965. Likewise, his correspondence is addressed to the new Father General, the Very Rev. Pedro Arrupe, S.J., in Rome. In his first formal Rector's letter, in January 1966, Father Burns emphasized his concern with the continued trend of the growing lay faculty: "It seems to me that we have a rather large number of paid teachers, which in truth is the biggest item in our financial needs."[16] The following summer, in August 1967, Father Burns again echoes financial concerns and puts a precise figure on a different type of shortage. Previous correspondences focused on large scale, long-term debt based on campus expansion. Here, the emphasis is on a more pressing, immediate, and growing challenge in light of the shifting ranks of employees:

We are experiencing considerable financial [challenge] in maintaining the school. This is due mainly to the need for increasing the salaries of the lay teachers. Last year we operated at a deficit of $42,000.00.[17]

Later in the same letter, however, some good news is reported concerning a matter that had burdened Fr. Burns' predecessors for the better part of two decades:

We have sold the property on which Canisius High School originally stood on Washington Street for a very fine price of $250,000. The down payment will alleviate some of our deficit of this past year.[18]

---

counselor, for example, to be a "teacher." In this case, by Father Kirsch's count, apparently not. Regardless of these ambiguities, one can conclusively say that the mid-1960s saw the end of majority-Jesuit staffing at CHS.

Amidst the correspondence of the late 1960s, we learn of the merging of the Buffalo Province with the New York Province.[19] During this time of transition, in his letter dated January 20, 1968, Father Burns again expresses financial concerns and some of the school's efforts to address them, including the removal of the bowling alleys and a substantial tuition hike:

In the eighth year of a ten-year lease for machines needed in the bowling alleys we terminated the lease and closed the operation of the alleys... The space afforded by the discontinuance of the alleys will be matter for consultation...it should prove advantageous.

Our school continues to enjoy a reputation for excellence.... We had 575 applicants.... [However,] Our financial situation is not good. We have not been meeting our operating costs with regular and extraordinary sources of income.... The new treasurer, Fr. Alvin Mahlmeister, has...organized a committee from among the fathers of the students to study the problem and help in the solution. They have recommended a rise in tuition from $400 to $500 next year, but with a stipulation that deductions be given generously to a greater number where this is needed.[20]

A somber note is included in an untitled, undated, and unattributed "history of the 1967-1968" school year, which was located along with several documents associated with the 1969 Middle States Accreditation process: "Canisius High School was much saddened by the loss of its greatest benefactor, George Frauenheim. Mr. Frauenheim died suddenly on April 5, 1968. His benefactions to the school and Jesuit community over a period of more than 20 years totaled more than a half-million dollars!"[21]

The school embarked on an ambitious "Second Century Fund," with a transparent advertising campaign that laid out the stark fiscal reality and presented a challenging appeal:

The Second Century Fund has been conceived as a $1,000,000 bulwark against the waves of inflation---$1,000,000 to be presented to Canisius High School as a perpetual endowment and invested so as to yield an annual interest that will secure the future of the school.[22]

(See materials on following pages).

YEAR AFTER YEAR
CLASS AFTER CLASS
CANISIUS HIGH SCHOOL
HAS CONTINUED
TO EDUCATE
DIVERSIFIED YOUNG
MEN IN A
MOST SINGULAR WAY!

NOW CANISIUS HIGH
MUST COME TO ITS
FRIENDS TO ASK
A SINGULAR AND
MOST PROFOUND
QUESTION . . .

THE QUESTION:
SHOULD THERE BE A CANISIUS FOR TOMORROW?

6,000 alumni say
A grateful community says
778 students say
38 Jesuits, 24 lay faculty and coaches say
Thousands of future Canisians say

YES!

THE ECONOMIC FACTS SAY NO!

A TRADITION

Today, when Canisius High is realizing its finest achievements, its future is threatened by the spiraling costs of our inflationary economy. Tuition income does not cover the full cost of the school's operation. It never has, nor will it in the future because it is the policy of Canisius to maintain a balance of qualified boys from all parts of the community who can share with one another the experience of their diverse backgrounds.

WORTH MAINTAINING

In these times when every basic Christian value is in jeopardy and morality is so loosely defined it becomes almost absent, the work of Canisius High is more vital than ever. It is important to remember that the most critical and formative years of a young person's life occur during his high school experience. The demand for Canisius graduates, young men of character, in all communities has new urgency.

THE DILEMMA

☐ Raise tuition so only the few can attend.

☐ Have a series of multiple annual appeals and fund-raising functions.

☐ Close Canisius High.

THE SOLUTION

With no endowment other than a limited and restricted Scholarship Fund, with no reserves for faculty salaries or rising maintenance costs, with a pressing need for renovation of some facilities, a new communication arts center, additions and improvements to the library, cafeteria and science laboratories — the way to guarantee Canisius' future is through the establishment of a special Fund.

Thus The Second Century Fund has been created — a $1,000,000 campaign for major gifts to be presented to the High School for a perpetual general endowment Scholarship Fund and Capital Renovations on the occasion of its entrance into its second century of service.

Income from the investment Fund will provide the capital needed annually to meet rising costs for as far into the future as we can reasonably project.

23

Middle States Accreditation Process

The Citadel of February 6, 1969, proclaimed "Middle States Advises Needed Improvements." This student reflection offers only a limited perspective on what amounted to a multi-year process, which Canisius has now undertaken several times to date. The article provided some basic context:

The Middle States Association of Schools and Colleges is a voluntary organization which rates high schools and colleges on the basis of demanding evaluator criteria. The association sets these standards and revises them every ten years...

Among the areas of evaluation are the philosophy and objectives of the school, the students and their backgrounds, the school in the community, and the program of studies.[24]

The article cited commendations from the visiting panel, which included Father Francis J. Taylor, principal of Lancaster Catholic High School of Lancaster, Pennsylvania, who said "A CHS student has a fine faculty, an interested student body, and an opportunity to get an awful lot out of his education."

Recommendations included a tuition hike and curricular developments:

Although the final report has not been completed the committee put forth several major recommendations: a raise in tuition to provide for 4-year courses in modern languages, the addition of other languages to the course of study, more teachers and smaller classes, and a larger expenditure for the library. The addition of a sixth student counselor and the expansion of Student Council powers to include those of a student court completed the preliminary recommendations.[25]

Internal correspondence, located in the CHS Archives, provides some background and context to this accreditation journey. Generally, the process of preparing for an accreditation involves substantial institutional reflection and comprehensive self-study. It is fitting, then, to examine some of those self-assessments to gather authentic insights about the state of the school in the latter part of the decade.

Presumably part of the initial self-study, a document outlining the mission and objectives of Canisius High School was located amidst accreditation materials. Entitled "Objectives" with a header labeled, "Philosophy," (one of the categories of Middle States review), the document lists seven goals of the high school:

The objectives of Jesuit education were first set down in the 1586 edition of the Ratio Studiorum. We still follow the spirit of this document.

- *To help the students come to a practical awareness of their relationship to God, to family, to the school and civic community.*
- *To provide a course of studies geared to develop the powers of insight, logical analysis and synthesis, effective written and oral expression.*
- *To help boys prepare for admission to a four-year college. (This objective restricts our registration to boys who have the ability and the desire to receive a college education.)*
- *To give a solid foundation in the languages, mathematics, science, and history. (The time required to do this well precludes the possibility of including in the curriculum extensive programs in the fine arts.)*
- *To develop the whole man, by providing spiritual, physical, and social activities as an extension of the intellectual activities of the classroom.*
- *To help boys acquire study habits that enable them to pursue private study with the economic use of time and the goal of mastery.*
- *To help students discover the need for an ordered way of life by providing an environment that is demanding in terms of punctuality, personal appearance, and social responsibility.[26]*

Notably, the priority given to the Fine Arts was admittedly low, the rationale for this revealing much about the academic culture of the time. Certainly, throughout the curricular changes that both preceded and followed this accreditation process, one can discern tension surrounding this issue.

Another document that accompanied this one was a report entitled "Canisius and the Community." Again, it is logical to assume that this comprised a portion of the accreditation self-study; likewise, it offers telling insights as to the culture of CHS in the 60s.

Canisius draws its student body from the slightly more than one million population of a Greater Buffalo Area approximately conterminal with Erie County. Originally a center for people of Irish and German ancestry, Buffalo later gained substantial Italian and Polish communities. With these earlier residents gradually moving to suburban areas, the city proper has newer communities of Negro and Puerto Rican heritage.

Greater Buffalo's industrial balance reflects national trends with two exceptions: there is only a slight agricultural community and manufacturing engages almost half of the male population. This imbalance shows up in the occupations of the fathers of Canisius students. But at the same time, fifty percent of these fathers are in professional, technical, or managerial capacities compared to twenty percent in the general population. Canisius, therefore, does not draw evenly from the area's national mix; rather many of the students at present come from suburban residences. It should be noted however, that ten percent of Canisius students receive grants from the school.

Census figures on the educational achievement of the local population are surprisingly low; less than ten percent are college graduates and fully twenty percent did not complete grade school. Canisius is strictly a college preparatory school; students come from families whose educational backgrounds out of line with local norms. Only six percent of their fathers failed to complete high school and fifty-five percent had at least some college.

Canisius, therefore, while not drawing exclusively from the educationally or socio-economically advantaged, tends to attract from a mindset where higher education is a value and a possibility.[27]

Culturally, it is telling that the demographic breakdown offered in this self-study reflects the still-true-today "conventional wisdom" about

Canisius relative to other area schools: It is regarded, generally, as "elite" but not "elitist." Likewise, the demographic composition of the student body is representative of a broad socioeconomic range.

The First "Mr. Canisius" Award - 1962

The Citadel ran a front-page story on February 2, 1962, entitled "WANTED: 'CANISIUS MAN OF THE YEAR.' STUDENT BODY TO BALLOT FOR 'MR. CANISIUS'. It describes the criteria for this inaugural award:

The fellow chosen is to be a composite of all the qualities previously assigned to individuals, such as best speaker, best dressed, best athlete...best summarized in these words: 'Let him be chosen for what he has given Canisius, not for what he has gotten from Canisius.'

Look for the fellow who is athletic, but not an all-sport, who is a good student, but not a 'brain,' who has a personality, but not a glamor boy, practices his Faith, but not pharisaically, and who is a gentleman at all times, but not a 'goody-goody'—then cast your ballot for him...

...Father Edward Dolan, S.J., principal, expressed interest in having a contest of this type and wholeheartedly approved its inception.[28]

The current language of the Mr. Canisius Award, fortunately, has been considerably refined since this initial, student-authored description of its criteria.[*] In place of the admonitions against being a "goody-goody" are more specific admirable qualities: "The Mr. Canisius Award is presented annually to the graduating senior who, in the estimation of his peers, epitomizes all for which Canisius stands. Typically, he is a student who has used his heart, spirit, strength, and mind to an exceptional degree in

---

[*] (Although this author would like to credit the editorial staff for introducing him, nearly at the age of forty and at an advanced stage of his writing and teaching career, to the word 'pharisaically' for the first time.)

service to others and love for God. Mr. Canisius possesses and lives up to each of these characteristics."[29]

A follow-up article later in February 1962 includes faculty commentary about the new award, for which a ballot-counting committee was being assembled, and for which Joe Mendola '62, Associate Editor of *The Citadel*, had been appointed Chair:

Here are some opinions volunteered by three members of the faculty...Father Fleming, S.J., remarked that this person would be one who 'is trying to enhance the prestige of Canisius by generous contributions of his talents.' Mr. Mirabile, S.J., said that 'he should be aware of the feelings of other people.' He also added that this person should have 'the ability to assume responsibilities, a certain amount of personality, varied interests, and a sense of humor.' Mr. Kessler, registrar, cited one extremely important quality, humility linked with talent.[30]

"FACULTY MEMBERS CONSENT TO OVERSEE MR. 'C' VOTING" was the headline in *The Citadel*'s March 23, 1962, issue. It underscored the importance of peer selection, while mentioning that faculty members Rev. Thomas Fleming, S.J., Mr. Robert Mirabile, S.J., and Mr. Ronald Hastreiter would supervise the process. "This title, 'Mr. Canisius,' represents an honor which can be determined only by the decision of the fellow students of this particular senior. Therefore, the election of 'Mr. C' is solely in the hands of the students under the direction of...these three faculty members." It emphasizes, concerning the teachers, that "neither their personal opinions nor their decisions will affect the nomination or the election."[31]

Students were reminded not to treat the process as a popularity contest. In the April 18, 1962, *Citadel*: "Formal campaigning for such a title is not necessary nor in accordance with the rules of the contest. The voting should be spontaneous, an automatic recognition.... Those students who are not familiar with the candidates should make an effort to find out why each is deserving of this title. In this way, they will...avoid the chance of the 'Mr. C' contest from becoming a popularity poll."[32]

The recipient of the first "Mr. Canisius" award—Jerome Best '62—was recognized on the cover of *The Citadel* dated June 1, 1962.

Mr. Canisius 1962

Senior Jerome Best has been chosen by the student body as "Mr. Canisius." The purpose of THE CITADEL-sponsored contest was to find the Crusader whom the students regarded as the one most representative of Canisius, the person who best served and thereby enhanced the glory of Canisius by generous contributions of his scholastic as well as extra-curricular achievements.

In his four years at Canisius, Jerry has distinguished himself in many ways. His major athletic participation included four years of football, baseball, and intramurals. Jerry is in the Greek Honors Course and has been in dramatics for several years. This year he served as president of the Student Council. The first "Mr. Canisius" is in the estimation of his fellow students "the best."

Athletics in the 1960s

Prominent Intramural Program

The October 6, 1961, *Citadel* included a report on the strong intramural tradition at CHS. "The intramural program here is without a doubt one of the finest offered in any high school in the United States. It provides an opportunity for every boy, whether he be a natural, average, or poor athlete, to take an active part in sports with his fellow students. With Fr. Sturm, S.J., at the helm for the past few years, the intramural program here at Canisius has moved forward with an accelerated pace."[33] Prominent contests included basketball, baseball, volleyball, and football.

However strong the support for intramurals, however, there was strong pushback against the idea of their supplanting interscholastic competition—a real proposition at the time. Talk of dropping interscholastic sports in favor of intramurals was a hot topic in issues of *The Citadel* from the early 1960s. The first reference to it comes in a tiny note in the bottom right corner of page 3 in the November 17, 1961 issue, referring to a November 11 article published in *America*, the Jesuit magazine: "'Eliminate interschool competition and get back to intramural sports.' This comment brought many letters to the Nov. 11 issue of *America* from professors and teachers, but none from students. Let's hear what you have to say!"[34]

The Citadel's Sports Editor, Charles Lesh '61, penned an informed editorial for the December 20, 1961, issue. His essay offers a nicely stated expression of the balanced approach to athletic priorities to which Canisius and its fellow Jesuit high schools have long aspired:

...The chief arguments used by those against interscholastic athletics are that they do not add to a student's education; they give him a false sense of values, and they injure the school machine in finances and quality of teaching. Henry Steele Commager, professor of history and American studies at Amherst College, puts it this way, 'As now organized...Athletics contribute nothing whatever to education. They simply distract the time, energy, and attention of the whole community from the main business of education.' And he exhorts, 'An end to the building or maintenance of costly stadia! Let us make drastic reductions in expenditures for athletic equipment....no more travel expenses.'

...The solution is a mean not unlike the moderation of all things inherent in Jesuit education. I offer our own school as a good example of this mean in practice. We all have the benefits of extensive interscholastic athletic competition along with an excellent intramural program. Yet through a competent administration and faculty and cooperative student attitude, we have few of the unwanted abuses. Varsity athletics and winning ball games has not become the end of scholastic life. We have been willing to accept losing seasons rather than to lower academic standards through such practices as giving athletic scholarships to grammar school graduates and passing students on their athletic ability alone.... A large percentage of the student body competes in athletics yet maintains high classroom averages.... At our school athletics takes its proper place in the balanced education of the whole man.[35]

The response was definitive. In a follow-up article on December 20th, students were quick to shoot down the idea, citing a variety of reasons. Joseph Sansonese '64, a sophomore at the time, offered perhaps the most compelling rationale: "Definitely not, for the simple reason that at intramural games there are no girls and what's a game without girls. At least when we play Timon there are girls from the Mount and other schools."[36]

In any case, history has made clear: interscholastic athletics were here to stay.

An Assortment of Firsts

1961 marked the inauguration of the Buffalo Province football championship rivalry; this was essentially a contest between Canisius and the relatively new McQuaid Jesuit of Rochester. "This game will be just the beginning of the inevitable rivalry between the two Jesuit high schools in the Buffalo Province. A rivalry which I predict will grow and grow to such dimensions that it will someday even surpass in the eyes of our students the St. Joe's-Canisius rivalry."[37] So wrote Charles Lesh '61, sports editor. Little could Mr. Lesh know that the Buffalo Province would shortly be dissolved, merged with the New York Province—thus significantly diminishing the potential for a Province Rivalry such as he envisioned.

In another first—or rather, the first after a long interlude—1961 marked the resurgence of the senior motorcade before the St. Joe's football game. "After an interval of over eight years the senior class this year was extended the privilege of celebrating the annual football classic with St. Joe's by holding a motorcade," proclaimed *The Citadel*.[38]

The Citadel of March 23, 1962, reported that CHS hosted the First all Catholic Swimming Meet on March 31, 1962; CHS swimmers won the championship.[39]

A Legend in Discipline and Love: Father John Sturm, S.J., '35

On September 26, 2017, the Fr. John G. Sturm, S.J. '35 Legacy Fund Luncheon was held at the KeyBank Center in Buffalo. The fund was established by "the Downtown Priest Committee," a group of associates and former students of Father Sturm, to support scholarships and athletics at

Father Sturm with Tim Russert '68. Photo from CHS Archives.

Canisius. The name came from a moniker for Father Sturm that emerged following his time at Canisius, during his tenure at Saint Michael's Church. His book, *Life's a Dance, Not a Dress Rehearsal*, contains his reflections and conveys many of the lessons he shared with so many. On the back cover, Tim Russert '68 is quoted: "These words of faith and inspiration are as powerful and unique as Father Sturm himself. Long live the Downtown Priest!"[40] In Russert's own book, *Big Russ & Me: Father & Son: Lessons of Life*, he described Sturm's significant impact during his formative years at Canisius: "Sturm was a stocky man with huge, Popeye-like forearms; people said he had once been a Golden Gloves boxer, although nobody knew for sure. He roamed the halls like a drill sergeant.... With a mere look, he could stop you dead in your tracks and improve your attitude.... He grilled everyone, all the time. His persistent, powerful, prosecutorial style elicited fast and honest responses even from those who hadn't planned to tell the truth.... He was smart, earthy, and tough, but he was also fair—at least some of the time. If you were a football hero or the son of a wealthy donor, you were treated the same as everybody else.... He had an intrinsic sense of proportionality, and saved his toughest tactics for the most incorrigible students."[41]

During his senior year in November 2000, Dan Zak '01 (now a feature writer and reporter for *The Washington Post*) conducted a *Citadel* interview with Tom Fontana '69, the prominent creator of NBC's *Homicide: Life on the Street* and HBO's *Oz*. When asked about his "overriding image or memory from Canisius," Fontana responded, "The thing that I will probably remember the most of all was the discipline.... I remember the fact that everything I did learn was in terms of how to discipline myself. I know it's a weird thing to say that the best thing is discipline [but] you have to motivate yourself to have all that capacity to call on yourself to be the best person you can be because nobody else is going to expect that.... That's the discipline.... So I didn't learn so much about writing here as I did about how to have everything ready when I needed it to be ready."[42]

Much of the discipline to which Fontana attributes so much importance found its source in one man, who figured massively in the experience of thousands of 20th century Canisius students: Rev. John Sturm, S.J. '35 According to Father Ron Sams, S.J. '46, any history of Canisius would be incomplete without recollections of "the nineteen years of Father Sturm."[43] Father Sams, in his interview for this book, shared his thoughts on the iconic figure who served CHS from 1951-1969:

Everybody from those years knew Father Sturm. And when he left here after nineteen years, he went to St. Michael's and he started working in Marriage Encounter. And he had a complete change over in personality. He was all discipline here...and down there he was all love, peace, and joy. And he claims...he told me.... "I had a conversion."

Here's a great story. I'm not sure if I should mention this. There was one class who decided they were going to pull a prank at graduation. It had to do with the auditorium. One of the guys involved got a little uneasy...so he said to Father Sturm, "Father, you oughta take a look above the aud stage." So Sturm took the hint and he went up. And now, above the stage...it's three stories high...these characters who were planning the event...they had gotten an old-style [fire] extinguisher...when you tip it, the acid would react and it would shoot foam...they had it up there on a tilt. There was a time clock. The idea was that the clock was gonna be set for the middle of graduation. And when the clock went off, it would knock out the thing holding the tank, the reaction would happen, the foam would shoot out, and it would look like that big eagle let go all over the faculty below!

JOHNNY STURM
. . . showing his speed

Fr. Sturm's Heroic Days Are in Canisius Tradition

Sturm found it. He called in the whole class. And he said, "Not funny, fellas." He could talk turkey to these guys. And he said, "If the ones responsible do not come to me and admit it, none of you are going to graduate from the stage. None of you!" And that put the pressure on from the other guys. So three or four of the guys, maybe five that did it, they went to Sturm and admitted it. So he said, "Okay fellas. You five will not graduate from the stage. You'll get your diplomas quietly in August. Cause this is a serious thing. I want you to realize that.... We won't throw you outta school. You had the courage to admit it. But actions have reactions." So those five got their diplomas in August, and everyone else graduated normally.

He always said, "Mercy comes from God. I deliver justice." He was a controversial prefect of discipline, but the fellas that he dealt with canonized him. He's a saint to this day to them....[44]

Joe Lucenti '73 likewise offered some perspectives on his memories.

He probably was as scary a man as you could ever meet. Back then you could smoke in the school, and Father Sturm smoked cigars. There were times when he talked to you when he would blow that cigar smoke right into your face....

Father Sturm as prefect was tough and no nonsense. Very guttural in terms of his delivery.... John Sturm was definitely a blue-collar Jesuit. So, in 1985 I was named Dean of Students on Graduation Day.... Celebrating the Jubilee class, the class of 1935, were attend-

ing graduation and receiving an hon-orary diploma.... Father Sturm was a member of that class.... I'm sitting on stage, and suddenly, when he gets his diploma, it hits me: "Oh my God. I'm him." And again, that doubt comes in.

Like, I can't do this. I can't be Father Sturm. He's legendary. Iconic. So after-ward, there's a reception for the Jubilarians. Now I knew Father Sturm from marriage encounter. I shared this story with him. He looked at me and he said, "Joe, don't you dare ever try to be me. You need to be you." And he gave me wise words, because he said, "John Sturm could not do this job today." Because he recognized when his time had passed...the importance of fit and chemistry and that what kids needed in 1985 was very different in 1955 and 1965...and those are words that I took with me for the rest of my career, to this day: Just be me.

...Maybe his greatest influence was...that no matter how tough he was, you knew he cared. And I also learned that he treated freshmen different than seniors...you better damn well recognize the difference between a fourteen-year-old and an eighteen-year-old.[45]

"We Swam Naked in Gym Class!"

Alumni whose tenure at Canisius began before the mid-seventies—even if they've forgotten most everything else—might retain one clear, vivid memory: swimming naked in gym class.

According to longtime Phys. Ed. teacher and former Athletic Director Jeff Gemmer, this practice ended only in 1969 following a change to the health code. Prior to that, when it was time to swim in gym class, it was done in the nude.

This author inquired as to the rationale for swimming naked. A few reasonable assumptions come to mind for the pondering alumnus: Perhaps it was due to the practical difficulties that wet swimsuits would entail. But that didn't make sense, because wet towels would be an issue anyway. Or maybe it was a simple matter of expediency: class periods are short, we're all boys here, and swimming in the buff would trim the time required to get ready. But no, that didn't make sense either, because it's hard to imagine how donning and ditching a swimsuit could add much more than about twenty-three seconds at most.

No. It was nothing quite so obvious. Rather, according to Mr. Gemmer, naked swimming was simply a Health Code rule, although he remained perplexed as to the logic:

It was the Health Code at the time. I went to Kenmore East, and we swam naked there, in junior high and the high school. And when I came here, I was told, yeah, guys swim nude.... What sense did it make, because the swim team wore suits?

Every reunion it comes up. It's the guys' wives who always ask about it! Anyway, it ended shortly after Title IX, a few years after that, sometime in the early seventies.

The introduction of swimsuits marked the end of an era among physical education classes both at Canisius and other high schools with pools. It is safe to say that more than likely, it was a welcome change among many boys who dreaded the prospect of baring all in front of their peers during those sometimes-awkward years.

All the same, it's equally likely that among the alumni attending reunions, there will be at least a few sporting t-shirts that proclaim boldly, "I SWAM NAKED IN GYM CLASS AT CHS!"

Gallery: 1960s

Enquiring Reporter

Should Canisius Be Co-Ed?

| T. Vella | G. Harig | R. Tuyn | R. Lee |

Tony Vella, 3C: "Well, now that's a question I like! If it could be done, it would please a lot of guys (including myself, of course!). Separate swimming classes would be necessary, and I don't think many guys would like that. But I'm sure everyone will agree that C.H.S. should be co-ed!"

Gary Harig, 2B: "Definitely! I think very highly of the idea. If the faculty went for it, I'm sure the students would go along with it totally. As for my personal opinion I think it would be great working out on the football field with the new students!"

Robert Tuyn, 3C: "It would be a good idea, but then there is the problem of not getting homework, or anything else done. If this fine institution was co-'ed, how would the teachers get anything done? Let's have Canisius all-boy if we want to get a decent education."

Richard Lee, 3E: "Yes co-education at Canisius would keep the students awake in classes and would make Fr. Sturm's job much easier. (Ed's Note—How I'll never know!) Also the cheerleaders would be much better to look at than old Vince Cotroneo!"

Students on a potentially co-ed CHS. The Citadel, October 27, 1961, p.4

When Crusaders Come Cruising Along

Precisely at 1 p.m., Oct. 11, while all within and without the walls of Canisius was quiet (the rest of the Student Body was in class or on retreat), the Seniors went merrily up Delaware Avenue to let the northern section of the City know the St. Joe's game was going to be fought to the last whistle. The enthusiasm of the seniors failed to tie up traffic, but the fighting eleven tied the game.

See page four for more on this exciting re-awakening of spirit.

The St. Joe's game motorcade. The Citadel, October 27, 1961, p.1

By NICK NOWOSAD and TERRY ROY

Bob Crowell recently remarked to Father LaCombe that his pie was in desperate need of Extreme Unction . . . T.V. commercials confirm the fact that one meal from the Canisius cafeteria and a multiple vitamin pill will give one all the minimum daily requirements one normally needs to take.

When Father Sturm arrived at the restaurant, where class 4A was out to dinner, he was greeted by the juke box, playing his favorite song—Big John . . . Realizing that every man has an obligation to make a living, the Prefect has asked Mike Cotton to give the barber a break.

Three out of four Assistant Prefects of Discipline recommend aspirin for minor headaches of school distress, and four out of four of them take them themselves.

Mr. O'Connor sympathetically told some of his sophomore geometry students that the theorems were by no means easy—they're simple!

Mr. Palisano, an algebra teacher, told class 1D they should be in the army with him as sergeant—like, help?

George Washington would have been glad to know that Canisius did not forget his birthday; the school held a big all-day party in his honor compulsively open to all students.

A certain senior commented that Brother Rosenecker is the "Jesuit's answer to Friar Tuck."

Jack Haggerty, 2C, tried an electrical experiment in Latin class one ambitious day. He stuck the steel point of his compass in the electrical outlet—the results were shocking!

Will someone please tell some of the senior "smokers," that Fr. Mooney's office is not the center of the universe?

Amazingly, class 4C collected five dollars for the missions in two minutes—the only way they could get a teacher to forget about the quiz marks.

"All roads lead to Rome—Delaware leads to Canisius!"

Boost Canisius! (it's the only way to keep the building from falling apart.)

"Sounding Off" - Random news and notes from *The Citadel*, March 23, 1962, p.2

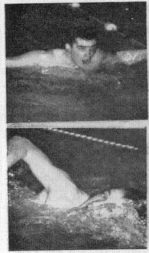

UPPER LEFT: Dave Burke butterflies. LOWER LEFT: Bill Bernbeck freestyles. RIGHT: Urban, Burke (1st row), Bernbeck, Bill Kean, Callaghan (2nd row), Cannamela, Zernentsch, Mc-Naughton, Noonan, and Art Kean (3rd row) reflect the glory of their victories. All except McNaughton who is from Duffy High are Coach Lamb's mermen.

Lambkins Overwhelm Opposition, Secure Nine First Place Wins In A-C Swim Meet

Led by double-winner Bill Bernbeck, the Canisius High Swimming Team stroked up nine of the ten first-place finishes in the first All-Catholic Swimming Meet held in the Crusaders' Pool three weeks ago, March 31.

Bernbeck, a senior, making his final appearance in an official meet as a finlambkin, took first place in the 200-yard freestyle and the 200-yard individual medley.

Other Canisius winners finishing first were: Pete Burke, 100-yard butterfly; Bill Kean, 100-yard backstroke; Walt Urban, 100-yard breaststroke.

Freshman Art Kean outclassed all opposition by taking first place in the 400-yard freestyle. Kev Noonan, a junior, grabbed the number one spot in the 100-yard freestyle.

In the 200-yard medley relay the Crusaders catapulted into first place with seniors Bill Kean, Pete Burke, Vince Callaghan, and junior, Walt Urman, stealing the victory.

Canisius' smallest men, Charley Zernentsch, Kev Noonan, Don Cannamella, and Art Kean, snatched the 200-yard free relay.

The only non-Canisius winner was Tom McNaughton from Bishop Duffy High School, who showed that interest in swimming in other Buffalo Catholic high schools is increasing rapidly. The swimmers from Dougherty, Timon, Turner, and Fallon were congratulated by the officials for their fine spirit and determination in this first event of its kind.

Swimming news from the first All-Catholic Swimming Meet held in the CHS pool. The Citadel, April 18, 1962, p.3

us At National Regatta

Coach Charley Fontana's oarsmen won two national championships in the finals of the 28th annual American Scholastic Regatta on the murky Schuykill River in Philadelphia, May 26.

By a boat length ahead of St. Catharines High School, Ontario, the senior crown came again to Fontana's last year's winning team — Tim O'Connor, Walt Urban, Kev Cheeley, G. Schwartzmueller, and Coxswain Bill Fenzel. The time was 5:40.

A sensational victory, since only two feet marked the lead over Washington-Lee High from Arlington, Va., crowned the junior crew champs. Maneuvering the winning shell were Tom O'Connor, Joe Krakowiak, Dick McCormick, Bill Cromwell, and Coxswain Arsene Gerber. Their time was 5:39.

The water gliders put in many strenuous hours of practice to prepare for this event. Coach Fontana had the fellows limbering up early in the year by trotting around the auditorium.

An embellished plaque will be forwarded to the winners commemorating their victories as soon as it is inscribed.

Each team member was presented with a jacket with the school emblem sewed on it.

Returning to 1180 Sunday afternoon, all smiles, with a cigar as big as an oar, Father John Sturm, S.J., moderator of Athletics, declared "Those guys pull mighty mean shells."

Two National titles for the rowing team, earned by legendary Coach Charles Fontana's crews. The Citadel, June 1, 1962, p.5. Images of the crews below.

Paul Cumbo

Father Sturm Gets In Citadel
Pic Draws Many Speculations

Never let it be said that The Citadel does not give everyone in the school full coverage. Because of a very urgent personal request, the picture to the right is being printed.

Who is the most talked about faculty member at Canisius? Who is the most well-known among students of other schools? When a Canisius man takes a girl to a school function who is the priest he always points out? Of course that person is Rev. John G. Sturm, S.J., Prefect of Discipline at Canisius High School.

Students and faculty were asked to deduce from the picture what Father Sturm was doing or saying. A sampling of their opinions will indicate to some extent the numerous duties of a Prefect of Discipline in a Jesuit High School.

One of the first opinions received was that he was watching the grass grow on the field. This was quickly contradicted by a student who said Father Sturm was resisting the temptation to stick his thumb out as he waited for a bus.

A frequent absentee commented that Father had just realized that the "mother" who had called in about her son's "illness" sounded a lot like a girl Father had talked to at a recent dance.

Other various thoughts were that he was trying to be the first person to disintegrate a freshman by a dirty look, or that he had discovered a new method of isometric contraction.

Many people thought Father Sturm was saying something. Most people usually open their mouth when they talk. But then again most people do not sound like Father Sturm.

Here are some of the imagined comments: "The second bell rang!" "Are these bermudas or pants?" "Did you swallow that cigarette?" "Discipline is our most important product!" "One

in the jug room is worth two in the third floor smoking room." "Didn't I see you go out the back door Friday? I don't care if you weren't in school Friday." "I don't care what the pizza tastes like. No riots in the cafeteria."

After all the good fun is finished one thing is left to be said. Although it is Father Sturm's often unpleasant task to see that the students do not enjoy themselves too much, he is one of the best liked

Fr. John G. Sturm, S.J.
... "All right! Youse Guys!"

priests at the school. At different sporting events and especially football games he is given a big hand by the Canisius crowd. At Christmas time he is the only one who receives a gift from the whole school.

An amusing look at Father Sturm's tremendous presence in CHS life in the 1960s. The Citadel, May 10, 1963, p. 3

Army Presents Canisians With Christmas 'Surprise'

Pvt. Donald A. Casciano, U.S.A., formerly Mr. Donald A. Casciano, history teacher at Canisius High School, is presently enjoying a six-month all-expenses-paid vacation through the courtesy of

Mr. Donald Casciano

Uncle Sam at picturesque Fort Dix, N. J.

In a recent visit to the home of Mr. Casciano's parents, Mr. and Mrs. Michael Casciano, **The Citadel** learned that "the Don" has finished basic training and is now engaged in clerical work. According to

Mr. 'C's" parents he is enjoying army life, and is in much better physical condition because of its rigors and maneuvers. Taking advantage of the camp's proximity to New York City, Mr. Casciano has attended the theater and football games there on the weekends.

Home for Christmas

The popular history mentor will fly to Buffalo for the holidays in order to be with his family. During his home stay he plans to visit the Blue and Gold Campus to extend his greetings to the faculty and his former pupils.

The senior Cascianos conjecture that their son's final day at Fort Dix will fall on or about the Ides of Feb.

Upon his release from the army, Mr. Casciano plans to continue his teaching career at Canisius.

His former students on many occasions have missed his colorful personality and his effective and interesting teaching methods.

Not only did Mr. Casciano rank highly as an instructor but gained wide renown as the coach of this year's undefeated tennis team.

A Christmas surprise "Mr. Cash" comes home on leave from Fort Dix, New Jersey. The Citadel, Dec. 18, 1963, p.8

Page Two

John Fitzgerald Kennedy
1917 - 1963

On a hill above the city of our nation's life,
there burns a flame.
The president is dead, "fallen like a mighty cedar."

Did he live in vain?

John Kennedy believed that men should not be hungry,
that they should not want for the basic necessities of life.
He lived in brotherhood with mankind.

Did he live in vain?

John Kennedy believed that the nations of the earth should be
free, that they are to be allowed to govern themselves,
and determine their own political destinies.

Did he live in vain?

John Kennedy held that all men must be free,
that their basic human rights cannot be denied them.
He held that all men are created equal.

Did he live in vain?

John Kennedy brought to this country a new sense of idealism,
a new sense of dedication to freedom's principles.
He was a martyr for an abiding peace.

Did he live in vain?

On a hill above the city of our nation's life,
there burns a flame.

CHS mourns the assassinated President John F. Kennedy. *The Citadel,*
Dec. 18, 1963, p.2

The Sports Chamber

By Andy Chambers, CITADEL Sports Editor

"THEY ARE THE GREATEST!" There's no two ways about it. This new, unoriginal, already overworked phrase is the only compact saying that could accurately describe Coach Connie and Company.

This fabulous five with a flare for the fantastic first overcame an eleven point deficit to tame a roaring Timon team. Then, after letting Captain Jeff Woeppel do a 16 minute solo act, Joe Michael's quartet teamed up with Wepp to give the Ryan Rams a run for the Cup, outscoring them 21-7 at one point, only to be outdone by one in the final outcome.

The 54-53 score at the end of 32 minutes reflects only a part of what really happened. Midway in the fourth quarter with the Rams rapidly retreating and the Crusaders fast closing the gap came the sudden splatter of a grade A fresh egg. With the help of slow clean-up job, Ryan received a precious gift of five minutes to recompose themselves and once again capitalize on their height and rebounding skills, the tall barrier which the Crusaders couldn't overcome.

After edging one point ahead, 49-48, Connie's quintet, lost its grasp of the coveted Cup as Paul Tokasz sunk both shots on a one and one with only seconds left.

IN THE LOCKER ROOM after the game there were no ranting, raving madmen shouting excuses for the loss, no horrified coach screaming angrily at the players for "letting him down," no tears shed for having lost this chance for glory; instead, pride shone on the faces of all. Replacing the expected ejectedness and sulking was the quiet murmur of congratulations and even a cake presented to Mr. Mack by the players to celebrate his 100th win as the Canisius coach, that victory coming over St. Mary's of Lancaster in the playoff quarterfinals.

When you lose a game of this type, when the players fight as ours did, when Greg Bonk had the stamina to limp out and play on an injury which pained him all season, when Jeff Woeppel, a standout in Canisius history, gives his greatest game in his three years on varsity, when the entire team employs an effective press to stage a fourth quarter come-from-behind rally, the second in three nights, when all this happens in one game it proves that there can be pride and glory in losing.

AS ANOTHER SPORTS WRITER said some years ago:
"For when the One Great Scorer
Goes to mark against your name,
He writes not that you won or lost,
But how you played the game." Grantland Rice

An insightful perspective on the type of sportsmanship Connie Mack cultivated. The Citadel, March 25, 1964, page 7.

Mr. Guariglia Named to Coach Canisius Matmen
Wrestlers Aim For Catholic League Competition

Wrestling made its way to Canisius last week under the auspices of Mr. Robert Guariglia. Although the team is still in the formative stage, 40 boys turned out enthusiastically with the first call.

Mr. Guariglia's immediate plans are mainly to familiarize the grapplers with various holds and positions taken in the matches.

The sport was installed at Canisius principally to give those boys athletically-inclined, but unsuted to other sports, the opportunity to participate. It also offers the fall and spring athlete the chance to keep in shape during the "off-season."

Match in February

There is a weight division in wrestling stretching all the way from 95 pounders to the unlimited class. This is the only limitation, that is, height is not a factor.

Coach Guariglia plans to hold the first two matches of the season in February, the first being with Kenmore East early in the month, the

COACH GUARIGLIA

second with Clarence Central later on.

The new mentor has hopes of seeing a Catholic wrestling league in the near future, since Turner and other schools are intrested. But for the time being, he is contented to campaign independently.

Wrestling comes to CHS. The Citadel, December 22, 1964, page 6.

272

Phys. Ed. Groups To Be Teamed Differently

Prior to this year the physical education teachers have found themselves in the predicament of facing class periods in which a wide range of abilities exists.

This ability range has run all the way from the physically gifted student to the obese and low-motor ability students. This common type of class organization is responsible to a degree for the inability of physical ed teachers to significantly affect mass development techniques. These techniques reach the majority of students but at present are not even being attempted.

However, starting with this year's freshman class, phys ed has been raised to the standards of the obvious. All one has to do now is glance at the patch sewn onto the front of a freshman's trunks in order to determine the condition of the student (i.e. unless Joe Schldbotnik is wearing Joe Atlas's equipment).

These patches are broken down into four color groups: white, royal blue, purple and gold. Any interscholastic athlete in good standing at the conclusion of a given season is eligible for silver.

To advance from one group to another, the student must attain ceiling performance in all fitness tests. Naturally the numbers and times change from group to group i.e. from 23 to 17 seconds in the agility run.

Among the tests taken are: pull-ups, push-ups, sit-ups, shuttle run, rope climb, agility run, 880 run, man lift and carry, and swimming. In order to advance, ceiling levels in all events must be attained.

According to Mr. Barnes, if any class were broken down, there would be five per cent who would stay in the white group, "the low-motor abilitied," who could just make it over the hump — and stay there.

Fireman's Carry

Chin-ups

A new Phys. Ed. policy involved classifying students by color-coded patches indicating their level of physical fitness. The author is not so sure this would fly in 2020! The Citadel, June 2, 1965, page 7.

Paul Cumbo

Ronald J. Hastreiter:
Varied activities take time
of veteran C.H.S. tutor

BY JAMES C. PLISZKA

During classtime you'll find Mr. Ronald Hastreiter driving home the intricacies of third year German. After school, during lunch, and in the morning before class he can be found in the Career Room. Here Mr. Hastreiter has aided many a bewildered senior plan his future.

Graduating from Canisius in 1950, Mr. Hastreiter has experienced those same moments. He went on to Canisius College to receive his Bachelor of Arts Degree. That year he began his teaching career here.

In 1956 his academic life was interrupted when he was issued a rifle and spent the next two years in the service. He served in the U.S. and Germany with a unit classified as top secret. As Sergeant First Class he was discharged in 1958. Though his duty was as an interpreter, he managed to teach at the base school.

From the army Mr. Hastreiter returned to Canisius to resume his career. In 1961 he obtained his Masters Degree in Education from Canisius College, and as a result he has taught basic and intermediate German at the college level.

Wed in 1960 to his wife June, he is the father of three, David five, Karen four, and Mariann nine months. Although he is now busy with his academic work and keeping up the house, he admits that his idle time is spent fishing and hunting.

A profile of Mr. Ronald Hastreiter, who would go on to serve CHS as a longtime faculty member. The Citadel, September 29, 1966.

A-C's McNaughton and White

Hermes Hoak wings home

Singers Handle Handel

Harriers Sweep AC's Jr. Varsity and Frosh Post Perfect Records

For the first time in the history of the Monsignor Martin League, one school captured the three coveted All-Catholic championships: Varsity, J.V., and Freshman. The 39 dedicated Canisius harriers achieved this pinnacle goal, in the words of coach James Skipper, "... with the ability and the desire, the hard work and determination" of a true team.

Varsity Cleans 8-1 Record

Captain Dan McNaughton, defeated three times during the regular season, let St. Joe's Marty Jacobi pace him for the first lap and for most of the final lap around the Delaware Lake course. Then, with about a quarter mile remaining McNaughton broke into a sprint to win decisively in 12:59.4.

The Crusader's next finisher was Senior Kev White, who capped a tremendous season of constant improvement, coming in fifth behind Mark Ryerson of Dougherty, John Hausle and Jacobi of St. Joe's, and McNaughton. Not far behind was Junior Bill Fisher in eighth, and an improved Herm Mogavero in eleventh.

Both Fisher and Mogavero worked hard and moved up several slots during the fatal second lap. Mogavero, like White, climaxed his rapid improvement in the November 3 meet.

Perhaps the most forgotten, but necessary factor to the A-C and season victories, is Senior Ted Wantuch. Placing twenty-third, he was often the crucial fifth place finisher for the Blue and Gold. Five men, however, don't make a team. Coach Skipper doesn't hesitate to say that each victory is a team effort.

Big news for the Cross-Country team. The Citadel, November 23, 1966, page 4.

275

Paul Cumbo

Citadel Takes Consensus Survey
Poll Reveals Harmony of Opinion

BY DAVE KOSIUR

During the past few weeks, students of CHS have had the opportunity to express their opinions and tastes through the recent poll conducted by the *Citadel*. Although the *Citadel* received less than helf of the forms it distributed, the forms returned provided an adequate cross-section of student opinions and tastes.

A large majority (85.4%) of the students felt that they would benefit from choosing their own courses, drawing on equally heavy support from every year, including 100% agreement from the Freshmen. Powered by reinforcements from the frosh and Seniors (76.7% and 82.4%, respectively), compulsory Summer reading received a small majority (62.5%). A great number (64.6%) felt that CHS needed only a two-year Latin program, with all others running far behind.

The *Citadel* received enormous support from the students concerning its articles. More than three-fourths of the students (77%) read *Citadel* editorials, generally considering them to be "better than those in the past". However, fewer students (72.9%) liked the Damsel of the Month column, some stating the often-heard views, "it's good for a few laughs" or "we don't need a monthly reminder of what girls look like".

Sports are an easy pushover for the most impressive activity (54.6%), drama, the next closest, far behind (16.8%). Many felt that the school now needs a comedy play (37.8%), with musical plays the closest second (23.1%).

Movies played a large role in influencing student tastes concerning modern literature, as Ian Fleming is considered the most widely read author (20.7%), though his works might be more widely seen than read. Hemingway was second with half as many votes (10.5%), with his largest number of supporters coming from the Seniors. Surprisingly, Fleming was not the favorite modern author (10.5%), as Salinger edged him out (12.6%) with heavy support from third and fourth years, showing the influence of their English classes.

As might be expected, television is the most favored medium of entertainment (39.6%), with music, radio, theater, and movies not far behind.

The most popular girls' school is Mt. St. Joseph's (29.4%), with Mt. St. Mary's (14.7%), Mount Mercy (10.5%) and Holy Angels (also 10.5%) following.

Student interests varied greatly, as shown by their favorite publications. *Time* was first (21%), with *Life* (18.9%) and *Sports Illustrated* (12.6%) close behind.

A great number of the students (85.4%) agreed that the US should be in Viet Nam under its present status, although many felt that LBJ would be unseated in the next election by Romney (56.7%). Some (21%) felt that Nixon would stage a comeback and upset LBJ.

Drawing on firm support from the Seniors (76.5%), while the other years gave shaky agreement, the general opinion is that there are such things as UFOs (64.6%).

Led by the Sophomores (77.7%), CHS students felt that the modern views on sex are not too radical (54.1%).

All in all, the cross-section of student views and opinions produced general student harmony.

An opinion poll reveals aspects of the school culture in the mid-1960s. The Citadel, December 14, 1966, page 3.

Mackmen Shock St. Joe's 62-61
1300 Witness Marauder Clipping

Fran Cosgrove played the mighty role of the spoiler as a spirited audience of some 1,300 spectators overflowed the Canisius Auditorium to enjoy a basketball war set in storybook fashion. St. Joe's high-riding Maroon invaded Canisius sitting on first place, flashing a 7-1 record and left marooned in second place in the Burke Division, losers to our Crusaders.

Fran poured in 29 pressure points on 9 buckets and 11 free throws, all highlighted by a game-winning charity shot during the last 10 seconds of the tangle. He and his counterpart, Joe Alessi who contributed 19 more points, were superlative off the boards, saving the Crusaders a life time and again. The third member of the "trio", Dave Amborski, played a stellar defensive game, contributing 9 points.

Kevin Spitler paced the Marauders with 21 points. All WNY Dale Tepas, troubled by a box-on one thrown up by the Blue and Gold, meshed 19 but fouled out at the game's most crucial point and killed most of the St. Joe punch.

The game climaxed in a wild frenzy as the loyal Canisius crowd flooded the floor to congratulate their gallant charges.

Tigers End Six-Game Streak

A brilliant six-game win streak was shattered at Timon in a "heated" contest witnessed by a packed house in the South Buffalo gym. Even though Fran Cosgrove meshed a generous 31 points and Joe Alessi melted the ribs for 30 more, the Tigers squeezed by 83-82 on an errant in-bounds pass which subsequently set up the game-winning free throw for Roger Kremblas with four seconds remaining in the game.

Paul Grys clicked for 22 points to lead the Tigers, followed by Rog Kremblas with 21.

Three days earlier, the Crusaders silenced Turner's Terriers after experiencing three quarters of stiff opposition. The Terriers held single-point leads in each of the first three stanzas, but the Crusaders went on to win 61-47.

The "Big 3" of Alessi, Cosgrove and Amborski accounted for 57 of Canisius' 73 points to lead the "Dandies" to a 73-58 thumping of Dougherty's Cards. Cosgrove with 22, Alessi with 19, and Amborski with 16 points set the pace for Canisius. Guard Joe Provenzano led with 16 points for the Cards.

The Duffy Rapideers roared into the Delaware auditorium on January 13, eager to upset Canisius and capture second place. After the evening was over, the Crusaders had posted a convincing 74-52 triumph.

Joe Alessi
....who needs Law?

Dave Amborski tallied a career high of 31 points on 12 field goals and 7 charity shots to lead the Crusader scoring spree. Fran Cosgrove contributed 14 more. Gary Bevilacqua led the Rapideers with 14 points.

Crusaders Get 84-71 Victory

The Canisians visited Tonawanda on January 8th to tangle with O'Hara. Alessi, Cosgrove and Amborski manhandled the Hawks off the boards as the Crusaders returned with a decisive 84-71 victory.

Previously, Canisius had defeated Neumann 70-55, and Fallon's Flyers 61-40, in a string of six straight victories.

Coach McGillicuddy's trio of forecourtmen has made the big difference this year, as hustle has been emphasized to defeat many quicker teams. Amborski, Cosgrove and Alessi are all among the top 15 in the league scoring race.

"...a basketball war set in storybook fashion..." The Citadel, Feb. 8, 1967, page 3.

Paul Cumbo

Debaters Qualify At NYS Finals
Clabeaux Shines In Nationals

CHS debaters are now culminating the end of a busy season and in the past few weeks have added numerous triumphs to an already successful season.

In the past weeks the debaters have traveled to many parts of the country and now are winding up the season with contests in Jamestown, Albany, Atlantic City, Oswego, and Washington, D. C.

Herman Mogavero, Ronald Huebsch, Herbert Sturm, and Timothy McNeill led the Junior Varsity team to second place in the March 18th New York State Regional Tournament in Jamestown, which qualified them for the New York State Finals held in Albany on April 14 and 15. At the same tournament the two Canisius Novice teams consisting of Chriss, Kris, Kelly, and Weiss on Team A, and Mezei, Zyla, Herman, and Moleski on Team B took first and second places. These two novice teams also participated in the New York State Finals.

Canisius Squads were also competed in Oswego on April 21 and 22 to defend their first place lead in the National Forensic League District. The winners of these district finals are being sent to the national finals in Louisville, Kentucky.

Individual success qualifies Timothy McNeill to compete in the National Catholic Oratory League Finals on May 4, 5 and 6 in Atlantic City. McNeill was the only Canisius orator to qualify for the finals during the preliminaries held here at Canisius. Success has also come to another Canisius orator, Thomas Clabeaux, at the National CYO Boy's Finals held in Washington, D.C., in which he won second place.

Figure 1 The Behrens Debate Society earned notable successes in this era. The Citadel, Apr 26, 1967, page 6.

fr. arrupe to visit

Very Rev. Fr. Arrupe SJ

Jesuits, their families and devoted friends will have the honor of greeting Very Reverend Peter Arrupe SJ, Superior General of the Society of Jesus in Rome, when he visits the three major cities of the Buffalo Province for the first time on May 4-5.

A private plane will bring Father Arrupe, otherwise known as Father General, from Cleveland to Buffalo on Thursday, May 4, at 3:15 p.m. Jesuit superiors in the Buffalo area will meet Father General at the airport and travel by limousine directly to Canisius High School for a private reception by Buffalo area Jesuits.

In the school foyer, each Jesuit priest, brother and scholastic will personally meet Father General. To record this historic occasion, pictures will be taken of Father General with each Jesuit community.

Then a private dinner for the Buffalo area Jesuits is scheduled in the Canisius High School Library. At this special gathering, Father General will address the fellow members of his Jesuit family.

After dinner, Father General will be escorted to Canisius College where he will meet His Excellency James A. McNulty, Bishop of Buffalo, at 7 p.m. A civic reception will begin at 7:30 in the Canisius College Student Center where the families of Jesuits will have the opportunity to greet Father General. Then, because time is limited, groups and organizations associated with Buffalo area Jesuits will have only selected representatives meet Father General.

At 9 p.m., Father General will conclude his first visit to Buffalo. He plans to fly directly to Syracuse where he will spend the night at the Jesuit Provincial's Residence.

On the morning of May 5, Father General will concelebrate Mass at Le-Moyne College in Syracuse. Then, after a brief reception by the Jesuits, lay faculty and students of LeMoyne, he will fly to Rochester for a similar reception at McQuaid Jesuit High School. At 2 p.m., Father General's historic visit to the Buffalo Province will end as he leaves by private plane for Montreal.

In Montreal, Father General's primary objective will be to address a gathering of all the Jesuit Missions Directors in North America. Rounding out his busy itinerary, Father General will visit three Canadian Jesuit Provinces before returning to his official residence at the Jesuit Curia in Rome.

Canisius High School hosted Very Reverend Peter Arrupe, S.J., Superior General of the Society of Jesus, in 1967. It is Father Arrupe who coined and popularized the phrase, "Men for Others." The Citadel, April 26, 1967, page 1.

James E. Hennessy
Faculty Focus:
Teacher, Traveler and Two-stepper

A man of varied interests and pursuits is Mr. James Hennessy, four year veteran on the faculty. Mr. Hennessy taught Latin his first two years, but now teaches German I and II. Rounding out his student-teacher relations, Mr. Hennessy moderates the Canisius bowling team.

After graduating from CHS in '58, he proceeded to Canisius College where he received his B.A. in Education in '63, and completed work on his Master's Degree there in '66.

When the school day ends, Mr. H. turns his attention to athletic and social activities. In sports he is a member of hockey, baskeball, and bowling teams, while in social circles he belongs to the Amherst Male Glee Club and as a bachelor, enjoys another favorite pastime, dancing.

Having traveled all around the United States and to parts of Europe, Mr. Hennessy will again be traveling abroad this summer with several Canisius students destined to study German in Kitzbuehel, Austria, and Cologne, Germany.

Auf Wiedersehen!

A profile of Mr. James Hennessy, longtime faculty member. The Citadel, June 1, 1967, page 2.

Russert Takes Up CYO Duties
Sweeps Into Unanimous Victory

Taking the helm of the Catholic Youth Organization of the Buffalo Diocese this year is Senior Tim Russert of 4G.

Elections took place at the Diocesan Youth Convention at the Statler Hilton Hotel

Tim Russert

earlier last month. An installation ceremony followed at St. Joseph's Old Cathedral, presided over by Auxiliary Bishop Stanislaus Brzana. Among the many congratulations Russert received was a surprise telegram from Senator Robert Kennedy.

"My main objective as CYO Diocesan President," said Russert at the Youth Convention, "will be to develop a mutual rapport among all Christian youth and help them realize their religious, cultural, social, and athletic responsibilities."

Russert's duties as president include conducting regular meetings of the Junior Senate, which consists of divisional CYO representatives, and attending New York State and national CYO meetings.

Russert is also one of nine officers elected recently by the American Legion Boy's State convention.

NOTARO ROOFING CO.

Above: Tim Russert '68 featured as CYO Diocesan President. *The Citadel*, Nov 2, 1967, page 6. Below: Photographic evidence of hockey on the back field. Undated photo. Included in a 20-year retrospective picture page. *The Citadel*, Dec. 18, 1968, page 3.

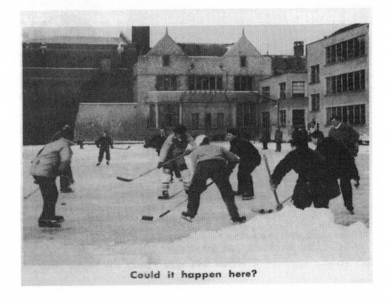

Could it happen here?

Paul Cumbo

Fr. Paul Naumann SJ:
belief and unbelief

Once upon a time a grammar school student from Ellsmere (near Albany) was heard but not seen in a Sunday School pageant. While his brother was on stage as a shepherd, he was off stage in the chorus. This greatly influenced the life of Fr. Pal Naumann SJ.

Not until he attended LeMoyne College as an English major did he come into his own as an actor in *The Man Who Came to Dinner* and *Macbeth.*

After three years at LeMoyne, Father entered the Society of Jesus at St. Andrew-on-Hudson in Poughkeepsie, New York, where he completed his Classics studies. He later attended Fordham University and Weston College in Massachusetts for studies in Philosophy and Theology.

A favorite pass-time during his philosophical studies was collaborating with his fellow Jesuit seminarians in the production of original musicals and skits. This experience led to his becoming dramatics moderator during Reegncy at St. Peter's Prep in Jersey City.

During the past summer the Jesuit General, Very Rev. Pedro Arrupe SJ, appointed Father Naumann as one of the delegates from the United States to study the problems of belief and unbelief in contemporary life. He journeyed to Denver, Colorado, to attend a seminar with American Jesuits studying the problem and its relationship to American life. "I'm sort of the 'Village Atheist,'" Father remarked.

Father Naumann has contributed to various publications in his "spare time," including *Perspective, Catholic Educational Quarterly,* and *Worship.* He co-authored the experimental English syllabus now in use at Canisius and at several high schools throughout the country. He is also writing a book about the poetic imagination and knowledge of God.

As a member of the CHS faculty, he teaches Junior and Senior English. Moreover, he has directed *The Fantastiks, Inspector General,* and recently *Hamlet.*

Father Paul Dugan SJ

Once a high school student cheering for arch-rival St. Joe's, Father Paul Dugan S.J., with roles reversed, has become one of the Crusaders' most loyal fans, encouraging the Blue and Gold both during the games and at practice.

Father Dugan, a graduate of St. Joe's class of 1941, went on to Canisius College before entering the Society of Jesus. He taught for seven years at McQuaid High School in Rochester before coming to Canisius in 1965.

The only Jesuit faithfully attending every football and basketball practice as well as every game, Father Dugan knows where the action is.

Perhaps Father Dugan's greatest triumph is on the slopes of Glenwood Acres, where he travels every Friday night with members of the Ski Club. Not only has he become an accomplished skier, but also has made it possible for many students to develop interest and skill in the sport.

Besides teaching Freshman and Sophomore Religion, Father Dugan moderates the Loyola Guild, an organization for the relatives of Buffalo area Jesuits.

Profiles of Jesuit faculty members Father Paul Naumann, S.J., and Father Paul Dugan, S.J., *The Citadel* Nov 29, 1967, page 2 and Feb 14, 1968, page 2, respectively.

Our Neighbors are watching.

Each day countless Crusaders turn their bored gaze from their classrooms to the windows, across the athletic field, and finally on to the tall red West Ferry apartment building. Some try to calculate the best way to put a ball through the windows; others try to figure out what those carvings really are; it's even been reported that some freshmen used to think it was a dorm! But everybody looks at it one time or another. But guess what — they're looking back!

Two of the many pairs of eyes belong to Mr. and Mrs. Richard Danahy, seven year residents of the building. And what are their comments on the swinging seven years of gym classes, dances, and football games, what is their opinion of their neighbors? "We're proud to have Canisius as a neighbor. I imagine everybody feels this way."

Mr. Danahy believes that Canisius men are "real gentlemen, a tribute to the administration and faculty." He believes they're neat, cautious, and they even carry over this courtesy to their classes. In fact, they can't remember any dance or social event ever disturbing them!

They even enjoy watching such things as

On a Clear Day...

gym classes. "Sometimes when we sleep in," says Mrs. Danahy, "we're awakened by "1-2-3-4." Mr. Danahy, "gets a kick" out of the football games as well.

Even during the summer the Danahy's are entertained by their neighbors. This time the students are younger in the Canisius Day Camp. The daily raising of the flag, with everybody at attention, is a special favorite.

Furthermore, says Mr. Danahy, "Nothing has changed the years we've been here, nothing has changed. It always was a good school."

As for the future, the Danahy's have but two suggestions. First, Mr. Danahy would like to see the old rivalry between CHS, St. Joe's and his own alma mater, Nichols, renewed.

Lastly, they complained of their furniture being soiled by flying ashes from our outdoor incinerator.

So beware students — and janitors — Mr. and Mrs. Danahy are watching you!

—M. Barnas

. . . you can even see N. Tonawanda

Some perspectives on the view from 800 West Ferry, which has loomed over thousands of CHS students for years. *The Citadel*, November 6, 1968, page 2.

UPPERCLASSMEN DEBATE SMOKING ISSUE

Early this year a group of non-smoking seniors and lay faculty members presented a petition to the administration requesting that it "review its policy concerning smoking in the senior lounge.

Swish: A Solution . . .

Contending that smoking seniors "had no right to endanger our health," seniors Mike Perley and Dick Hoar drew up the NO SMOKING petition just before Christmas vacation. This document urged "that another place be appropriated for senior smoking." Eventually this sheet obtained seventy-three valid senior signatures. They were supported by all the physical education instructors and nine other lay faculty members.

Principal Asks Students Advice

The administration in turn handed the "hot-sheet" over to the Senior and Junior Year Committees for their advice noting that another location for smokers was unavailable. The Seniors and Junior Committees unanimously recommended the retention of smoking.

As a basis for this decision the committees issued a joint recommendation, a portion of which stated, "We feel that if smoking were removed, attendance in the lounge would be held to a minimum as it was last year. The lounge as a meeting place for seniors would no longer exist. "In addition, the health hazard problem has greatly lessened with the installation of the Student Council financed fans.

On behalf of the petitioners, senior Mike

Puff: Privilege or Problem?

Perely commented, "As far as I am concerned with the fans put in and the proper ventilation provided, the issue is as good as settled."

Several side issues came into the air from this movement. One concerned the process in which this petition was handled. Senior Robert Martin expressed the general view of the committees saying, "I feel that this petition was definitely out of place. It should have been presented to the Student Council or year committees and action could have been started on it there."

The cover story of the March 5, 1969, *Citadel* reveals just what a different world it was back then.

Arena Dedications: 1961-1970

1961 - Ryrie E. MacTaggart

"The man and his work at Canisius will not soon be forgotten, and though Canisius mourns his loss, she rejoices to have received the benefit of his generous labors."

1962 - Charles I. Diemert, John F. Barnes, & Nicholas H. Kessler

"The above members of our faculty have contributed their time and talents to our school for a total of 128 years. Inspired by the example which they have shown us and in gratitude for their labors, we dedicate to them this 1962 *Arena* Yearbook."

Msrs. Charles I. Diemert; John F. Barnes; Nicholas H. Kessler.

1963 - Coaches John Barnes, Charles Fontana, Connie McGillicuddy, Paul Lamb, & Robert Murray

"We here at Canisius High School are fortunate in having a coaching staff who are not only able to teach boys to succeed in athletic contests but who can also lead them down the road to success as good Catholic gentlemen. For they know that the boy who wins as a competitor but loses as a man is a failure. Therefore, with this in mind, we dedicate the 1963 *Arena* to the varsity coaches."

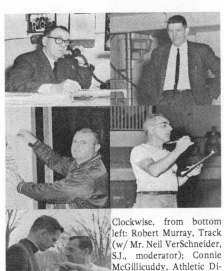

Clockwise, from bottom left: Robert Murray, Track (w/ Mr. Neil VerSchneider, S.J., moderator); Connie McGillicuddy, Athletic Director & Basketball; John Barnes, Football & Baseball; Charles Fontana, Crew; Paul Lamb, Swimming.

1964 - No dedication given.

1965 - Brother Paul A. Rosenecker, S.J.,

"It was the first day of school in early September, 1939, when a slightly chubby young Jesuit Brother unlocked a door marked 'Assistant Treasurer' for the first time.... The boys who came in wore knickers and close-cropped hair, and paid $120.00 a year in tuition.... But one thing has not changed...there has always been a crowd of smiling boys squeezed into Brother Rosie's office before school, during recess, during lunch, and even after school. Seniors and Freshmen alike...like being near him and he likes having them around. Twenty-five classes have graduated since Brother arrived, almost four-thousand boys have passed through his office, paid their tuition, and found a lasting friend"

1966 - In Memoriam - Brother Paul A. Rosenecker, S.J.,

"A year ago the *Arena* proudly dedicated its Golden Anniversary Issue to Brother Paul A. Rosenecker, S.J., and wished him well as he began his second quarter-century of devoted service to Canisius High School. Now, less than a year later, Brother has been called by God to his eternal reward...*Requiescat in Pace.*"

1967 - No dedication given.

1968 - Edward T. Mayer

"His work as a teacher and his influence as a friend has been felt by Canisius students for the last thirty years. Beneath his stern expression, Mr. Mayer is a man of dedication and devotion...His name is synonymous with Canisius, and innumerable students have known his kindness and interest. Adherence to one's principles is a rare trait in the world today and so it is fitting that we dedicate the 1968 *Arena* to a man who possesses such great integrity."

1969 - Connie McGillicuddy

Although not containing any entry explicitly labeled as an *Arena* dedication, the 1969 *Arena* opens with an honor for Mr. McGillicuddy upon his twenty-fifth year at the school. "During the last twenty-five years...[he] has held the unique responsibility of instructing Canisius students both in the classroom and on the playing field. This unusual ability is indicative of his sincere devotion."

1970 - No specific dedication; tribute to Mr. Edward Mayer upon his retirement (see 1968 dedication, above).

Notes

[1] *Arena,* The Canisius High School Yearbook, 1949, p.80-87.

[2] "History, Heritage, and Tradition." Article on the website of the Wendell August Forge Company. Accessed August 8, 2017. https://www.wendellaugust.com/page/history

[3] Notes from Apr. 16, 2010, interview between CHS library staff and Mr. Joseph Pisoni. Source: CHS Archives

[4] Interview at CHS with Rev. Richard Zanoni, S.J., January 27, 2017.

[5] *Ibid.*

[6] *Ibid.*

[7] Letter from Rev. Donald L. Kirsch, S.J., to Very Rev. John B. Janssens, S.J., Dated Jan. 15, 1961. Source: CHS Archives.

[8] *Ibid.*

[9] *Ibid.*

[10] Letter from Rev. Donald L. Kirsch, S.J., to Very Rev. John B. Janssens, S.J., Dated Feb. 27, 1962. Source: CHS Archives.

[11] Letter from Rev. Donald L. Kirsch, S.J., to Very Rev. John B. Janssens, S.J., Dated Sep. 14, 1962. Source: CHS Archives.

[12] Letter from Rev. Donald L. Kirsch, S.J., to Very Rev. John B. Janssens, S.J., Dated Jan. 4, 1963. Source: CHS Archives.

[13] Letter from Rev. Donald L. Kirsch, S.J., to Very Rev. John B. Janssens, S.J., Dated Jul. 22, 1963. Source: CHS Archives.

[14] Letter from Rev. Donald L. Kirsch, S.J., to Very Rev. John B. Janssens, S.J., Dated Jan. 10, 1964. Source: CHS Archives.

[15] Letter from Rev. Donald L. Kirsch, S.J., to Very Rev. John B. Janssens, S.J., Dated Aug. 25, 1964. Source: CHS Archives.

[16] Letter from Rev. Robert Burns, S.J., to Very Rev. Pedro Arrupe, S.J., Dated Jan. 17, 1966. Source: CHS Archives.

[17] Letter from Rev. Robert Burns, S.J., to Very Rev. Pedro Arrupe, S.J., Dated Aug. 26, 1967. Source: CHS Archives.

[18] *Ibid.*

[19] Letter from Pedro Arrupe, S.J., Superior General, to constituents of the Buffalo and New York Provinces. Dated November 13, 1967.

[20] Letter from Rev. Robert Burns, S.J., to Very Rev. Pedro Arrupe, S.J., Dated Jan. 20, 1968. Source: CHS Archives.

[21] Undated and untitled history of the 1967-1968 academic year, located alongside other materials related to the 1969 Middle States Accreditation process. Source: CHS Archives.

[22] Second Century Fund brochure, 1969.

[23] Second Century Fund appeal mailing, 1969.

[24] *The Citadel* student newspaper. Vol. 20, No. 4. Feb. 6, 1969. "Middle States Advises Needed Improvements."

[25] *Ibid.*

[26] From the Middle States Accreditation Self Study for 1969 accreditation; no author noted. Source, CHS Archives.

[27] *Ibid.*

[28] *The Citadel* student newspaper. Vol. 13, No. 5. Feb. 2, 1962. "Wanted: Canisius Man of the Year."

[29] Source: Mr. Canisius Award Plaque.

[30] *The Citadel* student newspaper. Vol. 13, No. 6. Feb. 23, 1962. "Sing to Me About Mr. C., Says Chairman Joe Mendola."

[31] *The Citadel* student newspaper. Vol. 13, No. 7. Mar. 23, 1962. "Faculty Members Consent to Oversee Mr. C Voting."

[32] *The Citadel* student newspaper. Vol. 13, No. 8. Apr. 18, 1962. "Not a Popularity Contest, Students Are Reminded."

[33] *The Citadel* student newspaper. Vol. 13, No. 2. Oct. 6, 1961. "Intramural Report."

[34] *The Citadel* student newspaper. Vol. 13, No. 3. Nov. 17, 1961. "Sportsman's Corner."

[35] *Ibid.*

[36] *The Citadel* student newspaper. Vol. 13, No. 4. Dec. 20, 1961. "Drop Interscholastic Sports for Intramurals?"

[37] *The Citadel* student newspaper. Vol. 13, No. 2. Oct. 6, 1961. "Intramural Report."

[38] *The Citadel* student newspaper. Vol. 13, No. 3. Oct. 27, 1961. "St. Joe's Motorcade Meets Seniors, Sees New Canisius High Spirit."

[39] *The Citadel* student newspaper. March 23, 1962.

[40] Sturm, John, S.J., *Life's a Dance, Not a Dress Rehearsal.* Tony Walker Books. Buffalo, NY. 2003.

[41] Russert, Tim. *Big Russ & Me – Father and Son: Lessons of Life.* Tenth Anniversary Edition. Weinstein Books. New York, NY. 2014

[42] Zak, Dan '01. "Follow the Yellow Brick Road." *The Citadel*, Volume 52, Issue 4. December 2000.

[43] Personal interview with Rev. Ronald Sams, S.J., '46. October 3, 2016.

[44] *Ibid.*

[45] Personal interview with Joe Lucenti '73. Dec 21, 2016.

CHAPTER 10

The 1970s

THE SEVENTIES MARKED a significant period of transition on
multiple levels. Academically, the school underwent a radical transformation in terms of curricular approach and philosophy—a change that
would see a pendulum shift toward progressive pedagogical theory followed soon thereafter by a return to more traditional norms. Culturally,
one perhaps needed look no further than the elimination of ties from the
100-year-old tradition for a fitting sign of the times. A relaxed dress code
might be viewed as tremendously symbolic of many aspects of these

changes. Rev. Jim Van Dyke, S.J., '77,* whose time as a student gave him witness to the core of the decade, offered some reflective insight during an interview for this book.

I think the most important thing to understand about Canisius High School in the seventies was the enormous flux, and sense of flux, in the period... The sixties had a very powerful effect, especially for those of us who had older brothers. We had come out of a very WWII, Korean, Eisenhower world—a JFK world fraught with idealism, but also with the turmoil of a growing Civil Rights Movement. A very public one. A world that very quickly became very violent, in a way that nobody quite expected. There was an enormous sense that cities were falling apart. Buffalo changed very radically.... There was a lot of injustice. Redlining and blockbusting was very prominent.... It was a pretty volatile world.

One of our first and most prominent memories would be the assassination of John F. Kennedy. It was very televised. Robert Kennedy and Martin Luther King being assassinated looms large in people's imagination at that time as well.

The popularization of the "soundtrack of the time," the popularity and availability of transistor radios was really remarkable...the massive spread of rock n' roll and protest music [was notable].

The very public nature of the Vietnam War, and a growing sense of the injustice...and the uselessness of that...a real polarization of young people and old people. I think, here in Buffalo, maybe even more [than other places] because of the size of the college population and the proximity to the Canadian border. The possibility of someone's brother being drafted and going across the border was a real one.

Certainly, when I was a freshman, I had no idea whether I might be drafted, or if my brother might, and there was really no end in sight.... [At Canisius]

---

* Father Van Dyke, S.J., is serving as President of Georgetown Preparatory School at the time of this book's initial publication.

we were able to "stave it off," but the rest of the cultural ferment couldn't be staved off.

The beginning of drug culture was not a small part of life here at Canisius.... We were aware that there were kids very actively smoking dope very regularly, and that it was impacting them. It was certainly very easily available.... There was a pretty free easy drinking culture as well.

A lot of that added up here to a situation at the school where there was not a lot of acceptance of authority for authority's sake. The breakdown of discipline was pretty drastic and pretty radical.... Part of it was that we'd had those long years under [Father] John Sturm [S.J.], who was a real disciplinarian. Some people would say that he was "draconian." After that, there was a series of less authoritative presences in the Dean's office.

One of the things that was positive was that good teaching was good teaching. People who were genuinely seen as interested in our education; genuinely challenging to our thinking; genuinely challenging to our growth—they were very powerful. [1]

Fr. Van Dyke's perspectives echo those of longtime Dean of Students Joe Lucenti '73.

It was scary. It was frightening. I remember taking the bus at the time, and I would transfer on Delaware, and I would walk from Delaware to Washington Street, around where the convention center is now. I can remember when the anti-war protests were taking place. There was a march coming down Delaware Avenue from U.B. All these students had come down Main Street to Niagara Square. All the sudden there's this massive amount of people. Now, I'm a clean-cut Canisius kid, in my shirt and tie and sport coat and proper hair and everything. And here come these long-hair hippies. And what I remember most shocking to me—and here's a little naivete—was the chant: "One, two, three, four, we don't want your fucking war!" And I remember thinking, "Wow, they're really shouting that." And of course, I didn't understand the politics of the war. I grew up, much like Tim Russert, you know, "God, country, family." Those were the three things that mattered in life. And you don't diss your country. You don't protest soldiers fighting for your country. Of course, that was my own naivete, and obliviousness to what was going on. But at the same time, one of the things about Canisius that affected me as I grew older was understanding what was wrong about the war.

Rev. Enrico Raulli, S.J.

I had an English teacher my sophomore year by the name of Father Rico Raulli.⁹ Great guy. Jesuit priest. And he was as radical as the day was long. His mantra was the clenched fist, power to the people. And one day, we're in 1E4. Back then, the windows in that wing were big. All the sudden, like five hippies, for lack of a better word, were standing right outside our classroom window. Father Raulli stops teaching, goes over to his desk, and gets all these sheets of paper, and starts handing them out the window to these hippies. We're all sitting there, like, what's going on?

That night, I'm at home. We just got done eating dinner. My parents had the news on. And there's Father Raulli being escorted out of the Buffalo Common Council Chambers. He was part of a social activist groups that had presented the Buffalo Mayor with a gold brick.¹⁰ I remember saying to my mother, "Hey, that's my English teacher!" Didn't go over so well. But he, as a teacher both of English and of kind of activism, though it was somewhat extreme, began to develop a social consciousness in me that I'd never had before. I mean, my upbringing was very traditional Italian and Polish. Felician nuns. Very traditionally conservative. Blind faith, blind obedience, don't question this. And so, these were experiences for me that were saying, wait a minute, you've gotta question authority. You've gotta question the why. And it was just one more thing in this enormous puzzle...things that shaped me for the rest of my life.

---

⁹ Rev. Enrico Raulli, S.J., taught at CHS from 1967-1977, then went on to spend the rest of his career at Saint Peter's Prep. He died in 2016 at the age of 83.

¹⁰ A reference to "goldbricking," a military slang term of the era for shirking one's duty or intentionally neglecting one's responsibilities.

That mentality was more widespread than I had thought. Canisius was a microcosm of what was going on in our country. It was a divided country. It was not just the war. You had everything changing. The whole idea of anti-establishment, the whole idea of questioning politicians and government and anyone in authority had said for years...the idea of questioning that just wasn't part of the consciousness. So when you got into things like race and homosexuality and things like that...oh my God. Canisius was that microcosm. A great deal of the Jesuit influence was that liberal theology that said we need to question whether we're true to principles and values and faith and beliefs and not just sit there and blindly accept what someone in authority says is the way it should be. And I think the truth lies somewhere in between.

There was a lot of fear about the war among the guys. I still know my draft number: 187. You know, when you're a freshman, you're not really thinking about the draft. But when you're a senior, and you've registered, and you have a number, and to me 187 was right in the middle of the back, it became a very real possibility. And I think as the war was getting uglier, and the protests were becoming more, not only violent, but constant on a daily basis. And you have to remember, too, that today, when we look at Afghanistan or whenever we have causalities, there's outrage. But there were 50,000 servicemen killed then. I can't imagine how we would react in this nation today if we lost 50,000. But every day, that was the headline. I remember they were trying to spin it positive. You know, 35 Americans killed, but 150 V.C. dead. So, then we went into Cambodia. There was genuine fear. There was talk among classmates about going to Canada. For me that wasn't an option. I think my family values were so ingrained. That if you were called, you serve your country. But of course, the safety net was the college deferral. So I think in a school like ours, when 99% were going to college, that fear was more about what's going to happen after, or if I don't make it through college.

One thing I remember well was the music of the time. Music with teenagers is powerful no matter what era. But what I remember about the late 60s and the early 70s, the music representing so much of the voice of what was going in this country—Bob Dylan, James Taylor, Carly Simon, Carol King, all your Greenwich Village poets.... It wasn't just the war. People forget. You were still in a time when the Civil Rights Act had only recently been passed. You still had signs in Buffalo that said, whites only, colored over here. And so the music represented some of the very thing the Jesuits were reinforcing, and that is, questioning. Why. Why is it this way? You have to remember. I had three major assassinations in my childhood. John Kennedy, Bobby Kennedy, and Martin Luther King. And just that kind of violence—I mean, when you take down a President, a candidate for President, a civil rights leader—those are some momentous times. And the music reflected that. The music also reflected anger. I remember I was in a study hall. A classmate was playing a cassette player. It was Jimi Hendrix's rendition of The Star-Spangled Banner. And it's funny how I listen to it today versus back then, but it really was an expression of anger. And even Neil Young and Southern Man...the bottom line is that music is a big part of high school. It brings back tough memories, because of the emotion of what was going on back then. One of my favorite songs is a song called Signs by the Five Man Electrical Band. And it talked about signs— no trespassing, you can't do this, you can't do that, man, can't you read the signs. But the last verse talks about coming across a church, where the sign says, 'All are welcome to come in and pray. And at the end of it all, it's about gratitude, and the lyrics say something like, "Thank God I'm alive." And that's really what that time was about. Getting to the core of what we are as human beings, as Christians, as Catholics, as "Men for Others." And that's not meant as a plug. It's meant because it's at the core of why we exist.

You know, that was a time when Father Berrigan[11] was making front page news. And even though he never taught here, the fact that he was a Jesuit...those were the kinds of things that really broadened my horizons. Eventually, it really culminated in my senior retreat.

It wasn't an Emmaus. It was a three-day, two-night retreat. I remember going to confession. My whole life, confession was basically in a box. Like a phone booth. You don't even see the priest, you just go through the mantra. And I

---

[11] Rev. Daniel J. Berrigan, S.J., (1921-2016) was a Jesuit priest, writer, and anti-war activist. He, along with his brother Philip, also a priest, were featured on the cover of the January 25, 1971 issue of *Time* magazine with the headline, *Rebel Priests: The Curious Case of the Berrigans.*

don't even remember which Jesuit it was, but it was face to face, sitting on the floor, talking. And I remember leaving that more fulfilled than I had ever been in my life. Probably at no time in my life was I ever more serious about becoming a priest than my senior year of high school. Because what it really exposed me to was the truest understanding of the message of the Gospel. It wasn't about all these rules. It was about reconciling yourself with your maker in your relationship with your fellow man. It wasn't about not eating meat on Friday. It was really about what was at the core.

And so my four years as a student, whether in the academic realm or the spiritual realm...it was really an evolution over four years that broadened my horizons like I'd never imagined. It was the greatest period of growth than any other in my life. Far more than college.

Now, the war ended and wound down during my freshman and sophomore year of college. So all those fears subsided. But they were very real.[2]

Both Van Dyke's and Lucenti's recollections underscore the signs of the times—radical transition and cultural transformation. In keeping with this, similarly radical change was afoot at Canisius High School. A radical revisioning of the academic approach—arguably a progressive one in philosophical terms—saw students and faculty engaging in a very different learning process. A shift toward less regimented structure ostensibly placed more intellectual freedom in the hands of all involved, while creating an ongoing series of "teachable moments" rooted in the need for students to take personal responsibility for their behavior in this context of reduced structure. At best, this broad set of cultural changes was a progressive move away from limited pedagogical approaches toward a more nuanced vision of learning that celebrated authentic intellectual curiosity. At worst, however, it might be viewed as a problematic loosening of discipline, both in terms of academic expectations and behavioral norms.

As is the case when looking back upon any period of substantial change, the benefit of hindsight affords us additional perspective; thus, the likely reality is that the changes of the 1970s lay somewhere in the middle ground between these two interpretations. Certainly, some of the most important and lasting elements of Canisius culture emerged out of the 1970s—consider the advent of Campus Ministry and the retreat program as we now know it, as well as traditions like GAMBIT, the Walkathon, and the hanging of class portraits in Alumni Hall. A transformation of classroom approaches away from principally lecture-style lessons toward more modern collaborative "deep learning" styles, derived from contemporary research in educational theory, invited new possibilities for curricular evolutions. An admirable focus on *cura personalis*—"care of the individual person"—permeates the efforts of the era, and it is apparent that many of the changes in policy and approach were rooted in the best of intentions to more fully foster the intellectual, spiritual, social, and moral growth of young men.

In large part, however, the success of many of these rapidly implemented changes—which generally tended toward loosening restrictions and encouraging personal freedom—relied heavily on the supposition that students would respond to said freedom with consistent responsibility. This was not, as evidenced by various challenges that presented themselves throughout the decade, always the case.

All of these changes, moreover, existed against a backdrop of continued, ongoing financial struggle. As insights to budgetary challenges will show in the coming pages, the decade continued the longstanding reality faced by previous school leaders: the unending tension between limited financial resources and a desire to provide an accessible education to a wide array of students by keeping tuition manageable. These struggles are manifestly clear in the fundamental questions of school identity raised at the highest levels of leadership. Indeed, Board discussions of the decade return again and again to the most existential questions: What kind of school should Canisius be? Is co-education the inevitable course for fiscal sustainability? Should the school re-think its essential orientation toward college preparation? Is opening a seventh and eighth grade the key to maintaining a healthy enrollment?

Ultimately, however one judges the perceived successes or failures of the 1970s, it is undeniable that the decade marked a time of radical change and modernization. This turbulence was, arguably, reflective of "the signs of the times." Indeed, the speech from which that quote derives, offered by Superior General Pedro Arrupe in 1973, issued some of the most important and challenging existential questions for every institution undertaking the mission of Jesuit education. What does it mean to be a school charged with the formation of "men for others" in the modern age? The associated questions were vital then; they remain so now.

At the Board Level: An Inside Look at the 1970s

While the previous three decades have been chronicled with a presentation of Jesuit correspondence, we shift now to excerpts from Minutes of the Board of Trustees and other leadership groups. (The change is rooted principally in the availability and accessibility of archived resources.) Like the Rector's Letters of decades prior, these selections offer a telling view of the school's development during this time. Through these excerpts, the reader will see that the 1970s brought significant change in a wide variety of school-life contexts, perhaps most importantly in terms of pedagogical methods. Concurrently, one can observe the ongoing financial struggles. Perhaps, as the 1970s reach their end, an astute eye might begin to see "the writing on the wall" in terms of the financial near-disaster that nearly crippled the school in the 1980s.

Financial Struggles & Creative Thinking

Financial concerns loomed over the 1970s. We see this at the onset of the 1970s, when, in the minutes of the "Permanent Advisors to the Board of Directors of the Founders of the New Canisius High School," a rather stark forecast centered on "the financial problems...and the lack of sound economic planning and budget controls... The situation is deteriorating...."[3] The same concerns are reflected in Minutes of the Trustees' meeting in October, 1969, including "the increased deficit...increased costs in school activities...and a slight drop in enrollment." The suggestion of "an incentive...to parents who pay the entire year's tuition at once" underscores the issues with cash flow.[4]

By March 1971, there was hope for "an improvement in...loss operation for the current year...and...a possible break-even or slight surplus...."[5]

Unfortunately, by midsummer of that year, "Brother Mauro [Treasurer] noted [that] in summary, the school operated at a deficit of $28,000 on a gross of about $800,000." The tenor of the financial concerns takes on a notable uptick, citing continuing inflation as a central factor in those making "it difficult to hold the tuition fee at its present figure" and noting "rigid control of expenditures." Alongside these financial frustrations are early signs of the curricular evolution that would mark the decade. "The curriculum for 1971-1972 will offer more electives." Also, on the positive side, a broader-thinking mindset was being applied in the context of admissions and recruiting: "Father Devine mentioned the public relation efforts of Fr. John Rohr, speaking to 6th and 7th grade elementary school students; the English Skills and Writing Contest for elementary school pupils, the Open House...and the Field Day."[6] The success of the Open House was noted in subsequent Minutes.

By fall 1971, financial concerns continued to weigh on school leadership. "Brother Mauro...indicated that expenditures will be much higher in subsequent quarters with no increase in income.... The $80,000 listed in...State Aid will most probably not be given in view of recent U.S. Supreme Court rulings. The yield of our Scholarship portfolio...has diminished. A correction for the financial planning must be found." Echoing these concerns were those of enrollment: "With the drop in the number of students (50 fewer than last year), a further drop in revenue must be met with a raise in the tuition.... The alternative of bringing the student population up to 800 would require an open admission policy that would inevitably lower the school's academic standards. In addition to the drop in revenue, there is the continuing increase in costs of operation, due to the general inflation." It was moved that "the tuition be raised to $850 for the next school year."[7] Along with these practical matters was the call for a market study that would, more holistically, look at how Canisius fit into the Western New York education picture.

Board Minutes from January 1972 allude to the Five-Year planning process "in the four specified areas: 1. Personnel, 2. Curriculum, 3. Finance, and 4. Philosophy." Along with enrollment challenges, there is yet another reference to the increasing proportion of lay to Jesuit faculty: "With the reduction in Jesuit faculty, a study is underway on the most efficient use of the teachers." As for curriculum development, the Minutes note that the entire faculty attended a presentation by Father Vincent Duminuco, S.J., Principal of Xavier High School in New York City. This presentation focused on "the need for change and the difficulties of change" to curricula at Jesuit high schools throughout the Province. As for finance, there is reference to an appeal by school leadership to the Province "requesting $20,000 from the 'Brooklyn Prep Fund' for scholarship help for underprivileged boys." Along with the obvious financial relevance, this request also indicates the rising sensitivity to the need for ethnic and socioeconomic diversity at Canisius. Finally, in the area of philosophy, there is a call for the philosophy of the school to be revised in order to be "expressed in terms of the student's psychology and his personal goals" and to be less "faculty oriented."[8]

According to Mr. Thomas Beecher '52, who would serve on the Board of Trustees (including the role of Chair), a family donation solicited by the school's President resulted in the dedication of the classroom wing as the Beecher Classroom Wing in late 1972. The exterior lettering now visible from Delaware Avenue was added in September, 2009, to match that on the Montante Academic Center and the Kennedy Field House.[9]

Board minutes from the early 1970s also include what appears to be the first—or one of the first—official references to what would become GAMBIT: "Harold Troidl suggested having a cocktail party, or a dance in the pattern of the public fundraising affairs, calling upon the whole city to support Canisius High School. Mr. Osteander mentioned that we already have an Alumni Ball, which might be expanded to a 'Friends of Canisius' night and reach far outside the immediate associates of the school."[10]

Financially, there was a sense of some relief at this juncture. "Brother Mauro...indicated that the current controls on expenditures will bring the year's deficit down to under $10,000.... The five-year projection...foreshadows small deficits each year" Another nominal rise in tuition is noted:

to $850 plus a $50.00 activities fee. "Federal and State Aid to Schools seems very unlikely."[11]

A small note in October 1973 in the "Founders" notes indicates the inception of "a plan for Corporate Giving—a community service—'Sponsor a boy at Canisius High School.' A number of business firms and individuals are sponsoring students at Canisius High School for full and half scholarships." There is no additional information provided about this program in the notes.[12]

Leadership Changes and Existential Questions

The end of the 1972-1973 school year saw the end of the tenure of Father Donald G. Devine, S.J., as Principal, and the arrival of Rev. Joseph A. Papaj, S.J., He was a graduate of Canisius High School, Class of 1957, and was, at that time, completing Doctoral studies in education at Columbia University, with a specialization in curriculum development.[13] It is apparent that with the arrival of Father Papaj, curricular evolutions accelerated at a rapid pace.

The task of identifying a new President began in earnest in fall 1973. In the midst of the Trustee's Minutes from November lies insight about an important change, namely the separation of duties between the school's President and the Rector of the Jesuit community. "The Rector has always been the President...[and] religious Superior...a full-time job for one man without the responsibilities of the school administration." Thus, the change: "Recently, a 'Superior' has been appointed to take responsibility for the Community, with all of the Rector's powers delegated to him permanently."[14] This marked a significant change in the roles and responsibilities, making the duties of the school's President distinct from those associated with oversight of the Jesuit community. The qualifications developed for the position of President were "1. A man of prayer, 2. Gracious in dealing with people, 3. Proven ability in administration, 4. Acquaintance with the Buffalo area, 5. Knowledge of budgeting and finance, and 6. Age between 40 and 55 years."[15] During an interview for this book, Father Van Dyke, S.J., '77 commented on this change: "At that time, a lot of guys [Jesuits] who came here to work at Canisius were sent here...for a variety of reasons." The implication was that Buffalo was not among the most sought-after places for a Jesuit to be sent. "But [despite that]," he continued, "it became one of the most remarkable communities. But it took a Superior to look after that. The other part of the puzzle is...the financial issues of the school. It took a full-time President to really be President of the school. That was not unique to Canisius, but it very pressing here. And so those two pieces *had* to get full consideration."[16]

The Finance Committee recommended yet another tuition hike, this time by $125.00, noting a rise nearly twice this large among the diocesan schools. The tuition raise was encouraged, but with emphatic focus on making sure that financial aid continued to be offered, advertised, and made available.[17]

At the mid-fiscal-year point of January 1974, tension is palpable: "Brother Mauro...noted that the budget was originally predicted on 730 students; presently there are 701...Brother Mauro concluded that the year-end will show a deficit of between $20,000 and $30,000."[18]

On the bright side, there is encouraging commentary about the effectiveness of the Higher Achievement Program (HAP) both at improving enrollment and diversifying the applicant pool. "Of the 45 HAP students (30 black and 15 white), 20 (15 black and 5 white) were accepted as freshmen for the fall term. A total of 41 black students and 1 Puerto Rican were among the applicants.... The present student body includes 34 black students."[19] In parallel with these efforts to diversify the student body, there was an effort cited later on that year to do the same with the Board of Trustees, including reaching out to potential candidates from the non-alumni, Protestant, downstate, and nonwhite communities.[20]

Along with the announcement that Rev. Robert G. Cregan, S.J., would be the next President of Canisius High School, Board Minutes from April 1974 indicate a formalized effort to establish what would eventually become GAMBIT. In response to a projection of a $30,000 deficit for the coming year, "...new sources of revenue must be found.... The benefit auction, 'BASH' held at McQuaid Jesuit...realized a $61,000 net profit. If we should put on an auction here...McQuaid would be willing to help us get it under way."[21]

Father Papaj also emphasized some of the curricular and cultural changes in the works at the school, which would include "a reduction in formal class time, the time thus freed...used by the student under the supervision of a faculty advisor.... More variation in the method of instruction...[and] a learning center available for each department of study."[22]

By midsummer 1974, there are signs of continued deficit reductions, along with the evolving plans to create a benefit auction. A solid incoming class of 203 freshmen compared to 145 graduating seniors indicates a positive trend, and Brother Mauro cited "a number of unexpected gifts" that proved helpful. Despite this encouraging news, however, it is again pointed out that "the largest increase in operating expense continues to be teachers' salaries and this trend evidently continues since there are fewer Jesuits available for teaching assignments." Along with more concrete discussions about the benefit auction that would eventually take form as GAMBIT, several creative possibilities were mentioned to cut costs and raise revenues. These included "weekly Bingo [as conducted] at St. Joseph's Collegiate Institute...and a plan in place at Nichols "where each student is expected to give thirty hours of required maintenance work around the school."[23] Apparently, neither of these two suggestions gained much traction.

January 1975 marked "the first time in ten years that the [financial] report showed a surplus at the end of the year."[24] However, this was due to a legacy gift counted as immediate income that would not, in fact, be realized immediately. Thus a more sober financial outlook remained, with the realization that enrollment had again dropped from 690 to 675—projecting an annual fiscal year deficit of $70,000. On the positive side, Father Papaj remarked that "school spirit has obviously gone up." Father Sams offered an update on GAMBIT, to be held for the first time on Saturday, April 19, 1975: "If GAMBIT reaches its potential it could wipe out the expected deficit."[25] Likewise, Father Sams announced a new program of Living Endowments related to life insurance policies. The success of GAMBIT, under the leadership of Father Sams and Robert B. Mayer, GAMBIT Chairman, was reported at the Board level in late April, with a net profit of $47,000. (More details about GAMBIT are provided in a separate section of this chapter.) Indeed, GAMBIT made the difference and eliminated the projected deficit, in fact leading, rather, to a projected $16,000 fiscal year surplus. At this time, it was noted that this surplus might be used to chip away at the school's debt balance of $280,000.[26]

In an effort to realize new revenue streams, the Board approved an arrangement whereby the Bryant and Stratton Business Institute would rent eight classrooms, four nights per week, for evening classes.[27]

Extensive notes about a disciplinary situation involving inappropriate material in the 1975 *Arena* yearbook are noted at the Board level—a scenario that at least one Jesuit priest suggests was actually "quite telling" of the lax disciplinary culture at the time. Following these notes, however, comes mention of an interesting milestone: "Copies of the new seal of Canisius High School were shown to the Trustees, and they voted for its adoption as the school's official seal as of July 24, 1975."[28]

Father Papaj offered a "State of the School" report in fall 1975, in which it was noted that "the new system of modular scheduling and advisor programs seems to be working more smoothly this year," and that "discipline is being worked out well by the Assistant Principal." Renovations to the "learning center" (the current library) included carpeting. Notably, there were 31 voluntary withdrawals from the school over the summer, in addition to those dismissed for academic reasons, yielding a 1975-1976 enrollment of only 675.[29] Thus "publicity and recruitment were next discussed as being very crucial to Canisius."[30] These concerns were balanced by a fiscal report that noted the second consecutive annual surplus, as well as plans to continue with a second GAMBIT under the Chairmanship of Minot Ortolani '47. Finally, Father Cregan commented on "Jesuit Project One, the thrust of which was 'to emphasize the service of faith and the promotion of justice as a means for a stronger religious dimension to our high schools.'" Notably, these words directly echo the tremendously influential address of Father General Pedro Arrupe, S.J., in Valencia, Spain in 1973—the challenging speech to Jesuit school alumni during which Arrupe coined the phrase "Men for Others." This would go on to become a motto for Jesuit education.

By early 1976, there were mixed outlooks on the financial front. Early projections forecasted yet another sizeable deficit ($38,000), but the Bryant and Stratton rental arrangement was profitable, and the school managed to make a $10,000 debt service payment. Relevant to the financial picture was a ten-year enrollment and tuition perspective offered by Father Papaj at the January meeting of the Board. He noted that "enrollment has declined from 925 to 682 with tuition rising from a total of $365 to $1050" and that there existed "obvious risk in losing students due to a significant increase in tuition." Yet again, exploring the possibility of co-education was advocated at the Board level, specifically the potential for partnership with Nardin Academy. In light of the fact that other independent schools were charging "over $2500 per year in tuition and do not seem to have a decreasing enrollment problem," there was apparent debate about whether or not tuition was truly an issue. To counter this, however, "Father Cregan stated that we do have a clear philosophy, that we aim at as wide an enrollment as possible which includes underprivileged and poor as well and that our goal is to provide this type of education not just to those who can afford the high tuition."[31] Nonetheless, a resolution passed to raise tuition by $75 for 1976-1977, increasing the total including fees to $1,125.00.

A blow to the school's finances came with the Federal District Court decision ruling unconstitutional the law by which New York State reimbursed church-related schools for performing certain services mandated by the State, such as keeping attendance records and administering State-mandated exams. This "Mandated Services Act" had provided $17,000 annually; this funding would end following the current school year, further reducing revenue.[32]

Underscoring the Board's awareness of enrollment and financial challenges, an explicit list of eventualities was assembled:

POSSIBLE LINES OF ACTION IN THE FACE OF ENROLLMENT DECLINE
- *Change of admissions standards with consequent change in curriculum away from college preparatory program.*
- *Expansion of enrollment through introduction of an eighth or seventh-eighth grade.*
- *Introduction of adult education.*
- *Increased use of facilities to augment income.*

- *Reduction of faculty and staff; savings through other economy measures.*
- *Increased income through development.*
- *Increased efforts in recruitment and/or publicity.*
- *Merger with one or more other high schools.*
- *Cooperative program with Canisius College in a six year "three-three" instructional sequence, similar to that now existing at Seattle University.*
- *Introduction of "cost tuition" similar to program now existing at Colegio San Ignacio in Puerto Rico.[33]*

Under the financial pressures, existential debate continued. "The question was raised by [a Jesuit] whether we must water down our religious dimension and strive primarily for academic excellence. Father Cregan emphasized that this would not be according to the Jesuit educational thrust today." Indeed, counter to this narrowing idea, the Board notes go on to focus on diversifying initiatives. The school adopted its first official non-discrimination policy in keeping with new government regulations, and Board members redoubled efforts to fund the HAP program in light of reduced Province-level funding.

Notably, "the religious life of the school has been enhanced recently with the appointment with a full-time chaplain, Father Gerald W. Aman, S.J., New opportunities are being offered to the students and the faculty for retreats and days of prayer. This is all in keeping with the thrust of *Project One* for a Jesuit high school of today."[34] The appointment of Father Aman can arguably be marked as the beginning of the Campus Ministry Department as we think of it now. In subsequent years, Father Aman would initiate the Emmaus retreat, which has served as the baseline model for countless variations on the Ignatian retreat experience for Canisius students ever since.

GAMBIT II, held in April 1976, was a success with a net income of $50,000, and Gambit III was quickly scheduled for March 1977.[35]

Following a visitation by the Province Coordinator of Secondary Schools, Father Daniel Fitzpatrick, S.J., Father Papaj reported that "the new position of the school chaplain has been quite effective. There are new days of recollection, a retreat program, and a plan of Christian Service. There is also a coordinated four-year effort in the religious program. Daily attendance at Mass in the school chapel has increased."[36]

Revisiting the potential solutions to ongoing enrollment challenges, Board "consensus was that the first priority in research be given to the possibility of experimenting with an eighth or seventh and eighth grade program." This was notably juxtaposed with Father Papaj's reminder that the Catholic high schools were, at this time, "prohibited from recruitment in the parochial schools...."[37] Ostensibly, the establishment of a middle-school division was seen as a potential avenue for improved enrollment. "Father Cregan was urged to look into this seventh/eighth grade possibility as a workable experiment in the near future. The Board also urged a study of what coeducation could mean for the school, even though such a change is remote now."[38]

By the start of the 1976-1977 fiscal year, financial concerns continued. With the loss of $17,000 from the repeal of the Mandated Services Act, along with ongoing lower enrollment (675), even the nominal tuition increase to $1,125.00 still yielded a projected deficit.[39] School leadership had already begun exploring middle school development in earnest, including issuing a faculty survey (which indicated more support than skepticism) and visiting McQuaid Jesuit in Rochester, which had an eighth grade. It was resolved that study of this possibility would continue.

Notably, a report on new data from the survey begun the year prior entitled "Canisius High School: Its Public Image" indicated some mounting concerns in the area of school culture:

The new replies came from the present graduating class and their parents. The overall tone seemed to be more negative toward the school than were previous years. A number of students felt that they should have been kept busier during the school day. Mr. Hastreiter commented on this, saying that the majority of students didn't know how to use "unstructured time" and sometimes the faculty were not giving clear guidelines on its use themselves.[40]

Enrollment stood at 670 in the fall of 1976, although the faculty was smaller by one teacher, yielding an average class size of 24-27 students.

Board minutes point out that the third consecutive fiscal year was projected "in the black," and yet one can understand how these larger classes against essentially unchanged enrollment presented another challenge, especially in light of the ongoing concerns about school culture and unstructured time.

A note from Brother Lou Mauro, S.J., Treasurer, to the President, Father Cregan, provides good insight into the financial tension of the era while, arguably, foreshadowing the fiscal crisis of the coming decade:

...We must learn that we cannot burn the candle at both ends. If we do not raise the tuition, then it is only right we do not increase our expenses. Major renovations and improvements or changes in the facilities would have to go by the wayside. Hiring an Academic Assistant Principal would have to be negated. If there is a need for a new teacher, forget it. The increases alone would wipe out the additional 25 students.

Cost [sic] have not oriented the school but the school has oriented the cost. This has been obvious in the increase of manpower and the changes in facilities. Whatever was needed was done in little or no relationship to cost or do we have the money to pay for it. The debt at the bank proves this out.[41]

Net enrollment in 1977-1978 had dropped to 660—although enrollment of freshmen was up to 192—and a deficit was again recorded in 1977 at the year's end. There is an uptick of focus on the "Founders" in leadership notes, especially upon the success of events like GAMBIT (which netted a larger profit in its second year) and a show presented by Mark Russell '50. The Russell show attracted 650 guests and netted the school $5,300.[42] Tuition debates continued in January 1977, with serious discussions about the school's mission relative to affordability.

Tuition was stressed as the school's surest source of income. The increased number of applicants and the evident positive attitude toward the school among parents argues for their willingness to pay more for a Canisius education. On the other hand, the school is in danger of becoming ever more elitist. Fewer of current applicants are from poorer neighborhoods....We are at risk of excluding students whom we want to serve if we overprice a Canisius education.[43]

Board Minutes of April 1977 mention the increased success of GAMBIT, which netted $53,000 in its third year under Chairman Mr. James R. Greer. Another new initiative, the "Annual Support Fund," was announced—what is now known as the "Annual Fund." Another Mark Russell show was announced for October. Notably, the establishment of the Father Kirsch Alumni Memorial Hall (now known as Alumni Hall) was scheduled for dedication on May 22, 1977.[44]

By fall 1977, enrollment stood at 661 and a troubling disparity was noted in Board minutes—that between a larger incoming freshman class (192) and a sizeable exodus of withdrawing upperclassmen. "The perplexing situation is that about 50 upperclassmen chose to withdraw from Canisius and there does not seem to be any perceivable pattern as to why."[45]

GAMBIT 1978 continued the trend of success, netting $64,000, and enrollment climbed to 688 in the fall of 1978. A Capital Development Drive called "PROJECT 80s" totaled more than $440,000 in gifts and pledges as of November 1978.[46] Also encouraging was the audit report for fiscal year '78-'79, which showed a surplus of $67,000 compared to the previous year's deficit of $38,000—and seemed to indicate that cost increases were significantly favorable to the rate of inflation. Some of this optimism, however, hung on the continued funding from the Mandated Services Act, the constitutionality of which continued to be debated at the legislative level. Emphasis was placed on keeping a principal objective of the PROJECT 80s drive the complete elimination of the school's debt, "so that we can get beyond operating expenses...[and] begin to do the things we project." The total pledged amount for the Drive was $564,000.[47]

The first Walkathon was mentioned, which netted $24,000. Gambit VI was set for April 1980, and the early stages of a search process for Father Cregan's successor were begun.

Academic Changes & Educational Technology

According to one alumnus from the 1970s who is now a Jesuit, the early part of the decade contained what came to be called by some in the school "The October Revolution of 1973." This is a reference to a sweeping set of relatively rapid changes that took place on curricular, cultural, and arguably existential levels. Certainly, elements of the Board minutes, etc., in the previous section provided some context for this; however, it is only a closer examination of the sweeping changes on a policy level that provides a full appreciation for just how significant this "revolution" was in terms of school culture. Thus, it is worth taking a detailed look at "The Canisius High School Program."

The "Program" was an educational plan that laid out a detailed set of objectives and strategies along with a contextual rationale. In spirit, it reflected an attempt to integrate traditional principles of Ignatian pedagogy with contemporary educational trends. According to the Program, the Five-Year Plan was developed in 1971-1972 for implementation beginning in September 1974 "as part of a New York State Province effort to reflect on the apostolate of secondary education and to increase the effectiveness of the Jesuit high school at the local level."[48]

Upon commencing the 1973-1974 academic year, the faculty met to review the plan against a contemporaneous statement from the Jesuit Secondary Education Association (JSEA) on "Values and Trends of the Jesuit High School." From this faculty review emerged four objectives for the year:

1. *Re-examination and redefinition of the roles of teachers and students.*
2. *Re-arrangement of organizational patterns so as to place greater emphasis on the centrality of the individual student.*
3. *Development of educational processes which reflect and foster goals 1 & 2.*
4. *Development of faculty and student attitudes which are directed to a shared purpose.*[49]

The plan had four stages: Analysis, Formulation, Development, and Research & Communication. A considerable quantity of committee and subcommittee work took place, with a hierarchical breakdown of responsibilities and objectives presented. In addition to an architectural study on space utilization, *ad hoc* committees focused on five areas:

1. *The role of the advisor*
2. *Self-Directed Time (including resources and materials)*
3. *Student preparation and adaptation*
4. *Faculty preparation and adaptation*
5. *Evaluation and accountability*[50]

The "Program" takes on a less procedural and more philosophical tone in its delineation of the rationale for the initiative. Excerpts of this rationale provide a telling window into the educational context of the time:

Like others involved in Jesuit education, Canisius has been seriously examining the significance and effectiveness of its contribution to the high school apostolate. It has accepted the assertion that it must not remain content with its accomplishments.... Recognizing them, it sees the need to go beyond the simple provision of good college preparatory education by accenting more forcefully its Jesuit heritage in forms consonant with today's world.

Two striking qualities of that heritage have stood out—the personal involvement, contact, and concern of teachers for students (what was called the Jesuit 'cura personalis alumnorum'); [and] the emphasis on helping students to grow as self-motivating, self-initiating learners even after they have graduated.

In the not too distant past these qualities were best realized in a carefully organized structure where teachers and authorities controlled student choices and actions. The course of studies was uniformly prescribed, with minor variations allowed on a limited scale. School rules applied to a collective student body in a uniform way. Surveillance and punishment ensured their observance.

Gradually, due to changing social situations as well as to developments in educational theory and practice, school settings began to move away from that kind of structure toward more flexible arrangements in time, space, instructional methods, and content. The point is not whether particular manifestations of these were good or bad as much as it is the recognition that all individuals do not learn in the same way, and that learning cannot be confined to only what happens in a classroom.

Canisius did not isolate itself from the shift...it must be admitted, however, that what changes did take place...lacked a sense of integration with any larger movement at Canisius toward coherence and to a planned, unified, specific direction for the school.

The work of the Five-Year Plan and last year's planning gave voice to the faculty's need and desire to specify a direction and coherence. Three features offered a starting point:

1. An instructional program rooted in contacts between teachers and students on a daily, academic, and personal basis...teachers would function not only as information-givers but also as guides, organizers, and facilitators of student experiences. Students would function as actively involved, responsible, and self-determining learners.

2. A school setting characterized by a thorough and reflective adaptation to the unique talents and needs of the individual student, one which allows persons to emerge from the group, and which encourages the teacher to withdraw so that the less Canisius students need their teachers, the more they have succeeded.

3. An emphasis on the Christian dimension of education, one built upon hope, service, charity, and the love of Christ as he lives in us and in His Church.

A number of values emerged from these features and from a consideration of the strengths and traditions of Canisius...these values provide the program with a sense of direction and give it a special character. Specifically, they are:

- *An explicit concern and emphasis on the development...of each student as a unique, complex person...*
- *The willingness to provide students, faculty, and administration with an environment in which they can make and learn from mistakes.*
- *A renewed stress on...the development of mature, dynamic Christian leaders...[and] a new stress on values and personal reflection...*
- *A re-interpretation of cura personalis, manifested in new patterns of interaction between faculty and student...*
- *A decrease in the amount of structure imposed upon students, coupled with a corresponding increase in the amount of guidance, direction, and personal contact...*
- *A re-interpretation of freedom as grounded in discipline & accountability...*
- *Practical realization that learning takes place not only within the classroom; that other sources are, or should be, available...*
- *Greater flexibility in the use of time, space, and personnel...*
- *A school tone that sets high expectations...to build students' pride rather than emphasize their failings...*[51]

These philosophical underpinnings were coupled with some very specific, concrete changes that arguably transformed the daily life of Canisius High School students. This was true to such an extent that those who attended the school prior to these changes would have, most likely, barely recognized the new daily patterns.

The Module System

One of the most prominent planned changes included scheduling, both in terms of the academic calendar and the daily use of time. Namely, this meant a departure "from the 40 minutes per period, 6 periods per day arrangement of time and [adoption of] a modular scheduling system." The "mod system," as it came to be known, was based on the idea of dividing the day into 20-minute segments ("modules") that could be arranged in varying patterns to suit a variety of scheduling structures. On the calendar level, there was planned movement from semesters to trimesters, which "makes possible earlier identification of problems and a greater variety of contact with more teachers." These changes were rooted in "a need and desire to reduce the rigidity of the school's former temporal arrangements...which may more effectively allow for greater adaptation of time and groupings to the particular needs of what different departments and courses are trying to accomplish."[52]

The concept of "Guided, Self-Directed Time" figures prominently in the Program, and involved "a reduction in the amount of time spent in regularly scheduled classes." The stated rationale was "to foster student growth in the exercise of self-responsibility and self-determination, in order to encourage more actively involved learners." Furthermore, the Plan explicates that "the wise, productive use of such [self-directed] time is a learned skill." Accordingly, the Plan called for a gradually increasing proportion of a student's time to be designated as self-directed: "Freshmen and Sophomores will be provided with self-directed time amounting to approximately 15% of the 96 modules available each cycle; Juniors with approximately 20 to 25%; and Seniors with about 25 to 30%. This will vary depending on the decisions a student makes relative to engaging in elective courses."[53]

The Program offers a defense against any allegations that it would simply loosen expectations, or that it would "give students a break from classes or learning," or that it would "lack controls and a structure." Indeed, six specific counters to these concerns are offered, which range from the argument that students need to learn to manage unstructured time to succeed in college to the suggestion that by limiting class time, it would become "a more precious commodity, eliciting a more carefully planned, intelligent, efficient, and stimulating use of such time."[54]

The Advisor System

One of the most resilient (and still active) elements of the Program included the establishment of the Advisor system, which is described as "the element that forms the core...[of] a system designed to ensure that students are accountable for their use of the time...[wherein] students will be given materials to make up a 'planbook.' On these sheets, a student is expected to maintain an accurate, up-to-date record of test/project deadlines, of what he plans to do during his self-directed periods, and what he has actually accomplished. The student will review his planbook with his advisor at regular intervals."[55]

At the most practical level, the Advisement system was rooted in a desire to provide "an increased amount of academic guidance" as a necessary complement to the lessened structure. To this point, the Program acknowledges that "experiences at Canisius with Seniors in recent years who have enjoyed less structured class time are good examples to illustrate the risks involved in decreasing structure without providing greater guidance."

More holistically, the Program justifies the Advisor system by pointing out that historically, the homeroom teacher was a "concrete manifestation" of *cura personalis*; whereas, "...as instruction became departmentalized and more specialized, the strong personal relationship between students and homeroom teacher grew weaker. Generally speaking, he became mainly a clerical assistant passing along messages and recording attendance." With this historical perspective in mind, the Program laid out a series of responsibilities for advisors under the new model. Among them:

- *"...a faculty member who takes a special interest in [the student's] academic and personal adjustment and development...by serving as a guide and facilitator...*
- *"...an awareness of a student's need for assistance and reinforcement...."*
- *"...[they would] not [be] expected to perform the functions...of the Counselor...however, [they would be] expected to be sensitive to possible personal implications...[and] to demonstrate an awareness of a student's need for counseling...and to be active in helping him to seek such help...."*
- *"...the key link in communications between the school and a student's home...."*

The schedule, per the Program, called for three daily meetings between students and advisors, beginning in fall of 1974: "5 minutes at the beginning of the day; 5 minutes at the end of the day; and a 30-minute advisement period in mid-morning." During these times, the Advisor "has the option of dealing with this group as a whole, with a subgroup, or with an individual advisee. During this time, he familiarizes himself with the work habits and personal discipline of his advisees...assists them in the formation of reliable study habits, effective note-taking...organization, and...other activities to foster the goals of the advisement function."[56] (It should be noted that the details as to what exactly this should comprise on a practical level are rather conspicuously absent.)

"New Role for Teachers"

The Program proclaimed, quite bluntly, that "the changes being introduced into the Canisius program are carefully organized to shift the emphases placed on the meaning of 'teacher' and 'student.'" A detailed contextual rationale is provided, which gets at a philosophical shift generally aimed at "an eagerness to bring students into contact with a learning stimulus and then move out of the students' way so that they need the teacher less and less...[coupled with] a willingness to guide more and direct less." Put another way, the changes called for a shift from teacher as "information-giver" to "one who guides and facilitates students."[57]

On a nuts and bolts level, this philosophical shift called for some significant changes to the dynamics of staffing assignments. "Previously, [these were] based on the number of classes a teacher taught and a predetermined number of assigned hours per week for teaching, proctoring, and executing other duties. Thus, a teacher's assignment was thought of, typically, as 5 class periods a day, a proctoring period, and two, perhaps three, class preparations." In place of this longtime system, the Program called for the implementation of one "using as the determining factor a concept known as 'teacher-student contact units.'" An explanation is provided as follows:

Under this arrangement staffing is determined on the principle that each department would have the services of one full-time teacher for every 115 students taking courses in that department. Because of the duties incumbent on department chairmen, an additional $1/4^{th}$ teacher would be added to each department. Calculating staff needs in this way...has provided for a teacher-pupil ratio of approximately 1:17.4. This is highly favorable if one considers that the New York State requirement is 1 teacher for every 150 students, and that *available figures show the teacher-pupil ratio is 1:19.4 in the Buffalo Schools; 1:20.6 in East Aurora; 1:21.4 in Lancaster; 1:22 in Williamsville; and the New York State public school average is 1:19.3...*

In addition, the basis for staffing enjoys the value of decentralizing decision-making with respect to the uses of departmental personnel resources since each department chair, in consultation with his colleagues and with the approval of the Principal, will be able to decide how teaching personnel can best be utilized...

Along with these changes, teachers were "urged to ask themselves" the following, more holistic questions "in terms of their teaching methods...organization...and their ways of testing."

- *Are all of your students studying the same material...or are different individuals or groups within the class allowed to work on different objectives, either those they have chosen or you have prescribed? Will the subject matter of the next test be the same for every student?*
- *Are all of your students achieving the same objectives the same way or are your students provided different ways in which similar objectives can be accomplished?*
- *Are all of your students proceeding at the same rate? Are all kept at the same pace whether they could go faster or should go more slowly?*

Ultimately, while the Program notes that "teachers will have to provide the direction, support, and discrimination which is precisely theirs alone because of their experience and expertise," they are also "being asked to do much less for students and considerably more with students." The Program emphasizes that in this way, "the learning process at Canisius will truly become a corporate effort whose success involves a genuine mutuality of capabilities, concern, and responsibility."[58]

Longtime faculty member Russ White offered a teacher's perspective on these changes during an interview for this book:

When I started, the school was very traditional. The faculty all wore black academic gowns.... I went to a public high school, so I'd never seen anything like that. The students had a dress code...shirt and tie, and a jacket.... I was a young teacher, so I was actually closer to the students in age than the faculty. I identified more with them, so I would let them take their jackets off in class on the hot days. I had to make sure they put them back on or we'd all be in trouble.

I think a big turning point was when we got a new principal...Father Joseph Papaj, S.J. As Jesuit principals go, he was a fairly young man and he had very progressive ideas. He was going to change the school. He did. There was talk among the faculty that he was working on an advanced degree—I don't really know if that's true—but the feeling was that we were his "project." He came in with a lot of ideas, and we adopted a lot of them.

He got rid of the black academic gowns. That was big stuff. Greatly relaxed the dress code with the student body; they were allowed to wear turtlenecks, stuff like that. Most important thing is he...Well, let me back up. The lay faculty at the time met [in the current Campus Ministry office]. All the administrative positions were Jesuit. Part of Father Papaj's approach was to set up what he called "Learning Centers." There were three departments out in the library: English, Modern Language, and History. The History Department was closest to the Faculty Room.... It was called Fort McPherson. It looked like a fort. The Science Department was up in 3E3.... There was talk in the faculty that this was a way to "de-centralize" the lay faculty. As there were fewer Jesuits, there was a higher percentage of lay teachers. The lay faculty was becoming larger and more influential in school politics, I guess you'd say. The feeling was that maybe this was a way...to break us up a bit. I don't know if that's true or not, but...that was the talk.

[He] changed the scheduling that we worked in mods [Modules] instead of periods. We had 20-minute mods. Most classes were 2 mods long, but labs were 3 mods, which was perfect, because we would have an hour. The problem was as you can imagine that just changed the whole schedule operation. You throw one one-hour block in the middle of the day and it throws everything

else off. But part of his plan was to have the students have free time. He called it 'unstructured time.' Ideally, they would sit and study; in reality they would "un-structure" the school!

It was a nice idea.... I think a lot of his ideas were good; [but] it was too much, too soon.... We were always told the Principal's position was three years; he knew his time was limited.... He had to do it all at once.... We thought maybe we were a Ph.D. program.... But I think he was on the right track.

After that we had Fr. Ken Boller, S.J. I thought he was a very good principal. He kind of brought us back. He slowly got rid of some of those ideas, but...we retained some of them.... The dress code came back a little.[59]

Likewise, Fr. Van Dyke, S.J. '77 again offered this student perspective, informed, of course, by many years of teaching and administration since his student days:

Largely what we saw at the time were functional changes...the move to a block schedule, the move to a computerized schedule. Unfortunately, the execution on those was not an easy transition. For example, there was a time they had to cancel school for a week because it didn't work out.... They had to go back and do the schedule by hand.

The idea behind the mod schedule was the learning centers.... That our use of unstructured time was to be mentored; well, by and large it really, practically, wasn't. So, to some extent, there was a fair amount of hanging out.... Eventually people got sick enough of hanging out that they actually began arranging independent studies.

The one place where I would say that there was a strengthening in the curriculum was in English and language arts. For instance, we had a separate course in language arts, grammar, and writing in our freshman year.... It dabbled a little bit in linguistics...and I think it helped a lot of kids who were coming in weaker in that area.... And at that time, the English Department was creating a curriculum...in which they were trying to address the needs of the students they saw coming in...guys like Naumann, Durkin, McIntyre, Tudini...created a really outstanding curriculum. [60]

"New Role for Students"

"The most important change at Canisius is the shift that has occurred in the student's role," proclaims the Program. "His role has been shifted to stress the student as an active person engaged in a mutual learning process with his fellow students and teachers.... He will be a person who assumes a greater part in defining his own learning objectives, in devising procedures for their attainment at his own pace.... In such a process, Canisius students will be learning to do for themselves much of what they had previously expected the faculty to be doing for them; they will be 'learning how to learn.'"[61]

Insofar as this philosophical shift would necessitate different expectations for students, these are likewise spelled out in the Program: "But as he grows more aware that he is in a school environment which invites his own initiative and entrusts more to his own care, the Canisius student will also find a corresponding demand for responsibility and accountability—at once a joy and a burden.... His role, then, will require that he be true to his newfound obligations, that he answer both to himself and to others. Without this there can be neither true freedom nor genuine learning."[62]

Physical Space Changes

Along with changes to the schedules and roles, there were modifications to the placement of students, teachers, and the corresponding use of physical spaces. One element included variability of class sizes, ostensibly rooted in varying modes of teaching and learning. "Variations in the sizes of group meetings will occur. The schedule has been arranged in such a way that in some classes, students will meet at times in groups of 30, at other times in groups of 60 or 90 (Freshmen History and Mathematics). In other classes (e.g., upper-class Religion) students will meet at times in groups of about 30, at other times in a group of about 12 to 15."[63]

A comprehensive physical space study was associated with the Five-Year Plan and the Program. "Assisted by architectural consultants, the faculty and students investigated needs and possibilities which pertained to the physical set-up of Canisius in light of the changing educational program." The following physical changes occurred:

- *Each Department has been provided with a Learning Center...located throughout the building...open to students during the entire school day.... The Centers...will also serve as faculty offices, thereby allowing teachers to be constantly available to work with students.... Teachers have been scheduled for definite periods of time...to ensure that at least one member of each department would be present in each Center at all times of the day with no responsibility other than to be available for students.*
- *All Science facilities are now located in one area of the school.*
- *A new Library Center has been established for silent study and research.*
- *Two rooms have been provided on the second floor of Berchmans Hall for seminar and small group-type instruction. A Conference Room has also been made available for general use.*
- *Under the direction of the school's first full-time Educational Television Coordinator since the facilities were installed, the Television Studio has been renovated...[for] more intensive use of our closed-circuit television resources...*
- *The Art Department has added a lecture room to complement its studio facilities and to assist its implementation of a new Fine Arts Program being introduced to all Sophomores this year.*
- *To increase the effectiveness of the school's Physical Education program, an exercise room has been established. This room is equipped with a Universal Gym—a multi-station machine capable of accommodating 16 people.*
- *A section of the Cafeteria has been converted to a school Commons for faculty and student relaxation and an informal gathering area.*[64]

A Noble Effort; a Mixed Result in Hindsight; The Pendulum Swings Back

The curricular changes implemented in the 1970s were, arguably, rooted in the best of intentions. "All of the changes called for...represent a coherent, school-wide effort to locate the student of Canisius in the center of what the school can offer.... The difference now is that the structure is aimed at self-initiative," claimed the Program. Furthermore, it went on to contextualize the changes in light of the school's tradition and history: "Canisius has always prided itself on its accomplishments...[and] the changes...are not meant to deny that tradition. They are, however...a gradual shift...[that] seeks to strengthen CHS's academic excellence while accenting more forcefully its Jesuit heritage.[65]

Notably, of course, one need only look to the end of the decade to see the pendulum swinging back toward a more traditional schedule structure. The sudden reduction in the liberty afforded students under the "mod system" created an understandable level of angst. The student editorial section of the December 1979 issue of *The Citadel* contains plenty of evidence:

Ineffective use of free time by students was a major cause for the institution of a new system here at Canisius. Mandatory study halls theoretically solves [sic] this problem but also eliminates the opportunity for students and teachers to take time out from the routine of a full day...After three years of high school and three years of self-directed time, shouldn't senior year afford some privileges? ... Is there an alternative? – Peter Ciotta

...There are definitely some advantages to the structural system. The number of students roaming the halls has been reduced. Vandalism has decreased to a certain extent. Also, it is much easier to trace where a student is.... But, there is the other side of the story to consider also.... There is also the psychological result from completely structured time. Tension is built up to greater height because of having to be in a certain place at a certain time, five days a week, eight periods a day. This pressure makes for a more strained learning atmosphere. – David Barnas

...Let's face it, the old system wasn't working for some students. However, it was just right for others. Those others should not have had all their freedom taken away after proving they could use the system with success. Granted, some kind of change had to be made, but I feel that such a drastic move was wrong. – Wally Biffl

Schedule management is a continuous process of discernment within schools. Ultimately, the experimental approach to modular flexibility in the 1970s afforded an institutional learning experience that has informed several subsequent revisions of the schedule.

The Origins of Contemporary Campus Ministry

Ms. Andrea Tyrpak-Endres provided some insight as to the evolution of both Religious Studies and Campus Ministry during an interview for this book.

[When I first arrived here to teach] my first reaction was, I spent four years in college and how many thousands of dollars for this? Because in the '70s, it was, "let's go paint rocks." Not quite so severe here, but that's how religion was. Collages...lots of collages. There was a "Jesus Magazine" called "EMIT" because it was "TIME" spelled backwards.... I did not need educational background to teach here.

But then [Father] Jack Ryan [S.J.,] taught seniors, and he was doing Meeting the Living God[12], *so in the upper levels it probably was a little bit more academic.... But in quick time that changed. We had Jim Keenan, Jr. come here; he's now a Biblical scholar. He started our Christian Service Program, actually, or the skeletal structure for it. We didn't have Campus Ministry; we had a Chaplain...Gerry Aman, who was just starting to get the idea for doing the first Emmaus. I replaced him first in the classroom, and then as Campus Minister when he went to Africa.[66]*

---

[12] *Meeting the Living God* is a theology text by Rev. William O'Malley '49 written for the upper secondary student. It has been widely used in religious studies courses throughout the country.

Father James Van Dyke, S.J. '77 offered a perspective—both as an alum and a Jesuit—on the evolution of the Campus Ministry program during the 1970s:

I would say that it was nothing near what we have now. There was a freshman retreat.... I think it was two homerooms went together. The only significant thing I remember is that somebody broke his teeth on the statue of the Blessed Mother at the retreat house in Clarence.

There was a Big Brother program. I don't think there was any sort of orientation for us—what being a big brother meant and how we should be going about that.

Toward the end of my time, [Father] Gerry Aman S.J., arrived here. And he's the person who began the retreat program [at the root of what] we have now, with the Emmaus retreat, and a much more intentional form of peer leadership.

He came in as a classroom teacher, [but] he was not comfortable being a classroom teacher. Out of his discomfort with being in the classroom, he became Chaplain. There were a few guys that sort of kind of tried to do retreat work, but it was very spotty along the way.... I would say this was a fairly simultaneous reality [at other Jesuit schools].... At the same time, in the ministries of Spirituality, no one was quite sure what to do. You had the idea of a retreat house start in the early 20th century, and into the 1960s those were places where guys came in for a weekend and had talks.... Only in the 1970s and 1980s did the idea of a directed retreat really become a serious idea...that this is what we should be doing with retreat direction.

I know that to a lot of the stuff that came into the Emmaus, Kairos, and Quest, the Cursillo Movement was not unimportant. Jesuit priests who were involved in those movements had an impact in the student retreat program. Emmaus started at Saint Peter's Prep in Jersey City, under Ned Coughlin, S.J., It would be fair to call him the "author" of it. As for Christian Service, it was a trimester religion course, and it was in the last trimester that we were able to go out to a local place.

These early days of the structured retreat program at Canisius would lead to one of the most cherished and respected elements of the CHS experience. They initiated the evolution of retreats from a series of isolated activities to a cohesive curriculum of spiritual formation now highly regarded as a key component of Jesuit secondary education.

The Allman Brothers At Canisius

Brian Prochnal '77, according to the June 4, 2017, *Buffalo News* article that tells the story in considerable detail, at first took Gregg Allman for a prank caller: "Prochnal said he began to curse at his caller, assuming it was a hoax.... It wasn't. It was Allman, the Southern rock legend."[67]

Following the lead of classmate Mike Militello '77, Prochnal, then 17, had managed to get a personal letter into the hands of the famous rocker. Eventually, after a series of conversations, the unbelievable happened: Allman met with Prochnal and, soon after, arranged with school administrators to put on a surprise concert under the guise of a school assembly.

When the students had gathered in the auditorium, they were treated with a remarkable surprise: a concert that had been kept under wraps and the celebrity visit of Allman, his wife Cher, their son, Elijah Blue, and their daughter, Chastity. The December 1, 1976 *Citadel* describes the concert:

The plan for Gregg's introduction was to have Militello, O'Shea, Irwin, Prochnal, and Curran go out front to introduce Allman. The curtain would remain closed during the first two songs so as not to reveal the presence of "Freeze."[13] This would create an added surprise, as Gregg would pretend he was going to leave, step behind the curtain and then break into the exalting sound of "One Way Out."

---

[13] Freeze was a Syracuse band who were scheduled to perform for a December dance at CHS; they joined Allmann for the impromptu concert, according to *The Citadel*.

Sparked by the cheers received by Cher and the children, Allmann, Cameron, and "Freeze" encored with another rendition of "One Way Out." Speculation was made as to whether Cher would sing or not, but the fact that she and Gregg plan to release a joint album was more than likely the reason why she didn't (so as not to reveal any new hits.) At the reception afterwards Allmann granted an exclusive Citadel interview on a variety of questions.

In response to why he accepted the invitation to visit Canisius, Gregg explained his mood and circumstances at the time Prochnal's letter arrived. "I was just sitting around...and I got the letter. To tell you the truth, I was bored at the time." The boredom he was enduring was due, as Gregg admitted, to his "missing a live audience. Because the people really make it."

He expressed his impressions of Canisius as being "very, very peaceful" compared to the military school he attended during high school. "There," he continued, "everything was done by a bell...even getting up in the morning."[68]

Image from the December 1, 1976 issue of *The Citadel*, taken by Fr. Ron Sams, S.J., '46. Allman is seated at the keyboard with the CHS student body seated in the auditorium in the background.

Page 148 of the *Arena* 1977 Yearbook. Allman & Cher at CHS. "To Canisius, 'Don't forget to Boogie'! Love, Gregory L. Allman & Cher & Elijah Blue," wrote Allman (below).

The Blizzard of '77

"The 1976-1977 School Year was marked by an unappreciated record. That record was the most days off on account of snow. Several separate storms hit the Buffalo Area, with the monstrous January-February Blizzard topping things off,"[69] proclaims the 1977 *Arena*. Nearly two weeks of snow-closure abbreviated the semester, which provided a respite from classes for Canisius students. The storm was no holiday, however—the death toll across the region was twenty-nine.

Snow puns pile up in the February 23, 1977 edition of *The Citadel*.

Some Athletic Notes From the 1970s

Establishment of Formalized Weight Training

According to Jeff Gemmer, "More than anything, [Phys. Ed.] offers opportunities for exposure to a lot of different things.... It enables kids to decide for themselves if a sport or skill is something they might want to pursue." Among the skills students learn in a physical education curriculum, Gemmer believes weight training is the most important because of its life-long utility. The school made an investment in this in the early 1970s.

Saving money by cancelling the $1,500 towel service, the department was able to purchase a universal training machine and begin to teach skills. Prior to 1972, there was no formalized weight training, even for the football team. Bodyweight resistance was the only thing, or kids would work out individually at other gyms. The first dedicated weight training facility began in the fall of 1973, according to Gemmer. "It became a fourth facility for gym," said Gemmer, referring to the aud, the small gym, the pool, and the weight room. It was located in the room at end of the corridor leading to the top of the stairs near the pool (currently Room 0B7). It was eventually moved in the late 1970s into the current space, which had been divided into a weight space and wrestling room. Gemmer explained that the weight collection was built gradually with money from the Phys. Ed. budget through the second half of the decade.[70]

An Undefeated Football Streak: 1972-1977

The Crusaders achieved what was, at the time, a state and local record in a remarkable unbeaten streak of 42-0-1 from 1972 to 1977. Bryce Hopkins '08, an Assistant Coach and team archivist, offered this description:

The Crusader football teams of the 1970s achieved a feat—the longest undefeated streak—which has yet to be surpassed in Western New York. With long-time head coach Johnny Barnes retiring as the nation's winningest high school football coach at the conclusion of the 1972 season, the first season of the streak, the program turned to his assistant, Richard "Bus" Werder, to lead the Crusaders.

In Buffalo, Canisius was the power program of the 1970s, compiling a team record of 42 wins and 1 tie from 1972 through 1977—the "Streak" years—to establish the local record for most consecutive games without a loss. In that time, Canisius kept opponents guessing by mixing schemes and play calls. Bill Koessler helped showcase the Crusaders' power run game and became the first Canisius player to rush for over 1,000 yards in 1973, running for a then-league record 1,238 yards; two years later in 1975, Mark Butler and the Crusaders took predominately to the air with Butler becoming the first Canisius player to throw for over 1,000 yards.

While the teams certainly had their share of talent, including All-Catholic stars such as Joe Bremer, Mark Butler, Kevin Curran, Art Eve, Bill Koessler, Phil McConkey, and Bryan Tenney, only a small handful of Crusaders from those "streak" teams went on to play at Division 1 programs, and only McConkey would go on to play professionally in the NFL, doing so after concluding his naval service following his graduation from the Naval Academy.

Just as dominant as the streak itself was Canisius' dominance of local rival St. Joe's. The Crusaders won all five games over the Marauders during the streak years, outscoring St. Joe's 134 to 25 over the stretch, including shutting them out twice. Those victories were part of a decade-long run for Canisius without a loss to their archival, as Canisius went 9-0-1 from 1968 through 1977, a streak only just recently surpassed in 2018 as the Crusaders won their 10th straight over the Marauders.

There have been many successful Crusader football teams over the years, but the legend of the "Streak" teams of the 1970s carries on even to this day as inspiration for the next generation of Crusaders. As Canisius continues to thrive on the gridiron, outsiders can find the origins of the modern-day success go back to the time of Barnes, "Bus," and the boys of the 1970s.[71]

Return of the Hockey Program: 1972

According to Jeff Gemmer, he brought hockey back in 1972, which had been gone since the mid-1950s. "The Sabres were brand new. Hockey fever was at a pitch; kids were asking if we could bring it back." There was some resistance to it among coaches of other programs. "First year we were 21 and 2, and beat Canisius College twice. Who knows what would have happened if we'd had a losing season. I've always questioned that. But we were blessed that we had a lot of good hockey players. My coaching experience was limited. In fact, I'd use the kids. They'd diagram stuff. We'd have off-ice chalk talks and I'd let them speak. I coached until 1977 when my son was born."[72]

GAMBIT is Born - 1975

Your author had the fortunate opportunity to interview Father Ron Sams, S.J., '46 in October 2016, less than a year before his death in June 2017. As the founder of GAMBIT—as well as its steward, champion, and face for many years—Father Sams was able to offer perhaps the most authentic perspective on its origins and relevance to the school.

Gambit has been a unique operation. The first Gambit was 1975. I came in 1974 from Guam. When I came here, we were just getting a new President...Bob Cregan became President my first year.... I was told by the administration that the school really needs money. So that's gonna be one of your major jobs...alumni and development...to raise money for the school.

I was given two options. We've gotta raise money in a major way. One possibility was to have Bingo every week on a big scale, which other places had done to make money. Or, another choice would be, we'd heard from other Jesuit high schools around the country that they are running what they are calling an auction, and they could teach us how to do it. But nobody knew any details...just that there was an auction making a lot of money.

My reaction was, I'm not going to run a big Bingo deal every week. So let's try this auction. I didn't know anything about it, but I'd learn. The first place I went was Rochester. McQuaid. And they had started just one year ahead of us. I went over to McQuaid after they'd done their first one in 1974, so I missed it. They called it BASH...an acronym for "Building a Scholastic Heritage." I found out there were several schools in the Midwest that McQuaid had learned from. I went to Cincinnati and saw theirs, and the one outside of Chicago, and got information from several others...Seattle, Spokane, San Francisco...that's how McQuaid got their start.

Interesting little story about how we got the name Gambit...all the schools had a different name, and they were always distinctive. For example, the one in Marquette was Topper, as in the top hat, to evoke class. The one at Xavier in Cincinnati, well, they were always known as "Saint X.,"so they call it "Xtravaganza." I can't remember all the others. So we had a Jesuit community, about twenty-five or thirty guys or so living over at Frauenheim Hall. So one evening, we had a brainstorming session. Just the Jesuits. I gave my presentation about the auction, about why we wanted a special name like the other schools.

So we brainstormed. What was distinctive about Canisius that we could build on for a name? So we said, it looks like a castle. And someone says, the game in a castle is chess. You know, the king and the queen, and the pawns. Now I don't know how to play chess. But somebody else says, you know, there's a move in chess where you sacrifice one of your pieces in order to be in a better position for the future. And I said, that's it. That sounds great! We're asking our people to sacrifice that the school may be in a better position. Perfect name. So that's how we got Gambit.

We used the old English letter style to evoke the castle idea. It was just at that time that the Super Bowl football game was getting started...and they always used Roman numerals. So, I said, let's use Roman numerals. And that's what we did.

Believe it or not, the first year gave us a net profit of $41,000. We were encouraged by that. And I remember talking to someone that night, one of our attendees. And I said, "You know, next year I want...." and he said, "Next year?! You don't want to do this again? You're out of your mind! You think

you're gonna get these people to do this again and donate all these things?"
He thought I was out of my mind to do it a second time. And we've been going
forty-two years...haven't skipped a year.

It was a large crowd in 1975. I don't remember actually, but I would guess we
had about three or four hundred.... It wasn't always on campus. And that was
unfortunate, but I understand why. A number of years ago...the administra-
tion here saw a problem with facilities. We only had one venue here...the aud.
We used to have to close the auditorium down for about a month...we used to
build tables over the aud seats. It was...interesting.

Anyway, we only had the one place for a lot of school activities. And the Stat-
ler was available. So for about five years, it was held at the Statler. It was
always held here until about 2004.... But we lost something during those five
or six years down at the Statler. Because it was just another auction, because
it wasn't at Canisius.... Now, with the new construction...having the Kennedy
Field House available for the dinner and the oral auction meant that we didn't
have to do as much in the auditorium, and the auditorium wasn't needed for
sports, so we would work it out for the play, and it worked out very well.[73]

Father Sams, S.J., '46 at Gambit XLII in 2017.

Alumni Hall - 1977

In the same interview, Father Ron Sams '46 also shared his account of the origins of Alumni Hall.

The idea of alumni hall came to my mind because when I came here as Alumni Director in 1974, I saw some of the Alumni pictures around the school falling apart. Several were great big frames...but no one took care of them. The pictures inside were individual pictures that were glued onto the backing, and they had fallen down. They looked awful. They were all different sizes, and they were all over the school, and they were not complete. So I said to myself, if I don't do anything else in my years here, I'm going to take care of those alumni pictures.

So what I did was this. A gentleman named Bob Koch was a professional photographer, a friend of mine. He came to take pictures for various events at the school. I talked to him one day about my plan. I said I want to have all of the alumni class pictures the same size...we'll put them in a place in common in the school...the entrance to the auditorium would be the perfect place; you know, everyone goes through there and sees everything.... [We chose]...the perfect size...some of them were huge...[and] had to be re-photographed and cut down to size. Then we'd have to figure out what we don't have.

I said the school began here separate from the College in 1912-1913... when the College segment moved down to Jefferson and Main...the high school...had its first graduation on its own in 1913, and I said I think we have pictures from then. And I wanted this thing to be complete, and it is. That's the first one down in Alumni Hall...

Fortunately, everything worked out well, because we had the old yearbooks. And so I had to take a few old yearbooks and cut them up and make a whole new montage of the class. And Bob [Koch] would come in when he had free time...it took us almost two years. He would come in the afternoon and we'd work in the room that's the Neil Conference Room now...that was our little studio and we'd set up the originals and work on it. We started off with putting up about forty or forty-five pictures in 1977. We had them all and we put them up in the entrance to the auditorium...and when Gambit came, we took them all down because we needed that as a display area for gifts and paintings...and then put them up again.

It was dedicated to Father Donald Kirsch, S.J., one of the previous presidents and principals.... I think it's one of the treasures of the school. That we have all the alumni pictures since we started independent as a high school...the fact that we have them all the way back to 1913...when people come, they see their grandfathers, their great grandfathers, and what a tradition it is. It's the first thing that attracts you.[74]

Alumni Hall. Photo by Ginger Geoffrey.

The First Female Faculty Members

Up until the Fall of 1970, Canisius had an all-male faculty. The addition of just a few female faculty members began the significant shift toward what is now a nearly even mix of men and women on the faculty. Ms. Andrea Tyrpak-Endres offered some perspectives on the integration of female faculty at Canisius during an interview for this book. At the time of the interview she was serving as the first female Principal in the school's history. Her first year at Canisius was 1975-1976.

There had been women here previously...randomly, a nun...as far as teachers go. Women were certainly here in secretarial positions. When I came in there were two others—Liz Friedman, an art teacher—and Mary Johnson, a French teacher—and I taught religion.... The Jesuits were very welcoming.[75]

Father James Van Dyke, S.J., '77 offered some perspectives as a student attending the school in the middle of the decade:

When I arrived here there was only really one female teacher, and that was Liz Friedman. There were some other women on the staff: Eleanor Houlihan, Lee Clark, Alice Leech, Andrea Tyrpak-Endres, and Kathleen Horrigan in the Guidance Office...she in many ways helped a lot of us get into college...she played an important role for all of us in College applications.... It was still a very small universe.

The more interesting thing is when I returned as a teacher...there were any number of female teachers who arrived and became very important in the life of students.... It was a huge change. One of the things that is helpful to set the context is this: grammar school was largely an experience of woman teachers. For us, coming here and realizing that intelligence and learning were also male enterprises was an incredibly important realization.... The interesting thing, also, was to see women who were very much a dynamic part of the faculty...in this very masculine preserve, there were very respected female teachers. That's a testimony.[76]

School publications contend that Mrs. Elizabeth Friedman and Miss Roselyn Wasserman were the first female teachers at the school. The *Citadel* issued October 21, 1970, reports that "when Miss Wasserman first came here, she understandably was worried about fitting in, but, as she put it, 'the boys have made me feel right at home.'"[77] As for Mrs. Friedman, the follow-up article pictured here (*The Citadel*, Dec. 1970) provides more insight into her initial experience.

Again, it is notable that today, Canisius benefits from a faculty that has nearly equal percentages of men and women—an important balancing element for an all-male student body.

Mrs. Friedman Expands Art Program
More Cultural Activities Planned

No one would have thought, even last year, that one of the questions asked of a new faculty member would be: "What did women's liberation have to do with your being hired?" The teacher, of course, is Mrs. Elizabeth Friedman, and the answer is "Nothing." "I didn't know you had an all-male faculty here," she says. "I heard they were looking for an art teacher, so I applied and got the job."

Mrs. Friedman, a graduate of Rosary Hill College, is now working on her master's degree at SUNYAB. She is involved in many Canisius activities and has already promoted the student art show that was held from Dec. 7-11. She feels that show had a two-fold purpose: First, to give students, many of whom cannot fit art into their schedule, a chance to exhibit their works; and, second, to give the student body a view of what is being done in the art classes. Her aim as a teacher is more than to produce artists: "Not every student can be a Picasso, but each one can learn to experiment with art and to appreciate it."

Mrs. Friedman feels art is neglected at Canisius. She would like to see Canisius' curriculum revised to allow a three year art program available to all students. She invites anyone interested to see her or talk to an administrator about it. For next year she plans an after-school art workshop. Students from all years could participate without their schedules being affected. Art, she feels, should be given a more important position not only because of its cultural value but also because it is relaxing.

Mrs. Friedman has not found being among the small minority of two female teachers at Canisius difficult. "Everyone is very nice and friendly," she said. She expects to remain here as a teacher for a long time and is very satisfied with the challenge. She would like to see coeducation at Canisius. "I think an all-male school and faculty is unnatural, and eventually you are going to go into the outside world and live alongside women. I don't expect it to happen soon but I think coeducation will eventually come here."

For now, however, she is kept busy with the time-consuming task of building up an art room. "We collected furniture from all over the school and made a work area and lecture area," she explained. "Then we had a paint-in one day after school." The desks are bright with stripes and colors and flags.

We can only hope.

She seldom finds being a woman a detriment. "But," she complains, "I'm always getting letters inviting me to programs at Canisius that say, 'Bring Your Wife'."

S. Desmond

338

Gallery: 1970s

'Big Brother' Steps In

Big Brother Is Watching

Every school year finds the senior class enjoying its inevitable "high-man" position while the freshmen are spending half the year getting to know the building.

This year a new program designed by Fr. Edmund Nagle SJ and developed by Joe Macmanus, with the help of Kevin McCarthy, Pat Tunney and Tony Ragusa, will attempt to curb this form of school disunity. The Senior-Freshman Counseling Program is arranged so that interested Seniors assume the responsibility of helping incoming freshmen adust to high school life.

Strong Senior Support

Approximately 140 of 190 Seniors indicated support and participation in the program.

Advantages of this counseling are twofold: first, it creates an understanding between freshmen and seniors, the seeming opposite interests of the school, and secondly introduces incoming freshmen to Canisius in terms of scholastic, athletic and extracurricular applications.

Personal Interest Called For

The Senior is asked to assume a personal interest in the freshman and display CHS not as a building of learning but as a community of understanding.

Counseling can help the Senior learn to accept a degree of responsibility in human affairs. Although no official moderator will be announced, the Guidance Department offers its assistance. The degree of success, however, will depend on how much personal initiative is taken by the Seniors.

C. DiNatale

The Big Brother program is established under Fr. Ed Nagle, S.J., The Citadel, September 11, 1970.

Editorial /
/ Teach Your Children

War has never been a spawning ground for intellectual advancement. The most war-torn ages have been the darkest ages and the most hostile times the most mind-stifling.

There is an honest-to-goodness war being waged at Canisius.

"Takes the worry out of being close"

Student-teacher relations are anything but close in the majority of instances. The learning process, undoubtedly meant to be a journey made by two sets of friends, has deteriorated into a forced march. Teachers keep searching for new and better methods of forcing learning down teenaged throats while students sit up nights trying to contrive novel ways of keeping their mouths shut tight enough when they spot a teacher approaching. The climate that results from such lunacy is hardly conducive to the acquisition of knowledge.

The blame for the Student-Teacher War of 1971 lies partly on both sides.

A major contributor is the fact that a lot of pupils just don't want to learn anything the school has to offer. They approach Canisius as an elaborate game, and, as anyone will tell you, if you can cheat at a game while the umpire isn't looking you're nothing but better off for it.

Students are openly hostile to their instructors. They view them with skepticism and downright distrust as just a few more challenges to be overcome.

"Say it ain't so"

While it is sad that our students see their teachers in such a light, it is even sadder that their reservations are not totally unfounded.

If CHS isn't a game to the faculty, why do they keep an inning-by-inning score in their mark books? If they really care about their partner, the student, why do so many flee from after-school activities? If they desire a warm, friendly basis to work on, why do they so hotly contest so many new student proposals? If they deserve to be trusted, why do they play word games and avoid issues when presented with them?

Insight and creation flourish in peace. Ignorance and destruction prevail in war.

Only time will tell which of these will find a permanent home here.

An editorial expresses some of the apparent curricular and cultural challenges CHS faced in the early 1970s. The Citadel, May 13, 1971, page 3.

Joe's CHS: What's behind the rivalry

Many Canisius students consider a game in which Canisius opposes a school in their own neighborhood to be of great importance. For example, the Timon games are important to South Buffalonians, as are the Neumann games to Williamsville residents. However, one opponent remains uppermost in the minds of every CHS student, that one school over which a win is most climactic, the St. Joe's Marauders. The Canisius-St. Joe's rivalry is without a doubt the fiercest and oldest in the city.

It began back in the early 1920's at which time Canisius and St. Joe's were the only two Catholic high schools in Buffalo, certainly a contributory factor in the rivalry. In the years 1921-1931, CHS played the Marauders only in football. The games were held in the now non-existant Offerman Stadium before huge crowds. From 1931-1941 the series was for some reason suspended. In 1941 the two schools once again engaged in athletic competition, this time in basketball as well as in football. The basketball rivalry began with a flurry as the teams met three times. St. Joe's won the first game in double overtime, but the Crusaders stormed back to win the next two. From then until 1948, the Crusaders continually dominated the Marauders. During the fall of 1948 the Catholic League was formed, causing many to question the strength of the rivalry.

They felt that with so many other schools, it would slacken off. However, obviously this rivalry has continued right up to the present.

In football CHS outscored St. Joe's regularly for the first seven years. At this time the games were played at War Memorial Stadium and televised locally. The first league meeting of the two was at this setting, before 1,200 fans in 1948. The Blue and Gold registered a victory and continued winning for the next six years, from 1949 to 1954. Then before 27,000 people in War Memorial Stadium, St. Joe's beat Canisius for the first time in league play. The Marauders also emerged victorious for the next five years, with the teams tying in the next one. From 1960 to 1967 the two rivals alternated winning. However, the last four years show Canisius with the upper hand with three wins and one tie. Overall the two have stalemated in football, with fifteen wins apiece and three ties.

In basketball they are also almost even in wins and losses. From 1941-1948 the Crusaders prevailed. Then St. Joe's got moving and dominated CHS for the next 11 years, the first years of the Catholic League. In 1959 the Marauders held a 12-4 edge at which point Canisius began to even up the score. This is due especially to Canisius victories in eight of the last nine games. Also it can be noted that in the last 14 seasons Canisius has emerged with 7 league championships.

The rivalry has also continued into track. St. Joe's has had extremely strong teams for the last 5 or 6 years, but early in the league, around 1955, when track competition began, Canisius was the league power.

Even though the athletes change, as do the places of competition, the rivalry has continued to run strong. So let the cry that has been heard for nearly fifty years continue to be heard for many years to come. Beat Joe's!

Understanding the rivalry. The Citadel, December 20, 1971.

Paul Cumbo

Program Helps Boys Achieve Higher

Under the direction of Mr. Charles Chimera, Canisius High School is offering a program for the 7th grade disadvantaged boys willing to spend part of their summer in improving themselves mentally and physically. It is also designed to assist both culturally and economically in their education. This program, called the Higher Achievement Program or simply H.A.P. is limited to students of low-income families with the academic potential to attend one of the better high schools, but who fail to do so because of inadequate counseling, insufficient motivation, and deficiency in verbal skills. Without special assistance, it is unlikely that the student will succeed in the competition involved in interesting high schools.

The program is free. Most expenses are paid for by the New York Province of the Society of Jesus.

This summer, the program will be limited to boys from the public and parochial elementary schools from the area often designated as inner-city. The financial status of the applicant's family should be between $3,000-$7,000 annual income. Occasionally, however, boys from large families with an annual income over this amount are accepted. The program is open to boys of all faiths.

The program runs from July 3 to August 8, 1972, from 9:00 to 3:00. A typical day would run as follows, 9:00-12:00 classes of English, Math, and Remedial Reading. An hour is then set aside for lunch. From 1:00 to 2:15, the student may choose to spend his own time on an elective, which includes electronics, Mechanical Drawing, reading or a movie. He next gets away from the mental works and concentrates on sports activities (soft ball, swimming, basketball). The program then concludes at 3:00.

Above all, the program tries to provide motivation to make the youngster aware of his potential and to create an atmosphere for ultimate success in high school.

Francis Downey

An article by Francis Downey announces the establishment of the HAP Program in summer 1972, under the direction of Mr. Chimera. *The Citadel,* May 25, 1972.

342

Johnny Barnes Retires After 42 Years of Service

If you do anything long enough, you can pile up statistics. If you work hard enough you can one day achieve recognition as the best. To make your name synonymous with success, however, takes a special kind of man. In his forty-two years at Canisius, Coach Johnny Barnes has succeeded both on the playing field and off. The nation's "winningest" school boy coach, Mr. Barnes has had only two losing seasons in seventy-nine combined sports campaigns.

Three times he has been chosen the prep-school coach of the year and has sent numerous crusaders on to later and greater stardom. Besides coaching football for forty-two seasons, basketball for twenty-two and baseball for thirty-five, Mr. Barnes ran the school's intramural program and was the only phys-ed instructor when Canisius had over one thousand students.

Mr. Barnes' career has been filled with highlights. Five times his baseball teams made it to the American Legion finals only to lose by one run. A twenty-three game winning streak of the early fifties and the legendary "Hurricane Hazel" game of the 1954 season stand out in Mr. Barnes' football coaching career. In 1933, the Crusaders had the low point of their football history when they went winless but Mr. Barnes came back the next year with an undefeated team and the first of eleven championships.

Coach Barnes not only knew how to win but also how to end his career on a positive note as he did with last fall's undefeated, first place finish.

Canisius College recognized Coach Barnes' contribution to the community last fall when they conferred on him an honorary Doctor of Humane Letters degree. Mr. Barnes, a fixture at Canisius for forty-two years, will remain a legend here forever.

—Joseph Sellers

Milestones to Remember

—Born in Louisiana: 1908

—August 30, 1931: came to Canisius from Loyola University

—Became head coach in football, baseball, and basketball

—1963: received a complementary letter from President Kennedy commending Coach Barnes on his fine work with young men

—In 22 seasons of Basketball he compiled 342 victories

—In 35 years of Baseball he compiled close to 400 victories

—In 42 years of Football he compiled a 286-68-16 record including 11 championships

—Worst season: winless football campaign in 1933

—Best season: undefeated campaign of 1972

—Named prep-school Coach of the year for 3rd time by the Chicago diocesan newspaper New World in 1972-73

From The Citadel, Apr. 6, 1973.

Paul Cumbo

Cregan, Papaj View Co-Education

Co-education at Canisius — there's a topic for you. *Citadel* decided to look into the area and see what exactly the school's stand on the subject of co-education was, or better yet, to find out if they even had a stand. *Citadel* talked with Frs. Cregan and Papaj to hear their official thoughts on the matter.

When asked if the topic of co-education had ever been considered at any meetings of Jesuit secondary school Principals Fr. Papaj stated quite matter of factly, "yes, it has." He continued by saying that at such meetings they have taken time to discuss and think about the matter. Fr. Cregan related that co-education had also been brought up by the Jesuit Secondary Education Association. This group has gathered together ideas, pro and con, on co-education from 7 Jesuit high schools that have changed over in the last 5 years. Fr. Cregan added that co-education was also discussed at a meeting of the Presidents of Jesuit high schools last October.

The final decision, or statement which has been issued from all these Jesuit Administrative meetings boils down to this; before any real decisions are made, co-education must be studied much more. If these meetings have brought about anything it's a realization that they're dealing with a situation that Fr. Cregan considers, "much bigger than can first be appreciated."

Within our own school situation Fr. Papaj revealed there has been "no serious thought" on the part of faculty and administration regarding co-education. He does say however they "have brainstormed the topic with the conclusion that co-education should be thought about." Fr. Cregan explained that it's "been brought up as something we must have ideas about."

Considering the rise in tuition of many if not all Catholic high schools in the years to come the next question put forth dealt with merging Catholic high schools as a means of staying in operation and at the same time going co-ed. Fr. Papaj related that as we are a Jesuit school we are under the direction of a Provincial who is in turn guided by a national province. "These people," Fr. Papaj stated, "have been thoughtful about co-education and they have expressed their thoughts: under no condition could they see going co-ed just to stay in operation" Fr. Papaj went on the explain that to go co-ed Canisius would need a good, sound educational basis for it. There must be, among other things, "sociological proof that it's needed in our community." Fr. Papaj

went on to point out that, "if you look at the Catholic high schools in Buffalo you can't say girls aren't receiving a good secondary education." He said the Buffalo areas does not have the problem other communities have in the area of a girl's high school education.

When asked what, in their opinions, would have to change at Canisius were we to co-ed, both Frs. Cregan and Papaj replied they couldn't answer because, "Too many prior questions would have to be answered." After a few moments of thought however, they began to list some of their questions:" What type of person would we accept as a student? How would we change our requirements? Would we have to make course changes? Physical Education must be kept in mind here. Fr. Cregan pointed out the "huge problem in physical education. This school was never built with that (co-education) in mind." Ideally you could attract the most intelligent people to a co-ed school; what then would happen to the less smart boys who normally would have been accepted but now are left out due to the added competition? How would the school character change, the relationship of faculty/student? How would teachers change their courses to fit the co-ed system? How would you revamp the entire area of extra-curriculars to suit the change? As Fr. Papaj said, "the question of co-education becomes more complex than it is first seen to be."

In closing Fr. Papaj stated, "at some point we ought to study the possibility, of co-education. Now, however, there is no pressing need to do it. As we do consider the possibility there are all kinds of things which must be considered. . . . No decision will be made until a great deal of study goes into co-education."

As Frs. Cregan and Papaj both stated, no school should choose the option of co-education without consulting nearly everyone beforehand. This is an area which cannot be considered independently, it must involve other groups. Such groups would include all private schools of Buffalo, the Buffalo Diocese, parents, alumni, the Board of Trustees of the school and the entire Jesuit educational organization which includes Provincials and the General in Rome among others.

As Fr. Cregan made very clear, "when speaking of co-education you're making a change, you're refounding your school."

—Mike Tunney

Co-ed possibilities examined in *The Citadel* Mar. 25, 1976.

344

Fr. Nagel, Fr. Aman and senior Harold Harden discuss Chapel's "new image." —Arena

Chapel Has Relaxed Look

The Canisius Student Chapel has a new look this year. During this past summer under the direction of Chaplain Fr. Gerald Aman, S.J. and Br. James Dennehey, S.J., the chapel was remodeled to accommodate the changes in the Mass and Catholic faith in recent years.

During the 1960's, the Catholic church attempted to narrow the gap between the secular and laity. "Everything was too rigid," says Fr. Aman. "Now they are trying to make the Mass more comfortable for the people by making things simpler." Making the liturgy easier to understand, and the moving of the altar to face the people, are two of the changes.

The renovation offers a whole new atmosphere. "It proves that beauty can be more than status," states Fr. Aman. In order to brighten the room, the permanent altar was removed from in front of a large window. The pews are no longer in rows but are arranged around the altar. Everything, except the stations of

the cross, was taken off the walls to bring out the beauty of the wood panelling and chandeliers. "It's really a beautiful room," adds Fr. Aman.

The chapel is now versatile and adaptable to the different groups of people using it. "We handle anywhere from 2 to 150 people," says Fr. Aman. "This arrangement lets us have a Liturgy closer to the type of liturgy we wanted to run." Everything is portable and can be easily rearranged if necessary. All materials removed such as the altar, statues and the second confessional have been stored away for the time being.

The cost of the whole project has been minimal. Work on the chapel started immediately after school ended last year and is just about complete. No new materials were purchased but a new beige rug has been donated by J.C. Penney's to help out with the acoustics.

— Mike Militello

Fr. Aman, S.J., comments on the Chapel redesign in *The Citadel*, Oct. 12, 1976.

Icers Get Reprieve

As a result of the revenue received from the "Mr. Bukowski for a day" raffle, which exceeded $350.00, the varsity hockey team will be able to complete its present season. Still, upon completion of this campaign, the problem of future funding will again confront the squad. The controversy surrounding this dilemna centers around who is going to appropriate funding to assist the financially troubled club.

Coach Jeff Gemmer personally feels his team should receive financial assistance from the school since many of the other school teams are subsidized by the administration. Furthermore, Mr. Gemmer emphasizes that the goalsters have performed admirably in previous years thus meriting financial aid. Obviously, the team cannot receive total assistance. However, proportionate budgeting has been mentioned as a possible solution on numerous occasions.

All excess money in the team treasury has been exhausted due to the fact that some necessary equipment (including a medical kit) was purchased by the squad before the commencement of the season. Additional assets would have been taken in during the regular season, however the league does not charge an admission fee therefore limiting the profits the team otherwise would have received.

Mr. Gemmer hopes to acquire $100.00 in admission revenues during the course of the play-offs and points out that although this is a small sum of money, "every little bit helps." Nevertheless, $100.00 is far short of the amount needed to complete a full hockey season. Ideas for fund raising events are presently being sought by general manager, Mr. Aldo Narduzzo, father of senior captain Paul Narduzzo. "Mr. Narduzzo has handled all the financial activities for the past two years and hasn't received any recognition for his excellent work," points out coach Gemmer.

However, even the excellent job performed by Mr. Narduzzo has been unable to solve the team's financial woes and it appears when next year's athletic budget is drawn up, the plight of the Canisius hockey franchise could well be determined.

— *Tom Perez*

The hockey program faced financial struggles in its early years. *The Citadel* Mar. 25, 1977.

Canisius "Behind Closed Doors"

Canisius High School is fortunate in having a number of distinguished alumni. Few, if any, are as famous or as popular as comedian Mark Russell of the class of 1950.

On Saturday night, Oct. 9, Russell came to Canisius for a benefit performance which added approximately $6,000 to the school's coffers.

After his performance, Fr. Robert Cregan, S.J., and Fr. Ronald Sams, S.J. presented a certificate to Mr. Russell, inducting him into the CHS Hall of Fame. Upon receiving the certificate, Mr. Russell quipped, "It's in Latin. I can't read it!"

Mark Russell has become one of America's foremost political satirists through his daily syndicated column, his personal appearances and his television shows. He is very modest in describing himself, however: "The Jesuits made me what I am today . . . a semi-name in show business, a slow-rising comedian."

The benefit performance was first suggested to Mr. Russell by Fr. Cregan's secretary, Mrs. Eleanor Hoolihan, in June of 1976. He agreed to the suggestion, thanking Mrs. Hoolihan for the invitation; the planning of the details encompassed over a year of work.

The show opened with musical entertainment provided by the "Tintinabulation Ragtime Trilogy," composed of Keith Konopa, '74, Marty Quebral, '76 and Canisius senior Darryl Nettles.

Mr. Russell's academic career at Canisius was less distinguished but just as exciting as his career afterwords. Graduating "about 169th" in a class of 211 graduates, Russell remembers attending summer school for geometry and French; his entry in the 1950 yearbook (under the name Ruslander) lists him as a member of the French Club. "That doesn't mean anything. They've got me on the tennis team in there too, I think. I never played tennis in my life."

Some of his anecdotes would seem to indicate that he believes that Canisius was more difficult when he attended. "I was chatting with some of the students earlier. I said, 'How are you doing in Latin?' They said, 'What?' They think Caesar is a salad."

He remembers his days at Canisius, when some of his classmates, who are now "respected pillars of the community," were fond of dropping bags of water from the balcony onto the auditorium's lower seats. He claims this is "one reason the balcony is closed

today." During his performance he told his audience that "in honor of your presence here this evening, one of the seats will be restuffed." He described the auditorium's decor as "early Ben-Hur" and remarked that it looked like "Charlton Heston's game room." Observed Mr. Russell, "Any room with no windows has a lot to hide." Mr. Russell told his audience at one point that he had both good news and bad news. "Good news, I brought a check for $50,000. Bad news, the check was signed by Bert Lance."

Mark Russell enrolled at Canisius because of its traditions and its academic excellence. Many of his friends also came here, so he attended even though it was difficult and he lived a "long way" from the school — in Kenmore ("when it was upper-middle class"). Back then, he wanted to become a musician, and was a member of the CHS orchestra. After visiting Canisius recently, he was impressed by the variety in today's curriculum. Courses in art, music and media were not offered when he was a student.

Through "a lot of luck" (as well as a great cynical wit and a great deal of work), Mark Russell has come to where he is today. He spends about three to four hours each day writing his jokes and songs, and he uses the material he writes for his column and his live shows.

Mr. Russell was asked by this reporter what advice he would give to students who would like a career in comedy, and secondly, what he would suggest for those who wish to enter politics. After thinking for a moment, he replied, "I see no difference between the two."

—Richard Biffl

Mark Russell, a "class clown" who made it.

The Oct 27, 1977 edition of *The Citadel* contained this profile by Richard Biffl of Mark Russell '50.

347

Paul Cumbo

Mr. Mac Retires as Coach

Recalls 22 Years of Cager Competition

As the Canisius varsity hoopsters approach the climax of their campaign, an "off the court" development looms as the big story of the season. After 22 years as head coach of varsity basketball, Mr. Cornelius V. McGuillicuddy has announced his retirement, effective at the end of the season.

The large amount of time which must be spent during the rigorous four month campaign was the motivating factor which influenced Mr. Mac to step down. "During basketball season, I'm active every night whether it is coaching or scouting other teams," points out Mr. Mac. Furthermore, being athletic director he is involved with every other sport. Along with this responsibility, he teachs three subjects. Hence, he found himself with minimal spare time.

Stepping down as basketball coach doesn't terminate Mr. Mac's involvement in the roundball program. Being athletic director, he looks over the basketball budget and organizes many basketball-related activities.

Many memorable moments were witnessed by Mr. Mac during his 22-year tenure as head coach. "Winning the Manhattan Cup during my first year as coach was probably my greatest thrill," reflects Mr. Mac. He went on to capture three more titles during the next twenty years and "would like to go out as a winner." Everything wasn't roses, however, as the Crusaders lost four Manhattan Cup encounters by one point. These were his most frustrating moments.

Many changes have occurred in basketball since the commencement of his coaching days. "Basketball has made the most significant change of any sport," points out Mr. Mac. "The players are bigger, stronger, and more agile than in previous years." Mr. Mac feels that this year's squad posesses the most talent of any squad which he has coached. Still, the Crusaders must battle for a spot in the playoffs as the quality of play is on the upswing.

A busy future lies in store for Mr. Mac. Spring marks the beginning of the baseball season. This means three months of vigorous toil en route to a possible Georgetown Cup.

As Mr. Mac ruminates on his 22-year coaching career in basketball, he has accumulated a highly successful record of over 265 victories. This adds up to many hours which he sacrificed for the benefit of the Canisius basketball program. Hence, as Mr. Mac exits the roundball scene, he leaves behind him an era of pride and success and truly merits recognition from the entire Canisius community.

—T. Perez

Werder Ends Coaching Career

The Citadel issues from Feb 9, 1978 (top) and Jun 2, 1978 (bottom)

With the football season still five months away, the varsity squad hasn't begun to develop its annual form, although one drastic change has already been made. Mr. Bus Werder, 5-year head coach of Canisius varsity football and 12-year assistant, has announced his retirement from coaching.

"It had become a full time job for me, and I have other things to consider such as my family and work," explains Mr. Werder. During football season, his daily routine was centered around football. It dominated his time after work as well as weekends. "It just became too time consuming."

Mr. Werder's head coaching career was not one of mediocrity, but one of excellence. Canisius captured the Burke League Championship in each of his 5 years. He led his team in defeating archrival St. Joe's 5 years in a row. The Crusaders smashed the Western New York record with 43 consecutive undefeated games. This streak was terminated by Niagara Catholic, which in fact, was the only loss encountered by Mr. Werder since taking over "sideline duty" in 1973.

Mr. Werder holds many memories from his glory-filled career. Among the most vivid was breaking the record on September 24, 1977 against Dougherty. "I also remember the 1973 St. Joe's game. They were rated #2 in the state and we were heavy underdogs, but we went out and beat them, 32-12."

Because his teams were all champions, Mr. Werder came in contact with many outstanding athletes. He declined to name any of the players for fear that he might slight someone. "We had great players on every team. I can't even begin to name them all.

"I have no regrets in all my years of coaching," comments Mr. Werder. "I loved every minute of it and I will certainly miss it."

An essential element of a championship is the coach. Mr. Werder fulfilled the role of an "ideal coach" by displaying perseverance, patience, and knowledge. Through many years of dedication, he made the Crusaders "the team to beat."

Mr. Bill Johnson, last year's assistant, will most likely take over head coach duties in the fall.   *—Tom Fanning*

348

Schedule Undergoes Changes

Take a Walk For Canisius

Attention Students:
SOMETHING NEW
ON THE HORIZON
FOR NEXT FALL

Have you grown weary of selling raffle chances every November and December?

Would you like to try something different — something very healthful — something you can do for your school from your own energy and talent?

There will be a WALK-FOR-CANISIUS HIGH and it will be held this September. The way it will work is this: each student will be asked to obtain sponsors to pay so much for the distance covered in the walk. Then we will have a special day to do the walking and there will be check points along the route to verify that the distance was covered. The student then takes his proof of the walk to the sponsors, collects from them, and brings the money to the school. Sponsors can be individuals (parents, brothers, sisters, uncles [especially *rich* ones!], aunts, grandparents, friends) or they can be businesses (neighborhood stores, organizations, etc.). We also expect that some of the "old" faculty will join in the walk, too! Valuable prizes will be given for obtaining the most sponsors.

So, plan ahead this summer for sponsors and you will get all the details in September. And be sure you get in good physical shape, too — for the first annual WALK-FOR-CANISIUS HIGH!

Canisius High School has always been a pacesetting and innovative school. During the past six years, one of these innovative ideas was engaging in a modular system. The school day was comprised of 17 mods with both structured and unstructured time alloted to each student. The system, though, was on a trial basis, and it has become apparent that the modular system must be revamped.

On Friday, April 6th, the faculty and administrative board met to deal with the delicate and intricate problem of changing the present system so that the students and teachers of Canisius could benefit dually from its assets. After hours of deliberation, the following guidelines were adopted.

1.) 1979-80 be scheduled as a structured system. All activities will be definite, and self-directed time will be eliminated. It is possible, though, that students will be given certain unstructured time based on academic achievement, greater learning advantages and the instructor's approval.

2.) Students will be involved in the organization of the new schedule and will participate in meetings pertaining to the matter. Students will not be able to cast votes or directly affect the decisions made by the committee, however.

3.) The 1979-80 school year will be scheduled as a structured system, but the objectives of the modular system will not be rejected, but suspended for better implementation in the future.

The set-up of departmental Learning Centers will also be changed in order to coincide with the new structured system.

Advisement groups will remain in the set-up because they are an integral and valuable aid to the Canisius student.

If the new system is to be successful, we, the student body of Canisius High School, must support its strong points and also help to improve its flaws. We must also remember the quality education we are receiving will not change, but will be presented in a more beneficial fashion.

The Citadel's June 5, 1979, edition announces the end of the "mod system" of structured and unstructured time in the academic schedule (right). The same issue announced the departure of Fr. Joseph Papaj, S.J., as Principal after six years. Also, notably, the first CHS Walkathon is announced (left).

349

Canisius used to have cheerleaders! Image from *The Citadel*, December 1979.

Fr. Boller Assumes Principal Post

Along with the many new things here at Canisius this year—new schedules, more study halls, new mid-trimester grades, new teachers—there is one new and important face in the crowd. This is, of course, our new principal, Fr. Kenneth Boller, S.J.

Succeeding Fr. Joseph Papaj, Fr. Boller assumed the duties of principal last May. Previously Fr. Boller had taught at Xavier High School in New York from 1969 to 1972. In 1975 he became assistant headmaster at Xavier until his transfer to Canisius in 1978.

A native New Yorker, Fr. Boller attended Archbishop Mallory as a high school student. He commented, however, that he is "in love with the Buffalo area."

On Canisius students he said, "They are very friendly and open; fairly hard-working." In his experience with other Jesuit high schools across the nation, he said that the Canisius student "compares favorably with them." —*Christopher Sion*

Fr. Boller in action. —*photo by Kuczkowski*

The Citadel, December 1979, introduces Rev. Kenneth Boller, S.J., as the new Principal of Canisius.

Arena Dedications: 1971-1980

1971 - In Memoriam: Rev. Thomas M. Harvey, S.J., 1914-1970

1972 - Mr. John F. Barnes

"John F. Barnes has completed his forty-first year as a member of the Canisius High School faculty. His dedication to Canisius and his boundless determination as a coach have earned him a unique reputation as a truly outstanding educator.... Mr. Barnes has won recognition not only at Canisius but throughout Western New York. Recently, for example, he was named the Athletic Director at the Buffalo Athletic Club."

1973 - Nicholas H. Kessler

"Graduating himself from Canisius himself in 1928, Mr. Kessler has presently completed his 39th year teaching.... In honor of Mr. Kessler's many years of sincere devotion to the education of the 'Canisius Man,' and also in honor of the spirited integrity and classic individuality of this man, we dedicate the 1973 *Arena* Yearbook to him."

1974 - No dedication offered.

1975 - Dedication to "People [who must] live like this."

The 1975 *Arena*'s dedication is unique. It contains three photos, two depicting minority children in city locations, and a third simply of a door with a "FOR RENT" sign. The caption is "in this age of prosperity, we wonder why people must live like this. the [sic] arena '75 is dedicated

in this age of prosperity, we wonder why people must live like this. the arena '75 is dedicated to these people.

to these people." Perhaps the senior quote of editor Kevin Curran '75, lyrics from "Donkey Jaw" by the band America, offers some further insight: "Does it take the children to make you understand? Does it take the children to make a better land."

1976 - Nicholas H. Kessler

1977 - J. Gregory Werder '77

Gregory J. LoTempio '77 composed the dedication to his classmate: "On behalf of the 1977 graduating class of Canisius High School, it is with great pride and feeling that we dedicate this yearbook to the memory of our very special classmate, J. Gregory Werder. All of the students who were associated with Greg personally knew him to be a wonderful friend, someone you could talk to, someone who cared, and someone who would be honest.... Greg gave enjoyment to those who were together with him, even though we knew him for only a short time."

1978 - James Lancaster '78

Michael Barney '78, likewise, composed another reflection in memory of his classmate, James Lancaster, to whom the 1978 *Arena* is dedicated. "Jim had the rare ability to make people laugh with him...so overflowing with joy, happiness, and life.... It would be very selfish for us to continually feel sad about his departure because of the love he had unceasingly given to all of us. Those  of us who knew and loved him should realize that he has just gone to receive the payment for services rendered."

1979 - Rev. Edward N. May, S.J.

Continuing the in-memoriam tradition of the preced-
ing two years, the 1979 *Arena* was dedicated in
memory of Fr. Edward May, with the following reflection composed by Marc D. Landsberg '79: "What he
elicited from his students was the confidence and previously unknown ability to do the difficult work on our
own. Yet he was always there when anyone needed him.... Fr. May...was
dedication personified. Not only did he concern himself with our
knowledge in mathematics, but as a Jesuit he accepted the responsibility
of teaching the word of God.... He is no longer with us in this world, but I
know that in all of us his presence will linger on."

1980 - Thomas Hogenkamp

 "On December 16, 1979, the entire Canisius commu-
nity was grief stricken by news of the death of fresh-
man Thomas Hogenkamp.... [He] was always willing to
give of himself in order to share what he had with others. Whether by sharing his lunch with friends or his
intelligence by helping classmates with schoolwork,
Tom always embodied the true Christian spirit of giving.... The memory
of this friendly freshman who gave his all—in academics, in athletics, and
to his friends—will serve as an inspiration to all and will not soon be forgotten." The Hogenkamp Award was established in his memory and is one
of the highest honors bestowed annually upon a graduating senior at Commencement.

Notes

[1] Interview with Father James R. Van Dyke, S.J., '77. Thu, Nov 16, 2017.

[2] Interview with Mr. Joseph Lucenti '73. Wed, Dec 21, 2016.

[3] "Minutes of the Permanent Advisors and the Board of Directors of the Founders of the New Canisius High School." Nov. 19, 1969. Source: CHS Archives.

[4] "Minutes of the Board of Trustees.". October 22, 1969.

[5] "Minutes of the Permanent Advisors and the Board of Directors of the Founders of the New Canisius High School." Mar 29, 1971. Source: CHS Archives.

[6] "Minutes of the Board of Trustees." Jul 22, 1971.

[7] "Minutes of the Board of Trustees." Oct 28, 1971.

[8] "Minutes of the Board of Trustees." Jan 27, 1972.

[9] Phone Interview with Tom Beecher '52. February, 2019.

[10] *Ibid.*

[11] *Ibid.*

[12] "Minutes of the Permanent Advisors and the Board of Directors of the Founders of the New Canisius High School." Oct 18, 1973.

[13] "Minutes of the Board of Trustees." May 3, 1973.

[14] "Minutes of the Board of Trustees." Nov 7, 1973.

[15] "Minutes of the Board of Trustees." Jan 24, 1974.

[16] Interview with Father James R. Van Dyke, S.J., '77. Thu, Nov 16, 2017.

[17] "Minutes of the Board of Trustees." Nov 7, 1973.

[18] "Minutes of the Board of Trustees." Jan 24, 1974.

[19] *Ibid.*

[20] "Minutes of the Board of Trustees." Oct 24, 1974.

[21] "Minutes of the Board of Trustees." Apr 24, 1974.

[22] *Ibid.*

[23] "Minutes of the Board of Trustees." Jul 25, 1974.

[24] "Minutes of the Board of Trustees." Jan 23, 1975

[25] *Ibid.*

[26] "Minutes of the Board of Trustees." April 24, 1975.

[27] "Minutes of the Board of Trustees." July 24, 1975.

[28] *Ibid.*

[29] *Ibid.*

[30] *Ibid.*

[31] "Minutes of the Board of Trustees." January 22, 1976.

[32] *Ibid.*

[33] *Ibid.*

[34] *Ibid.*

[35] "Minutes of the Board of Trustees." April 29, 1976.

[36] *Ibid.*

[37] *Ibid.*

[38] *Ibid.*

[39] "Minutes of the Board of Trustees." July 22, 1976.

[40] *Ibid.*

[41] Correspondence on file from the Treasurer's Office to the President's Office, January 28, 1977. Source: CHS Archives.

[42] "Minutes of the Founders of Canisius High School." November 16, 1977.

[43] "Minutes of the Board of Trustees." January 27, 1977.

[44] "Minutes of the Board of Trustees." April 22, 1977.

[45] "Minutes of the Board of Trustees." October 27, 1977.

[46] "Minutes of the Board of Directors of the Founders of Canisius High School." November 14, 1978.

[47] "Minutes of the Board of Trustees." November 29, 1979.

[48] "The Canisius High School Program." September, 1974. Source: CHS Archives.

[49] *Ibid*, p. 1.

[50] *Ibid*, p. 3.

[51] *Ibid*, pp. 4-5.

[52] *Ibid*, p. 6.

[53] *Ibid*, p. 8

[54] *Ibid*, p. 8

[55] *Ibid*, p. 8.

[56] *Ibid*, p. 10.

[57] *Ibid*, p. 10.

[58] *Ibid*, p. 11.

[59] Interview with Mr. Russell White. Thu, Dec 22, 2016.

[60] Interview with Father James R. Van Dyke, S.J. '77. Thu, Nov 16, 2017.

[61] *Ibid*, p. 11.

[62] *Ibid*, p. 11.

[63] *Ibid*, p. 6.

[64] *Ibid*, p. 7.

[65] *Ibid*, p. 13.

[66] Interview with Andrea Tyrpak-Endres. Mar 7, 2018.

[67] Kirst, Sean. "How Gregg Allman and Cher Stunned Canisius High 'assembly' in 1976." *The Buffalo News*, 4 June 2017, http://buffalonews.com/2017/06/04/dream-sequence-gregg-allman-cher-lighted-canisius-high/

[68] *The Citadel.* December 1, 1976. Page 3.

[69] *Arena* 1977. Page 56. Source: CHS Archives.

[70] Personal interview with Jeff Gemmer. Jan 11, 2017.

[71] Hopkins, Bryce '08. Written response to interview question. Feb 6, 2019.

[72] *Ibid.*

[73] Personal interview with Father Ron Sams, S.J., '46. Oct 3, 2016.

[74] *Ibid.*

[75] Personal interview with Andrea Tyrpak-Endres. Mar 12, 2018.

[76] Personal interview with Father James R. Van Dyke, S.J., '77. Nov 16, 2017.

[77] *The Citadel.* October 21, 1970, page 1, story by P. Adornetto, M. Collard, and J. Millemaci.

CHAPTER 11

The 1980s

ASK ANY LONGTIME FACULTY MEMBER about Canisius High School in the 1980s, and the nearly universal, immediate response is something to this effect: "That's when CHS almost closed its doors."

Now, of course, it's certainly reductive to characterize an entire decade of an institution's life based on financial struggle. However, the fiscal challenges loom so large in the picture that they were—and remain—impossible to ignore. (Consider: a great many events unrelated to the stock market crash took place in 1929, but that year and the years following will forever be associated with the Great Depression.) Certainly, while the 80s saw Canisius develop in myriad ways, they also demanded an existential reckoning. What emerged as the school's most critical fiscal (and, argua-bly, enrollment-related) crisis would lead—due to the tremendous effort, sacrifice, and generosity on the part of many—into a period of rebirth in the 1990s marked by many milestones, perhaps chief among them the "burning" of the mortgage in 1991 and the emergence of a long-awaited debt-free status. They also serve as a stark reminder and cautionary tale, underscoring the need for measured fiduciary management of an institu-tion so heavily dependent on annual tuition revenues.

Perhaps no other period of the school's (relatively) recent history can stimulate such strong and visceral reaction among those whose insti-tutional memory stretches back to that time. The slings and arrows of blame are quick to be loosed when conversation harkens back to such a painful period; however, it's important to bear in mind the benefit and privilege of hindsight when accounting for the challenges that faced the school. Certainly, questions emerge about the fiscal management, priori-ties, and decisions. Connecting the dots is easier in retrospect, of course, although one might reasonably ask why some weren't connected at the time. Regardless of this, ultimately, the most lasting testament is to the sacrifice and generosity so keenly apparent among so many in the com-munity. Where missteps and miscommunication alike may well have played a role; fervent commitment, unwavering faith, and dedication to the mission would see the school through this tumultuous decade.

An Alumnus-Turned-Teacher Recalls the 1980s

Dennis Beecher '88, now a longtime faculty member at Canisius, offered insights on student life in the mid-1980s.

Canisius was transformational. You walked in the door at thirteen and walked out a confident young man, ready for college. Cura personalis was alive and well, despite the fiscal challenges. We had no idea. We were cared for. We had tremendous pride. We built lasting bonds.

I was unaware how dire the enrollment situation was becoming, but my brother, who followed right after me, noticed it. We eventually became well aware that Canisius was on the verge of closing. But the fact that most students were unaware of it says a lot about the professionalism of our teachers.

In the 1970s, Canisius got extremely liberal and a lot less rigid. It was actually the students who brought back the rules in the early 1980s. They petitioned to the school to return to the strict dress code with a tie. Compared to today, the CHS of my student days was much stricter. I remember walking in freshman year on the first day of school, and a kid had a tail...like, a rat tail. A Jesuit took him aside, took out a pair of scissors, and just cut it. You couldn't get away with that today, of course. It set the tone. Like, "these guys mean business."

There were more Jesuits around, so I think you had a little more of that old school philosophy. If you were a second late for class, you had to get a pass, and you got JUG. Or you got the promptness sheet. And that's not just anecdotal. It was the case across the board. And those tiny little details—top buttons, for example—that we sometimes don't pay attention to and let slide, they did not let slide. I remember sitting in the Aud the first day. They said look right and look left. One of you will not make it to graduation.

There was more of a sense that this is a challenging school academically, and you're going to have to work very hard to make it. And if you don't, you're gone. I think now, we probably do a lot more to work with students who are struggling to try to keep them here; then, there was more of a sink or swim mentality with academics. Certainly, there weren't the after school programs we have nowadays to help students.

Day to Day Academic Life

Every school day was a different schedule and everything dropped out a day, so you had every subject just five out of six days, and every lunch was a double period and a double lab period for science. With AP's, now, you can't really do that.

Something that would happen very frequently, which was very funny, was that you'd be sitting in a class and ten or fifteen minutes in you'd look around and realize wait...these aren't the students in my class. You'd raise your hands and say I'm in the wrong class. It's weird, because the students seemed to notice it more often than the teachers. Teachers would often forget their lunch periods, because their lunch periods would change all the time. You'd go to your class and your teacher wouldn't be there, because the teacher thought it was his lunch period. I can see the benefit that you'd catch kids at different times of the day, but all in all, it caused a lot of chaos.

We didn't really take foreign language in our grammar schools. So when you got here freshman year, you took a little bit of Latin, a little bit of German, a little bit of Spanish, and a little bit of French. And then you chose, but didn't start a language full time until sophomore year. As for the other half of freshman year, you had a half-year language arts course—separate from English class—that was just grammar, designed to get everyone up to speed.

There was no Advanced Placement, and I don't recall that there were honors designated classes. Today, our AP and Honors courses take the top performing kids and put them in a top set of classes. There were some real advantages to not having those distinctions and the de-facto tracking. Look, I was an average student. I would see the top students in the class and see what they did and how they worked, and how they interacted. It helped me. I'd say, hey, I want to do what Greg Fenzl's doing. I would see how he would study. How much he would study. We were in the same class, and we'd sit down and go over Shakespeare together.

Daily Life as a Student

There was no consultation. School got out at 2:50. Everybody was out. Kids didn't really hang out after school. There weren't anywhere near as many clubs or this kind of community that we have now, where kids are hanging out on campus and in the library after school.

That being said, I remember a real sense by senior year that everybody got along. I really felt that community—that brotherhood that we talk about to-day, although we didn't really call it that—was very real. I definitely felt that sense of spirit. When we played at Pilot Field in the baseball championship, everybody was there. We weren't great athletically, across the board. I didn't see us beat Saint Joe's...we didn't have that dominance in most sports. We were good in some sports, but we definitely didn't dominate it. But there was a kind of underdog spirit. The rivalry was real. The sense of community was real. The brotherhood was there. And that was despite the fact that we were struggling to get kids in the door. We didn't know that. I loved every minute of my time here, and I know the same is true for a lot of guys.

Ministry & Formation

Emmaus senior year was one of the most important events of my life. It was unquestionably transformational. You had one real retreat while you were here. That's the only similarity to what we have now—the impact of that sin-gular experience. But we didn't have a memorable progression of retreats out-side of that. I think the retreat program we have now is the reason why many people walk out of Canisius and say this is the best high school in Western New York. For guys my age, that singular experience was just as important.

When I was a student, we didn't have religion the second half of senior year. We all were assigned service locations throughout the city. I was assigned to a nursing home. It was a great opportunity. It led me to see that when you get old and infirmed, it's pretty tough. I gained a lot of perspective on life from that. But all that was required was logging the hours. It was during a lunch period and another free period. It was all about just doing the action. Not a lot of guidance on the process, and there really wasn't a follow-up or reflective component like we have now.

Veteran Faculty Recollections

According to Mr. Russ White, who retired in 2016 after having served a remarkably long tenure at Canisius, the period of the late 1980s was defining for the school. A substantial excerpt from his interview with the author is included here for its contextual value:

Obviously, we [the faculty] weren't really privy to all the inside financial deal- ings of the school, but we knew something. I was on the Faculty Senate at the time...although it wasn't even called the Faculty Senate...I think it was called the "Negotiating Committee," actually.

Financially, things were going down the drain in '89. The feeling was that it was the school's own fault. I think we tried to hold tuition down, and we just got deeper and deeper into the hole until everything started to fall apart. There was some mismanagement. We were going down the drain, and there was still talk about artificial turf. I don't think we can blame anybody but ourselves.

Now, I can't give you numbers. But when I started in the 1960s we were prob- ably running about 900 kids.... I look back; I don't know how we did it. My typical chemistry class...if I had a class of 32, that was a nice size. 35 was not unusual.... And you know the size of those classrooms. We were packing them in. There was no room to move. But that was the norm.

As enrollment went down, I recall we had a retention and recruitment com- mittee. We were down in the high 400's. Plus there's word gets out that Canis- ius is in trouble, and if you've got a kid that's in 6th grade, maybe you don't even think about it. Self-perpetuating.

But 1989 was tough. The lay faculty...gave up a lot. Well, the Jesuits did too. We gave up a lot. We gave up raises; bigger than that, we gave up three per- cent of retirement, and that's...as you can imagine, the three percent is part of it, but the growth of that three percent over twenty years, that's another story. So we paid a price to keep the building open.... Prior to that, to the best of my knowledge, they were giving us 6%.

We bottomed out. We were told...there were times when making the payroll was tight. And Federal law says if you can't make the payroll, all sorts of things happen. I was led to believe we were maybe weeks away from going under.

We were cutting back. It was not a pretty time. There was a lot of stuff going on, but to the best of my knowledge, it didn't get into the classroom. People did their jobs. I don't even think the kids knew. Back then I don't think it was as well known. As far as the kids knew, everything was fine. It was far from fine. But we made it through. Father Keenan came in, and that was a major financial turning point.

When Father Keenan came in—and he turned out to be the savior of the school—Father Keenan was the good guy.... Father Zimpfer was cast as the bad guy...it was truly good cop / bad cop...Father Zimpfer had to be the hatchet man.... It was an ugly job, but it was a job that probably needed to be done, and it was usually laid at Father Zimpfer's feet. He took the heat. And he wasn't really like that. It's unfortunate, but it was his job.

[Father Keenan] was an excellent fund-raiser. We had a sense that we were in good shape. He just...gave you that feeling. He was very personable. People liked him. We had a feeling that he could fix things.

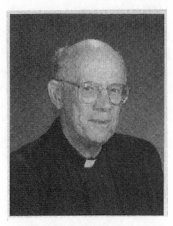

Certainly, the 1980s were a long and difficult road for Canisius High School. From early signs of fiscal trouble to, as Mr. White put it, the point where the school "bottomed out," the decade would confront the school with arguably its most painful period of reckoning to date.

Rev. Eugene Zimpfer, S.J., '49

An Inside Look at the 1980s

A degree of urgency is palpable in the "Minutes of the Trustees' Physical Plant Committee" from late December, 1980. Regarding a number of planned campus improvements, the minutes note that "considering the immediate need of the school for this renovation and the predictable rise in costs of at least 10% per year if the project is postponed, the Committee decided that the renovation should be planned for 1981."[1] Specifically, these improvements included the following:

- Roof work for Berchmans Hall, including a year's worth of pointing, totaling $25,000
- Renovation of the Science facilities, based on the fact that "Reports of both the Middle States Association of Colleges and Secondary Schools and of Jesuit Province visiting committees have emphasized this need." The total estimate quoted for this work in the summer of 1981 was "$450,000 which is divided into $200,000 for work on the building and $250,000 for equipment."[2]

Discussion is noted as to incorporating these expenditures as the next phase of the "PROJECT 80s" campaign, including the recommendation that "we look for a plan of long-term financing at low interest to cover the cost and include in this the school's debt. The paying off of this amount could be made a goal of the second phase of PROJECT 80s."[3]

Finally, it was again emphasized that the project should move forward despite its significant cost: "The Committee was well aware that this is a major undertaking for the school, but was convinced that the need for modernization of the Science area was so great that it should not be postponed."[4]

The Board's minutes from the end-of-school-year meeting (May 1980) reference the anticipation of an incoming class of 225, with a waiting list begun—this regardless of an announced tuition hike. Confidence remained in the fiscal arena, bolstered by a $10,000 payment on outstanding debt and projections that envisioned only a nominal deficit for the upcoming school year based on an enrollment of 700 students. A report on development activities indicated that GAMBIT VI grossed more than $100,000, a new record, and netted approximately $84,000. With regard to PROJECT 80s, the notes indicate, "...income has slowed a bit, but the overall pledge total just passed the $600,000 mark." Additional notes include a commitment to renew the Walkathon for a second year, and a new type of appeal for deferred funds and estate planning under the direction of Fr. Ron Sams, S.J.[5]

With regard to school life, the same report indicated renewed commitment to the HAP program, as well as underscoring the importance of two surveys. The first was "conducted among the students in conjunction with the New York State Bureau on the use of alcohol and drugs" in order to inform school programs related to this matter. The second was "an informal survey to ascertain how our 30 black students (4% of student body) are finding life here at Canisius High. In general, positive attitudes appear to outweigh the negatives."[6]

In a notable final insight labeled "new business," there is attention to "a suggestion made at a previous meeting that we look into the advisability of selecting a chairman of the Board who is not also the president of the school."[7]

In the notes of February 1981, there was considerable Board-level attention to faculty salaries and benefits. In hindsight, and in light of the salary freeze that would loom large in the lives of faculty later in the decade, it is interesting to note these observations:

Brother Mauro reported that discussions were centering around a 10% increase including the Blue Cross-Blue Shield insurance plan and a 1% increase in the school payment to the pension plan. The total cost of this increase would be about $70,000. Mr. McPherson commented that it is necessary for the school to continue to upgrade its faculty salaries in order to attract and keep good teachers. At present the Canisius High School salaries are on top of the list of all the local Catholic independent schools and compare favorably with the local public-school teachers' salaries. After a brief discussion, Mr. McPherson assured the Board that the faculty considers the school as theirs, too, and are determined to cooperate for the good of the institution.[8]

The fiscal challenges were no small matter, and there were significant factors that might well have caused some anxiety. One of these was the question of admissions numbers: "Father Boller reported that the present enrollment for next September's freshman class stands at 194—off a bit from last year's record enrollment, but still quite good.... Staffing needs will probably require the hiring of one new teacher (to replace a Jesuit going to a new assignment.)" Another significant concern lay with the rising cost projections for the planned physical plant work: "The architect's projected total costs approach $500,000.... The crucial question of how to finance such a major project was discussed. Since the school now has a bank debt of $235,000, the Finance Committee feels we should add that to the financial package needed, thus making the figure about $725,000. It was agreed by all that while the Science facilities renovation is needed academically as soon as possible, it will take some time to put together a proper financial package to handle this large amount. Therefore, the actual work will have to be postponed to the summer of 1982."[9] Further detail is provide in the Minutes, including various plans for initiating a new element of the PROJECT 80s fund drive, and the possibility of securing a[n additional] mortgage on the school.

Notably, it is mentioned that the incoming President, Father Joseph E. Billotti, S.J., had supplied a letter "giving his personal support for both the renovations and the fund drive." Closing notes clarified that "the renovation of the Science facilities is approved in concept, providing that the proper financing plan can be arranged...."

Finally, there was considerable focus on tuition revenue, both from an annual perspective and in light of long-term financing for major projects:

Brother Mauro pointed out that in order to seek a loan from any source we would have to present a balanced budget for the school with assurances of an ability to repay the loan. In order to balance next year's projected budget, an increase of $275 would be needed.... Up to the present time, our annual proposed budget was always projected with a deficit. The Board agreed that this was the time to make a tuition increase which would raise the actual money needed to balance the budget.... Thus, by a unanimous vote of the Board, it was decided that an increase of $275 be announced for next year with the full tuition and fees amounting to $1,765.

The Board also approved that in negotiating with the lay faculty and staff a 10% increase in the financial package be approved. Amidst all the focus on expenditures and financing, it is also noted that GAMBIT VII preparations were moving well, the Alumni Fund had reached nearly all of its $20,000 goal, and that pledges for PROJECT 80s totaled nearly $630,000, with $415,000 collected to date.[10]

Certainly, then, it is clear that the turn of the decade brought with it great anticipation, ambitious vision, and perhaps just enough fiscal support to keep cool heads supportive of a considerable financial outlay.

A lengthy letter dated March 4, 1982, was sent to the parents of the students from CHS President Rev. Joseph E. Billotti, S.J., and Board Chair Eugene P. Vukelic '48. In it, they provided a reasonably detailed summary of the school's concurrent financial challenges, including an explanation of the effective subsidy applied to each student in light of the actual-cost-to-educate vs. tuition charged. Likewise, the letter explained the interplay between several years of attempted "net zero" budgeting while avoiding substantial tuition hikes and the accumulation of expensive deferred maintenance. Finally, underscoring the principled commitment to maintaining an excellent teaching faculty (and alluding to the sacrifices made by teachers), they announced a tuition hike effective July 1, 1982. It would raise the total (tuition and fees) nearly 20% from $1765.00 to $2100.00. As part of this announcement, the school offered a new payment structure based on ten installments of $210.00. The letter closed by assuring the parents that "you are in our prayers as you sacrifice for the education of your sons. Please remember us as we labor to live up to the trust you have placed in us."[11]

Good news came in May, when Father Billotti was able to report that the bids for the renovation of the Science Center came in "at a level about 20% lower than estimated...[they] totaled $401,000 (vs. the original estimate of $504,000)." With this lower estimate, plans were added to install a new roof at a cost of $30,000. 202 freshmen had registered; about 210 were expected. Furthermore, "Father Sams reported...that the Science Center pledge total now stood at $335,000, that GAMBIT VIII...expected to net about $82,000."[12] Along with this good news, however, there existed a serious matter of unpaid tuition, "which amounted to over $100,000," but that "Brother [Mauro] said he expected that most of this would be paid by the end of the school year."[13]

By midwinter 1983, the Board Academic and Faculty Affairs Committee reported that they "had met with the Science Department members, who in turn conveyed that they overwhelmingly approved of the Science Center." On the down side, enrollment was "off by about 10% from last year" with only 161 students registered in January. Indicating a continued interest in diversifying the largely white student body, it was noted that "about 4% of the freshman student body are black."[14]

Along with discussion about reexamining the school's portfolio based on cash yield, there was optimistic news citing an increased Annual Fund Drive yield for the period from July 1982 to January 1983 ($100,082) over the *twelve*-month period prior to that, which had yielded only $91,272. A motion passed unanimously that resolved, with regard to the 1983-1984 fiscal year, to: "1.) Present a balanced budget; 2) Cap the Grant-in-Aid at $180,000; 3) [include a] $300 Tuition raise; and 4) [include a] 3% faculty raise."[15]

By the end of the 1982-1983 school year, a draft of a "long range plan" was presented to the board by an outside consultant, along with some adjustments to tuition and fee structures. Continued growth in Annual Fund and Gambit revenues is noted. On the expense side of things, the Minutes state that "Berchmans Hall and the Auditorium will be needing new roofs in the next two years and the cost has been estimated at $120,000 for the project."[16]

On the school life front, notably, the Faculty Steering Committee completed the profile of a Canisius High School graduate at graduation. A new Dean of Students was announced (Mr. Patrick Plunkett '77).[17] In the Board Minutes of February 11, 1984, it is noted that "Fr. Billotti made a presentation that had been prepared by Lawlor F. Quinlan, Jr., for the Student Recruitment Committee. His firm organized all of our publications—everything that goes out to the public—he developed a new logo and thrust—Jesuit excellence— 'Jesuit education for college for life.'"[18] This logo and motto would be used on school materials for many years.

An undated memo (although physically attached to the hard copy February 1984 Minutes in the archives) appears to contain summary copy intended for promotional publication related to this initiative and talking points for Father Billotti related to announcing a "Capital Needs

Campaign." It is printed on letterhead from the President's office, directed to the Greater Buffalo Press (ostensibly for publication) and contains a sort of "state of the school" summary, including this: "In the summer of 1983, we carried out a complete renovation of our Science Center, gutting and rebuilding the entire third floor of the Beecher School Wing. We took the opportunity afforded by lower than expected bids to also lower ceilings, install insulation, and replace all three floors of windows as well as the roof of this wing." The same memo indicates that the "next major projects which must be undertaken are the repair of the roof and repointing of the one-time Masonic Consistory" and that "as we were encountering difficulties in our student recruitment efforts due to the condition of our science facilities before our renovation, we are again hearing quite negative comments on the condition of our athletic facilities—locker rooms and showers, exercise rooms, gymnasium, and so on."

The memo also summarizes the tuition and financial aid realities of the era: "In 1983, 26% of the student body received $186,752 in scholarship and financial aid. Over 70% of this aid is unfunded and therefore is obtained through fund raising efforts...[because] no young man should be denied a Canisius education solely because of family financial difficulties...." Specifically, it names the need for the years ahead: "We must add $1,600,000 to our scholarship fund in order to endow this financial aid program and remove this burden from our operating budget.... We have also begun to plan for a contingency budget to maintain our buildings...to remove all capital expenditures from our operating budget."[19]

Based on an Annual Fund report from Mr. James P. Corcoran, Director of Development and Alumni, the Annual Fund had healthy returns: "In seven months this year we are more than $3,000 over the full twelve-month Annual Fund last year," with a total reported of $173,689 in seven months versus $123,483 for the twelve months prior to that period. (Of this, approximately $46,000 was attributed to the Walkathon, the revenues of which were nearly double those of each of the previous two events). Reflective of a desire to pass a non-deficit budget and in light of a projected enrollment of 680 students, a $200 tuition hike was carried for 1984-1985, representing an 8% rise. At the time of the hike's passage,

"188 students [had] registered for the class of 1988...[while] two hundred students are expected, compared to 182 last year."[20]

In the Minutes of May 17, 1984, there is a tone of optimism, including a report that "the Capital Gifts program...fund had $1,020,00 in pledges." Furthermore, the Annual Fund stood at $207,737 at the ten-month mark, "compared to $170,465 for all of last year." As for Gambit X, the net was a record $105,878, and enrollment was projected to rise with 201 registered freshmen for Fall 1984 (with 10 more expected).[21] Later in 1984, the November Board Minutes include news of steady enrollment, continued fundraising progress, and continued renovations to the athletic areas and various infrastructure projects. "By the summer of 1985 it is hoped that the Counseling Center will be renovated."[22]

As of May 1985, it is noted that the Science Center renovation debt was "reduced from $360,000 to $280,000" and that several gifts had been received to increase the scholarship endowment. Capital Improvements are listed as "the Auditorium roof" and "the Johnson Control Automated Heating System." Items "Planned or in Progress" included "The Bedie N. Joseph Counselling Center, Tiling of Classrooms and Cafeteria, Auditorium Seats, Athletic Complex, and Restoration of the Library." Juxtaposed with this challenging set of initiatives is a note that "173 are enrolled for the Class of 1989." This was a marked drop in enrollment from the preceding years.[23] By November 1985, the enrollment had proved to be even lower than anticipated: only 168 freshmen and a total enrollment of 651.[24]

The Board Minutes from February 1986 illuminate the rising financial concerns facing school leadership. Admissions became an increasing area of focus. A significant portion of the Minutes is dedicated to matters of enrollment, most notably this discouraging reality: "As of February 1 [1986] incoming freshman registration was 135, as of now the figure is 149. The projection is 150 to 160 incoming freshmen. The total enrollment for September is projected at 623." A detailed description of enhanced admissions strategy follows, including redoubled efforts in the areas of advertising, recruitment visits, and outreach. The Student Recruitment Committee was made into a Standing Committee of the Board of Trustees, with unanimous approval. In the President's Report, it is noted that "some reasons for our difficulties" include "[a] decrease in the student population in Erie County; Western New York is a depressed economic area; rising costs in utilities, insurance, fringes, debt; deteriorating buildings; Jesuit numbers have decreased so that the Jesuit contribution is lower; commitment to educating cross section of students without regard to financial status; contract agreements with faculty." Additionally, "Frs. Billotti and Boller also stressed that this is not our unique problem. All schools are beginning to face enrollment problems. We have probably come face to face with them earlier due to our commitment to quality over quantity (filling the school without regard to ability to do college preparatory work) and our higher cost at present."[25]

Interestingly, juxtaposed with this concern over enrollment was this note: "A committee is being set up to explore different programs for students on the therapeutic approach to the abuse of drugs and alcohol at Canisius High School."[26] No additional commentary or explanation is included; however, this coincides with programming initiated by Mr. Joseph Lucenti '73 as Dean of Students.

The fiscal reality was stark. Father Billotti's report concluded with a list of "the major necessary building improvements over the past five years." Considered together, these expenses indeed comprise an intimidating expense figure:

- *$565,000   Science Center*
- *$52,000   Bedie N. Joseph Counseling Center*
- *$181,000   New roofs*
- *$22,000   Auditorium lights and insulation*
- *$25,000   Auditorium seats*
- *$60,000   Johnson Heat Control System*
- *$45,000   South parking lot and upper field*
- *$50,000   Miscellaneous[27]*

It is noted that "no decision on tuition or salaries has been decided for 1986-1987. The Board referred this matter back to the Finance Committee. The budget will have to be cut $106,890 to keep tuition under $3,000."[28]

By the end of the 1985-1986 school year, enrollment challenges continued: "160 freshman [sic] are presently enrolled for next September. Expecting student body to be in the 625 range." Movements of staff from teaching to support and administrative roles, as well as the reduction of the teaching ranks in Language, Science, and Religion, underscore the dropping numbers.[29]

Along with the concurrent issue of enrollment, increasing emphasis lay with matters of faculty morale: "Morale of the Faculty is very poor due to the fact that there is a perception that when the budget is passed the Faculty raises are considered a low priority item." To this end, a Faculty Life Committee was established "to serve as a conduit between the Faculty and the Board of Trustees."[30]

There was some encouraging financial news: Annual Fund numbers "went over the top...of goal $270,000" and "alumni contributors also went over the goal by $160,000. Almost 400 more alumni contributed this year over last year (1901 to 1478)." The Finance Committee, meanwhile, engaged in "discussion on the possibility of liquidating the 2nd Century Fund to pay off the current loans of $125,000 and $325,000." There was also discussion about "the possibility of taking out a mortgage loan for a 20 to 30-year period coupled with liquidating the 2nd Century Fund to eliminate our debt."[31]

Finally, the potential for a major existential change emerged yet again—one that underscores the deep concern that existed about the financial future of the school: "The Composition Task Force recommended that a study be made of the feasibility of Canisius going co-ed. This stage should be completed by September, 1986.... Fr. Boller restated the school's position—at this point WE ARE NOT PLANNING TO GO CO-ED—BUT WE ARE INVESTIGATING THE POSSIBILITY" [Emphasis included in original document].[32]

Midwinter 1987's Board Minutes indicate that only 124 students had registered. Fr. Sweitzer's Principal's Report emphasized that "the two main goals this year has [sic] been student recruitment and student retention." Also, it detailed a reduction of personnel "based on an average academic class size of 25," the equivalent of 7.2 full-time positions: "1 in English, 1 in Science (History teacher will teach part time), 1 in History retires, 1 in Arts/Media (English teacher will do an elective), 1 Secretary (Teachers to fill in part time in Principal's Office, Bookstore, and Recruitment)." At the request of the Faculty Life Committee, further discussion of the faculty pay scale continued; this included focus on both the scale's structure and gradations as well as the real numbers relative to the Consumer Price Index. While a vote passed to adopt a revised scale, "The faculty salary commitment for next year was sent back to the Finance Committee for study." A tuition hike of $85.00 was approved.[33] Finally, it's clear that the question of co-education had remained an open one for some time but was, again, shelved: "Although the school received approval from Bishop Head there is no plan at this time to pursue this course of action."[34]

At this point, it is worth looking at the archives from a few years later to garner some perspective. A "Fact Sheet" dated August 13, 1991, associated with the "Burn the Mortgage" Project offered an insightful summary of factors which, in hindsight, can be viewed as complicating elements of the fiscal crisis that would come to a head in 1989. It lists building projects (which have been mentioned throughout this section), and traces the declining. This author added enrollment data from 1981-1986 to provide a more demonstrative visual of the trend:[35]

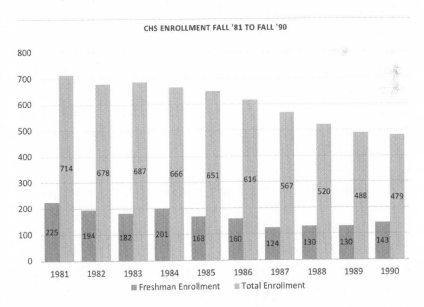

CHS ENROLLMENT FALL '81 TO FALL '90

■ Freshman Enrollment   ■ Total Enrollment

The decline in enrollment combined with the aggressive schedule of building improvements makes, in hindsight, for a perfect storm in terms of financial stress. This was not the total picture, however, and another powerful force played a role in making for fiscal crisis. Beginning in the mid-1980s, there is documentation of ongoing negotiations, proposals, and counter-proposals in the context of faculty compensation. It would be simplistic to place blame on the advocates for bolstering teacher pay; indeed, the salary schedule was anything but generous. In fact, a comprehensive body of correspondence assembled by the Faculty Life Committee goes into painstaking detail, outlining in stark terms the disparity between the Canisius scale and those of comparable institutions, namely McQuaid Jesuit in Rochester and Saint Joseph's Collegiate Institute. Moreover, in a comprehensive analysis tracing the Canisius salaries relative to the Consumer Price Index (CPI), the Faculty Life Committee was able to illustrate that not only was the school's pay scale significantly low compared to these other schools, but also far from even a conservative degree of parity to the CPI.

To fully appreciate the challenge posed by this declining enrollment coupled with a commitment to faculty raises, it is useful, again, to consider the substantial building expenses undertaken in the same timeframe. For this we can cite the summary of "Building Projects Since 1982" offered in the same "Fact Sheet" document:

- *The 1982 "renovation of the science facility, thereafter named the Fr. James J. Redmond, S.J., Science Center.... The entire third floor was reconstructed to form the physics, chemistry, biology and general science areas...Two teacher preparation rooms were also constructed."*
- *The 1985 construction of "a centrally located counseling center...named for 1959 alumnus Bedie N. Joseph," which featured "a large conference area, a computer for college research information, and private offices for each of the four counselors."*
- *The 1987 renovation, "with our high school coaches and our students doing the work...of the old...bowling alleys into two separate facilities...a*

wrestling/workout room...[and] an ultramodern, completely equipped
weight training facility."

- The 1988 dedication of "the Michael P. Montante Computer Center,"
  which was a "state of the art teaching facility...[with] 3 computer
  rooms...[and]...30 computers."
- The 1989 renovation of the cafeteria, "featuring new windows, ventila-
  tion/heating system; ceiling, wall, floor covering; lighting, sound system,
  emergency lighting, etc."[36]

The document indicates that as of June 30, 1989, the school's mortgage
balance stood at $1,123,597. In nothing short of an amazing turnaround,
just two years later, on June 30, 1991, the balance would be reduced to
$329,000. Shortly after, it would be eliminated altogether, and CHS would
be essentially debt free for the first time in its existence. This remarkable
recovery is a testament to perseverance, good stewardship, and profound
generosity on the part of many in the community, and will be detailed in
the next chapter.[37]

Now that we've had a look at some of the factors leading up to the
fiscal crisis of the late 1980s, we turn again to reflections from Mr. Joe
Lucenti '73, who was serving as Dean of Students during that time.

It was a frightening time to be here as an alumnus and an employee. We were
two weeks from not meeting payroll. That statement would tell anyone how
bad it was.

It was frightening because you were talking about so many significant parts
of your life being in doubt. First, your living. You're talking about providing
for a family, so you are talking about survival. Your job. You're talking about
a school that you love. I think that's one of the most unique things about the
faculty...nothing could replace the collegiality that existed here among our
faculty and staff during the 19 years I was there during good and bad. It was
family.

And I think the fact that this could be lost was frightening in and of itself. I
think it also was that, when I first came here as a student, Canisius was larger

than life. You're talking about an institution that was at least perceived to be indestructible. 1870, come on! You're talking about a four-hundred-year Jesuit tradition. It was unthinkable. You had those three major negative potential impacts, not just inside your own head, but you could see it and feel it everywhere. There were massive cuts to staff. There were cuts to pensions, frozen salaries. It was very constricting. Why would you even work here, other than love of the place?

It was mismanagement. Financially, you were giving out more money, whether through financial assistance or spending it, than you were taking in. Again, it's pretty simple math. There was very little, if any, foresight. There weren't endowments and funds that recognized that with all the character that these buildings have, they are costly, not just to maintain, but when something needs to be replaced. And you couple that with the fact that in the 1980s, the economy in Western New York went to hell. You lost, from its peak in the 60s to when it closed, 20,000 jobs at Bethlehem Steel. You lost Republic Steel. You lost the Trico plants. You lost so much manufacturing in this area, that we were an economically depressed area. You had a perfect storm of poor planning, spending more than we got, and a dwindling enrollment. Because the population was venting. I look at myself. My father wasn't a doctor, a lawyer, or college educated. He worked at General Mills. But his dream was to give his children a better life and he understood that education was important. So when you lose 20,000 steel workers, thousands more in these plants, and now they're moving to Georgia and North Carolina and out West, your enrollment is in trouble.

Our enrollment was definitely north of 700 when I started, and by the worst of times we were in the 400's. One event that I remember vividly was registration day, because it was a benchmark every year. During that time, when all the sudden, we'd see numbers like 120, 115, and we'd look at each other, like, "That's it? This can't be right." And when you think that a few years later it was in the 200's, that was a wake-up call and a half.

People made sacrifices. It started with things that were handed to us. When you start with a zero percent salary increase and inflation is whatever it was, you're already taking a hit. When your pension contribution is reduced, you're taking a hit. And you have to remember, you're already starting where your counterparts in the public schools are already well above where you are. Because you're not regulated by the state, you have a lot more flexibility as to who teaches what. So there were a lot of people stepping forward to teach a subject out of their specialty. There was the recognition that our survival as a school depended on us meeting the needs of our students. You couldn't simply say, "Hey, screw this." Because you were signing your own death warrant.

People really stepped up volunteering with extracurriculars. Some of the best of our morale came in the midst of those challenging moments. In 1987 or so, we had frozen salaries and morale was pretty low. So I went to Father Billotti, and I told him we have to do something for these people. Christmas is coming, there have been all these cuts. The least we can do is throw a Christmas party. I suggested we go out to Bennigan's Grill and Tavern on Maple, and that the school pay for it. We just meet out there, advertise it, let people order off the menu and get drinks. So he said okay. We had probably the most people attend the Christmas party ever.

Joe Billotti is going out of town the night of this Christmas party, so he gives me his credit card and tells me to pay the bill. So, it's about 11:00 and the manager comes over and asks who's in charge? Everybody points at me. I asked him what's the problem. He says, "Your bar bill. It's $1200." Now this was 1987. That was a lot of money. So I pull out the credit card.

When he got the credit card bill, I think I can still hear his voice echoing through the halls screaming my name. It was like something out of a movie. But the important thing is, people had a good time. And it was so important. Because when you're low in morale, nothing can do what camaraderie does. One of the things that I chose to focus on was people's birthdays, I would go out and find coffee mugs that somehow related to that person. Usually in a humorous way. Remember Bob Krum? He was one of our first computer teachers. I found this mug with a picture of this guy peeing on a table of computers, and the caption says, "Computer Whiz." I got our switchboard operator a mug with a handle shaped like a telephone receiver. She cried, she was so touched. Those were the kinds of things that brought this faculty together. Despite losing colleagues to budget cuts and being scared, we stuck together. And I think we found that support from one another. Some was from humor, some was from venting. Those were some of the things that got us through that. What was nice was, there was a divide between some of the lay faculty and some of the Jesuits. In a very negative way, there was a school of thought often articulated that when things are going well, it's a Jesuit school, but when things are going bad, we're collegiate and we all have ownership. As a lay person, that's a tough pill to swallow. But you had Jesuits like Gerry McIntyre and Rich Zanoni who understood what laypeople were going through.

There was a lot of talk and theory that one of the reasons we got into the mess we did was because CHS never left the attitude of the 1950s and 1960s, and that was that they were knocking the doors down in terms of enrollment. We had 900-plus guys. But Canisius had never recognized what was happening around us, that we needed to do more to recruit kids and get them into this building than just say here we are and wait for them to come. That was one of the biggest changes. That after 1989, the recognition, finally, that we could not just sit on our laurels. You couldn't just say hey, we're Jesuit. Hey, we've been here since 1870.[38]

Notably, according to Father Rich Zanoni, S.J., it is with this realization that Fathers Gerry McIntyre, S.J., David Ciancimino, S.J., and Michael Corcoran, S.J. '76, were charged with ramping up recruitment efforts in the Admissions Office.[39]

Early Forays Into Computer Science

Three men figure prominently in the early days of computer integration at Canisius High School. According to *CHS Today* magazine, "In the late 1980s the Rev. Eugene Zimpfer, S.J., '49 introduced personal computers to the school. He authorized a computer lab for administrative support staff, who wore t-shirts saying 'I boot for Zimpfer,' in recognition of the momentous occasion."[40]

Mr. Dennis Linda served in 1983 as Administrative Assistant to the Principal. He would later serve as Assistant Principal following a long tenure on the faculty as a chemistry teacher; following this, he would return to the faculty for many more years until his retirement in 2016.

Mr. Robert Krum, who since departing from Canisius in 2008 has moved on to be a Program Host at Classical 94.5 WNED Buffalo, taught computer science and math at Canisius for twenty-four years. He taught the first computer programming courses at the school.

Father Zimpfer, Mr. Linda, and Mr. Krum were adamant that computers would figure centrally in the future of education at Canisius and everywhere else. Certainly, their embrace of programming instruction and advocacy for technology integration positioned the school well to be ready for the digital transformation of the 21st Century. Of course, the students of 2020 would barely recognize the technology first introduced to the school in 1983. In a press release dated October 11, 1983, Mr. Linda offered details of the school's new computer center.[14]

Two images that accompanied the October 1983 press release depict Mr. Robert Krum and students in his computer programming course.

On Saturday, September 24, 1983, Fr. Joseph Billotti, S.J., President of Canisius High School, pronounced a blessing on the school's new computer center. The equipment includes 12 new Radio Shack TRS-80 Color Computers with disk drives and makes a total of 19 computers available for faculty and student use. Canisius High School presently offers courses in introductory programming with practical applications. The students are given the opportunity to learn word processing and programming in BASIC and PASCAL.[41]

---

[14] This center is not to be confused with the Montante Computer Center, which was opened in 1988 on the basement level of Berchmans Hall (the Rand Mansion) at the foot of the spiral stairs.

The Montante Computer Center, added in 1988.

Later, the Montante Computer Center would open in 1988, representing a substantial expansion and investment in computer integration with the curriculum. With its installation, word processing and keyboarding became standard, required courses.

Gallery: 1981-1990

First Annual Canisius Run Ran Well

THE First Annual Canisius Crusader 3.1 Mile (5,000 Meter) Road Race took place on Sunday, March 1, 1981. The race was sponsored bt the Canisius High School Cross Country/Track Teams, the Canisius Alumni Office, and the Locker Room Athletic Club Running Club. The race was sanctioned by the Niagara Association of the A.A.U. The race was coordinated by Mr. Jeffrey Gemmer.

Awards were presented to the overall male and female winners, and to the first three places in each A.A.U. age group. Awards were given to each winner of the special Canisius student, faculty, and alumni divisions.

THE race started and finished at Canisius High School. It proceeded south on Delaware Avenue to West Utica Street, to Elmwood Avenue, and then north to Forest Avenue. Racers turned right on Forest Avenue and proceeded east to Lincoln Parkway. A right turn on Lincoln Parkway took the

Runners participate in road race.

runners to Soldiers Place, on to Chapin Parkway, up to Gates Circle, and up Delaware Avenue to Canisius High School.

Mr. Gemmer says the race was started because of the great interest in

running found at Canisius. Alumni were introduced into the event to make it a larger, family affair. From early returns, both Mr. James Skipper, the cross country coach, and Mr. Gemmer were confident of success in this endeavor.

The inaugural Crusader 5k, which would come to be known as the "Chilly Challenge," was held March 1, 1981, under the direction of Mr. Jeff Gemmer and Mr. Jim Skipper.

Skiers Glide Along Smoothly

Skier checks out slopes.

THE Canisius High School Ski Club is halfway through its 1980-81 season, which began in December, and should end sometime in February. It is under the direction of Miss Gretchen Kessler and Mr. Joseph Lucenti, both faculty members at Canisius. Under the program, forty-seven students are enjoying the slopes at Kissing Bridge Ski resort every Friday. The members ski from after school to 11:00 p.m. This includes a one hour lesson from one of the

Kissing Bridge instructors. On occasion, Mrs. Pendolino and Mr. Tutak join the club for an evening of entertainment.

One of the members of the club, Mike Skretny, feels that the best part of the club activity is the bus ride home. "It's like a party!" he says. Jim Runfola also comments that "it is a great relief after a long week of school, and an exciting way to begin a week-end."

Although it is her first year as moderator, Miss Kessler is an experienced skier, and enjoys taking the students out on the slopes. The club has a few more weeks of skiing left this year — as long as the snow continues to fall.

THE little advertised but widely known Canisius High ski team, headed by captain Mark Carey and co-captain Keith Joslyn, both juniors, is moving towards its fourth consecutive championship season. According to Carey, the team is off to an excellent start, winning its first slalom competition at Kissing Bridge on Wednesday, February fourth. The best time of the evening was turned in by sophomore Bill Mead, who was clocked at 24.95 seconds. The next Crusader in was freshman John Deck, with a time of 27.45 seconds. Following Deck were Juniors Keith Joslyn (28.5), Mark Carey (30.13), Donato Borrillo (31.53), and Kelly Brannen (32.45).

Sid Binks

The CHS Ski Club, along with the "little advertised but widely known Canisius High ski team," gets some press. *The Citadel,* Mar. 1981.

Paul Cumbo

Coach Skipper leads runners

When a Crusader cross-country team member competes for Canisius, always behind him stands the harriers' coach, Mr. James L. Skipper. The key to the runner's victory is in his coach's formula for success. "Everyone has a place on the team," Mr. Skipper explains, "and everyone has a special gift. My job is to help that individual find his gift and show him that he is an important part of this team."

A graduate of Father Baker High and Ithaca College, Mr. Skipper came to Canisius High School in 1964. For thirteen years he coached the track team. He coached junior varsity basketball, and for eighteen years he has coached the cross-country team. In that time he has gained the highest respect and has been labeled among Canisius' best coaches.

It was not until three or four years after he graduated from high school that Mr. Skipper decided to major in physical education. Over the years, however, his choice proved to be the correct one, and he continued his post-graduate studies in night school at the University of Buffalo. The reason Mr. Skipper chose to teach gym and to coach sports was that he felt it was an important area where the student could express himself differently while he is having fun.

In the past eighteen years, Mr. Skipper has learned from the best

Canisius has to offer. Mr. John Barnes, who at one time coached every CHS sports team, taught the young Mr. Skipper very much. He proved that experience is the best teacher, for Barnes spent more than forty years in both the Delaware Avenue and Washington Street Canisius High Schools.

When he started in 1964, Mr. Skipper replaced Mr. Murray as cross-country team coach and as gym teacher. The cross-country team had won their championship the previous year, so he stepped into a good spot. Not to be outdone, however, the team under new coach Skipper won the championship the following four years.

Coach Skipper, one of the most successful coaches at CHS, attributes his success and the success of the team to the pride, closeness, and the attitude of the members of his cross-country team. Although the team is ranked second in Western New York, the coach never looks to the future, but takes things season by season, meet by meet. Mr. Skipper also takes pride in the fact that he never had to recruit younger players because the image his team reflects draws members to try out.

After eighteen years of coaching and teaching, Mr. Jim Skipper has experienced the feeling of victory and of defeat, but still relies on the basics that so many other teams lack. He stresses

Mr. Skipper discusses strategy with Jim Fisher and Mike O'Rourke.

fun while growing and maturing, and supplies a feeling of self worth to freshmen as well as to seniors in his classes. The characteristics will surely make the name of Mr. James L. Skipper one of the most popular in the history of Canisius High.

—Bob Reiser

October 1981 profile of longtime faculty member and coach Jim Skipper.

CHS student rules revised

As most students know by now, this year a revised "jug" system is being implemented. This year's rulebreakers will be serving jug in what Mr. Bukowski refers to as "silent meditation."

When it was proposed that an updated jug system be created, members of a student committee met with members of the faculty to discuss ideas. Fr. Aman was moderator of this mini-congress. Once the committee generated its suggestions for changes and shortenings of the old rules, Fr. Boller and Mr. Bukowski polished and approved the ideas. Finally, Fr. Zanoni and Mr. Durkin transformed all of these into one concise written document.

The new jug setup basically says that students will now serve jug on the day they receive it by sitting in a room at the end of the day. The room will be moderated by one of two proctors — Fr. Greer three times a week and Mr. Tudini twice a week. Their job is to see that students serve their jug by doing nothing but remaining quiet and inactive.

The length of one's stay in the new "jug room" is determined by Mr. Bukowski. When a faculty member feels that a student should receive jug, he or she will advise Mr. Bukowski. He will then administer "units" of jug according to the severity of the offense. One unit of jug is equal to twenty minutes.

Another notable change in the rules is the dress code. Each student is to wear a shirt, with all buttons secured, and a tie. One final change worth noting is that seniors no longer have smoking privileges. Surprisingly, one member of the student committee has called the new rules "excellent changes". Parents and alumni were also very much in favor. Our associate principal of student services, Mr. Bukowski, summed it all up by saying that he is "very optimistic (about the) potential of the new rule changes to create a positive attitude around the school."

—Mark Siwiec

Mr. Bukowski will oversee the enforcement of the new rules.

Above: September 1982's issue of *The Citadel* summarizes several changes in disciplinary rules, including a return to ties in the dress code after an eight-year reprieve that began in the fall of 1974. Below, left: A tongue-in-cheek student perspective on the new Science Wing vs. the locker room facility (*Citadel,* Jan '83). Below, right, in the same issue: coverage of the Emmaus retreat, which began as an experience for seniors in the early 1980s.

Emmaus retreat "breaks bread"

Last year, for the second year in a row, a special retreat was planned for Canisius seniors. This retreat, called the Emmaus retreat, lasted for two-and-a-half days. The word Emmaus comes from the name of a town in Israel where Jesus met and broke bread with two of his disciples shortly after his resurrection. This retreat allows these seniors to "break bread" with each other and to spend time reflecting on their relationships with God, their inner selves, and others. This year's retreat ran from Tuesday, December 7 to Thursday evening, December 9. About 20 seniors went on the retreat, along with Father Billotti, Father French, Mr. Skipper, and Father Aman, the moderator. The retreat occurred at Camp Asbury at Silver Lake, near Rochester.

— *Ronald J. Granieri*

January, 1983

383

Gambit X Equals the Feats of the Past: "A Success"

The work on Gambit X began in October. Gambit is the dinner-auction held by Canisius in order to raise money to meet the expenses that tuition doesn't cover. The tuition charged by Canisius is lower than the actual cost of one year's education for a student, so the difference must be made up elsewhere. Gambit is one way that these additional funds are raised. Other methods include the CHS Walkathon, and the Annual Fund Drive. The money raised through these activities is used to pay operating expenses for the school, grant-in-aid money, and many other things.

Running and planning Gambit is no small task. Work begins in early fall and runs through mid May. This year the co-

bit are donated by many different people and companies. These gifts are collected at "gift-giving parties" held by various individuals prior to the evening of Gambit itself. Some of this year's largest attractions were a 1958 Lincoln Continental, an Apple II computer, a cruise in the Virgin islands, a windsurfer, and a trip to the Kentucky Derby including hotel accommodations.

The auction itself was split into various parts including a written auction, and an oral auction to be run by Mr. Lew Bronstein and Barbara Jones.

More than 390 people attended last year's Gambit and about 465 attended this year's Gambit. Gambit IX grossed over

Mark Romanowski and Matt Brennan, caught during a candid moment of laughter and excitement at Gambit X.

chairmen were Mr. Paul Bauer and Mr. William Lawley, while the co-ordinator was Mr. James Corcoran. These people attend all the gift-giving parties. This may sound like fun, but it often requires that they give up entire weekends for the benefit of Gambit. It is not unusual for these men to put in 70 hours a week working on just Gambit alone. Other key gears in the huge Gambit machine include secretaries Mrs. Anita Utech and Mrs. Pat McCarthy.

There are also many people that give their time on the night of Gambit doing volunteer work. Of the approximate 300 people that work on the evening of Gambit, about 175 are students.

The gifts that are auctioned off at Gam-

$118,000 and after expenses were paid the school had made close to $90,000. This was roughly twice as much as the first Gambit grossed nine years ago. This year Canisius is expecting to gross close to $150,000 with a net profit of over $100,000. The items that were not sold at Gambit were reauctioned at a smaller following auction for the adult workers. The profits raised here will also go to Canisius.

Gambit is one of the many activities though the year that unites the Canisius Community; and it would not be possible without the work and co-operation of the Alumni, the faculty, friends, and students of Canisius High School.

— *Marcus Romanowski*

Gambit X: Ten years strong, profiled in *The Citadel*, May 1984.

Crew Returns

For the first time since 1975 Canisius has put together a rowing team, headed by Coach Joe Krakowiak. The reason for this long absence in a sport which Canisius was once nationally prominent was a fire at the West Side Rowing Club. Coach Krakowiak, a former national rowing champion, says the team started "land training" in early March around the school five days a week. Once April came around the team moved to the Rowing Club for "water training" six days a week in which a typical practice was rowing six to eight miles and lifting weights.

Contrary to popular belief, rowing is a sport for people of any size since there are lightweight and heavyweight divisions. Rowers can compete in teams of four or eight which consist of oars (guys who row) and coxies (guys who steer). At last count, this year's Crusader team listed twenty-two oars and four coxies.

Archrival St. Joes is the only local male rowing team the oarsmen face this year with all other regattas (races) against assorted Canadian and American teams. Despite this lack of local competition and apparent lack of experience, the team is working hard to reestablish Canisius High School as a national rowing power.

(Right) By December 1984, *The Citadel* boasts of the team's quick return to national prominence under the leadership of Coach Joe Krakowiak.

(Left) *The Citadel* of May, 1984 reports on the return of the CHS rowing team after a nearly 10-year hiatus following the catastrophic fire that destroyed the West Side Rowing Club.

Crew Team Gains National Recognition

The Head of the Charles, one of rowing's most distinguished events, took place on Sunday, October 21, on the Charles River in Boston, Massachusetts.

One hundred various organizations, including seventy colleges, from across the nation were present. Included in the competition were teams from such colleges as Harvard, Yale, Princeton, and Georgetown.

The West Side Rowing Club represented the Buffalo area with two crews. Canisius' Marc Romanowski rowed in the coxed four which placed 13th out of 28 with a 17 minute and 30 second time. Paul Joyce, Bob Kubiniec, and Jed Dietrich rowed in an eight man shell which finished 24th out of 40 with a 16 minute and 30 second time.

The rebirth of competitive crew at Canisius has been a welcome addition to our family of sports teams. Renewed interest and enthusiasm about a sport long neglected is encouraging. Congratulations to the oarsmen for a fine showing at such a prestigious event.

— *David A. DiVita*

Crusader Hockey Team Ices the Cake

The Canisius Crusaders hockey team, spearheaded by the amazing hat tricks of Sean Green (how *does* he do it?) continues to pour on the coal (or is it "goal"), melt the confidence of their opponents and assure a complete ice-ing of their victory cake!

Joe T. tries out for the choir.

The team, boasting a very successful winning record to date, also relieve heavily on the excellent performances of the following players: center Joe Teresi; defensemen Tom Grimm, Jon Lockwood and John Schratz; goalies Chris Thomas and Art Bascomb; wings Joe Donovan and Brian Duffett.

In their first tournament of the season, the Ithaca Tournament at Cornell University, they defeated Irondequoit in the first game 5-4 after Sean Green helped correct a 4-goal deficit with a 3-goal hat trick in the 3rd period. Canisius then went on to defeat Ithaca 4-3 and win the championship.

On January 3 the Crusaders squeaked by arch-rival St. Joes 4-3, with junior goalie Art Bascomb giving his all in an outstanding performance.

A 7-3 loss the following week, however, did not dampen the Crusaders' spirit and by the end of January they were ranked 15th in the state. By this time they have surely moved up even higher.

In early February the Alexandria Bay Tournament saw Canisius defeat Auburn 7-3 in the first game and then go on to defeat Alexandreia Bay 6-3 for the championship. Sean Green's hat trick and a stopped penalty shot in the third period by Chris Thomas were undoubtedly the highlights of this game. The tournament's MVP award went to Sean Green for his total of seven points, and Chris Thomas and Joe Teresi were named to the all-tournament team for their strong outstanding performances.

February 8-9 found the Canisius team battling the number one team in the state, Messina, in a tournament at Messina. On the weekend of February 16, the Canisius Crusaders faced a competitive group of eight teams from the United States and Canada. All teams vied for a top spot in a challenging tournament in Toronto, Canada. Unfortunately, scores for these tournaments were unavailable at press time.

As statistics for the year begin to emerge, the Canisius Crusaders cannot help but be proud of the numbers they have compiled.

So far, they have a win-tie record of 87.5%, compared to a loss record of only 12.5%. The statistics available show that the Crusaders are scoring an average of 4.8 goals per game, which is 26% more than their opponents.

The Junior Varsity Crusaders, with a win-tie record of 96%, compared to a loss record of only 4%, appear to have some excellent prospects for next year's Varsity Crusaders with Paul Donovan (center and

> *Congratulations*
> *League*
> *Champions!*
>
> Canisius: 6
> St. Joes: 4

wing), Marc Fortner (goalie), and Wally Iwanenko (defense).

Miss Szafran, faculty moderator of the teams, is very much pleased with the teams' success thus far. She feels that the tournaments are both a great experience and exposure. With such a sparkling season

The iceman cometh and the puck goeth!

to date, how can the Canisius Crusaders hockey teams be headed for anything else but glory?

— *Raymond Flannery*

This profile of the hockey team in the March 1985 *Citadel* describes a relatively new program that had by then come into its own at CHS.

CITADEL

THE CANISIUS HIGH SCHOOL NEWS MAGAZINE

OCTOBER, 1985   VOL. 38 / NO. 1

Walk-A-Thon Wednesday

The CHS Walkathon was a well-established tradition and vital fundraising initiative by the time it was the cover story of this special edition of *The Citadel* in October 1985. Buffalo Mayor James Griffin was present for the start of the 1985 Walk.

Adventure on the Truk Islands

I recently had the opportunity to interview Fr. Zanoni, S.J. If you are unfamiliar with this name, he is the new Jesuit who teaches sophomore geometry and freshmen religion. We talked mostly about the two times ('76 - '79, '85 - '86) during which he was stationed at a boarding school in the Truk Islands. The Truk Islands are a group of about 2000 very small islands in the

South Pacific. They are northeast of Australia and southeast of the Phillipines. Fr. Zanoni told me that it was very difficult living on the islands. The school building was at one time a Japanese communications center. There were no telephones or radios, and no running water. The basic diet of all the people on the islands was fish and rice, mainly because both of these foods were easy to store.

Fr. Zanoni said what he liked most about teaching on the islands was the attitude of the students. He said they have a great interest in learning and are very cooperative. There are about 140 students who attend this school, which was the first high school opened in all the islands. The students in the school are both male and female and, just like in any other high school, range in age from 13-19 years old. Fr. Zanoni said that the majority of them will go back to their islands and help their people when they graduate. Others want to become priests or doctors so that they can help the mostly uneducated people of the Truk Islands.

The most popular sports on the islands are basketball, softball and track. Fr. Zanoni enjoyed teaching in the Truk Islands and hopes he will be able to teach there again someday.

— Mark Crittenden

A profile of "new" teacher Rev. Richard Zanoni, S.J., in *The Citadel*, Feb, 1987.

Coach Johnson Retires After 40 Years

Mr. James L. Skipper, Canisius High School Athletic Director, announced last December that William A. "Bill" Johnson is retiring as varsity football coach after forty years of dedicated and unselfish service in various capacities at the school.

Bill enrolled at the Jesuit school as a student in the Fall of 1946. He was an All Catholic guard on Johnny Barnes' 1948 gridiron championship team and he graduated with honors from Canisius in 1950. He played collegiate football at Bowling Green University in Ohio and holds a bachelor's degree from the University of Buffalo.

Except for four years of Army service in Germany, where he continued his active football career, Bill coached Crusader Junior Varsity football teams from 1952 to 1972. He served as Bus Werder's assistant on the varsity level for the next five years, a period when Canisius' teams went forty-three games without a loss. For the last nine years, Coach Johnson has directed the Blue and Gold varsity football program, with championship seasons in 1978 and 1980.

Pacing the sidelines during more than two-hundred-fifty gridiron contests, spread out over thirty-one campaigns, Bill Johnson has been instrumental in the development and guidance of over twelve-hundred athletes and has seen Canisius football teams win over eighty percent of their contests.

Mr. Johnson is president of the Johnson Fastener Company, a Buffalo-based business. For the past twenty-seven years, he has been the official play-by-play typist in the press box at every Buffalo Bills game, whether in War Memorial or Rich Stadium. He plans to continue being active in both these endeavors.

Retiring from active coaching will give Bill more time to pursue his hobby of the last nine years, namely competitive sailing. A familiar figure in Lake Erie and Lake Ontario summer regattas, he has earned a reputation as a skilful and daring sailor; numerous trophies and plaques attest to his successes.

"Forty years is enough time," says Bill, "for one person to be in one institution. My years at Canisius have been fun and most rewarding. Now it's time for someone else to take over." That "someone else" will be announced at a later date, according to Athletics Director Jim Skipper.

A profile of retiring football coach Bill Johnson after 40 years. *The Citadel*, February 1987.

The Doctor Is In

A doctorate, according to *Webster's* Dictionary, is the degree of a doctor conferred by a university. It is also the result, by my estimations, of a person who works very hard at something to do it perfectly. A member of the Canisius faculty, Mr. Thomas McPherson, exemplifies this description and will receive an honorary doctorate of humane letters from his alma mater, Canisius College, during their graduation ceremonies later this year.

Mr. McPherson has been a history teacher at Canisius High School for thirty-eight years, and one of the reasons why he's been here so long is that he "likes the school and working with the great students at Canisius," and that the Canisius community is like a family.

Probably the most respected member of the faculty, Mr. McPherson had these humble words to say about his doctorate: "I'm very flattered and pleased, but many other teachers are just as deserving as I."

Fr. Billotti, president of Canisius High School, had these words about Mr. McPherson and his great honor: "This was an honor well deserved for his thirty-eight years teaching and his high degree of professionalism. He is such a professional that a few years ago, a graduating class established an Outstanding Teacher Award, and, at their graduation, they presented it to Mr. McPherson.

"I think this is an honor to him and for him, but I believe it is one honor to the teaching profession, that Mr. McPherson receives it for teachers in general. In addition, it shows the interest and the caring Canisius College has for the teaching profession."

— *Tom Enstice*

March, 1987 *Citadel* profile of "Doc" McPherson.

Jug, An Institution

Jug is as old as Canisius High School itself. It was established back in 1870 when the school was founded. Jug does not stand for "Justice Under God" as most people think. Jug was a slang term used for jail at the time it was created. In the 1920's and 1930's punishment was served by writing out the day's Latin vocabulary. In the 1940's the Prefect of Discipline's office was the mailroom. There were about twenty to twenty-five seats outside his office. Jug was served by sitting in a chair and writing out a composition. In the late 1940's and 1950's Jug became physically administered. One form of this punishment was to walk around the foyer and run up and down the marble stairs. In nice weather students serving Jug would walk around the track a certain number of times. Another form of physical Jug was standing on one of the brass fit-

A history of JUG, as offered by Gerald Whelan '88 in *The Citadel*, February 1988.

tings in the foyer floor for forty minutes to one hour without talking to anyone.

The most legendary era of discipline at Canisius was while Fr. Sturm was Prefect of Discipline. He held this post for seventeen years, stretching from the late 1950's until the early 1970's when he retired. In the changing times of the late 1960's and early 1970's, Fr. Sturm's idea about discipline was "the way Jesuit discipline used to be." The punishment always fit the crime. He once caught a student throwing snowballs. The student had to make one thousand snowballs and put them into piles of one hundred. After he finished Fr. Sturm told him to put the snow back where he got it from.

The standard form of Jug in this period was to write a four-hundred to seven-hundred word composition on a selected topic such as doorknobs, salt on crackers, or the inside of a bubble. There was a daily writing formula, for example, start on the third line and skip every fourth line. The student then had to read the composition to Fr. Sturm. If he did not like it the student had to come back the next day to serve his Jug again.

At that time Fr. Greer was his associate. His method of administering Jug was to write out the Time Tables for all the train stops in Texas, which he provided from memory.

Mr. Grotke said, "Fr. Sturm was very strict but I found out that he had a keen sense of humor, by seeing him from the point of view as a student and later as a teacher." Every year this "humor" was shown when Fr. Sturm read a Christmas poem after Mass, in which all the seniors names' were mentioned in rhyme.

A few years ago the position of Prefect of Discipline was transformed into the position of Dean of Students. Discipline is only one of many parts that the Dean's Office handles. I discussed this discipline factor with Dean of Students Mr. Lucenti. He explained "I do not like Jug. Ideally I would hope students would cooperate behavior-wise and Jug would not be necessary. I am a realist though, therefore Jug is needed to deal with the petty offenses that arise."

He further went on to say that Jug is only one of many tools to help the student realize what he did wrong and learn from it. Jug is meant to be unpleasant to deter students from breaking school rules. Mr. Lucenti changed the policy of not being able to get out of Jug even with a reasonable excuse. "I wanted to promote a mentality of openness between myself and the students. In the past three years the system has worked."

— *Gerald Whelan*

Keenan Takes C.H.S. Helm

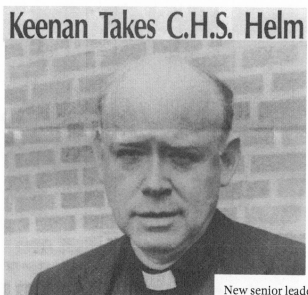

New senior leadership of CHS is introduced in *The Citadel*, October 1989, including President Rev. James F. Keenan, S.J., (top) and Principal Rev. John Costello, S.J., (bottom).

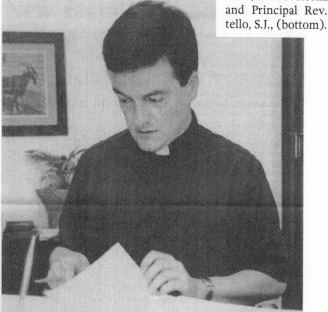

Fr. John Costello, S.J. outlines the year's agenda.   Photo by Flammer

Costello Upholds Canisius Ideals

(photo by Whelan) (photo by Whelan)

(photo by Whelan) (photo by Whelan)

...As tumbled over rim and roundy wells stones ring... G. M. Hopkins, S.J.

A photo series by Gerry Whalen '90 illustrates several campus features visible in the '90s, but unknown to the 21st Century CHS student, including: the patio across from the Dean's office (top left); the entry to a storage area on the south fire escape of the auditorium (top right); the old field house building, which has been demolished (bottom right); the south entrance to the Beecher Classroom Wing, which is now where the old wing connects to the Montante Wing (bottom left).

Arena Dedications: 1981-1990

1981 - John M. Garrity III

The 1981 *Arena* is dedicated in memory of John M. Gar-
rity, who would have graduated in the Class of 1982, but
died in 1981. "He used all the talents God gave him to
the best of his ability. He excelled in the classroom, always willing to help his classmates, and enthusiastically
participated in sports. But the thing we will remember
most about John was the fun had in his company.... Everyone who knew him was his friend. John Garrity was a loyal, fun-loving
classmate, and a good teammate."

1982 -Rev. Francis M. Redmond, S.J.

 "From 1960 until he died, Fr. Redmond served as a
member of the Canisius High School faculty teaching
Latin and Language Studies.... He received the Father
Thomas M. Harvey, S.J., Award in recognition of
twenty-five years teaching in a Jesuit high school [and]
the Bene Meriti Award for twenty years of service to
Canisius.... Fr. Redmond is remembered most by his
students for his jokes and anecdotes from the past. Canisius' principal, Fr.
Boller, described Fr. Redmond as a 'humble man with a great love of kids
and a warm sense of humor. He was a self-effacing man who never took
credit for all he did.' The Canisius community misses this man who gave
so much of his life to us."

1983 - Charles S. Pizza

The memorials in the *Arena* Yearbook continued in
1983, with the publication dedicated in memory of
Charles S. Pizza, who would have graduated that year.
Mark Jaroszewski '83 wrote: "Charlie came to our
school as a transfer student just before his junior year
and immediately made himself noticed.... He was an

outstanding athlete...quiet but charismatic...the kind of leader who led by example.... Charlie always wore a friendly smile and was always the optimist. People like Charles Pizza are what make this world more enjoyable...[and] for many of us, he will be an inspiration."

1984 - Rev. James Greer, S.J.

While the 1984 *Arena* doesn't contain any explicit dedication, an article by Mark Zaccagnino '84 profiling 21-year veteran teacher Fr. Jim Greer, S.J., makes for the implicit one. "His tests challenge the constraints of time and memory; his philosophy challenges the bounds of reason.... But wait, behind that conservative and cynical exterior lurks a man ripened with wisdom and humor.... His unique outlook on life leads many to the false conclusion that he is a pessimist. Fr. Greer, however, considers himself a realist. He teaches people not to accept things at face value.... When asked about the students at Canisius, Father replied, 'The kid who goes here has two advantages—his parents.'"

1985 - Cornelius V. McGillicuddy

Like the year preceding, the 1985 *Arena* contains no specific dedication. However, a profile of "Mr. Mack" is the de facto dedication. Some excerpts: "Mr. Mack. A name synonymous with and paralleled by such adjectives as dedicated, competitive, dignified, profound.... On October 13, 1984, a testimonial roast was held...to recognize his forty years of service to Canisius in both the classroom  and behind the bench.... Throughout the evening, Mr. Mack accepted numerous well-deserved awards from a whole array of WNY sports personalities...the Buffalo Bills...the Buffalo Bisons.... Fr. Billotti...established an academic scholarship in Mr. McGillicuddy's name."

Paul Cumbo

1986 - No dedication given

1987 - Rev. Gerry Aman, S.J.

"*Arena* would like to give special recognition to a man who had been the backbone of many...institutions and activities. As moderator of the Student Senate and Pep Squad for many years, he was responsible for many previous Spirit Weeks and cultivating student morale. He also founded the Emmaus program at CHS before leaving for Nigeria."

1988 - Miss Gretchen Kessler

It is not entirely clear whether or not the following commentary by Oscar Piedad '88 constitutes a particular dedication to one person, but the language certainly can be interpreted as such: "We on the editorial staff would like to humbly thank Canisius and our companions for what they have given us—friendship. We thank Miss Kessler for being not only advisor, but a friend. In return, we give you our gift, the 1988 *Arena Yearbook*."

1989 - Rev. Carl Christian Beck, S.J.

As in several preceding issues of *Arena*, there is no explicit dedication offered in 1989. However, a memorial is offered for Rev. Carl Christian Beck, S.J., "Fr. Beck...joined the faculty of CHS and taught for three years.... Returning to Canisius in 1978, Fr. Beck worked as a guidance counselor where his calmness and patience instantly made him a favorite among students...until 1987.... Canisius misses the kind, warm disposition of Fr. Beck."

1990 - Mr. Cornelius V. McGillicuddy

"This past year, a man who is a tradition at CHS in his own right, Mr. Cornelius McGillicuddy...received the 'Buffalonian of the Year' award from Mayor James Griffin.... [Mr. Mack] is a portrait of the excellence that Canisius High School strives for." – Scott Celani.

Notes

[1] "Meeting of the Trustees' Physical Plant Committee." Friday, Dec 19, 1980.

[2] *Ibid.*

[3] *Ibid.*

[4] *Ibid.*

[5] "Minutes of the Board of Trustees." May 8, 1980.

[6] *Ibid.*

[7] *Ibid.*

[8] "Minutes of the Board of Trustees." February 19, 1981.

[9] *Ibid.*

[10] *Ibid.*

[11] Letter to Parents from CHS President Rev. Joseph E. Billotti, S.J., and Board Chair Eugene P. Vukelic '48. March 4, 1982.

[12] "Minutes of the Board of Trustees." May 20, 1982.

[13] *Ibid.*

[14] "Minutes of the Board of Trustees." Feb 5, 1983.

[15] *Ibid.*

[16] "Minutes of the Board of Trustees." May 19, 1983.

[17] *Ibid.*

[18] "Minutes of the Board of Trustees." Feb 11, 1984.

[19] Undated "Background" and "Capital Needs" memo from the President's Office, attached to Feb 11, 1984, Board Minutes in the CHS Archives.

[20] *Ibid.*

[21] "Minutes of the Board of Trustees." May 17, 1984.

[22] "Minutes of the Board of Trustees." Nov 15, 1984.

[23] "Minutes of the Board of Trustees." May 16, 1985.

[24] "Minutes of the Board of Trustees." Nov 21, 1985.

[25] "Minutes of the Board of Trustees." Feb 8, 1986.

[26] *Ibid.*

[27] *Ibid.*

[28] *Ibid.*

[29] "Minutes of the Board of Trustees." May 15, 1986.

[30] *Ibid.*

[31] *Ibid.*

[32] *Ibid.*

[33] *Ibid.*

[34] *Ibid.*

[35] "Fact Sheet" by James P. Corcoran, VP Institutional Advancement, connected to a series of Press Release materials sent to Rev. James F. Keenan, S.J., CHS President, related to the "Burn the Mortgage" announcement. Aug 14, 1991.

[36] *Ibid.*

[37] *Ibid.*

[38] Interview with Joe Lucenti '73. Dec 21, 2016.

[39] Editorial comment from Rev. Rich Zanoni, S.J., June 19, 2018.

[40] "One-to-One: Canisius Rolls Out iPad Initiative for Learning Results." *Summer 2012* issue.

[41] Linda, Dennis. Press Release dated October 11, 1983.

CHAPTER 12

The 1990s

IF THE 1980s MARKED AN EXISTENTIAL reckoning and what might arguably be called "The Dark Ages," then it could be said that the 1990s marked a renaissance for Canisius. To be fair, the 1980s were obviously not wholly defined by the financial crisis that defined the latter part of the decade. For the students who attended during that time, the fiscal woes of the institution were kept in the proper place, and to the extent possible, their experience was shielded from the challenges faced by their teachers and administrators. But those challenges were stark and real, and the 1990s brought a vital "sea change" to Canisius High School that was, according to multiple employees, long overdue.

Just as a confluence of factors led to the challenges of the previous decade, a number of elements would contribute to the school's economic recovery. However, it is undeniable that a shift in institutional leadership—and with it, a new approach to fiscal management—played a vital role in the stabilization of the school.

New Leadership & Clear Mission

An interview with Rev. David Ciancimino, S.J., in March 2018 provided considerable insight about the 1990s. Here, he sets the context for the beginning of the new decade, a time he—like many others—describes as a time of "rebuilding."

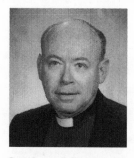

We were five Jesuits being missioned here: Father Jim Keenan, Father John Costello, Father Michael Tunney, [me], and Father Michael Corcoran.... Those years were challenging years for the high school. The number that sticks in my head is that we were about 484 students.... That had dropped from an eight-hundred number back in the day.... It was marked by a time of rebuilding.... We had a new President [and] a new Principal.

Rev. James F. Keenan, S.J.,

Those of us who were sent were charged with a clear mission. We had to address the issues that were facing the school. We had to build enrollment, handle the mortgage, and what was a very modest debt...but that also, somehow, public confidence had waned. So it was to rebuild that confidence, and that was certainly squarely at the feet of the President, Father Jim Keenan.

We all know that had a happy ending...the mortgage, which was very modest, was burned. Enrollment, even though in '89 when I began it was at 484 as I was leaving, enrollment would have opened at about 715...so we saw about a 50% increase in enrollment over those years, and we saw the tide of local public opinion move.

And it's not just at the feet of these five Jesuits. There was a very clear sense that everyone in the building those days—faculty, staff— [was] working very closely together, everyone pulling on an oar, in a united purpose, for the good of the high school.

Here's an example: Tom McPherson. One of the stories I remember from Tom is that when he told me he was ready to retire, I told him that I thought he had a few years in the classroom left in you. And he said, "You know, Dave, you're right. But that's the time to go. You don't want to stay to that very end. You don't want people to say, 'You know, Tom is great, but he stayed on too long and he should have been done a few years ago.'" I learned a lot from that, and about life, and when it's time to move on. It's good to move on when you're on top. I often have recounted that to Jesuits in the Province Office, when I would say it was time to move along. They'd say, "But I'm still doing great things!" And I'd say, "Perfect time to leave." There's a humility to that.

Just before the five of us arrived, there was a hero behind the scenes, who did a lot of difficult work: Father Gene Zimpfer, S.J., [Class of 1949]. He had to take a school that had been larger and had come down to 484—but was still staffed at a much larger size—and he pulled that down, "right sized it," that meant a lot of people either had to retire...or there was a reduction in force, or they were teaching out of their roles, but he really right-sized the place. He paved the way for Father Jim Keenan to come in, in his very genteel, avuncular, authentic, but kind way to do the repair work, of what had to be done in a post-right-sizing moment, if you will. But really, without the work that Father Gene Zimpfer did, I do not think we would be where we are today, and it would have taken us longer to dig out of what we had started.[1]

Joe Lucenti '73 echoed Father C.'s thoughts during his own interview for this book:

Gene Zimpfer had the finesse of a bull in a China shop. One of the most famous memos came out when he was named interim president. I still have it. He put out a memo that told it how it was. We're cutting salaries, we're cutting positions, etc. But on top of that, the memo also asked us to consider voluntarily taking a bigger cut individually. Maybe think about a sabbatical. Maybe consider going part time. And a lot of people were outraged. Now I'm sitting in the faculty room with Tom McPherson who, like Nick Kessler, was that classic calm, experienced, I guess you'd say "Dean" of the faculty. I'm shaking my head like, "Can you friggin' believe this?" And Tom looked at me and said, very quietly and calmly, "Joe, someday people are gonna look back on Gene Zimpfer and realize he saved this school."

Tom was right. Right on the money. Gene was only President for six months. And it was probably a brilliant move by the Jesuit hierarchy. Because they brought him in as a hatchet man. Someone had to come in to get blood on his hands to save this school. And he did. And then they brought in Jim Keenan. I remember I was speaking at a Province conference. A lot of the Jesuit presidents were there. And collectively they said, "Hey, you're at Canisius? Wow. You're getting Jim Keenan. We don't have anyone better than Jim Keenan." His reputation had already preceded him. What was brilliant from the hierarchy was that Gene had the blood on his hands, and Jim was able to come in and set the course straight.

Jim got it. We burned the mortgage before it was due. To this day, I would take a bullet for Father Keenan. He got it. He understood. And he understood it in the simplest of ways. Never once did I hear Father Keenan say, "I'm the President." Like Kessler and McPherson, you respected the man by his deeds. He didn't need to tell you he was the boss. And he understood our needs, what needed to be fixed. He was honest, and he proved that trusting him would pay off. It's funny how what was one of the darkest times in our school's history allowed it also to become one of the brightest.[2]

An October 1989 article in *The Citadel* provided insight into the perspectives of incoming President Rev. James F. Keenan, S.J.,:

The financial condition of the school is a major concern of Fr. Keenan. He discussed that due to several factors Canisius has accumulated a debt. The debt began with the construction of the Science Center, which was only half paid. Other costly projects like remodeling the library, waterproofing the school's brick face, fixing the roof, refurbishing the pool and weight room, and installing new boilers have set the school back. There also has been a decrease in the number of potential boys of high school age in the past few years. Keenan explained, "Now that those repairs are finished they will not cause any further expense for quite some time. Demographic studies of the Buffalo area also show that in two or three years the pool of high school boys will increase."[3]

He also addressed the cuts to faculty, with a hopeful eye to the future:

When asked whether the reduction in faculty was due to financial reasons he responded, "In the past few years the number of students has dropped from close to 700 to just over 500, while the number of faculty has remained the same. It was not feasible to keep a staff for 700 students when there are only 500 students. If there is a sizeable increase in enrollment, which I believe will be the case in the future, more faculty will be hired."[4]

This alone would be insufficient, of course, as financial stability without attention to campus culture, faculty morale, and continued development would be only a partial victory. Fortunately, as demographics fueled a positive trend in enrollment through the early 1990s, the school's population rose steadily (if not rapidly) while spending was kept under control. "My main goal," Keenan continued in the same article, "is to make Canisius number one and one important way to do that is to achieve financial stability."[5]

Along with a new President, CHS also welcomed new academic leadership in the Principal's Office. It was an unusual shift: rarely, since the very early days of the school's history, have simultaneous shifts in both offices taken place. This underscores the degree to which the transition from the 1980s to the 1990s was focused on substantial change. In an article published in the same issue of *The Citadel*, the student body was introduced to their new Principal, Fr. John Costello, S.J.:

This year Canisius is experiencing some momentous changes. One of the most significant is the arrival of our new principal, Fr. John Costello, S.J.... As a novice in 1976...[he] was very impressed and thought very highly of CHS and its Jesuit ideals...

As Principal, Father would like to continue supporting those ideals and hopefully enhance them. He explained, "The goal of a college preparatory school is to maximize the potential of its students and allow them to become more aware of their gifts." Father Costello feels that the process of developing a student's gifts extends far beyond academics and should include the means to help him grow spiritually. When asked how sports and extracurricular should tie into academics and a high school education he said, "Their relationships are incredibly close. All are critical. We are not here to produce brains alone, but well-rounded students who can interact and compete with their peers on all levels."[6]

Father Costello's tenure as Principal would not last long, however, and following an illness he was replaced by an Acting Principal well known to the student body and faculty. According to *The Citadel*, "The recent illness of Rev. John Costello, S.J., has brought to light all of the diligent efforts contributed by all of those within the Canisius community.... Rev. David S. Ciancimino, S.J., has assumed the position of Acting Principal.... Fr. C., as he is affectionately called throughout Canisius, was the logical choice.... Since his arrival approximately three years ago, he has regularly attended meetings held by the Board of Trustees. Functioning as Admissions Director [has provided him with]...a personal knowledge of all the students, [which] makes a principal more effective.... His functioning in the capacity of moderator of the Student Senate has and will continue to allow him to fully comprehend and solve the problems faced by the student body. Overall, Father C. was the best candidate for the position."[7]

Father Ciancimino offered further thoughts about his appointment during an interview for this book.

What I would share from that time was that I had tremendous support from faculty and staff. Some of that is that we were in tough straits.... But I had never been a principal before. I was thirty-one years old.... I say the difference between me back then is that I turned thirty while I was here, [whereas] if I stick around here for a couple more years I'll turn sixty! It's a large gap, right? So you [wound] up with a very young principal with no experience except having run some summer schools and having taught...but when I left here at the end of that time, I was very grateful for the patience of the faculty and the staff because they taught me how to be a school principal. They were very patient. Those were good years for me and I think for the school. But they really did teach me what it meant to be a high school principal. I was also very blessed to have Father Keenan as a very good mentor—you know, President-Principal type things; someone you could run things by—but you had a thirty-one-year-old who was trying to do the best he [could] and wasn't shy on work.

Outside of Father Keenan and myself [in terms of leadership], we also had great people like Pam Jacobs, who was a Board chair in those days, Anne Gioia, Tom Beecher...they were very key players. Bernie Kennedy was around...Jim McCarthy, Mike Madden, Mike Ryan...certainly Carl Montante...just a lot of good and helpful folks who were key trustees...Ron Ahrens, Sr. and Joe Michael...key people who were helping to push out the good word, but also advising, encouraging, being present, working with the board, working with Father Keenan...fully engaged.

Considering the devastating impact of the last decade upon the school in terms of faculty morale, the new leadership and "clear mission" that came with the beginning of the 1990s comprised a turning point in the life of Canisius. Father C. commented on how cooperation between formal school leaders and the "informal" leadership among faculty ranks helped usher in this period of rebuilding.

I think in those early days, there was a question about whether or not we would survive. Whether or not we would make it.... It didn't take long for [Fr. Keenan] along with Board people to change that narrative and build that confidence within the school.... I certainly never felt [that sense of desperation.] [We were] nose to the grindstone, do what you need to do, not dwelling on that. I think there was a pretty quick sense that we were gonna be okay. The tide started to change.

We also had some other key players. We had Joe Lucenti in the Dean's Office, Dennis Linda in the Principal's Office. Then you had Joe Lucenti move into the Assistant Principal's Office. We had Tom Keenan; we had Fran McGreevy moving into the Admissions Office. We had some really strong people who had been here and were assuming leadership roles or were already in them. I think of Gretchen Kessler who eventually joins that administrative team. Just incredibly strong people who helped to build that confidence and kept the ship going.

When I think of faculty, I think of Tom McPherson. He didn't say a lot, but if he spoke in a meeting, folks were going to listen. He was very supportive, he was very positive, and he was very good. When I think of Father Rich Zanoni...another guy to whom people would listen. There were many other great teachers. I'm just pulling out a few.[8]

Father C.'s fond recollections of Dr. Tom McPherson's teaching days have been shared by many. The 1993 *Arena* was dedicated to him (see end of this chapter). In a brief telephone interview with this author, he offered

a few spirited comments. Despite his "advanced" age, he was characteristically enthusiastic, positive, and upbeat. He began, in a humorous tone, by reminding me that, "You know I'm going on ninety-five, right, Paul?!" He went on to explain, "It was a wonderful place to teach. I didn't hang around there for so long because I was miserable. During my tenure, the faculty was fine, the administration was always helping, and the student

"Doc" Tom McPherson

body...the students...they were outstanding. You could trust them all. They were serious. You could push them. I think I did. It was the parents behind them. The parents were wonderful."[9]

"Doc" McPherson, throughout his very long tenure at CHS, served as a fine example of the kind of dedication and perseverance to which faculty at a Jesuit high school are called to aspire.

Changing Policies; Changing Campus

An article in the November, 1991 issue of *The Citadel* by Jason Young '92 entitled "Times of Change" offers a student perspective on the period between the '88-'89 to the '91-'92 school years. Here are some of its insights:

- *"In my freshman year, the school needed a great deal of change, and fast! This change, through the completion of the weight room and the computer center, was well on its way.... The weight room would not be in existence if not for the hard work of Mr. Gemmer.... The computer room has been open since the fall of 1988...and was made possible through many donations.... The center is open for student use until five because of the dedication of its chief operator, Miss Weber, D.H.M...."*

- *"The use of the Walk-a-thon money proved to be an instrumental factor in the completion of...[the newly renovated cafeteria]. This café gives the students a pleasant environment to share that all important meal...."*

- *"1989-90 brought about the greatest changes the school has seen in years. It began with the appointment of Fr. Keenan, who immediately began a 'crusade' to decrease the school's immense deficit. Over the past three years he has successfully accomplished his goal. The school plans a "mortgage burning" in 1992.... Father Costello...opened his doors to the Canisius community. By doing this, he was able to shrink the gap between the students and faculty."*

- *"During the '90-'91 school year, a few more pieces of the 'Beautify Canisius' puzzle were completed. One step was the completion of Tripifield.... The Walk-a-Thon money was used to renovate the locker rooms.... This year was also the premier of Channel One. This program informs and entertains the students during advisement."*

- *"This year...the new gym floor has been completed through the work of the Student Senate.... As for the money from the Walk-a-Thon, it will go to the completion of the new patio.*[*],10

---

* The patio was built in the courtyard where the Koessler Academic Center (the Rand mansion) meets the Beecher Classroom Wing; it became unusable following installation of the senior lounge beneath it approximately 20 years later. At time of this writing, the space is being eyed as the location for an atrium to house the Center for Global Learning as part of a Capital Campaign.

Screens Move In: From Channel One to Early Computers

Marty McCarthy '92 penned an editorial in the Fall, 1991 *Citadel* entitled "The Litmus Test on *Channel One*." By way of introduction, McCarthy writes, "*Channel One* has been here at Canisius for a year now, and according to *The Citadel* Student Poll, has the support of the majority of the students. However, there are many CHS students who would love to see *Channel One* banished from the Canisius community."[11]

Channel One, brought to the school as a technology and cultural initiative, provided a combination of news and lifestyle programming designed for the teenage demographic. It offered a daily use for the wall-mounted television screens, which had been installed some years prior through a grant. While the aforementioned *Citadel* poll indicated that most students enjoyed the daily news blast, support wasn't universal. McCarthy's commentary offered some perspective on some detrimental effects. "But what about the people who do not want to watch...What about the guy who must study for that killer first period history test? What about the guys who would rather talk among their friends than watch...? What should we do for them? We could set up a lounge for those who would want to talk. We could allow students who would rather study to go to the library for advisement."[12]

It is a testament to the rapid shift in the use of media in the classroom to consider the daily use of screens, projectors, tablets, and laptops in every classroom today. Indeed, comments McCarthy, "The only other thing CHS has used all the televisions for was the 'Bruce Friedhaber Report' during Spirit Days. I believe CHS should take advantage of the equipment given to them in a more substantial way. Perhaps a morning announcement show.... Also, more teachers should use the monitors and VCR's to display curriculum tapes.[13]

Burning the Mortgage

Readers of this history will certainly have noted the long history of debt associated with Canisius High School. From the earliest years of the institution's founding, through its momentous campus movement following WWII, various levels of debt imposed constant challenge and, occasionally, nearly-crippling obstacles. As the last chapter made clear, this was never clearer than in the latter part of the 1980s, when Canisius flirted with the possibility of closure in light of its dire financial situation. Always, it has been the generosity and sacrifice of benefactors, alumni, employees, and the Jesuits themselves that has sustained the school—all fundamentally rooted in a firm belief in its mission. That belief was bolstered and affirmed in 1992 by the "burning of the mortgage" when, for the first time in anyone's memory, Canisius stood truly free of burdensome debt.

Signs of the Times: Library Technology

Though it reads like ancient history today, the profile of the "Canisius High School Library Technology Project" in the Fall 1993 *CHS Today* newsletter marked an important development in the campus community.

Trustees and Administrators celebrate the "Burning of the Mortgage" in the CHS Auditorium. Pictured left to right are Paul Bauer, Pamela Jacobs, Fr. James Keenan, S.J., Tom Beecher '52, Fr. Thomas McMahon, S.J., and Fr. David Ciancimino, S.J., (Photo from CHS Archives, dated December 6, 1992.)

Penned by Father Ciancimino, the article laid out the vision and goals. These included:

- *30 computers with color monitors, extended keyboards, and mouse; networked to a central server and connected to the Montante Computer Center machines;*
- *Introduction of CD-ROM technology;*
- *Addition of bar codes to all library print resources for computerized cataloging;*
- *Six new printers (one color)*
- *Attachment of a modem*
- *Purchase new furniture*

As Father C. explained, "When students go off to competitive college programs and wish to do research they meet such new creations as the CD-ROM, on-line library cataloging, and modems to reach beyond the boundaries of the library within which they sit. We need to prepare our students not only with facts and knowledge, but also with the skills so they know how to learn, how to research.... 'It's not what's in here, it's what's out there.' Somewhere along the line, someone I met to talk about the future of high school libraries told me that.... Just use a modem to have your computer call Buff State's computer or maybe even a computer in another country. Once you're there...you can even check the latest stock report or weather forecast...Amazing! A wealth of knowledge at your fingertips travelling through phone lines and satellites. And all here at CHS...."[14]

Obviously, technology has come a long way since 1993. But it is telling indeed that even in this early phase of development, Canisius embraced technology as an essential component of contemporary Jesuit education.

125th Anniversary and The Campaign for Canisius High School

The Fall 1995 issue of *Canisius High Today* included several reflections on the school's 125th Anniversary. Among these was a series of perspectives from the President, Rev. Charles F. Kelley, S.J.

When Fr. Peter Spicher, superior of the Buffalo German Jesuit Mission, wrote to Bishop Stephen Ryan in March, 1869, to ask "permission for the German fathers to set up a Latin and a commercial school, if the opportunity arises, and to close them down if unsuccessful," he was keenly aware that three prior attempts within the last twenty years had, in fact, been unsuccessful. Though

Rev. Charles F. Kelley, S.J.,

land, money, and manpower were available, if not abundant, there was no certainty that the Catholics of Buffalo really wanted a school or would support one if they had one. No doubt, then, it was with a mixture of excitement and trepidation that his successor, Fr. William Becker, put the issue clearly and succinctly before the assembled faithful at St. Michael's Church on the last Sunday of August, 1870: "You have wanted [a high school] for a long time. Now you are about to get one. If it is not a success, if the people of Buffalo fail to give it the support it needs, we will close it down for good at the end of the year."

The school did not have to close at the end of that year, or for that matter, at the end of any of the 124 years that followed.... For 125 years, the one unchanging fact about Canisius is that it has been and continues to be a community of people resolved to make it a success. Canisius is not built out of bricks and mortar, but on the faith of men and women who believe in its mission and are resolved to see that mission fulfilled...

But we must not take God's will for granted or simply assume that everything we do is for God's greater glory. We can become neither complacent nor smug. God's activity in our lives is dynamic and fresh and new in every time and in every place. So, too, Canisius High School must remain dynamic and fresh and new so that we may give God glory in this time and in this place.[15]

The same issue also reported on an important milestone in the school's continued recovery from the economic troubles of the 1980s. The message was one of hopeful confidence, reinforced by the strong enroll-ment and solid footing that marked the first half of the 1990s.

On April 27, 1995, Canisius High School publicly announced the kick-off of its 125th Anniversary Campaign: A Foundation of Excellence...A Vision of the Future. *The announcement was made at a reception honoring faculty and staff hosted by Rev. Charles F. Kelley, S.J., President. This event was the cul-mination of eight months of behind-the-scenes work and was highlighted by the good news of a record setting $1-million-dollar gift from the Koessler fam-ily.16*

The eighteen-month, multi-phase campaign, which featured the larg-est gift to the school to date (the Koessler gift cited above), would aim to secure $4.5 million over a subsequent five-year period, with focus on building financial strength in three principal areas:

- A tuition endowment (Goal of $3.6 million)
- A faculty endowment (Goal of $450,000)
- A physical plant fund (Goal of $450,000)

End of a Losing Streak; Start of a Winning One

The 1999 CHS Football season marked the end of a seventeen-year losing streak against rival Saint Joseph's Collegiate Institute of Kenmore. While the focus of considerably less fanfare at the time, the fledgling volleyball team's Monsignor Martin Championship victory would mark a winning streak that has continued for nearly twenty years (including Fall 2018 as of this writing).

17-14: A Memorable Scoreboard

Sam Hartman '00 penned the *Arena* 2000 yearbook article that summa-rizes the victory, and it is offered here in its entirety:

About 7,000 people entered Crosby Field on a beautiful Saturday. The huge crowd entered through the same entrance, but they divided onto separate sides of the field. On one side were the St. Joe's Marauders fans, who had just another win for the ages in their minds. On the opposite side were the Canisius Crusaders fans, who had upset written all over their faces and bodies.

In the first half, it was obvious to everyone on hand that the Canisius Crusaders football team was out to break the streak that had plagued the team for the past 17 years. In the crowd, the fans all knew this was going to be the year for Canisius. At the end of the half, the score was 17-0 after a field goal by Tim Mack and two rushing touchdowns, one by John Mann and another by Erik Turner. During halftime, St. Joe's coach Bob O'Connor must have said something to his team because when they returned they appeared much more determined and prepared to win. Mike Capozzi caught a touchdown pass and Sandro DeAngelis ran in a 2-yard touchdown to make the score 17-14.

The fans got louder and the offense got ready to go back onto the field. With 5:44, the Crusaders started on the 20-yard line and began a drive that would go down in Canisius history. Facing third and 3 from the 27-yard line, quarterback John Mann completed an 18-yard pass to Mike Boryszak for the first down and the clock kept going. The fans became anxious waiting to see the clock hit zero. Later, with 3 minutes left in the game, Mann hit Chris Ganci with an 11-yard completion and another first down. Then, 2 minutes left, John Mann followed behind guard Dan Rinkerman and Dave Escoboles for another first down. The crowd was pumped as they realized that St. Joe's had used all their timeouts. Then, Howard Brackett connected with the finishing blow as he burst out and made a 27-yard run to the St. Joe's 3-yard line. That's when the fans knew they could begin their true celebration. With about a minute left, Canisius ran out the clock and the streak was broken after 17 years. Junior Howard Bracket described it as "the best feeling in the world." The feeling was mutual for the entire Canisius football team and all of the Crusader fans that rushed the field after the game. At that point, nothing else mattered. It was a wonderful time for everyone at Canisius. One that will be remembered forever.[17]

Paul Zablocki '01, Development Gifts Officer at the time of this writing, served for a number of years as the Director of Alumni Relations. As a member of the squad that played that day, he was able to offer some firsthand recollections. In order to fully understand Zablocki's commentary, it's important to know the team's context that year—a season marked as much by the tragic circumstances befalling a teammate as it was by historic victory.

On September 11, 1999, at the start of the second half of a game against Watertown High School, Christopher Cravatta '01 complained to trainer Sean Metz that he didn't feel good, then vomited and collapsed. Emergency surgery, induced comas, complications and the hope of recovery led to more surgeries, induced comas, complications and to a slow and painful realization that any recovery would be far from full. Chris was the type of teammate that worked his ass off. He wasn't the biggest or strongest but he was there, working hard, pushing himself to be better and pushed us to be better. We each wore a wrist wrap with the #44 on it, his jersey number. We each carried a piece of him onto the field.

What do I remember after the victory? I remember being numb, a sense of relief that we had done it, that it (the streak) was over. I had watched us lose to St. Joe's for years. I remember the snowy game at St. Joe's in 1996, the botched trick play that we had practiced so many times in practice in 1997, and I was on the field for the decimation at St. Joe's in 1999. We just didn't beat St. Joe's at football.

There were unbelievable passes for first downs thrown by John Mann '00. Passes caught by Mike Boryzak '00 and Chris Ganci '01. There was the running of Eric Turner '01 and the huge gain by Howard Bracket '01 that took us to the goal line with seconds to go that sealed the victory. The linemen pushed and pushed and pushed. Dan Rinkerman '00, Nick Rodgers '00, Peter Jay '00, Andrew Shaus '00, Mike Commorato '01, Paul Novotny '01, Dave Escobales '01, and me [Paul Zablocki '01].

I remember the students rushing the field and the unencumbered celebration. Teachers, students, alumni were all on that field sharing in the breaking of the streak. There was so much emotion that season. We were all dealing with the tragic loss of our teammate and friend... We were determined beyond belief. I don't think I can say it any better today. We were determined to break the streak—seventeen years of heartbreaking and embarrassing losses serving as inspiration to hold onto the football.... We were determined to do something within our control for Chris.... Winning that game was one thing we could do. We couldn't make him healthy, but we could hold onto that ball and win that game for Chris and for our school.[18]

The historic victory over SJCI. *Arena* 2000.

Junior Erik Turner carried 16 times for 50 yards.

Senior Mike Boryszak and Junior Paul Zablocki celebrate after another first down in the final drive.

The 1999 Varsity Football Team. From *Arena* 2000.

First Row: Howard Brackett, John Mann, Anthony McLaurin, Mike Boryszak, Josh Thomann, David Hooper, Tom Coppola, Andy Smith, Joe Mann, Ryan Cannon. Second Row: Chris Ganci, Erik Turner, Dayle Hodge, Joe Connelly, Jeff Tudini, Paul Zablocki, Nick Rodgers, Chris Cravatta, Tim Mack, Vinny Zuccaro. Third Row: Bob Travis, Mike Commaroto, Glenn Olejniczak, Pat O'Sullivan, Conor Drury, Dennis Abrams, Gant Brett, Dave Escobales, Peter Jay, Andrew Schaus, Paul Novotny, Dan Rinkerman, Ron Overs, Roland Davis, Matt Hy. Fourth Row: Adam Baker (mgr), Coach Bacon, Coach Troy, Paul Appleby (mgr)

Volleyball Begins Its Legacy

Volleyball began a championship-winning streak in 2000 that has continued to the date of this writing. Jay Josker '01, Director of Alumni Relations, shared his memories of the match that started the streak:

It was the culmination of two years of hard work and redemption for the '99 team that got beat bad in the championship the year before.... To finish my CHS career with a win as big as that one is something I'll always remember...For it to be the first of an almost twenty-year run of championships is really special.

The championship means so much to me because I got to share it with my friends. We did it together. We wanted to win for each other more than anything. And I think we wanted to extract a little vengeance not just for ourselves but for the seniors on the '99 team. Our championship really started with them.... They set a tone in '99 that we carried through...and the way we played that championship game was a pure celebration. A genuine joy and happiness for each other and a sense of togetherness that I never experienced before or after that...[19]

First Row: Charles Baldo, Andy Gangloff, Luke Darling, Kevin Buggs, Crosby Sommers. Second Row: Tim Short, Tim Buckley, Joe Zera, Jason Josker, Joe Battin, Mike Sellick, Mike Zlotkowski, Coach Walker

The 2000-2001 Varsity Volleyball Team. *Arena* 2001.

Arrival of Kairos

The Kairos retreat arrived at CHS in spring 1999 as a joint effort with McQuaid Jesuit. The first retreats were conducted *with* McQuaid staff and students at Camp Asbury on the shore of Silver Lake. Kairos was initiated at CHS under the direction of Rev. Robert Reiser, S.J., and, eventually, Rev. Peter Arabia, S.J., who would succeed him as Campus Minister.

CHS students of today would hardly recognize the retreat conducted in its original format, which was based on the traditional model imported from Loyola-Blakefield, a Jesuit high school in Baltimore. Most importantly, it was offered to seniors, not juniors. While most Jesuit schools offer Kairos to juniors, a number did and still do center the retreat on senior year. Another significant difference was the length: Kairos in its original form was a four-day, three-night retreat. (Again, this was changed

in the mid-2000s for practical reasons; details about these shifts are provided in the next chapter.) Of course, like Emmaus, which had been the junior retreat for many years, Kairos was held at Camp Asbury. This was the site of Kairos I through XIV, until CHS moved its partnership to Cradle Beach Camp in Angola beginning with Kairos XV in February 2003. Another significant difference was that it was standard practice for student leaders (the retreatants' peers, since both participants and leaders were seniors) to dress up formally in a shirt and tie for their talks.

The traditional "Kairos Cross" given to participants at the closing Commissioning Ceremony. It is a Jerusalem cross, used by CHS and most Jesuit high schools.

The *CHS Kairos Manual* has been modified and updated in various iterations across the years. A new introduction was written by this author when he served as Director of Student Formation Programs in 2007-2008. It offers some insights into the history and context of the retreat, and some excerpts are shared here:

"Kairos is a decisive, momentary unveiling of the eternal."
- C.S. Lewis

Building upon the foundations established as underclassmen, participants of Kairos engage in a more substantial and challenging reflective experience. An in-depth focus on relationships with family and friends helps clarify and deepen one's understanding of and relationship with Christ. Most significantly, Kairos challenges each student to embrace the Christian call to service. This, ultimately, becomes the primary focus of the retreat....

Named for the Greek term meaning, "The Lord's Time," Kairos is a nationwide spiritual growth program. It is not originally a Jesuit retreat per se. It was adapted from the Roman Catholic Cursillo *program, which was begun in Spain in 1944.* Cursillo *was adapted for youth by the Diocese of Brooklyn in 1965. Kairos made its main inroad into Jesuit circles when faculty at St. Ignatius HS in Chicago further adapted the retreat soon after, incorporating more specifically Ignatian elements and language. It has also been formed into a prison ministry movement.*

Just as did the original Cursillo *program from which it is derived, Kairos incorporates several fundamentals of Ignatian spirituality, with a strong influence from the* Spiritual Exercises. *Most Jesuit high schools and colleges in the United States now center their retreat programs around various adaptations of Kairos, retaining the basic structure and core elements of the retreat. The distinctive Jerusalem Cross has become associated with this experience, and alumni of the program often wear it, though some schools utilize different crosses.*

Kairos came to CHS in Spring 1999 in conjunction with McQuaid Jesuit in Rochester. It replaced the Companions retreat for seniors, which had been in place since 1997. It remained primarily a senior retreat until 2007, when it was repositioned to the junior year to replace Emmaus, which was shifted to sophomore year.[20]

It is difficult to overstate the impact Kairos has had upon the culture at Canisius. Serving as a critical juncture for deepening students' spirituality while strengthening the bonds among them, the retreat has established itself as a powerful fulcrum point in the formative mission at CHS for nearly twenty years.

Above: Kairos I, held April 28-May 1, 1999, at Camp Asbury on Silver Lake. Below: Student and faculty leaders of Kairos 100, held in March 2018 at Cradle Beach Camp in Angola.

Middle States Accreditation, 2000

Canisius underwent a comprehensive accreditation review by the Middle States organization in the 1999-2000 academic year. It is a fitting conclusion to the decade to consider objective, third-party impressions of the now fiscally stabilized school.

According to a May 2000 *Citadel* article by Timothy Buckley '02 and Nicholas Earley '01 entitled "Taking the Test – Middle States Gives Crusaders Pat on the Back," the school's stable financial status and rising enrollment provided conditions ripe for improvements to academic and cultural elements:

The three main objectives that were identified by the CHS Mid States Planning Committee as needing improvement are technology, Jesuit identity, and effective communication. Improvement in technology will include an increase in student and faculty access to computer labs before and after school, and expanded integration of education technology resources into the curriculum. To improve the school's Jesuit identity, students and faculty members will be educated about Jesuit heritage and the role of the Jesuit educator. In addition to this, students and faculty will see an increase in retreat and service opportunities, two key components in developing the "complete man." The effective communication of students [sic] will improve by incorporating into the curriculum more opportunities for students to present oral and group projects in class, increasing in number and time length across the four years of study.

...A student meeting with the Validation Team on April 12th raised a number of student concerns. The establishment of better outdoor and indoor sports facilities, the development and expansion of the Fine Arts Department, and the availability of technology to students are all major areas that were discussed. Students are also interested in seeing the curriculum expand to include more AP and elective courses. Additional concerns included the inability to retain staff members and the lack of diversity of the student body. One major concern noted by the Validation Team itself was the need for individual students to have the opportunity to voice their opinions and concerns. The administration and faculty must develop better ways to communicate to the general student body....

The Mid States visit has helped the administration and faculty to recognize and appreciate the strengths of CHS. Over the past ten years, CHS has developed into a flourishing and healthy community. The increasingly talented faculty and student body, the rigor of the academic program, and the supportive community spirit contribute to the school's pursuit of excellence.[21]

The "Blizzard of 2000"

While it wasn't technically a blizzard by meteorological standards, it's the only appropriate word for the massive winter storm that hit the Buffalo region on November 20, 2000. It was the first time most residents of the

The unexpected "Blizzard of 2000," which struck at the start of rush hour on November 20th, dumped approximately thirty inches of snow in the course of an evening, at rates of up to four inches per hour. Many students and staff, stranded at school, spent the night at Canisius. In this image, Principal Father Mattimore oversees students (both boys and girls) boarding busses the morning after the storm. *Arena* 2001.

city had heard the term "thundersnow," which was the only way to describe the freakish weather that combined snowfall with thunder and lightning. Gretchen Kessler, who was serving as Assistant Principal at the time, offered this recollection:

I remember watching the thundersnow hit, fast and furious. Teachers got out of the building that afternoon as fast as they could so they didn't get stuck. [Father] Jack Mattimore and I were there overnight with the kids and people coming off the street. I was interviewed by MSNBC the next morning about how we handled it. We ended up putting boys on one floor of the school wing, girls on the other. A school bus got stuck on Delaware and those kids all came in. Kids played basketball during the evening in the gym. Luckily, our food service had enough food in their storage that we could give people something to eat at night and again in the morning. By mid-morning four-wheel-drive vehicles were getting through and all the students were getting picked up.[22]

It took Andrea Tyrpak-Endres five and a half hours to get to Loyola Hall at Canisius College, and Charlie and Sandy Chimera enjoyed a seventeen-hour commute to Clarence. Jay Josker '01 had a memorable evening:

I got a ride from a fellow student. It took us four hours to get to somewhere between North Street and Allen. Delaware was down to one lane. It was so slow that along the way we jumped out of the car to help push people. One of us had a cell phone and our parents told us that there was no way we were getting home that night and to ditch the car and find a hotel. Tim had an emergency credit card, so the four of us put the car into a snow bank out front of the Best Western on Delaware and got a room. The next day we were still stuck so we made our way over to Ryan's brother's apartment.... Along the way we helped push out more cars. Finally, we found out that front loaders were on Delaware digging out cars. We headed back to ours just in time to see a front loader clearing it out. All told it took us 30+ hours to get home. When we got back to school a classmate told us that we made the newspaper. A lady had written in to say how nice it was to see students in Canisius gear helping other cars on Delaware. We think she ID'd us by the varsity jacket I was wearing.[23]

Gallery - 1991-2000

Fr. Costello and Mr. McGuire look on in festive spirits as Fr. Keenan officially opens the new backstage complex in the auditorium.

A celebration of a refurbished "backstage complex" in the aud, which would serve the Drama Guild and provide additional classroom space. *The Citadel*, April 1991.

One of the newly refurbished science center lecture halls, which featured tiered seating, on the 3rd floor of the Beecher Classroom Wing. Photo: *Arena* 1991.

Jim Neil – Olympian

Jim Neil was the first Buffalonian to be an Olympic oarsman since the '50's when Doug Turner, Jim Wynne, Jim McMullen, Ron Cardwell, Sonny Fox and cox Ed Masterson all represented the West Side Rowing Club in the 1956 Olympics.

The Olympic experience in Europe began with an encouraging second-place finish in Lucerne, behind Poland, in which both boats set course records, ahead of two German and two British boats. In the Olympic finals, on Lake Banyoles, the U.S. crew rowed its best time ever, 6:06.03, and finished in fourth place.

For Jim, the entire Neil family and his Canisius friends those were achievements that will remain long after the torch has been extinguished, along with the designation: Jim Neil, Olympian.

He brought honor to Western New York and its host rowing club, West Side, by his extraordinary performance. Hundreds of Buffalo fans shared the excitement of following Jim's pursuit of an Olympic medal, and were proud of his many accomplishments along the way.

His parents, Dick and Marilyn Neil, and family, Chris '84, Matthew '90, and Maribeth, said that the Olympics were the experience of a lifetime. They stayed at a hotel right across from the boathouse in Banyoles and could visit with Jim following races. Others who joined the contingent from Buffalo were Fr. Dugan of Canisius College and Peter Manias, who rowed with Jim at Canisius High School.

Sonny Fox, who rowed in the 1956 Olympics with Doug Turner in a four, joined the Neils for the finals. His daughter now lives in Majorca.

In his rowing career, Jim won most events in a four, straight or with cox. For Canisius High School, his four plus cox took both American and Canadian Schoolboys, becoming 1985 North American Champions. In 1986, the crew was selected as the US Junior National straight four and competed in the World Youth Championships in Prague, Czechoslovakia. That year Jim won the Outstanding High School Oarsman Award in Buffalo.

All four went on to row in college and each became captains of their respective teams. They are: Ted Haley, Georgetown, Jed Dietrich, Temple, Peter Manias, Brown. Peter travelled to Spain to join the Neils for the Olympics.

Jim attended Rutgers and was coached by Jim "Pops" Wagner. He was named Outstanding Athlete in Sport for Rowing in 1990, when he graduated.

During the pre-Olymics trials, Jim affiliated with the Vesper Rowing Club of Philadelphia.

Until 7/21 the teams were considered to be the U.S. National teams, and become the Olympics teams upon arriving for processing in Banyoles on 7/21.

Jim carries on a long tradition of Canisius and Buffalo rowing history, dating back to the era of the late Charlie Fontana, to today's successful Canisius four, comprised of Mike Rausch, John Lyons, Kirk Dorn, and Kevin Weigel who won six of seven regional, national and international regattas, finishing second in a photo finish in the seventh, under coach Mark Kostrzewki.

Jim's plans for the future include graduate school. His rowing career is uncertain at this moment, but could include a push for the 1996 Olympics and coaching.

Whatever path he chooses, he will always be able to claim the title, Jim Neil, Olympian.

Jim Neil '88, 1992 Olympian. Article and photo from the Fall 1992 *Canisius High Today.*

John McGowan takes matters into his own hands and attempts to cook a hotdog on the partially completed patio while Mr. Corcoran looks on.

3.

Top: *The Citadel,* February 1992, featured some tongue-in-cheek humor about the much anticipated, yet unfinished, patio project.

Left: The newly installed door made this photograph by the time *Arena* 1993 came around.

Bottom: This photo in *Arena* 1997 shows students enjoying full use of the finished project.

CHS Inaugurates New Team

It's fall at Canisius again and the football, cross country, soccer, and golf teams were all competitive in their quest for their respective Monsignor Martin Association crowns. However, this year marks the first time in Canisius' great history that it has had a volleyball team. The team is coached by Chris Webber, who is Holland's volleyball coach and a student at Buffalo State College. Our moderator is Mr. Don Leslie, who teaches history and math here at Canisius. After a relatively late start, a month full of vigorous tryouts and two series of cuts, the team has made incredible progress and is still learning. The Inaugural and Varsity consists of seniors John Brennan, Adam Cugalj, Tim Montante, and Doug Tonucci, juniors Stan Nowak, Joe Artanis, Pat Gallager, Alex Porter, and Bart Funk, and is led by sophomore sensation Jay Jakubowski. The Junior Varsity squad consists of sophomores Mark Starosilec, Mark Michaels, Joel Amico, Adam Ryan, Seth Trego, Ryan Grundtisch, and Dave Rooth, and freshmen Nathan Nowak and Pat Beecher. This bunch is led by outstanding sophomore Dan McDermid. The Varsity and JV teams are are off to a slow start, however, the team is still improving and in coming months and years looks to be one of Canisius' most promising sports team. Good luck team. Go Spikers.

- *Mark Starosielec*

The Results Are In

Top: The beginning of one of CHS's strongest athletic programs—Volleyball—is announced in the November 1992 *Citadel*.

Right: The same issue provides a glimpse into CHS student perspectives on the Bills, politics, *Channel One*, and school life concerns.

Here are the results of the poll Canisius students took a couple of weeks ago. There were 321 polls counted. 79% of us think the Bills will make it to the Super Bowl. 77% think the Bills need a new stadium. Results for best running back included 57% for Thurman Thomas; 21% for Barry Sanders; 13% for Emmett Smith; and 8% for others. 79% said we would be at the Joe's game. Where were the other 21%? 78% think we will win, shows what you know!

Results from our Presidential Poll: 56% Clinton; 35% Bush; 9% Perot.

Channel One worth our time, 50% yes/ 50% no (go figure). 112 of you said you would write for the *Citadel*, so where are you?

Best things about CHS included sports and educational programs; worse things about CHS include homework, JUG, and the lack of female students. Suggestions to improve CHS included NO JUG, renovate the Aud, and purchase new desks. There also seemed to be an desire for an influx of new female teachers.

- *Kris James*

Mr. Dennis Woods, a longtime custodian at Canisius whose tenure exceeds most of the faculty's, attends to the American Flag in front of the mansion. *Arena* '93.

Keenan New Varsity Basketball Coach

Coach Tom Keenan

Father Ciancimino announced that a committee selected Thomas Keenan as the new Varsity Basketball Coach at Canisius. Coach Keenan brings a wealth of experience both from the high school and college level to CHS. A long time coach at Nazareth and Xaverian High Schools in NYC, Coach Keenan then coached at Kingsborough Community College and the College of Staten Island. A move to Western New York found Coach Keenan as a Varsity Assistant at Division I Niagara University. Desires to spend time with his family and to do less travelling required for college recruiting and playing brought him back to the high school basketball court.

The Crusaders met Coach Keenan on the court at the Junior Varsity basketball games against St. Joe's this past season. Last year the Coach posted an undefeated season.

We welcome Coach Keenan and his basketball coaching staff to the "Home of the Crusaders."

Interview with Coach Keenan

"I hope that the players will be good listeners and play hard." Tom Keenan, the new varsity basketball coach, brings a philosophy of learning to his job at Canisius. That approach led to his being named Division III Coach of the year by Sport Magazine in 1986. His game style is to be on his feet in front of the bench. Referees only tagged him with one "T" last year, evidence of a man in control.

He most recently coached the St. Joe's JV to a 22-0 season, and is eager to bring a career of coaching experience to the Crusaders. The boys of the blue and gold will hear about his years with Jim Valvano's brother, Bob at St. Francis College of Brooklyn, and more recently, his stint with Jack Armstrong at Niagara U. Past head coaching positions included The College of Staten Island and Kingsborough Community College.

Coach Keenan observed that a coach might be able to take a team from an 18-4 record to 22-0 or 7-15 to 16-6, but that the team and talent are the real reasons for the wins. He added that the coming season will tell the rest of the story, for him and for the Canisius basketball team.

In the interview, Coach Keenan noted that he has already discovered the importance of participation at Canisius and expects to become a real part of the overall picture here. He mentioned anticipating the Open House and added that the boys could count on seeing him in the corridors regularly during the school year.

He and his wife, Kathy and two sons, Tom and Brian came from Brooklyn to Western New York three years ago and reside on Grand Island.

From *Canisius High Today*, Fall 1993

Father Keenan Leaves His Mark

Father James F. Keenan, S.J., came to Canisius High School in 1989. When he arrived he took on both the Presidency of the high school and the Rectorship of the Jesuit community. Upon his arrival he was faced with great financial problems. Throughout Fr. Keenan's four years at Canisius, he has mananged to curb the school's spending and reduce the debt of Canisius. He reduced spending within the school by setting a budget and holding the school accountable to that budget. Fr. Keenan was then able to secure funding to "Burn the Mortgage" of Canisius High School and thus eliminated Canisius's large debt.

In addition, Fr. Keenan has done wonders within the Canisius community. He has always found time to assist the many people of Cansisius. Whether he is keeping tabs on a student's academics, advising a brother priest within the community or helping a friend outside the community, Father Keenan has touched the hearts of many. When the Canisius community was informed of the departure of Fr. Keenan after the 1993-1994 school year, talk of all the good he has done throughout his five years at Canisius was heard echoing throughout the hallowed halls of Canisius.

Father Keenan has done great things for Canisius High School. He will be remembered and severely missed by all. It is with this in mind that Father James F. Keenan receives the dedication of the 1994 *Arena* yearbook.

—Bart Funk

FACING PAGE, TOP: It's the Canisius High School blue doors that welcome studen everyday. BOTTOM LEFT: Tim Beecher relaxes during Freshmen Fun Day. BOTTOM R Markiewicz is all smiles. THIS PAGE, TOP: "Heard any good jokes lately, Fr. Keenan? Fr. Keenan gives guidance to Mike Loehfelm.

The *Arena* 1994 was dedicated to Father Keenan, S.J., with this article marking his departure.

430

This new, custom-commissioned sign was installed above the newly-re-painted Blue Doors. Care and attention to the school's entrance was largely the work of Rev. Richard Zanoni, S.J., for many years.

Faculty collage, early 1990s. From *Arena* 1991-1995.

The fire that burns within: Seniors (from left to right) J.P. Leous, Jim Lilley, Paul Smaldone and Ron Parsons during the Games held in Ithaca, NY this past summer.

Top: The New York State Empire Games figured prominently in CHS athletics in the mid-1990s. From *The Citadel,* November 1995. Bottom: Father Dave Ciancimino, S.J., - the Jesuit Principal who also operates the snowplow.

It had been a really long losing streak for the CHS-SJCI football rivalry, and CHS students took bragging rights where they could find them to add spirit to the motorcade. *Arena* 1996.

Cast and crew of *Dark of the Moon* in *Arena* 1996.

CHS Juniors in a moment of reflection as they travel the road to Emmaus. (Left.)

The Emmaus retreat program was held for many years at Camp Asbury, in the Methodist Manor retreat house, on the shores of Silver Lake, New York. (Bottom.)

The 1996 *Arena* celebrated a number of athletic championships. Pictured here are Georgetown Cup champions (baseball) and Manhattan Cup champions (basketball). Seated at the center in the basketball portrait is longtime Dean of Students and varsity basketball coach Tom Keenan, whose untimely death greatly saddened the CHS community.

Rev. John J. Mattimore, S.J., (Principal) and Rev. Charles F. Kelly, S.J., (President), from *Arena* 1996.

Canadian Secondary Schools champions (L to R): Moderator Fr. Jim Van Dyke, S.J. '77, Coach Dr. David Bonfante, Patrick Haumesser '98, Tim Ernst '98, Chris Szczepanski '98 (coxswain, front), Nathan DeLuke '98, Matt Gerrish '98, Coach Jack Hailand, and Coach Tom Flaherty, Sr. From *Arena* 1998.

Arena 1999 included this portrait of alumni serving at the school (above); *Arena* 2001 shows us how many Jesuits were on staff (11) at the turn of the millennium (below). Not pictured: Father Richard Zanoni, S.J.,

Rev. James F. Fox, S.J., served as CHS President for a brief tenure before succumbing to illness.

Rev. Peter Hans Kolvenbach, S.J., Superior General of the Jesuits, shakes hands with student leaders during his visit to Canisius on October 7th, 1999.

Arena Dedications - 1991-2000

1991 - Rev. Richard Zanoni, S.J.

"Caring. Dedicated. Generous. These are only a few of the adjectives students and faculty use when describing Father Zanoni. His love for the school and passion for teaching combine to make him one of the most-liked and well-respected teachers at Canisius High School," wrote Stan Bowman '91 in the 1991 *Arena*. "Not to be lost in the shuffle of his work for God is Fr. Zanoni's extreme dedication to the betterment of Canisius High School...repainting the blue doors, numbering the lockers, and repairing broken tiles.... Being the modest person that the is, Fr. Zanoni enjoys working behind the scenes...and exemplifies the dedication to excellence that Canisius High School promotes. We thank him for the everlasting impression that he has left on every life that he has touched at Canisius, students and faculty alike."

1992 -No dedication offered.

1993 - Dr. Thomas McPherson

Steve Slawinski '93 wrote the 1993 *Arena* dedication: "Canisius has had a tradition of academic excellence. This tradition is founded upon a dedicated and personable faculty. One mainstay and pillar of Canisius has proven to be Dr. McPherson. Over the years, few have remained as long as and proven as dedicated as Dr. McPherson.... Expecting the utmost excellence of himself and his students has been a trait of 'Doc' since he began teaching at this Jesuit institute.... 'Doc' could be defined by the Canisius motto, as he has prepared and will continue to prepare his students for college, and for life."

1994 - Rev. James F. Keenan, S.J.

As Bart Funk '94 wrote in the 1994 *Arena*, "Father James F. Keenan, S.J., came to Canisius High School in 1989. When he arrived, he took on both the Presidency of the high school and the Rectorship of the Jesuit community. Upon his arrival, he was faced with great financial problems. Throughout Fr. Keenan's four years at Canisius, he has managed to curb the school's spending and reduce the debt.... [He] was then able to secure funding to

'Burn the Mortgage'.... In addition, [he] has done wonders within the Canisius community. He has always found time to assist the many people...a student's academics, advising a brother priest...or helping a friend.... Father Keenan has touched the hearts of many."

1995 - CHS on its 125th Anniversary

The 1995 *Arena* lacks a particular dedication; however, a substantial opening section is focused on celebrating the school's 125th Anniversary. As such, the yearbook is arguably dedicated to the school itself in recognition of this milestone.

1996 - Miss Loretta Weber, D.H.M. 1939-1995

"For twelve years, the Canisius High School community was graced with the presence of Miss Loretta Weber, D.H.M. With a witty, caring personality, Miss Weber personified the essence of Canisius.... She had a compassionate heart, an intelligent and dedicated mind, and an undying soul.... Through all of her years of service to God and community, Miss Loretta Weber influenced thousands of young minds and inspired the religious and intellectual growth of

all she associated with. [Her] trademark personality and energy often hid the fact that she was dying of cancer.... Miss Weber, through all her suffering, was able to put personal matters aside and teach with the vigor and energy of a teenager.... She will be always remembered as a woman of dedication, compassion, and love."

1997 - Mr. Richard Sniezak

"For the past twenty-six years," wrote Rev. Ronald Sams, S.J., in the 1997 *Arena*, "those who made the pilgrimage to the second-floor treasurer's office always found a smiling, helpful man ready to great them and assist them.... To the faculty and staff who knew him more personally than the students, he was always the life of the party with his warm sense of humor and his ready smile. We shall all miss our friend now that the Lord has called him to his reward in eternal life where each one's treasure is safe and sound."

1998 - Mr. Joseph Lucenti '73

Mr. Michael LiVigni, who went on after teaching at Canisius to serve as Assistant Headmaster and eventually Headmaster of Xavier High School in New York City, wrote the 1998 *Arena* dedication. "What is the definition of blue and gold? Anyone at Canisius for the past two decades would have to answer 'Joe Lucenti.' A graduate...a CHS Guidance Counselor, the Dean of Students, and the Assistant Principal, Mr. Lucenti was all of these things, and yet so much more.... We dedicate this book to the man who taught us all what it meant to be a Crusader, but more importantly what it meant to be men and women for others."

1999 - In Memoriam: David Patrick O'Brien '87

Rev. James R. Van Dyke, S.J., '77 wrote: "David O'Brien was always present...[he] emerged to take charge of the Food Drive.... In the 1987 *Arena*, David appears in more pictures than any other student...a tribute to his presence.... David attended Dartmouth and went on to study for master's degrees in nutrition, law, and diplomacy at Tufts.... [He] looked beyond what those achievements could mean for himself....

His interest led him literally around the globe to such places as Latin America, the Sudan, Kenya, and finally India...[where] he sought to be 'a man for others.' David took [that slogan] and ran with it. His sudden death in India while doing research on hunger shows how far those words can carry a man.... David met his God while doing what he most loved to do.... In life and death, he became a complete man."

2000 - Mr. Ronald Hastreiter '50 and Mr. Robert O'Connor '55

Robert O'Connor
Class of 1955

Math, Math Honors
From *Arena* 1999

Ronald Hastreiter
Class of 1950

Global Studies, Economics
From *Arena* 1999

The 2000 *Arena* is dedicated to two longtime faculty members upon their retirement: "Last year CHS said goodbye to two faculty legends. Mr. Ronald Hastreiter '50 and Mr. Robert O'Connor '55 retired last year after serving the Canisius community for over fifty of its one hundred thirty years. The gifts that they have shared with us and their students are incalculable. It is with gratitude then that we dedicate this volume of *Arena* in thanks for all they have given. May God bless them both and congratulations!"

Notes

[1] Interview, personal, with Rev. David S. Ciancimino, S.J., Mar 7, 2018.

[2] Interview with Joe Lucenti '73. Dec 21, 2016.

[3] Whelan, Gerald. "Keenan Takes CHS Helm." *The Citadel*, Volume 42, No. 1. October, 1989. p.1.

[4] *Ibid.*

[5] *Ibid.*

[6] Whelan, Gerald. "Costello Upholds Canisius Ideals." *The Citadel*, Volume 42, No. 1. October, 1989.

[7] Young, Harvey '93. "Principal Update." *The Citadel*, Volume 44, No. 5. March 1992.

[8] Interview, personal, with Rev. David S. Ciancimino, S.J., Mar 7, 2018.

[9] Telephone interview with Dr. Thomas McPherson. Jan 3, 2017.

[10] Young, Jason '92. "Times of Change." *The Citadel*, Volume 44, No. 3. Fall 1991.

[11] McCarthy, Marty '92. "The Litmus Test on *Channel One*." *The Citadel*, Volume 44, No. 3. Fall 1991.

[12] *Ibid.*

[13] *Ibid.*

[14] Ciancimino, David, S.J., "Library Technology Project." *CHS Today*. Vol. 24, No. 1. Fall 1993.

[15] "From the President." *Canisius High Today*. Vol. 26, No. 1. Fall 1995.

[16] "The Campaign for Canisius High School." *Canisius High Today*. Vol. 26, No. 1. Fall 1995.

[17] Hartman, Sam '00. "17-14". *Arena*, 2001.

[18] Electronic correspondence with Paul Zablocki '01. Mar 6, 2018.

[19] Interview via email with Jay Josker '01. Thursday, February 22, 2018.

[20] Cumbo, Paul. *Canisius High School Kairos Manual*. 2007. CHS Archives.

[21] Buckley, Timothy '02 and Earley, Nicholas '01. "Taking the Test – Middle States Gives Crusaders Pat on the Back." *The Citadel*. Volume 51, Issue 2. May, 2000.

[22] Email interview with Gretchen Kessler. February 22, 2018.

[23] Email interview with Jay Josker '01. February 22, 2018.

CHAPTER 13

The 2000s

THE FIRST DECADE OF THE NEW millennium was marked by substantial growth and expansion at Canisius. The physical campus saw extensive development and new property acquisitions. Just as importantly, however, the school changed in other ways. Enrollment climbed, diversity increased, curricular offerings became more varied, and programs increasingly connected CHS to organizations and communities outside of Western New York.

If the late 1980s brought a literal and figurative crash to the school's portfolio, the 1990s represented a slow, painstaking return to a stable market. Thus, considered in the context of previous decades, the ambitious expansion the school undertook in the 2000s might well be considered good evidence that the recovery period of the 1990s was a success. In terms of enrollment and school operations, it was arguably a "bullish" ride for a while—although in terms of personnel, the school saw a conspicuous period of high turnover and tension between faculty and administration. Of course, as could be said about the entire global economy, there was yet more turbulence in store, and yet again the leadership of Canisius would struggle with a challenging confluence of fiscal realities following the 2008 housing market crash.

By the close of the decade, Canisius had more than doubled its campus footprint, including substantial property acquisition and construction. It had massively expanded its programming and offerings. But change is messy, and along with the dust, noise, and energy of physical construction, stability in the ranks was a challenge as well. The Canisius community was hard pressed to keep up with the pace of transformation. Lest we underestimate the challenges in hindsight, we need only consider two remarkably telling facts: between the 1999-2000 and 2009-2010 academic years, Canisius High School was led by three different Presidents and three different Principals.

A Visionary Leader & Enrollment Expansion

Rev. James P. Higgins, S.J., '72, began his tenure following the untimely death of Rev. James F. Fox, S.J., and remained in office until summer 2008; he stepped down as President shortly before his own death. Father Higgins was fervently devoted to Canisius, and despite many controversies that roiled his presidency, it was always clear that he had an ambitious vision for the future of the school. Among these ambitions was a desire to see enrollment reach or exceed one thousand students.

In a 2005 conversation with this author, Fr. Higgins made it clear that he envisioned Canisius becoming a regional academic and athletic power-house—a massive academy rivaling the largest Jesuit high schools in the country, expanding its enrollment reach in all directions, including into

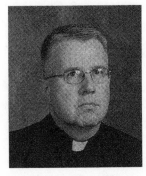

southern Ontario. He admired the size and scope of such large institutions as Saint Ignatius College Prep of Chicago, Illinois, with its enrollment well above one thousand students.

Coming as I had from Georgetown Prep, where I served as a Housemaster in the last remaining residential boarding program at an American Jesuit high school, Father Higgins had plenty of questions about Prep's programs

Rev. James P. Higgins, S.J., '72

and policies. He remarked that Canisius was too limited by Buffalo's "provincial mentality" that made people "think small when they should be thinking big." We needed to be open to all possibilities, including the potential for a boarding program and, eventually, the opening of a middle school. Opening a middle school along the lines of that at McQuaid Jesuit in Rochester would

be, according to Fr. Higgins, "an almost sure thing" somewhere in Canisius High School's relatively near future—he characterized it as only a matter of time. He mentioned his inclination to re-brand the school as Canisius Preparatory School or Canisius Preparatory Academy—nomenclature he believed would foster a more prestigious reputation. I joked that chants of "C.P.S." would perhaps be problematic at athletic events, and we shared a laugh.

Fr. Higgins, 1972 *Arena*

To say that Fr. Higgins had a broad vision for the potential of Canisius High School is an understatement. His most outspoken critics—and given his leadership style, he garnered several—say that his aspirational reach in terms of enrollment and facilities expansion exceeded the school's institutional grasp. He significantly expanded scholarship offerings, and redoubled efforts to attract a more diverse student body. His whole-hearted support of the HAP program gave rise, arguably, to one of the most successful and proven vectors for student recruitment. Given what many described as an often-tumultuous tenure, marked by an unprece-dented level of faculty, staff, and administrative turnover, there was no shortage of such critics, particularly among influential sectors of the fac-ulty. Countering the criticism of a frequently controversial tenure, how-ever, are the countless voices of admiration and gratitude for Higgins' undaunted belief in the school's potential, coupled with tireless and dog-ged efforts to achieve it. There is a strong case to be made that in many ways and on many levels, Canisius owes much of what it looks like to-day—in terms of enrollment, facilities, and, to some degree, financial chal-lenges—to the expansive vision of Father Higgins. His tenure—the longest for a CHS President since the 1980s—definitively set the school's course for the first part of the new century and the new millennium.

Following Father Higgins' death in 2009, the old Consistory's entry hall (known simply as "The Foyer") was dedicated in his memory as Hig-gins Hall. During a memorial service held there with family, friends, and colleagues, Rev. Patrick Lynch, S.J., commented, "Jim threw himself wholeheartedly into whatever he did; there were no half measures."[1] Hon. Lawrence J. Vilardo '73, during the same event, said, "One of the lessons of the Ignatian ideal of 'men and women for others' is that great-ness and generosity go hand in hand. A man who has vision and talent and

the capacity for hard work is blessed to be sure, but he is not great unless and until he puts those blessings to work for others."[2]

But a decade before Canisius would bid farewell to Father Higgins, the school was setting its course for the significant growth he envisioned. The enrollment declines of the late 1980s seemed a distant memory indeed as Canisius entered the 2000s. In *The Citadel* issue dated September 2000, Editor Dan Zak '01[*] penned a cover story focused on enrollment:

Fifteen advisements? That's a lot of freshmen. In fact, it's the largest fresh-man class this side of World War II. The official tally is 239, about fifty-five more students than the average class entering Canisius.... The jump can be attributed to many things. First of all, the shadow program[**] was refined last year. Shadows not only went to classes but met with upperclassmen to discuss the high school lifestyle.... Open House...was able to make a hugely effective and favorable impression.... As a result, Canisius received more qualified students.[3]

In fact, while impressive in its own right, this enrollment milestone wouldn't mean too much if not part of a broader trend of continued high enrollment. A look at graduating seniors over the course of the decade reveals this trend. (Counting graduating seniors, rather than incoming freshmen, accounts for attrition.) Indeed, the average graduating class size for the first half of the decade was 173, whereas for the second half it was 194—an 11% increase in average graduating class size across a relatively brief five-year period. Put another way, for illustrative purposes: enrollment in 2001 can be estimated at 681 (using these graduation numbers, which are post-attrition) compared to approximately 771 in 2007. This trend would continue, bringing enrollment well above 800 after 2009.

---

[*] Mr. Zak's editorial experience in *The Citadel* served him well; he went on to a career as an author and columnist for *The Washington Post*.

[**] The "shadow" program, now known as "Crusader for Day," is an admissions initiative that invites prospective students to spend a day at CHS with a designated host student—usually a freshman.

CHS GRADUATES SPRING '01 TO SPRING '10

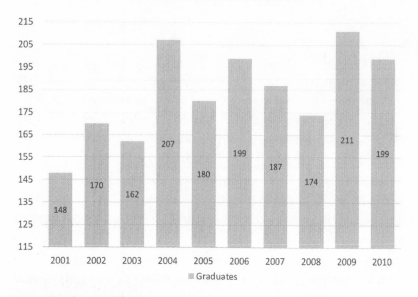

A New Era of HAP

The Higher Achievement Program (HAP) began in 1969 under the leadership of Mr. Charlie Chimera. It continued to evolve in the mid-1990s under the direction of Mr. Thomas Keenan, Dean of Students. 1995 marked its 27th year, and by that time it had expanded to a six-week program with 94 participants, eight full-time teachers, and several CHS student tutors. Along with its traditional academic and sports focus, HAP expanded its offerings with elective courses and field trips.[4] This growth continued through the end of the 1990s and into the early 2000s, with enrollment continuing to climb.

Under the vision and guidance of Father Higgins, along with the administrative leadership of Mr. Dennis Beecher '88, HAP continued to grow in diversity. Father Higgins saw HAP as an ideal means by which to be inclusive and demonstrate the opportunity of a Canisius education to young men throughout Western New York—including those who otherwise might not have considered attending. 133 students were enrolled in 2005, and HAP became increasingly important as an admissions factor. While not designed as an admissions or recruiting mechanism, the program nonetheless has played an important role in providing exposure to the community and inviting boys from around the area to experience what Canisius has to offer.

HAP students and a counselor at HAP 2006. Left to right: Bernard Williams '10, John Gibbons '05, and Matthew Wischerath '10.

A Transition to Lay Leadership

As mentioned above, CHS would see three Presidents and three Principals between 1999 and 2010—six senior administrators in the space of approximately one decade. In a crucial "sign of the times,"* a radical shift occurred amidst these leadership changes. For the first time in the institution's history, lay leadership took the helm in the offices of both the Principal and President.

---

* This phrase, in circles of Jesuit education, is a usually a nod to the seminal 1978 "Men for Others" address by Jesuit Superior General Pedro Arrupe, S.J. However, Fr. Arrupe was, of course, referencing Pope John XXIII's 1962 Apostolic Constitution, *Humanae salutis*, which began the Second Vatican Council. Ultimately, the phrase is a reference to Matthew 16:4.)

Succeeding Rev. John Mattimore, S.J., Mr. Frank Tudini '62 became the twenty-first—and first non-Jesuit—Principal of Canisius beginning with the 2002-2003 academic year. His four-year tenure as principal would follow thirty-five years of dedicated service on the faculty. While his time

in office faced numerous challenges related to personnel matters and some contentious issues that saw the Faculty Senate at odds with senior leadership, Tudini maintained the respect of his longtime colleagues on the faculty. In a 2006 *Citadel* interview with Ian Toner '08, Mr. Tudini remarked that rather than having people remember him after he leaves, "I would rather have people say, 'I remember in the first half of

Mr. Frank Tudini '62

the first decade of the twenty-first century, Canisius really was a great school.' And I'll know that I was on watch during that time."[5]

Tudini was succeeded by Mr. William Kopas, another lay administrator. Kopas, who was hired by Canisius following a national search, came from outside Western New York following a long tenure as a teacher and Assistant Principal for Student Affairs at Brophy College Preparatory, a Jesuit school in Phoenix, Arizona. Gerald Glose, board member and chair of the search committee that identified Kopas, offered a statement published in

Mr. William Kopas

April 2006 by *Buffalo Business First:* "The committee felt Kopas was a perfect fit for the educational, co-curricular and interscholastic program needs of Canisius High School.... He will appropriately carry on the fine Jesuit tradition that is currently in place at Canisius."[6]

Following the departure of Father Jim Higgins '72 after the 2007-2008 school year, Canisius saw another milestone in the appointment of Mr. John Knight as the school's first lay President. A husband, father, and native of Toledo, Ohio, Knight came to CHS from Milwaukee, Wisconsin, where he had been president of Catholic Memorial High School. Prior to this, he'd worked at University of Detroit Jesuit High School in Michigan and as a younger man had undergone some stages of formation as he discerned a potential vocation with the Jesuits. Underscoring the lay-Jesuit collaborative, he remarked, "My primary role is to be the Director of the Mission. The Provincial of the New York Province of the Jesuits, the Board of Members and the Board of Trustees have asked me to work to make sure that Canisius High School stays true to its Jesuit identity."

Mr. John Knight

In the years that have passed since the first appointment of laypeople to the senior leadership roles at Canisius, leadership has continued to evolve with another first: the first female Principal, Andrea Tyrpak-Endres, whose tenure began in Fall 2014. While the school has seen as many Jesuit presidents as lay presidents since the conclusion of Mr. Knight's term, there have been no Jesuit principals since the appointment of Mr. Tudini in 2002. Considering the demographics and personnel dynamics across the schools in the Jesuit Schools Network, it appears increasingly likely that academic administration of individual Jesuit schools will remain primarily the responsibility of lay "partners in mission," with Jesuits being prioritized either to the offices of President or, increasingly, roles related to vocations, formation, mission, and identity at the Province-wide level.

Facilities Development

Early Changes in Advance of Major Ones

Adam Baber '01, who would eventually return to CHS as a history teacher and, later, Assistant Principal, authored a *Citadel* article in the September 2000 issue entitled "All New, From Toilets to Classrooms" that focused on campus improvements at the outset of the 2000s. It is worth taking a look at these early campus enhancements, because they initiate a decade that would veritably transform CHS as the school grew, both in terms of physical plant and enrollment.

John Paul Sfeir '02 on the newly installed Astroturf. *Arena* 2001.

With close to 250 entering freshmen, the school faced a shortage of classrooms. This problem was solved by creating three new classrooms: 1B2, 2B1, and 2B8....

In addition to the new Astroturf, Walkathon money has gone into improving the locker rooms and bathrooms downstairs.... Plans call for the weight room to be moved into an expanded wrestling room, with the wrestling room then occupying the current weight room.

One of the less obvious but no less important changes to the Canisius landscape is the wiring of all classrooms for the Internet. "With the money from BISSNET [Buffalo Independent Secondary Schools Network] and our own additional funds from CHS, we were able to wire the entire building," says Fr. Mattimore of this exciting project. "This puts us in a position to use technology to better the education offered here at CHS."

Fr. Mattimore is also happy with the addition of a school nurse, the first in the school's history. She is Mrs. Maureen Conners, and her "Wellness Center" is in the old sick room across from the President's Office in Berchmans Hall.

Baber's article also mentions smaller improvements, ranging from refreshed blacktop and carpeting to central air conditioning of administrative offices.

The goal of the 2000 Walkathon was to fund the installation of turf on TripiField, which had been completed prior to the start of the school year.

Of course, these relatively minor improvements to the campus are barely perceptible next to the massive changes that were in store later in the decade.

The CHS Campus, Redefined

Without a doubt, the single most substantial and consequential evolution of the school's physical plant was the move from Washington Street to Delaware Avenue in the late 1940s. Obviously, such a radical move as the campus location represented nothing short of a paradigm shift.

It is debatable whether the 1950s contained the second-place period of campus change, or if that designation belongs to the second half of the first decade of the new millennium. There is a strong case to be made for the '50s, including the acquisition and demolition of residential properties along West Ferry Street and Cleveland Avenue, as well as the construction of Frauenheim Hall. Arguably, however, it was the few years leading up to 2010 that mark the second-place transition period in terms of campus development. This included the construction of the Kennedy Field House and Montante Academic Center on campus, along with a massively refurbished cafeteria, weight room, senior lounge, elevator system, and Campus Ministry center. Additionally, this period saw the opening of the Stransky Athletic Complex in West Seneca, which provided a true home field location for the first time.

There was great enthusiasm surrounding the "Walk for the Land" in 2005, and "the parcels" were word uttered frequently around campus. The phrase became synonymous with the land acquisition in West

Seneca. But years went by between the "Walk for the Land" and the groundbreaking, and among many students, the parcels became the butt of sarcastic jokes about unfulfilled ambitions. Finally, in the summer of 2007, following a number of hurdles, CHS was able to break ground on the new facility, as reported in *The Citadel*'s September 2007 cover story, headlined, "Land Ho! Three Years in the Making, Canisius Breaks Ground in West Seneca." This would become the Robert J. Stransky Memorial Athletic Complex.

It is a project that has been on the minds of CHS upperclassmen for three years. Funded in part by proceeds from the 2005 Walk-a-Thon, the athletic complex in West Seneca has progressed significantly. Located on 33.4 acres of land on Clinton Street, the site is expected to be the home away from home for all of Canisius High School's athletic teams....

Mr. Mauro [Athletic Director] has been impressed with the amount of work that the school had done in preparation for a task of this scale.... "[Canisius] investigated many different locations before deciding on the site on Clinton

Street," he noted. As the fields were being prepared for construction, "the plans and layouts have changed multiple times."[7]

By March 2008, excitement was ramping up among students for the coming construction. Again, *The Citadel* kept pace with the developments:

With the completion of the Clinton Street Fields occurring this spring, the Canisius community anxiously waits for the next step of the school's master plan of expansion to begin. The next step in Canisius' renovation will consist of the largest structural undertaking the school has ever witnessed. On March 17, 2008, Frauenheim Hall will be demolished, making space for a multimillion-dollar field house to be erected....

The new field house will feature a main gym floor, where the basketball and volleyball teams will play their games. The floor will also have three additional courts perpendicular to the feature court.... The project will also include new home and away locker rooms as well as both a training center and concession stand.

By late spring, Canisius plans to be involved in simultaneous construction projects, as the new math [and] science wing will also be being built at the same time as the field house. The first-year experience of the incoming Class of 2012 will be, for lack of a better word, chaotic. However, with the completion of both buildings projected to be in the fall of 2009, they will be able to enjoy the finished plan as sophomores.[8]

The incoming Class of 2012 read a cover story entitled "Ch-Ch-Ch-Changes...Construction Progress Brings Excitement, Challenges" in their first issue of *The Citadel*.

The continuing facelift of Canisius High School is, finally, becoming drastically more visible in the everyday lives of students. The Clinton Street fields were completed in the spring, and have since been dedicated to Robert J. Stransky, blessed by Bishop Edward U. Kmiec, and hosted several fall athletic events.

Construction proceeds on the new field house and math and science building. In the near future, these facilities will bring a plethora of benefits to CHS students, staff, and alumni; however, for the time being, they present several obstacles and challenges....

Construction has posed some navigational difficulties. "It's a challenge to get to class on time this year," stated Lucas Clotfelter '10. With only one stairwell available for use in the classroom wing, swarms of students crowded the staircase.... The parking lot has also created challenges with the elimination of the Cleveland Drive exit and changes to the flow of traffic.... The number of student parking spots has in fact decreased.

Construction is nevertheless on schedule and is expected to be completed by mid-August 2009...The new math and science wing will offer more classroom space, hopefully eliminating the problem of having "traveling" teachers. The new field house, with its large curved wall now standing where the old Frauenheim Hall stood, will be a state-of-the-art facility and conveniently located right on campus. It will consist of two locker rooms, a trainer room, a conference room, coaches' offices, additional storage space, and a handicapped-accessible elevator.

The new cafeteria will have a significantly different feel than the current one. According to Mr. Kopas, "The new cafeteria will have a more 'loungy' feel with a fireplace and more comfortable furniture.' There will be more space where students may socialize, allowing the library to (believe it or not) be a place for silent study. Also, as part of the Middle States initiative, changes will occur to the breakfast and lunch menus as CHS takes a healthy step in the right direction....

Mr. Kopas also added that, while bound to bring more challenges and headaches as progress continues, it should be remembered that these are the most dramatic changes this campus has ever undertaken and it will, in time, be more than worth it.[9]

By March 2009, students, faculty, staff, and administration had weathered the challenges of construction for the majority of the school year. A *Citadel* cover story investigated the ongoing project and provided some insights as to its magnitude.

Even in stable economic times, the undertaking of a project this massive is difficult. With the market currently unstable, it is truly remarkable that the buildings are still on schedule.

As of March 16th, the auditorium became the center of the school as the cafeteria was officially closed for renovation. A more limited menu is now being prepared by the cafeteria staff to one side of the gym, while students eat at tables spread out across the gym floor.... The new and expanded cafeteria...will allow Canisius to eliminate the third lunch period. The new "Starbucks" style café will allow the lunch team to serve up to 450 people per period...

The school plans to go wireless after the construction.... This will enable maintenance to operate lights, control room temperatures, and see any of the security cameras that will be installed. The switchboard will be moved to the current outdoor patio area and...1B1. It will be enclosed in glass and will serve as the main visitor entrance to CHS.* the campus overhaul will feature three elevators, allowing those with disabilities access to any point in the building, including the library and third floor.[10]

Board Chair Paul Koessler Sr. '55, one of the main catalysts for this project, had noted, "This project is even bigger than Canisius' move from Washington Street over 60 years ago."[11] From a certain perspective, in terms of earth moved and transformative development, Koessler was right. The following pages contain a number of construction photos.

---

* This aspect of the project was altered. The elevator located across from the Chapel was enclosed in glass, but the envisioned main entrance incorporating the patio and room 1B1 did not come to fruition. Instead, new glass doors were installed at the front of the Rand Mansion and the switchboard area was renovated and placed there.

The CHS campus as of spring 2008, pre-construction.

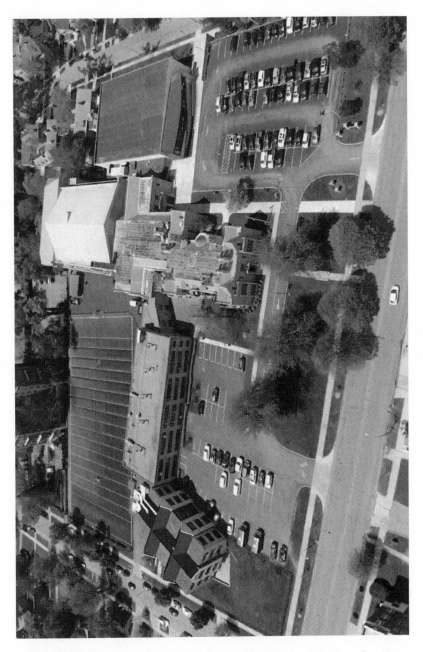

The CHS campus as of spring 2018. Drone photo by Eric Amodeo '94.

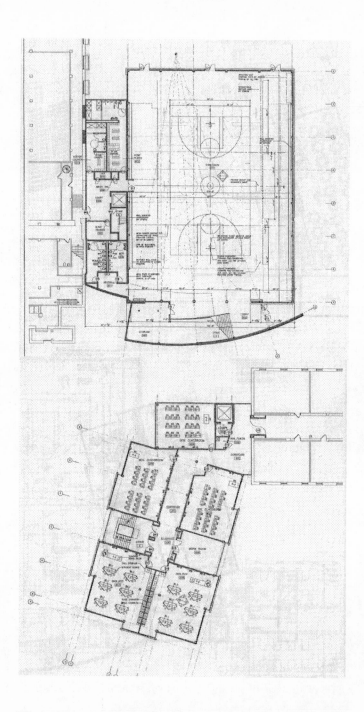

Ch-Ch-Ch-Changes...

Construction Progress Brings Excitement, Challenges

BY AARON DEUTSCHMAN '10 and WILLIAM H. BUTT '09

The continuing facelift of Canisius High School is, finally, becoming drastically more visible in the everyday lives of Canisius students. The Clinton Street fields were completed in the spring, and have since been dedicated to Robert J. Stransky, blessed by Bishop Edward U. Kmiec, and hosted several fall athletic events. Construction proceeds on the new field house and math and science building. In the near future, these facilities will bring forth a plethora of benefits for CHS students, staff, and alumni; however, for the time being, they present several obstacles and challenges for the Canisius community.

Construction has posed some navigational difficulties. "It is a challenge to get to class on time this year," stated Lucas Clotfelter '10. With only one stairwell available for use in the classroom wing, swarms of students crowd the staircase, sometimes turning the stairs into a sort of mosh pit. As a result, navigating to the third floor often requires some patience.

The parking lot has also created challenges. With the elimination of the Cleveland Drive exit and changes to the flow of traffic, there has, at times, been confusion in the parking lot. In addition, the student parking situation generated some chatter at the beginning of the year after many students had been under the impression that student parking on campus would actually increase. Of course, as anyone who has tried parking in the new student lot knows, the number of student spots has in fact decreased from last year. Also, the spots left for students are extremely close together.

CONTINUED ON PAGE 8

Above: The Beecher Wing, with the south stairwell removed and interior exposed. Below: Demolition of Frauenheim Hall.

Top: Cranes position concrete panels on the structure of the Kennedy Field House.

Bottom: Structural steel in place for the Field House.

Top: The Montante Academic Hall. Center: Bishop Kmiec blesses the new field house alongside Dillon Insalaco '10 and C.J. Montante '12. Bottom: The Bernard J. Kennedy Field House.

Campus Ministry Evolves & Expands

The arrival of the Kairos retreat set the stage for a transformation of the Campus Ministry program. To contextualize this, one must understand the changing nature of the demographics and spirituality of the Canisius student. According to current Principal Andrea Tyrpak-Endres, who has had the perspective of teaching Religious Studies and serving as Campus Minister at various times since the mid-1970s, there has been a change in the spirituality of students:

Religious studies has become more academic because of the evolution of Campus Ministry. Back in the day you had to do more of the formation in class. And yet, academically, it's becoming increasingly difficult now in terms of Religious Studies because there is a much lower level of religious preparation in the student body.

I'll say this, though. From ten and fifteen years ago, the number of kids proclaiming to be agnostic or atheist is way down. Way down. So, you can tell kids are searching for stuff. I think fifteen years ago, kids had some formation, and they were rejecting something they didn't like. But now they haven't had much, and it seems they're much more open to being introduced to these concepts.[12]

Ask Canisius alumni from the 1980s and 1990s about their retreat experience, and most of the feedback will center on Emmaus. For the better part of 21 years, from 1979 to 2000, it was the centerpiece of the retreat program at Canisius. A three-day, two-night program for Juniors, it was, for many young men (including this author) a transformative moment wherein the extraordinary met the ordinary and the popular Jesuit expression "finding God in all things" took on a new level of meaning. With the addition of Kairos in 1999, the school's investment in an iterative retreat process continued. For seven years, Emmaus for Juniors was followed by Kairos for seniors, and participation skyrocketed. For many students, the second half of their Canisius experience was defined—at least on a spiritual level—by this progression.

From Disparate Activities to a Unified Department

Perhaps no one can offer a more holistic commentary on the contemporary evolution of Campus Ministry than Rev. Frederick Betti, S.J., who served as Director for fourteen years, from 2002 to 2016 after being transferred from McQuaid Jesuit to Canisius in fall 2002. In an interview for this book, he explained,

I was assigned here to expand what we now call Campus Ministry. If the school were going to expand and have a really effective program, it needed a full-time position. Fr. Peter Arabia [S.J.,] was teaching and struggling to manage Emmaus, Kairos, and liturgy. Ron Ahrens '91 was assisting. Ron, a former Jesuit Volunteer, was the pioneer of the predecessor of the Companions Program, but it was a struggle for him to go once a year to Camden, N.J. or Appalachia. Mr. Joe Chernowski was a full-time teacher, assisting part time.

There was a Campus Ministry office, but no department. Building a true department was a revolutionary decision. The whole idea was that we'd have an umbrella department that covered service, formation, reflection, faculty formation, and even did some work with parents.

Ron put a ton of work into Emmaus. Dennis Linda did a lot with Kairos. He built an effective program for leadership development, and that really gave rise to the idea of a leadership corps model.

When I started, a service requirement was there, but it was nothing cohesive, and it didn't have the other components of education and reflection. We tried to tighten that up.

This was the first time there was a dedicated, full-time person in charge of the liturgical life of the school, retreats, and service. It was a very challenging, transformative time.[13]

Early Transitions of the Retreat Program

Two major transitions occurred in the Kairos program between 1999 and 2003. First, CHS began conducting its own retreats. (Kairos VI, in December 2000, was the first without McQuaid.) Second, CHS retreats found a new home: Cradle Beach Camp.

The first thirteen Kairos retreats were held at Camp Asbury in Silver Lake, from 1999 to fall 2002—the same location where Emmaus had been held for many years. Oddly enough, however, Kairos XIV was among these first thirteen. The disparity emerges because Kairos XIII was cancelled at the last minute. However, rather than call the next one XIII, it was considered XIV and was the last held at Silver Lake. Therefore, it was with "Kairos XV" that began the school's relationship with Cradle Beach Camp. Father Betti explained:

We had this freshman retreat where we'd bus the entire class out to Cradle Beach for the day. It was rough. We spent an exorbitant amount of money for food and busses just to go out there for a few hours. I knew it was time to cancel the program. Cradle Beach had just hired a new Director, Bonnie Brusk, and I assumed she'd be disappointed.

But Bonnie had actually just been commissioned by their board of directors to find non-summer programs to fill the camp from September to June. It turned out Bonnie was great to work with, and we made a good arrangement. So moved there with Kairos XV in 2003. At that point, we still used the original Blakefield Model*.

The spirit of the retreat remains the same, but we have been able to use the vision and leadership of many people to adapt it. The Blakefield model was great, but it was dated. Unlike other Jesuit high schools that follow that manual rigidly, we collaborated—students, teachers, Jesuits, the camp staff—and

---

* The "Blakefield Model" is the traditional script for Kairos that Canisius imported from McQuaid, which had been imported from Loyola Blakefield, a brother Jesuit school in Baltimore, Maryland.

we adapted it. The beauty of celebrating the recent Kairos 100 is that we were able to see how far we've come: discerning, listening, and adapting.

One of the big changes was shifting to a model that stuck to weekdays. Spiritual formation is integral to Jesuit education, so we had to prioritize it. We specifically decided to keep the retreats optional, but subscription kept growing. The next big paradigm shift took place in the mid-2000s.

This was the arrival of Principal William Kopas in 2006-2007. This would herald a period of rapid and substantial expansion of Campus Ministry, service learning, and formation programs.

Mr. Kopas was adamant about the department having a central, symbolic location. The second thing was staffing. He made it possible for us to keep several younger faculty members involved; specifically, he enabled Ron and me to bring another person in.

This author was the addition to the Campus Ministry Department in 2007, in the new role of Director of Student Formation. I'd come to Canisius after serving as Assistant Chaplain at Georgetown Prep, where I'd been responsible for co-directing retreats and running the international service program. At Prep—as is the case for most Jesuit high schools in the U.S. that have it—Kairos is a junior retreat. The logic is simple. Kairos couples a spiritual focus with a call to "Love in Action." It is a springboard for leadership. During my tenure at Prep, I witnessed the way Kairos served as the entre to a cohesive service-learning program for rising seniors; likewise, I came to respect the educational value of challenging older students to mentor younger ones. When I got back to Canisius, I envisioned a curricular approach to our retreat program, with junior year as the hinge point—a sort of fulcrum on which the formative curriculum should rest.

Senior year, we all agreed, should be a time of peer mentoring and community service, coupled with reflection. I suggested that would best be achieved by offering Kairos—and its implicit call to action—in junior year, followed by a service requirement with real teeth. On the front end of the fulcrum—the first half of high school—the work should be about self-knowledge and community building. I felt the Emmaus retreat could well be adapted for sophomores. A freshman retreat could usher in this progression. Finally, at the end, a Senior Service Portfolio Presentation would be required, wherein seniors would be challenged to reflect upon and share their spiritual and service-oriented journey in a seminar format. (This would eventually become, largely under the leadership of Ron Ahrens '91 and Chris Pitek '00, the current "Grad at Grad" Program.) A new Fourth Day retreat for seniors would provide focus on adult spirituality and the transition to college.

The proposals were approved, and the next couple of years saw a whirlwind of changes. We were moved to a new office complex on the first floor of the Rand Mansion, next to the Chapel. Kairos was redesigned and consolidated to a three-day, two-night model; Emmaus correspondingly was redesigned for a two-day, one-night model. During this same year we piloted a new, daylong, on-campus freshman retreat, as well as a new Fourth Day retreat. It was, indeed, a whirlwind. But this "downshifting," as Father Betti calls it, had a transformative effect.

Moving the retreats was the single best thing we ever did. At first, I thought it was nuts. But it was brilliant. It gave us the cohesiveness we needed to integrate spiritual formation and service education.

Shifting and consolidating the retreats eliminated some redundancy. We also realized that the first night was lost on retreatants, because they were shot by the end of the school day. Bringing them out fresh in the morning is so much better. It also facilitated more faculty getting involved, because it reduced the number of missed class days. This also made room for the student leaders' preparation night. This enabled groups to fine tune talks and to do their own team-building as leaders.

By doing this progression better from Emmaus to Kairos, guys were better equipped to do the heavy lifting of the Companions experience. They were ready to live together and engage in the kind of mature reflection required.[14]

The Companions Program: A Commitment to Service-Learning

Canisius had seen occasional immersive service experiences over the years to places including rural Appalachia in West Virginia and Camden, New Jersey. Despite a well-developed program of local service-learning opportunities, however, there was no widespread system of "immersion trips," such as those existing at other schools. In order to test the waters, Director of Christian Service Ron Ahrens '91 and I coordinated a week-long trip to Taos, New Mexico, with a group of eight seniors from the class of 2006 during spring break. Although their trip didn't mark the *official* start of the Companions Program, it was an essential step.

I had spent upward of four weeks in remote villages of the Dominican Republic directing the *Somos Amigos* program at Georgetown Prep. It had proved to be an effective program for more than ten years, but its scope was limited—only eight rising seniors were able to go each year. At Canisius, my aim was to help us build more than an annual service opportunity; rather, I hoped we could develop a curriculum of service-learning that could be adapted to various locations, both domestic and, eventually, international.

I found a kindred spirit in a fellow young faculty member, Adam Baber '01. He agreed to join me in starting this thing, and while Mr. Kopas wasn't ready to dive immediately into an international program, we got his support for a domestic trial. We wanted to push our students' boundaries as much as possible, so we aimed for the Mexican border. Mr. Kopas agreed to let us take an early spring scouting trip to south Texas.

Our budget was tight, and we stayed in a low-rent motel. But Companions was "born" along the San Antonio River Walk. At the base of Westin Hotel is an upscale lobby and coffee bar with plush leather chairs. It's there—over several cups of overpriced coffee in a luxurious venue paradoxical with the spirit of the program—that we hammered out the mission statement:

The Companions Program at Canisius High School offers the student an opportunity to respond to the Ignatian call to service. He is invited to grow in self-knowledge through an experience of service to and solidarity with the marginalized. A personal encounter with communities and individuals bearing the weight of poverty, weakness, and financial dependence challenges a young man to understand these conditions while acknowledging the poverty implicit in his own weaknesses, shortcomings, and dependence. Likewise, the companionship of this encounter affirms the goodness and potential implicit in his strengths. Drawing upon four central components of community, spirituality, justice, and simple living, Companions engages the Gospel message while challenging the student to embrace struggle and discomfort in an unfamiliar context. The program seeks to foster an ongoing desire to serve the needs of the other, coupled with a lifelong commitment to justice.[15]

COMPANIONS

The Companions logo designed by David M. Cumbo '00 (this book's cover artist), depicting the Jerusalem Cross superimposed over the globe.

The scouting trip enabled us to connect with Habitat for Humanity of Greater Laredo as well as Our Lady of Guadeloupe Parish in San Antonio. We sketched the basics of a curriculum. A few months later, we piloted the first Kairos for juniors. In order to facilitate this, we conducted part of the retreat in Buffalo and the remainder, including the Commissioning Service, in South Texas. As eight members of the Class of 2008 received their Jerusalem Crosses on the shores of Padre Island National Seashore facing the Gulf of Mexico, it was a fitting start to a program that sought to expand the educational horizons of Canisius students far beyond Western New York. With the first Companions immersion in place, the stage was set for the continued transformation of Campus Ministry. With Kairos now centrally located as the "fulcrum point" of spiritual formation, Canisius men were challenged earlier and more intensely to explore spirituality, faith, and service heading into their upper-class years.

Still hoping to provide an international experience, I was blessed with a serendipitous meeting. While attending a Kairos led by Mr. Dennis Linda, I heard a talk by Mr. Christopher O'Brien '81 about his younger brother, David O'Brien '87. Recalling his brother's untimely death to ill-

Left: Members of the inaugural Companions immersion during a family picnic at Lake Casa Blanca International State Park with members of the Laredo community in July, 2007.

ness in the course of famine relief work in India, Chris implored the seniors to undertake a life of service—and, especially, to help those most in need in the developing world. His words resonated deeply with me and my recent experiences in India, Nepal, the Dominican Republic, and Haiti. So, when Chris finished his talk, I literally chased him to his car to introduce myself and arrange a time to talk about my ideas for international service opportunities.

Within a matter of months, we had a green light to move forward with the first international immersion, which we would call *Compañeros*. 2008 would see two groups travel to the Dominican Republic. The first took me, Adam Baber '01, and Mr. Joe Zera '01, a new member of the Math Department, along with a group of juniors and seniors to the village of El Papayo for a week, where we assisted with the construction of a home for a family who had lost theirs to a propane tank explosion. The final half week saw us at the Crossroads Center, an ecumenical mission on the north coast that served the Haitian refugee population. The second trip, which lasted for three weeks later that July, saw the construction of the David O'Brien '87 Memorial Bridge, which provided access to the remote village of La Norita, along with a few days in ministry with the Crossroads Center.

Left: Memorial plaque for "Puente David" (David's Bridge) in memory of David O'Brien '87 (center).

Bottom: the July 2008 *Compañeros* group in front of the completed bridge.

Twelve years later, Companions has now seen nearly a thousand alumni serve across more than a dozen states and five nations,[15] including Biloxi, Mississippi; Buffalo, New York; The Dominican Republic; Cincinnati, Ohio; The Navajo Nation, New Mexico and Arizona; Erie, Pennsylvania; Nicaragua; Gulf Port, Alabama; The Pine Ridge Reservation, South Dakota; Laredo, Texas; Los Angeles, California; Wheeling, West Virginia; Newburgh, New York; New Orleans, Louisiana; Slidell, Louisiana; Niagara Falls, New York; San Antonio, Texas; and Washington, D.C. The program has worked with local agencies to support meaningful projects that benefit local communities; however, the primary focus of Companions—in keeping with the original mission statement—is upon the formative education of our students. It is for this reason that we have intentionally avoided employing the term "mission trip" when speaking about the program. While it is certainly grounded in the Ignatian mission, it differs in many ways from the often-more-evangelical approaches taken by other church groups and youth organizations.

A small group of alumni and friends kick-started what would become the David O'Brien '87 Companions Endowment, the balance of which is approaching the quarter million-dollar mark at the time of this book's publication. It guarantees that the Companions and *Compañeros* programs can operate on a "pay-as-you-can" basis, ensuring that any Canisius student with a desire to serve can apply and participate without regard to his financial resources. Likewise, the Neil R. Reilly '80 Companions Mentorship Fund was established in 2017 to support the training of faculty leaders.

The Companions/*Compañeros* programs will have been an integral part of the Canisius mission for more than a dozen years as the school celebrates its sesquicentennial year—a clear testament to the Jesuit commitment to global service and spiritual formation.

---

[15] The Companions Program names Native American Reservations, including the Navajo Nation and the Pine Ridge, South Dakota, international locations given their technical status as sovereign nations as well as their distinct culture.

Canisius in Gettysburg

Mr. Samuel Rizzo '97, who has taught United States History for many years, began the "CHS Gettysburg Trip" in 2006. Since that time, it has grown to become a storied tradition among the juniors of Canisius High School. Led by Mr. Rizzo, affectionately referred to as "The Colonel," the program sees approximately fifty students, along with several faculty and parent chaperones, visiting the battlefield site each summer.

Inspired by his own study of the Civil War under professor F. Gordon Shay at St. John Fisher College in Rochester, Mr. Rizzo interned with the National Parks Service in Gettysburg as an undergraduate student. He designed and continues to lead the trips for his own students at Canisius.

Top: The "195th NY Regiment" in front of The White House in 2016; bottom: the Regiment marches near the base of Little Round Top in Gettysburg in 2016.

"We are the 195th New York Volunteer Infantry Regiment. There were 194 regiments that were mustered out of New York State during the American Civil War, with some from the Western New York area. When I reached out to local reenactment groups about using their regimental number for our trip I was told no, so I figured we'd be the 195th New York, so as not to upset anyone," said Rizzo.[16]

In addition to reenacting various charges and maneuvers at the Gettysburg site, the Canisius students travel on to the nation's capital to visit the monuments and historic sites of the city. Further commenting on the meaning and purpose of the experience, Rizzo remarked: "I will often say when giving battlefield tours that it is my hope that students come back to Gettysburg someday with their parents and/or their children, so that what took place here some one hundred fifty odd years ago is never forgotten."[17]

A Scholarship in Memory of a Tragic Loss

From *Arena 2002*:

Shortly before Canisius graduate Sean Rooney ['69] was killed in the September 11, 2001, terrorist attack, he made a phone call home to his wife [Ms. Beverly Eckert]. They were able to say their last goodbyes as the building collapsed. Ms. Eckert described the experience, saying, "Sean, at the end, was so brave, resourceful, and calm...he helped me through the final moments." Ms. Eckert was grateful that she knew what happened to him, that she was able to say goodbye and that she was with him in the end. On what would have been his 51st birthday, Mr. Rooney's high school friend, Tom Fontana '69 premiered his new film Judas as well as the first scholarship to Canisius in the name of Sean Rooney. In attendance were Sean's wife, Beverly Eckert, Tom Fontana, as well as many other family members and friends.[18]

Sean Rooney '69

Ms. Beverly Eckert

In a cruel twist of fate, Beverly Eckert died on the wintry night of February 12th, 2009, aboard Continental Flight 3407 from Newark to Buffalo, which crashed in Clarence, N.Y., killing all 49 people on board and one person on the ground. She was headed to Buffalo to present the scholarship award in Sean's memory. She was fifty-seven at the time of her death. The two met at Canisius High School when they were both sixteen.[19]

The Sean Rooney Memorial Scholarship was established to assist a high-achieving student who demonstrates financial need. The inaugural award was presented to Remy Uwilingiyimana '06, who fled violence in Rwanda in 1995. According to a 2006 letter from Ms. Eckert to Canisius High School, the scholarship had "more than exceeded my expectations of finding some way to counteract the destructive intent of terrorism."

Remy Uwilingiyimana '06, the first recipient of the Rooney memorial scholarship, receives his award during a ceremony in the CHS Auditorium in 2002. From *Arena* 2002.

Gallery: 2001-2010

Students and Rev. Peter Arabia, S.J., on one of the first Kairos retreats at Silver Lake, NY. *Arena* 2001.

Mr. Ron Ahrens '91 and students working at the Romero Center in Camden, NJ, on an immersion trip before the era of the Companions Program. *Arena* 2003.

Faculty on a rafting adventure. *Arena* 2003.

CHS mourned the loss of Mr. James Lilley, longtime baseball coach and Assistant Dean of Students. *Arena* 2003.

Above: A group of Lighting Crew students, spearheaded by John Roach '05, restored the sun and other decorative lighting in the auditorium, including the replacement of 1600 light bulbs in the summer of 2003. *Arena* 2004. Below: A page from *Arena* 2006 highlights the Beecher Wing window project and athletic renovations, including the new weight room and wrestling room.

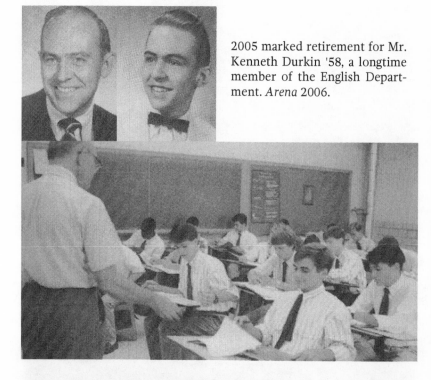

2005 marked retirement for Mr. Kenneth Durkin '58, a longtime member of the English Department. *Arena* 2006.

Rev. Fred Betti, S.J., presides at Mass using the altar built by Rev. Richard Zanoni, S.J., pictured here to Father Betti's right.

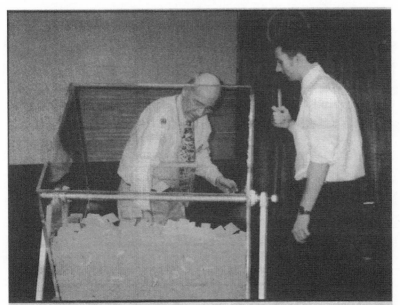

Fr. Lux S.J. reaches for "The Golden Ticket" during The Raffle drawing on December 23, 2005. Mr. Baber offers advice on random selection and barrel maneuvering.

Downed trees litter the front of campus after the "October Surprise" storm in 2006. School was closed for a week.

Left: Mr. Group and Mr. Pecori bring Christmas cheer to the annual holiday assembly.

Below: Mr. Ahrens '91 and Mr. Cumbo '97 along with seniors from the class of 2007 on a service immersion trip to Taos, New Mexico, in spring 2006. The trip was a precursor to the Companions program, which began the following year.

Above: Fired up CHS fans wield swords, crosses, and war paint—and the ubiquitous "Ragin' Rag," not to be confused with the "Rowdy Rags" of rival SJCI. *Arena* 2008. Below: Scenes from the 2008 Chilly Challenge. *Arena* 2008.

Top Left: Stage time at the *Casa de Café* "Coffee House." Top Right: An iconic Kairos moment at Cradle Beach. Bottom: Mr. Linda and Father McCurdy, S.J., lead one of the first Fourth Day retreats with '09 seniors. *Arena 2009.*

THE CITADEL

THE VOICE OF THE CRUSAD

September 2010   Canisius High School, Buffalo NY

THE WALK IS BACK

BY: KYLE LARKIN '11

September: the time for pressed pants, old friends, and neat folders. As we adjust to the rigors of the new school year, we also become familiar with the policy changes in the school. While some new policies have been established, other ones are returning to the school; namely the return of the Walk for Canisius. While no current Canisius student has actually participated in a Walk-a-Thon, it is a tradition that takes place in many Jesuit schools across the country. From 1979 to 2004, the Walk-a-Thon was

an annual tradition that all students looked forward to. Unlike many events at school that help the community around us, the Walk directly benefits the students. With the money raised, Canisius will install new lockers in the Montante Academic Hall. In addition to raising money for lockers, the Walk will help support the Canisius Tuition Assistance Program. "The Walk-a-Thon is a fantastic thing for Canisius High School because it is going to allow for students to relax outside of the classroom and raise money that will benefit the student body" says student senator Conor Mangan '11.

While many students are excited about

the return of the Walk, the question is raised: Why was it brought back this year? Mr. Baber, Director of Student Activities and defender of the Walk says, "The revival of a Walk-a-Thon was really brought about by the veteran faculty members like Mr. Ahrens and Mr. Fitzgerald, as well as support from president John Knight."

The best part about the Walk is the immediate benefit for the students. Mr. Baber expects the new lockers to be installed just weeks after the event. The tradition and excitement of the Canisius High School Walk-a-Thon is a brand new experience for all students and many teachers in the school are

A younger Mr. Coppola cheers for the Walk-a-Thon. [1999]

THE NE
Page 2
BEYON
Page 3
WHO'S
Page 4
MEET T
Page 3
FOOTB
Page 6
GOLF D
Page 5

Left: The September 2010 issue of *The Citadel* focused on the return of the Walkathon.

Below: The CHS Class of 2009 at Commencement. During this phase of graduation exercises, faculty were seated on the stage.

Arena Dedications: 2001-2010

2001 - Mrs. Diane Piscopo

Mrs. Diane Piscopo was a longtime Counselor at CHS. Mr. David Isbrandt of the Counseling Department authored the dedication to her in the 2001 *Arena*, which included the following student testimonies: "No matter what year I was in, or what kind of day I'd had, or if she was busy, she always had time to chat." "She helped me find what I wanted to do with my life."

2002 - Joshua Richards '02

In this second remembrance, classmates offered tributes. Jason Roche '02, said, "True friendship is like sound health; the value of it is seldom known until it is lost. We will remember you always. Friends forever."

2003 - Gretchen Kessler

Vincent Miranda '04 wrote: "...as [she] departs, she leaves behind a legacy of 24 outstanding years of service to the Canisius community." Rev. Louis Garaventa, S.J., remarked: "What a great gift she has been to our school community! Let this small dedication...only mirror the love and gratitude we have for your being in our midst so long and so well."

2004 - In Memoriam: Mr. Thomas H. Keenan

Mr. Thomas Keenan, longtime Dean of Students and Head Basketball Coach at Canisius, was remembered fondly by his students. Luke Haumesser '05: "The halls of Canisius will never be the same. Thank you for all you have done...remember, angels need JUG too." Dennis Baker '98: "Coach, thanks for showing me how to be a man. I'll never forget all of our good times and I will always miss you. You're

one of my heroes." Joseph Barill '04: "Mr. Keenan was the nicest and most selfless man I have ever had the privilege of meeting."

2005 - Mr. Charles Chimera

"It is entirely fitting that this year's yearbook be dedicated to Mr. Chimera because he is a man who symbolizes everything that Canisius stands for. He brought an uncommon level of excellence to his work and he strived to do his very best at educating men to go out into the world and be productive human beings. He was a man for others because he put forth nothing but his best effort and gave the majority of his valuable time to young men. He taught with obvious enthusiasm, like only someone who truly loved what he was doing could do." – Peter Snajczuk '05

2006 - Rev. Frederick J. Betti, S.J.

Christopher Wrobel '06 wrote: "While at Canisius, Father Betti has played a significant role in regard to student life. [He] has proven time and time again, through his actions and words, that he would do anything for anyone. He gives up his time to organize events and has seemingly insurmountable amounts of stress placed on him. Yet, he gracefully demonstrates that he is a Man for Others. He always puts others first and that is something for which we are all grateful."

2007 - The Maintenance Staff

"The members of our maintenance staff at Canisius High School not only strive to keep a century-old building in order on a daily basis, but they also continue to develop enhancements to improve the lives of students, faculty, and staff."

2008 - Rev. James P. Higgins, S.J., '72

"In its long, storied history, Canisius High School has seen thousands of students walk through its hallowed halls. Each has left his mark on the school, from the great to the minute. But one of these men, Fr. James P. Higgins, S.J., '72, has made, and continues to make, an unsurpassable impact on CHS.... His efforts will be recalled for years to come, and his legacy will be remembered."

2009 -Ms. Andrea Tyrpak-Endres

"This year, the dedication goes to a teacher in the religious studies department who came to Canisius over thirty years ago.... Mrs. Tyrpak-Endres has devoted herself to Canisius High School. She knows the in's and out's of the Crusader lifestyle, and she actively keeps herself connected to her students, both inside and outside of the classroom. And so, in thanks for her hard work, dedication, and commitment to our school, the *Arena* staff...is proud to dedicate this year's book to someone truly deserving the recognition."

2010 - Mrs. Sandra Chimera

"Since her arrival at Canisius 24 years ago, Mrs. Chimera has been dedicated to keeping the student body in line...More than two decades of dealing with teenagers at their smartest has made [her] an institution in her own right.... Many faculty members express with awe how it would take more than two people to do the work Mrs. Chimera does in the dean's office.... Mrs. Chimera has shown an undying dedication to Canisius and the student body...She lives the motto 'Men and Women for Others."

Notes

[1] Baach, Taylor '10 and Jonathan Schuta '10. "Higgins Hall Dedicated." *The Citadel.* Vol 50, Issue 3. Dec 2009.

[2] *Ibid.*

[3] Zak, Dan '01. "Fresh Start: Inside the Frosh Influx." *The Citadel.* Vol 42, Issue 1. September, 2000.

[4] "CHS Home to the Higher Achievement Program." *Canisius High Today.* Vol. 26, No. 1. Fall 1995.

[5] Toner, Ian '08. "Mr. Tudini Bids Farewell." *The Citadel.* Vol. 46, Issue 7. May, 2006.

[6] "Canisius High Names New Principal." *Buffalo Business First.* April 25, 2006.

[7] Johnson, Christopher. "Land Ho! Three years in the making, Canisius breaks ground in West Seneca." *The Citadel.* Vol 48, Issue 1. Sep 2007.

[8] Egnatchick, Robert '08. "Canisius Set to Begin Largest Project in School History." *The Citadel.* Vol 48, Issue 4. Mar 2008.

[9] Butt, William '09 and Aaron Deutschman '09. "Ch-Ch-Ch-Changes...Construction Progress Brings Excitement, Challenges." *The Citadel.* Vol 49, Issue 1. Sep 2008.

[10] Owen, Stephen '09. "School Community Anticipates Completion of Construction." *The Citadel.* Vol 49, Issue 5. Mar 2009.

[11] *Ibid.*

[12] Interview with Andrea Tyrpak-Endres. Mar 7, 2018.

[13] Interview with Rev. Fred Betti, S.J., Apr 15, 2018.

[14] *Ibid.*

[15] Baber, Adam '01 and Paul Cumbo '97. "Companions Program Mission Statement." From *The Companions Leaders Manual, 2007.*

[16] Personal interview with Sam Rizzo '97. May 22, 2018.

[17] *Ibid.*

[18] *Arena,* the Canisius High School Yearbook, 2002, p. 207.

[19] Chan, Sewell. "A 9/11 Widow, Killed in Crash Near Buffalo." *The New York Times.* Feb 13, 2009. Accessed from the Internet May 9, 2018.

CHAPTER 14

The 2010s

IT WAS AGAINST THE ODDS that Canisius entered the 2010s
with tremendous energy and momentum. The financial situation was
grim. The recession of 2008 had hit the school hard, just at a time when it
had taken on considerable bond debt to finance construction. Amidst the
fiscal woes at the end of the 2000s, a well-publicized scandal involving a
former employee's theft of approximately a half-million dollars over the
course of many years rocked the community. The fiscal troubles at the
turn of the decade mirrored a challenging period of physical upheaval due
to demolition and construction. Much of the campus had been, quite

literally, a hard hat zone—and it wasn't hard to spot debris and unfinished surfaces.

Despite all of this upheaval—or maybe *because* of it, in some ways—the beginning of the 2010s was a time of tremendous energy and momentum. With the dedication of new buildings came a long-sought-for return to normalcy. Along with the burgeoning debt and an endowment still licking its wounds, there were signs of financial recovery. And in terms of school life, growth was everywhere: the enrollment was high and more diverse than ever, academics were vibrant, athletic programs were achieving historic and sustained levels of accomplishment, and investment in campus ministry and formation programs (both for students and faculty) had reached record levels.

While riding this momentum, Canisius would continue to struggle with the challenges that come with administrative turnaround at the leadership level. Between 2010 and 2015, Canisius would see four Presidents, three Principals, and two Deans of Students. And yet things have stabilized—these offices have remained unchanged since 2015.

Evolution never stops. Since the turn of the decade, Canisius has become an increasingly more diverse school in terms of demographics, ethnicities, and religious backgrounds. The intentional and comprehensive integration of technology has veritably transformed the campus, the curriculum, and many aspects of student life. All of this has brought new challenges and opportunities.

Continued Campus Ministry Evolution

Early in the decade, Campus Ministry continued its evolution in earnest. The immersion program grew, a new freshman retreat was initiated, and the Grad at Grad program underwent further refinement. In the latter half of the decade, along with a transition to almost entirely new staffing, the department saw a move to a newly designed Campus Ministry Center on the second floor of Berchmans Hall.

Companions Continues Building

The Companions Program continued to grow, adding several domestic locations and three additional international placements: Nicaragua, the Navajo Nation in Arizona, and the Pine Ridge Reservation in South Dakota. Locally, the school took on a unique project and became the first high school in Western New York to fully sponsor the construction of a Habitat for Humanity home. Students, faculty and staff, parents, alumni, Board members, and friends all came together to work on the completion of a home for a family on Buffalo's East Side.

The David O'Brien '87 memorial endowment continued to grow and continues to finance scholarships that put Companions experience within reach of any Canisius family, regardless of financial resources. A new endowment, the Neil Reilly '80 Scholarship Fund, facilitates faculty development and training for immersion leaders. The school took its first International Leadership Development Cohort (ILDC) group to the Dominican Republic in 2016, with the aim of preparing a cadre of seven faculty to lead international service ventures. It worked—since that time, all faculty enrolled in the ILDC have led an international trip.

A New Freshman Retreat

While several versions of freshmen retreats have existed over the years, Chris Pitek '00 (Director of Student Formation at the time, and Principal of Nardin Elementary at the time of this writing) shadowed the Rockhurst Jesuit High School (Kansas City, MO) program to learn and bring it back to Canisius in 2012. Involving a range of activities and led by a large cadre of upperclassmen, the freshman retreat as it exists now centers on a brotherhood-related theme. Like other Canisius retreats such as Emmaus and Kairos, large group talks are followed by small group discussions. Freshmen are kept busy with a full slate of games, competitions, and contests. One of the highlights of the experience is "home time," wherein students gather at a junior or senior leader's home for dinner and an evening reflection offered by a guest faculty or staff member. Additionally, alumni offer a talk to small groups. One night of the retreat is spent at the school, with small groups sleeping in classrooms and enjoying a full twenty-four hours of talks, games, reflection, and shared meals.

The "Grad at Grad" Program

The Jesuit Secondary Education Association, now called the Jesuit Schools Network, undertook a 1980 initiative to establish a common set of qualities toward which any student at a Jesuit school should aspire. This resulted in the "Profile of the Graduate at Graduation," which was described in an introductory document. Excerpts of that document follow.

In one sense, the graduate is a threshold person: he or she is on or rapidly approaching the threshold of young adulthood. The world of childhood has been left behind definitively....

Fluctuating between highs and lows of fear and confidence, love and loneliness, confusion and success, the Jesuit student at graduation has negotiated during these years many of the shoals of adolescence. On the other hand, the graduate has not reached the maturity of the college senior. During the last year of high school, especially, the senior is beginning to awaken to complexity, to discover many puzzling things about the adult world....

In describing the graduate under five general categories, we chose those qualities that seem most desirable not only for this threshold period, but those which seem most desirable for adult life.... These categories are I. Open to Growth, II. Intellectually Competent, III. Religious, IV. Loving, and V. Committed to Doing Justice.[1]

The Grad-at-Grad was "re-visioned" in 2010 through a collaborative, comprehensive process involving faculty and leaders across a broad range of institutions. Upon this revision, a further note of explanation was included:

The characteristics of the Profile may tend to describe the graduate from various perspectives. Jesuit education, however, is, has been, and always will be focused on whole person education: mind, spirit, and body. Jesuit education accomplishes this through cura personalis (personalized care and concern for the individual) and through a holistic curriculum. Jesuit education aims to form life-long learners imbued with an Ignatian approach to living shaped by the knowledge, understanding, and use of the interplay of experience, reflection, and action (the dynamic at the heart of the Spiritual Exercises). Jesuit education also aims to graduate students who possess the desire and the personal resources to be men and women for and with others. Thus, the Profile always needs to be viewed within the context of the mission of Jesuit education and not merely as a list of achievable outcomes for the Jesuit high school graduate.[2]

Here at Canisius High School, the "Grad at Grad Program" represents a capstone reflection exercise for second semester seniors. Tasked with examining their journey through four years of education and development in adolescence, students are paired with a faculty or staff mentor for a several-months-long self-study process. Through a combination of guided reflection, open discussion, and critical inquiry, seniors are challenged to engage in an honest self-assessment in the context of the five traits central to the Grad at Grad document. This culminates in a twenty-minute talk before their peers and teachers.

This process now comprises a significant component of the senior religious studies curriculum.

A New Focus on Ignatian Identity

Following the trend of Jesuit schools across the country and around the world, Canisius began putting a new level of emphasis on faculty and staff formation. Universities and high schools alike saw new positions such as Vice President for Mission, Assistant Principal for Mission and Identity, and Director of Faculty and Staff Formation. Representing an intentional approach by Jesuit leadership to improve and expand formation measures for an increasingly lay-led educational apostolate, this trend has proven instrumental in maintaining the Ignatian identity of Jesuit schools.

A transformational approach to this area was brought to Canisius by Rev. Robert Pecoraro, S.J.,* who initiated a wide range of inclusive opportunities such as discernment groups, a book club, spiritual direction, and a "One School, One Book" program that aimed to have all members of the school community—faculty, staff, administration, and students—read a common text and engage in reflection.

Canisius Embraces the Digital Age

The fundamental pillars of a Canisius education have been consistent for 150 years, and they will remain so. Occasionally, however, there has come a paradigm shift so substantial as to redefine the nature of the educational experience for faculty and students alike. The adoption of the "1:1" Apple iPad program in 2011 certainly marks one such shift.

In order to appreciate fully the significance of the change, one must consider a variety of contexts. When every student and faculty member is equipped with a portable digital device with remarkable connectivity and the ability to create, edit, produce, and share multimedia content with impressive ease, few aspects of daily life remain unchanged. Since the adoption of widespread technology, nearly every element of what we do and how we do it has been affected—creating both remarkable opportunities and undeniable challenges.

Teachers received iPads in November 2011. This followed a considerable evolution of thinking and planning. According to then-Principal Mr. Tim Fitzgerald, "Technology is where the 21st century kid learns and expects to find information...we're meeting them where they already are." Eric Amodeo '94, who championed and shepherded many aspects of the 1:1 initiative and now serves as Director of Academic Technology, said, "If Canisius is a college preparatory program, students need to be well-versed in technology. Once kids hit college, they will be doing research online, submitting papers in electronic form, taking part in online activities and more. What if they didn't have those experiences already?"[3]

---

* Fr. Pecoraro would go on to serve as Director of Xavier High School in Chuuk, Micronesia, and then President of Cheverus High School in Maine, where he was at the time of this publication.

It became immediately apparent that the iPad was an ideal device. A combination of affordability, durability, simplicity, and universality of applications made it a clear choice. Moreover, according to Amodeo, "Apple has great education systems engineers. We didn't have to reinvent the wheel."

Curricular Adaptations

Putting a web-enabled device in the hands of every student and teacher had immediate and massive impact upon curricular design and execution. A remarkable range of opportunities arose quickly, and students and teachers alike embraced the widespread tools and resources in short order. Implementation of course management software enabled teachers to create, post, collect, and manage assignments in a paper-free environment. The same or accompanying software suites facilitated a transparent open gradebook, which enabled students, parents, and teachers alike to have a better sense of academic progress at any given moment. One of the most immediate benefits, according to many students, was the way the devices facilitated organization. As a demographic, teenage boys are not well known for their organizational skills—the iPad's proclivity for managing and organizing notes, calendars, notifications, and schedules in an electronic hub is a demonstrably useful tool.

Of course, beyond these practicalities, the 1:1 model equips each student with an incredible opportunity to expand the context of his education beyond the singular experience of the classroom. Many of these features, according to Mr. Amodeo, "expand classroom walls. They also contribute to the ways that Canisius engages with the 'flipped classroom' educational model, [in which] students watch lectures, do research, and read textbooks at home and learn at school through teacher-guided, hands-on activities." Students and teachers regularly access and produce multimedia content, engage in chat-based discussion forums regarding course materials, utilize interactive apps across their courses, and build a library of digital textbooks, notes, and other resources.

Technology & Infrastructure

The CHS Technology Department saw considerable growth in the first part of the 21ˢᵗ Century. Under the guidance of longtime Director of Technology Andre Foti, the school's infrastructure—both in terms of the physical network and support personnel—has developed to accommodate the ever-expanding integration of digital technology into the curriculum. In addition to massively expanding capabilities with fiber-optic wiring, this has involved the installation and maintenance of extremely high capacity wireless routers to meet the capacity needs of nearly 1000 daily users and even more devices.

Digital Citizenship for the Digital Age

Certainly, the school's embrace of academic technology involves a response to the "signs of the times," and wholly resisting the incorporation of such would be a disservice to students. Nonetheless, embracing these changes has proven to be a complex process—along with multitudinous benefits and opportunities come serious challenges in several realms: infrastructure, pedagogy, and campus culture.

Truthfully, whether or not Canisius had gone with the 1:1 iPad initiative, there would still be a powerful computer in nearly every student's pocket. Clearly, in terms of the formative period of adolescence, this poses some challenges, potential dangers, and corresponding learning opportunities.

Acting on concerns expressed by a variety of students, parents, and faculty members, Canisius High School initiated a "Digital Citizenship" curricular program in 2015. The Year End Report contextualizes the effort:

Most of our students are "digital natives" who have never known a world without smartphones, video games, and social media. The Internet has created tremendous opportunities, but this technology also presents challenges. Such interconnectedness, ironically, has created the potential for isolation, and the online landscape is a proverbial minefield where impulsive decisions can have

serious consequences. Of equal concern is the potentially addictive use of dig-
ital devices and content....

This is a "teachable moment," which calls for the development of a "Digital
Citizenship" curriculum focusing on a range of topics such as pornography,
social media and video games. Indeed, these broad categories are inclusive of
a vast digital landscape, the boundaries and definitions of which are blurred.
Regardless of particular focal areas, the need is clear: In keeping with our
mission, we have an obligation to meet our students where they are. As a Jesuit
school charged with the formation of boys into young men, we cannot ignore
the "digital lives" our students lead...

We are not taking an alarmist or chastising approach. We are not resisting
technology or progress. Quite the opposite—indeed, Canisius, like many Jesuit
schools, has been and remains on the leading edge of technology integration.
This applies not only to our embrace of devices or platforms, but also to our
very proactive curricular design efforts. We hope to educate students about
the scientific, psychological, behavioral, and ethical aspects of these topics—
a holistic approach at appropriate junctures such as classes, retreats, and ad-
visory groups.[4]

According to a study by Common Sense Media available at the time of
this writing, smartphone-using teens spend an average of four hours and
thirty-eight minutes directly interacting with their phones, two hours of
which comprise social media usage.[5] A survey issued to freshmen of the
Class of 2021 revealed that one-third of these young men never go no
more than one waking hour without checking at least one digital feed
(email, social media, notifications, gaming, etc.). Perhaps more strikingly,
seventy-eight percent said they never go more than a few hours without
checking at least one digital feed.

These statistics come as no surprise to the students and faculty of
Canisius, for whom it is a regular occurrence to observe a nearly silent
advisement room full of students focused intently on devices. This, and
other observations of apparently negative impact upon the social culture
of the school, have invited the community to broad conversations about

boundaries, limits, balance, and moderation with regard to technology and device usage. One area where this changing reality has manifested itself with clearly observable results is in the school's retreat program. Back in the '80s, '90s, and early 2000s it was nothing more than a simple novelty to require that students relinquish their watches and be "freed from the constraints of time" on an Emmaus or Kairos retreat. Fast forward to 2018—and time apart from smartphones poses a genuine challenge to students and faculty alike. So much so that a considerable portion of each retreat is now spent examining and considering the importance of "disconnecting to reconnect." In this author's opinion, one of the most important roles of our retreats and immersive service programs is the way in which they serve as a "technology detox" for our students—and faculty.

Canisius continues to make efforts to "read and respond to the signs of the times." That means keeping pace with and learning from the constantly changing landscape of technology integration. Young men need formative education that includes this influential aspect of daily life.

The Alumni Volunteer Corps (AVC)

With a desire to provide a service opportunity for young college graduates, the Alumni Volunteer Corps was established in 2010-2011 by this author and then Director of Alumni Relations Paul Zablocki '01. Similar programs exist at many Jesuit high schools. Designed to incorporate an intentional community as well as personal and spiritual development, the AVC program engages its participants with a curriculum aimed at deepening their self-knowledge while challenging them to embrace the JVC tenets of Community, Spirituality, Simplicity, and Justice. They are provided housing, a cafeteria allowance, use of school athletic facilities, and a nominal monthly stipend. AVs are hired based on their desire to serve the school community, and their talents are employed in a variety of roles, from academic and athletic to administrative and co-curricular.

To accommodate the AVs, the school entered a lease arrangement with Canisius College to secure a modest two-story residential property on Lafayette Avenue near Main, approximately one mile from the high school campus. The house can accommodate up to four AVs, two on each

of two floors, each with his own bedroom, sharing a bathroom and kitchen with his floormate. The high school furnished the house with basic furniture, kitchen and bathroom amenities, and appliances. The AV's enjoy same-floor laundry machines, off-street parking, high-speed wireless, and other basics.

AVs have served as part-time teachers, coaches, administrative assistants, retreat leaders, bus drivers, club moderators, immersion trip co-facilitators, and other roles. Along with their work at the school, the AVs maintain a connection with the Jesuits at Loyola Hall[*], where they are hosted for occasional community dinners, masses, and other events.

Continued Campus Expansion and Enhancement

While the pace of development of the previous decade would be nearly impossible to match, Canisius has nonetheless maintained a consistent commitment to developing its physical plant, expanding its campus when possible, and making capital improvements to existing facilities.

Stransky Athletic Complex Locker Rooms

Continuing the gradual development of the Stransky Complex, a set of locker rooms became open for use in the fall of 2014. These contain separate meeting/prep areas for home and away teams, lockers, and showers.

---

[*] Loyola Hall is the Jesuit residence at Canisius College, which houses men assigned to the high school as well as those working at the college.

Library Renovation and Transformation

The school's library underwent a major transformation over the summer of 2016 into a "learning commons," including a paint job, new carpeting, and the installation of two glass-enclosed, tech-equipped seminar rooms. Along with the physical changes, this represented a paradigm shift in the meaning of the term "library." The stacks of physical books were greatly reduced—by more than half—with an emphasis on increased access to digital resources. Mrs. Brigid Monica, Librarian at Canisius for nearly a decade at the time of this writing, has invested considerable time and effort in making the most of these resources for students. This includes building a digital portal to a wholly reorganized and archived suite of database tools.

The refurbished library.

The Maker Space

The middle of the decade brought about an increased emphasis on robotics and technology learning. Key to this development was the repurposing of a Montante Academic Hall classroom prior to the 2017-2018 year to facilitate the "maker space," in which students and faculty can engage various new technologies. The facility's equipment and curriculum connect students to drones, programming, and robotic design. Director of Academic Technology Eric Amodeo '94, describing the program, explained: "This year every freshman will take a new course called introduction to innovative technologies, where they'll do things like 3D printing, robotics, and basic app development."

Freshmen of the Class of 2021 work on robotics projects in the Maker Space.

New Campus Ministry Center & Chapel Refurbishment

Alongside the library renovation, the Campus Ministry Center was moved to a newly repurposed space on the second floor of Berchmans Hall. Featuring new carpeting, furniture, glassed-in staff offices, and multiple conference tables, the center is significantly larger than the old one.

Likewise, the Chapel underwent significant renovations in 2016-2017, with new carpet, furnishings, and attention paid to the wood paneling and painting. The aging pews were traded for more versatile, more comfortable individual chairs.

The new Campus Ministry Center (above) and refurbished Chapel (below).

The Canisius Center for the Arts

The historic Conners Mansion on Delaware Avenue, across West Ferry Street from the Montante Academic Center, was obtained by Canisius High School from Hospice Buffalo in 2018. It contains specially designed areas for music and chorus programs, studio classrooms for visual arts and architecture courses, and acoustically sound performance spaces. Likewise, the well-equipped kitchen and spacious, refurbished interior provide an inviting venue for social functions and special events.

Clockwise, from top: The Canisius Center for the Arts at 1140 Delaware Avenue. Students work on pottery projects in one of the art rooms. Rotating glass doors create a spacious, flexible, and airy studio classroom space on the second floor.

Smaller Projects

Amidst the larger and more notable campus improvements, a number of smaller but not insignificant projects were undertaken in this decade.

The replacement of the original, 1940s-era student lockers was the goal of a student walkathon fundraising initiative. Expanding the arrangement and layout of lockers throughout both wings of the school has enabled every student to have his own, whereas previous generations had locker partners. While the dimensions of each locker are a bit slimmer, Canisius students of today have plenty of space for their books, jackets, boots, and other paraphernalia.

The faculty lounge, located in the southeast corner of Berchmans Hall, second floor, was updated with new carpeting and furnishings.

The improved faculty lounge, located in the southeast corner, second floor, of the mansion.

The swimming pool was drained, re-grouted, and cleaned for the first time in many years. The weight room continues to see the installation of new systems and equipment, including a ventilation and air conditioning apparatus that keeps the environment optimal for workouts.

Center for Global Learning

The exploratory phase of a "Center for Global Learning" was announced at a faculty gathering in early 2018. The vision for the Center includes a glass-enclosed atrium in the courtyard space where the Beecher Classroom Wing meets Berchmans Hall. Promotional material for the new Capital Campaign, which carries the slogan, "Rich Tradition, Bold Vision," describes the initiative:

> With a highly visible planned location facing Delaware Avenue, the Center for Global Learning will provide a programmatic experience to enhance and promote learning by virtually connecting students with other Jesuit institutions and Canisius alumni worldwide. Faculty and students will be able to share a cultural and educational exchange, opening Canisius students to a world of knowledge beyond the classroom, and demonstrate "when theory meets practice" with the latest technology.

> A Global Learning Advisory Council, composed of Canisius faculty, alumni, and Jesuit faculty or professionals from other institutions, will collectively support the Global Learning Center....[6]

Curricular Evolution

Curriculum Design & Review Process (CDRP)

Early in the decade, Canisius began a Curriculum Design & Review Process (CDRP). While focus on this process waned for a period of several years during administrative turnover, it was reasserted in 2016-2017 with the redirection of the program under the model of "Understanding By Design," otherwise known as "Backward Design." This approach to curricular design, authored by educational researchers Jay McTighe and Grant Wiggins, has been adopted broadly in the secondary school world. It reconciles well with a traditional pedagogical maxim of the Jesuits: begin with the end in mind. The model challenges educators first to establish a clear set of goals, *before* thinking about content or activities. Secondarily, it requires curriculum planners to consider assessment methods—to determine how achievement or attainment of the stated goals will be measured. Only then, after these two steps have been completed, does it encourage consideration of specific content and lesson activities. This upends traditional methods, wherein courses have been built around certain content, activities, or materials—it puts the *why* before the *how*. It is a time-consuming process and remains ongoing.

Several specific changes to the overall curriculum have come out of a natural process of adaptation. A good example of this sort of "responding to the signs of the times" can be observed with how Canisius has modified the traditional "Freshman Seminar." Long a sort of catch-all course that merged study methods and practical skills with periodic guest speakers, it has been replaced with an Introduction to Technology course that integrates robotics and coding in the new Maker Space. Some of the time allotted to the old course is also designated for Digital Citizenship.

Sponsorship Review & Ongoing Commitment to Mission

As Canisius nears its sesquicentennial, it is appropriate that it has undergone the Jesuit Sponsorship Review Process. Designed to ensure that Jesuit schools are continuing to grow and strengthen their commitment to the collective mission of Jesuit education, Sponsorship is extended by the Provincial and certifies that the institution is officially a Jesuit school.

A document called *Our Way of Proceeding: Standards & Benchmarks for Jesuit Schools in the 21st Century* provides the framework for the Sponsorship Review. The introduction to *Our Way of Proceeding* cites Decree 26 of General Congregation 34, which articulates well the charism and mission of our school:

> As partners in mission, Jesuits and our colleagues are never content with the status quo, the known, the tried, the already existing. We are constantly driven to discover, redefine, and reach out for the magis. For us, frontiers and boundaries are not obstacles or ends, but new challenges to be faced, new opportunities to be welcomed. Indeed, ours is a holy boldness, "a certain apostolic aggressivity," typical of our way of proceeding. Our way of proceeding is a way of challenge."[7]

The process, which is aligned with fourteen standards organized across five thematic domains, called for an honest, multifaceted institutional self-reflection involving the entire faculty, staff, and administration. This yearlong collaborative undertaking tasked the community with the assembly of a self-study through committee discussion and writing. Once completed, the self-study was submitted to the Province Office for review by a visiting team of administrators from fellow schools. This team then spent two and a half days on campus conversing with varied constituencies, gathering insights, and drafting a report that articulates both commendations and recommendations. Their report included their recommendation to the Provincial, which will inform his decision regarding the renewal of sponsorship. At the time of this writing, the report is in queue at the Province Office; the renewal is expected in the coming months.

Introduction of the House System

At the time of this writing, Canisius is developing a "House System," which is planned for implementation in 2019-2020. The House System will introduce a time-tested organizational model intentionally designed to strengthen *cura personalis* through deeper community bonds and an enhanced formative curriculum. Though this is a new concept here, it has been an integral part of many independent boys' schools for centuries. It will welcome each incoming freshman into a group of peers with whom he will share a meaningful connection throughout his time at CHS.

A principal goal is to create a universal culture of student citizenship— that is, students regarding themselves as citizens of the community that comprises Canisius. Likewise, by prioritizing "vertical integration" among the grade levels within the Houses, the system will facilitate and promote peer leadership and mentoring in varied aspects of school life.

Enculturating a sense of belonging and ownership within the Houses will aim to bolster student engagement and school spirit. A proven mechanism for this will be the infusion of amicable competition among the Houses in a range of contexts—academic, athletic, extracurricular, and charitable. This competition will overlay existing activities and give rise to new ones. A House Points system will quantify achievements and promote participation with meaningful incentives.

Predicated on these core concepts of student citizenship and vertical integration, the House System will engage the skills and energy of dedicated faculty in meaningful mentoring roles that substantially enhance the current dynamics of the advisement system. The Head of each House will oversee programming implemented by House Mentors, who, in turn, will guide student leaders who hold House Offices.

Ultimately, the principal aim of the House System is to strengthen the CHS community by inviting each student to a peer group that will affirm and challenge him in meaningful ways, issuing a call to good citizenship throughout his four years at the school.

Arena Dedications: 2011 - 2018

2011 - Rev. Frederick J. Betti, S.J.

According to the 2011 *Arena* Editor-in-Chief Christopher Driscoll '11, "The title of Campus Minister does not nearly encompass all of the things

that Fr. Betti does for Canisius High School.... Most importantly, his concern for all students is exemplified as he knows everyone's name.... I am proud to dedicate the effort that has been put into this book to a man who is extraordinary beyond words. He is a perfect example of the tradition that Canisius seeks to give to young men."

2012 - Br. Christopher Derby, S.J.

"Br. Derby, S.J., professed his Final Vows into the Society of Jesus on September 16th, 2011, before his family, friends, students, colleagues, and fellow Jesuits. In light of this marked occasion, coupled with the determination, dedication, compassion, and integrity that Br. Derby exemplifies daily, this edition of the *Arena*

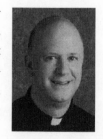

yearbook is fondly dedicated to him." – Nicholas Sawicki '12 & John Bassanello '12

2013 - Mrs. Anne Marie Moscovic & Mrs. Annette Sugg

"Every day they toil through the viscera that the senior class throws their way, asking for help with college and making demands that they always surmount.... They are dedicated to helping all their students get to where they want.... Each of them takes approximately half the senior class under her wing during college planning.... These two women have in-

fluenced the college careers of hundreds of Canisius grads over the past few years. The hard work and dedication...deserves more recognition than this article can provide."

2014 - Mr. Russell White & Mr. Dennis Linda

"With a combined teaching experience of over seven decades, Mr. White and Mr. Linda form the backbone of the Science Department. They stepped into the doors in 1968 and have been hydrogen bonding ever since.... The pair are often seen as the cornerstones of the Jesuit ideals stressed at Canisius. Mr. White was named the first recipient of the

Outstanding Ignatian Educator Award.... Mr. Linda has brought Kairos to life, having directed over a dozen retreats.... Ignatian virtues and leadership define the educators at Canisius.... Because of that, the *Arena* staff humbly dedicate the 2014 yearbook to Mr. Russell White and Mr. Dennis Linda."

2015 - Nathan Carducci '15

"The *Arena* staff would like to dedicate this book to Nathan Carducci. Nathan died unexpectedly his freshman year. He was a cheerful and creative student who brightened our lives when he was here, and is still sorely missed. Had he lived he would have walked across the stage as a proud member of the Class of 2015. Nathan, you will always be a Crusader."

2016 - Rev. David S. Ciancimino, S.J.

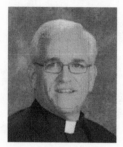

"[We] dedicate this year's 2016 Yearbook to Father Ciancimino for his tireless work as our new President. He inspired us in the beginning of the year with his 'One Canisius' speech, but even more importantly he has led Canisius by example.... Father C. often pitches in whenever and wherever needed."

2017 - Mr. David Saj

Mr. David Saj, a member of the CHS History Department, was diagnosed with multiple myeloma and succumbed during the 2016-2017 school year following a years-long battle. Known for his tenacious dedication to the CHS Food Drive for many years, as well as a lively classroom personality, Mr. Saj was loved by students and colleagues alike. Bernard Dent '17 wrote, "Mr. Saj will always be remembered for...leading us by example in how to be a man for others."

2018 - Rev. James R. Van Dyke, S.J., '77

Father Van Dyke, at time of this publication, had just completed his fourth "tour" at CHS—one as a student, one as a scholastic, and two as a priest—before beginning as President of Georgetown Prep in Maryland. The *Arena* dedication reads, "...For the last two years you have helped guide us with your characteristic humor, integrity, academic rigor, and class...."

2019 - Ms. Andrea Tyrpak-Endres

The dedication to CHS's first female principal reads, "Her keen ability to connect with and understand what is important to every generation is what gives her a unique teaching style. She holds her students accountable and responsible for what they learn.... She is authentic, honest, and caring.... Her love for the school is apparent each time she talks about Canisius."

Notes

[1] "Introduction to the Profile of the Graduate at Graduation (1980). Jesuit Schools Network online resources. Accessed from the internet May 16, 2018.

[2] "Preface to the 2010 Re-Visioned Profile of the Graduate at Graduation." Jesuit Schools Network online resources. Accessed from the internet May 16, 2018.

[3] "One to One: Canisius Rolls Out iPad Initiative for Learning Results." *Canisius High School Today*. Summer 2012 issue.

[4] Cumbo, Paul J. "Digital Citizenship: A Curricular Initiative for Jesuit Secondary Education in the 21st Century – 2015-2016 Year-End Report." Canisius High School internal publication.

[5] "Fact Sheet: Teens and Smartphones. The Common Sense Census: Media Use by Tweens and Teens." https://www.commonsensemedia.org/sites/default/files/uploads/pdfs/census_factsheet_teensandsmartphones.pdf. Accessed from the internet May 24, 2018.

[6] "Rich Tradition. Bold Vision." Canisius High School Capital Campaign promotional pamphlet, 2018.

[7] Provincial Assistants for Secondary Education. (2015) *Our Way of Proceeding: Standards & Benchmarks for Jesuit Schools in the 21st Century.* Jesuit Schools Network, Canada and United States Assistancy, Washington, D.C.

CHAPTER 15

2020 Vision: The Road Ahead

ONE CAN IMAGINE that it would have been hard for the founding Jesuits of Canisius to envision the school one hundred fifty years later. Indeed, as we know from Mr. Kessler's account of the early history, there was uncertainty as to whether the institution would even remain viable. Perhaps we can gain a fuller appreciation for their vision and faith by trying to put ourselves in a similar position: Can we try to imagine what the Canisius High School of 2170—after another 150 years have passed—will be like? It is daunting, and perhaps it seems a little bit audacious and presumptuous. But it's simultaneously compelling, because if the school has survived this long, who is to say it won't be here in another one hundred fifty years? Will it be here on Delaware Avenue? Going anywhere else seems inconceivable—and yet, we know that the move from Washington Street to our present campus was the essentially unplanned result of an unlikely coincidence. Will we remain an all-boys institution? Again, tradition dictates that we shall—but who knows what cultural, fiscal, and circumstantial dictates might yield changes to this in the future? What about the inevitable day to come when Canisius must function without a single Jesuit priest or brother on the staff? Might there be a day when there is a Canisius middle school? A boarding component?

These are all interesting propositions, indeed, but perhaps some are a little too distant and speculative. What we can and should do at this point, however, is consider where we've been and where we are as an institution, with an eye toward the immediate future of Jesuit education in Buffalo. Central to that, of course, is a consideration of the immediate future of Jesuit education more broadly. To gather some insight on this, we turn to the perspectives of three senior leaders of Canisius: Father David Ciancimino, S.J., President of Canisius at the time of this writing; Ms. Andrea Tyrpak-Endres, Principal; and Mr. Robert Reger '66, Chair of the Board of Trustees.

"Audacity for the Improbable"

Father Ciancimino began his reflections with insights from leaders in the Church and connected them with the past, present, and future of Canisius High School.

At this last General Congregation of the Jesuits—GC 36—the Master General of the Dominicans, Father Cadoré, said that we had to be marked by a certain "audacity." He said it's an "audacity for the improbable." And then Father General picked up on that—as did the Pope—and said sometimes we're being pushed in an "audacity for what seems impossible." That audacity should be a mark of who we are and what we do. It's an audacity for what seems improbable, and sometimes what seems impossible. I think that's what led the Congregation to talk about a real ministry of reconciliation that's so important in our world, whether it's a reconciliation with creation, or with peoples. So when we think of the future, and some of the challenges, it's the global nature; it's depth. It's that audacity. There's a certain audacity about the first folks who opened up the high school, right?

When I think of where we are today, we are a school of four Jesuits and a novice. When I look ahead, I see the likelihood of two Jesuits, maybe a third. And that's been the case for a long time now, that's nothing new.... What I see having grown instead is a lot of the non-Jesuits who carry a lot of the buckets with the mission. The Board is keenly aware of carrying the mission of the school....

And that's still an important and vibrant mission. We've always felt as Jesuits—and I know this is shared by those laypeople with whom we co-labor in ministry—that this is a really important time in the life of a young man. So to have the opportunity to plug into their lives at this stage of their growth is pretty important. When we think about the future, about being able to accompany these guys now as they grow and as we form them...we're in service to the Church, the city, the nation, because when we think about who's in front of us today, they are the people who will be the leaders in our school, Church, city, and nation. These kids today are going to be our faculty, staff, Deans, and Principals at Canisius—yes. But they're also going to be leaders in our city, nation, etc. We're trying to influence them for good and for great things now. And that's why I think the focus of what we need to do with them is focus on depth...going deeper...and keeping them reflective.

I look at the growth that has taken place on the campus, and it's hard to imagine that it's ever been in better shape. We have great facilities, faculty, and the students are in good shape...the curriculum is strong. The curb appeal is there. Our athletic programs, student formation, and faculty formation are strong. When we look at leadership, we see the first woman leading the school as Principal. I think the school has come miles from those early days of worrying about leadership.

In the Jesuit world, we don't talk about colleagueship in terms of declining numbers [of priests]; we talk about colleagueship as an essential element of how we do ministry today. But General Nicolas always felt that we Jesuits do better in number two or number three or number four positions, because it's always easier to talk about colleagueship when we're in charge...but when you're not in charge, and you have to be the support from the classroom or the middle management, or whatever, that can change the narrative. And that's where the rubber really hits the road, and I've always been keenly aware of that. He kind of pounded that into the heads of Jesuits during his time.

One of the things I tell alumni from over the past thirty years is that a lot has changed. The building, the courses, the whole wonder of technology and iPads and computers, the library...our programs, our maker space, eSports, etc. Much has changed. The retreat programs were always there, but they're different. Faith, service, academic scholarship—I always say they're kind of the pillars on which the foundation of the school rests. I don't think that's changed an iota. I think we've remained firm on all of those pieces. We want our students, as we always have, to lead meaningful lives, to lead holy lives, to lead just lives in that pursuit of excellence, their relationship with their families, others, and God.

If I have a concern, I go back to something Father General Adolfo Nicolas expressed. It's the challenge of superficiality. We have to be careful that we're not skipping stones when we use our "Ignatian terms" like "men for others" or "magis" or an "Arrupe-ism" or any of that Ignatian jargon. Because there can be a superficiality there, and it rings a little tinny. And Father Nicolas used to say that one of the challenges for the Society of Jesus and our colleagues today is that there is a "universality of superficiality," that he could see that from his vantage point. His real call to the Society was to go deeper. And that's what magis means—to go deeper. Not to do more, because we're great at doing more and keeping it thin. But how do you get roots; how do you go deeper? And that's a challenge that I do think we face today. Greater depth. For each of us, for our colleagues, for those we serve. It's got to start with us, and then it goes down into those we serve.

"Renaissance From Within and Without"

Mr. Robert Reger '66 (Mr. Canisius '66) offered these perspectives on the state of the school as we look ahead to 2020.

My observation, as someone who's not here every day, is that there's a better focus on the complexities of what it means to be a young adult and a young person and a willingness to identify with and accommodate and guide the struggles that manifest themselves in this very critical four-year period. There's more of a compassion for the experience of being young and not fully formed. So I see, at least in my conversations with faculty, I see that as a characteristic. In my conversations with the young men, I'm constantly impressed with their use of the word brotherhood, and that community, and their sense of commitment to one another, and their willingness to engage in all kinds of different [ideas].

It's an overused phrase, but I'll say [I'm impressed by their] intellectual curiosity. I think intellectual curiosity is really important throughout life. I think when you stop being intellectually curious, there's a part of you that just begins to die. And it's funny, because in a very highly disciplined approach to education, the intellectual curiosity component of education gets minimized. I see at Canisius now a situation where intellectual curiosity is encouraged, and it seems freer to me than it did when I was here. These young men—I can have a conversation with them, and I feel, at least for a while, like I'm a part of their community. They're willing to share their perspectives, they're not missing any words—they may be careful of the words they're using—but you get a real sense of them as people, as unique human beings.

I don't think that we would have felt that freedom when we were at Canisius. We would have been much more careful. Much more circumspect. Much more unwilling to say anything other than yes sir, no sir, and be polite. But being polite is a much different thing from sharing in each other's intellectual curiosity.

What do we say: one of our characteristics of our experience is our openness to growth. That's incredibly powerful, and it's a two-way street. Not just the students—*the faculty, administration, board, parents. It doesn't mean chaos. It means something short of that.*

I see Canisius as a more vibrant entity today than I would have seen it when I was here. I was on the Board in the early 2000s. Jim Higgins was the President. He was the man who asked me to be on the Board. I don't think that I was particularly devoted to Canisius at that particular point in time. But Jim was a very compelling advocate for Canisius and he convinced me to do this. I remember having a conversation on the Board level at that point and the idea was that we needed to be more willing to invite people from more diverse backgrounds.... And we were 100% behind it, as long as we made that investment and were willing to follow through. I don't think we're where we need to be yet, but the willingness to create a community that welcomes people of different backgrounds and skin colors and experiences, is, frankly, part of the intellectual curiosity and openness to growth to which I was alluding earlier.

Canisius has challenges. I mentioned earlier that the parochial schools that were feeder schools aren't anymore, because they're either very small or they've closed. Canisius has to find a way to penetrate the public-school constituency to continue to populate 1180 Delaware. Right now, the Board has focused on the issue of enrollment big time and is encouraging initiatives that are designed to crack that nut. That requires a different level of expertise and focus from just contacting pastors and knowing we'd be fine. I think the enrollment is going to continue to be a challenge, and we need to find the right size: I think about 800 kids, about 200 a class. I think that's right.... I think Canisius needs to find a way to invest in faculty. The education is only going to be as good as the faculty at Canisius and I think we ought to be more scientific about establishing Chairs and inviting faculty from different parts of the country to come to the school to see what they can do to expand the way we're operating.

I think the physical plant of the school is "right sized" right now. Maintaining it is a goal. I would personally like for there to be a conversation about a boarding school. I've said this for a number of years. There's always a reason not to do something. No matter what you want to do, there will be somebody who has good reasons why you shouldn't. But if we could figure out a way to bring to Western New York and to Canisius a different group of young men, it has to help in the whole diversity experience. Just coming from a different geographical area is part of diversity. That would be great. And I think it is consistent with the whole notion of the renaissance of Buffalo. Renaissance comes from within and from without. The way to encourage one is to bring people into the community and get them acclimated and rooted and focused and happy. Those four years [of adolescence] are a great time to do it.

"More Counter-Cultural Than Ever"

Andrea Tyrpak-Endres, longtime faculty member and Principal of Canisius, brings broad perspective to the current moment.

The biggest challenge that I've seen in recent years, and this is corroborated by teachers who are in the trenches, is that we have to be more countercultural than we've ever been. We have to call people to a depth of reflection on life, on our responsibilities in a world that no longer teaches responsibility. That's extremely difficult, and I see the next ten years becoming even more difficult....

If we're going to keep our identity, that can't be compromised. We are effectively countercultural by holding to our values as things change ever more rapidly. We've lost a lot of core values in our culture. The solution to problems is often to give up and give in, to compromise, or to react with violence, in destructive ways.

I'm glad to hear kids say that, generally, they know that if they have an issue or a problem, they have people here in the building to talk to. It says a lot about cura personalis. *I like teaching boys because they are resilient and flexible and they have wonderful senses of humor. Men can be very strong in a lot of ways...but they really need that* cura personalis *at this age. It's vital. This is a tough time to be a young man.*

[Because of that] we have to be more proactive in making sure that we are hiring for the mission. That's going to become very key, because as a Catholic institution with a Jesuit tradition, we have to stick to what we believe. We used to have society working with us more. Now we don't. That's why we have to be more countercultural than ever.

As for teaching, we need to be thinking about our formational role more than ever. It has to be more than providing information. Teaching has to be leading. Helping kids to wonder, to be curious, to want to go deeper. How do we get kids to want the "examined life"? Their need to be able to reflect and to empathize with others is vital.... Schooling as a whole is absolutely a different mission than it was twenty-five or even five or ten years ago. We are now in the business of helping them understand why things matter. Why knowledge matters.

The good thing is that we are not going to compromise our mission. We've been through difficult times in the world and we haven't compromised. So many of our programs and curricula have been in response to what's going on out there. We're on top of seeing that, and re-gearing to respond to it.

In Closing

The Blue Doors are central to the Canisius story for generations of young men. They mark the beginning of the four-year journey; likewise, they mark the entry point for each new day at the school. And yet, when Canisius alumni leave the building immediately following Commencement, it is not through those same doors by which they entered. Graduates depart through the front glass doors of the Rand Mansion. It is both a literal and symbolic "threshold moment." It marks a departure from the past and into the immediacy of the future.

Canisius is, in many ways, at a similar threshold moment as we approach our 150th Anniversary. Certainly, it is an important occasion to remember the past, celebrate the present, and turn a hopeful eye to the future. And yet in ways it is no more important a moment than any other. For as a community grounded in the tradition of Jesuit education, we know that *every* moment—no matter how challenging—is a gift from God. It is a continuous work we do, with and for each other—indeed, for all of God's people—*ad Majorem Dei Gloriam.*

CHAPTER 16

Appendix A: Alumni Awards and Recognitions

The Mr. Canisius Award

The Mr. Canisius Award was established in 1962 and is presented annually "to the graduating senior who, in the estimation of his peers, epitomizes all that Canisius stands for. Typically, he is a student who has used his heart, spirit, strength, and mind to an exceptional degree in service to others and love for God. Mr. Canisius possesses and lives up to each of these characteristics. The entire student body, with senior votes carrying the most weight, votes for this award."

1962	Jerry Best	1992	James Swartz, Jr.
1963	Tom Haney	1993	Harvey Young
1964	Jeff Woeppel	1994	Carlos Perez
1965	Tom Lombardo	1995	Noel Sutton
1966	Robert Reger	1996	Thaddeus Kresse
1967	Tim Harmon	1997	Paul Cumbo
1968	Greg Pratt	1998	Brian Lysiak
1969	Larry Chojecki	1999	Martin LaFalce
1970	Mike Connolly	2000	Timothy Leary
1971	Peter Curtin	2001	Timothy Short
1972	Mark McNamara	2002	Joshua Birdsall
1973	Scott Barry	2003	Michael Fitzgerald
1974	Gary Pollock	2004	Stanley Pietrak III
1975	Kevin Curran	2005	Theophilus Ossei-Anto
1976	Bryan Tenney	2006	Timothy Keating
1977	Patrick Plunkett	2007	Cosimo Polino
1978	Paul Gregory	2008	Stephen Brenner
1979	Mark Fitzgerald	2009	John Urschel
1980	Rick Divalerio	2010	Cameron Walsh
1981	Jerry Hokaj	2011	Gordon Lyons
1982	Mike O'Neill	2012	Russell Fiorella
1983	Ken Crosta	2013	John "Jack" Sardinia
1984	John McCarthy	2014	Kevin Driscoll
1985	Mike Naugton	2015	Frank Fialkiewicz III
1986	Hank Nowak	2016	Christopher "C.J." Wild
1987	Salvatore LaDuca	2017	Caleb Blodgett
1988	Timothy Rine	2018	George Burnett
1989	Ben Batory	2019	Joel Nicholas
1990	Thomas Enstice		
1991	Brendan Malley		

The Philippe B. Piedad '93 Accolade Award

The Accolade Award, "named in memory of Philippe B. Piedad '93, honors a graduating senior whose quiet inner strength exemplifies the essence of the Canisius Spirit through academics, athletics, and service."

1993	Jonathan M. Buscaglia & Christopher J. Dobbins
1994	Christopher P. Decker & Timothy J. Patronski
1995	Mitul D. Shah
1996	Craig G. Zakrzewski
1997	Keith T. Erazmus
1998	Joel M. Palachuvattil
1999	Benjamin D. Hamm
2000	John E. Turner
2001	Michael D. Kocher
2002	Nathan R. Menke
2003	Paul Riley
2004	Victor J. Perez, Jr.
2005	Phillip C. Mongiovi
2006	Bradley P. Bogdan
2007	Christopher J. Moy & Patrick T. Raab
2008	Andrew Wingerter
2009	John Brownschidle III
2010	John Michael Cotter
2011	Cole Nathaniel Townsend
2012	Jacob Daniel Foster
2013	William Walton McCauley
2014	William Patrick Christ
2015	John Thomas Marszalkowski
2016	Elliott James Jerge
2017	Christopher Octavious Augustin
2018	John P. Collins
2019	William C.M. Ezquerro

The Jesuit Schools Network (JSN) Award

The JSN Award, formerly known as the Jesuit Secondary Education Association (JSEA) Award, "is presented to the graduate who most closely resembles this ideal: A well rounded person who is intellectually competent, open to growth, religious, loving, and committed to doing justice in generous service to the people of God."

1987	Anthony J. Bellia
1988	Donald P. Leslie
1989	Sean C. O'Brien
1990	Gerald F. Whelan
1991	Richard J. Paolini, Jr.
1992	James J. Swartz, Jr.
1993	Adam P. Cucalj
1994	Kyle R. Cieply
1995	Joseph G. Chernowski
1996	Philip D. Young
1997	Jonathan J. Danner
1998	Nathan A. DeLuke
1999	Daniel A. D'Souza
2000	Dale Bauman
2001	Adam R. Baber
2002	Philip J. Revekant
2003	Daniel Vivacqua
2004	Matthew J. Kubus
2005	Kevin M. Kelley
2006	Gregory P. Cummings
2007	Mark A. Henry & William J. Becker
2008	Robert Egnatchik & Ian Toner
2009	Jacob J. Moy & Timothy J. Sardinia
2010	Zachary W. Deibel & David I. Karambizi
2011	Paul J. Riester & Timothy J. Hartigan
2012	Zachary D. Benfanti & Nicholas D. Sawicki
2013	Jacob C. Dittenhauser & Shane P. Fiust-Klink
2014	Kyle J. Clarey & Jared C. Negron
2015	Ken O. Ngoopos & Hunter R. McLean
2016	Jacob P. Bennett & Michael R. Tenney
2017	Levi M. Collier-Hezel & John J. Russ
2018	Raymond E. Miranda & Joseph A. Ricottone
2019	Nicholas A. Mecca & James F. Twist

The Midshipman 1/C Jeffrey R. Korn Memorial Award

The Korn Memorial Award is "presented to the Canisius High School senior who best exemplifies the characteristics which Jeff respected: outstanding moral integrity, leadership, and sportsmanship."

1983	Phillip Rados
1984	John J. McCarthy
1985	Michael A. Naughton
1986	Raymond L. Flannery
1987	Joseph P. Kennedy & David M. O'Brien
1988	Timothy D. Rine
1989	Robert E. Rice, Jr.
1990	Kevin M. Korn
1991	Jonathan D. Lamb
1992	Gregory F. Shea
1993	Michael E. Horn
1994	Matthew J. Carver
1995	John C. Christ
1996	Ronald F. Parsons
1997	Darren Fenn
1998	Jeffrey M. Kney
1999	James G. Egnatchik
2000	Timothy J. Leary
2001	Thomas W. Coppola
2002	D. Steven Coppola
2003	Thomas Keenan
2004	Herbert E. Glose
2005	Sean David O'Keeffe
2006	Michael J. LoFaso
2007	Peter C. Golinski
2008	Justin Young
2009	John Urschel
2010	Patrick Thomas Dearing
2011	Connor Joseph Mangan
2012	Brendan Eugene Tenney
2013	Massimo Bartholomew Capizzi
2014	Nicholas Jose Santos
2015	Andrew James Heitzhaus
2016	Patrick J. Collins
2017	Michael Mazzara, Jr.
2018	John P. Minogue
2019	Brendan G. Leong

The Thomas W. Hogencamp Memorial Award

The Thomas W. Hogencamp Award for Excellence in Scholarship is presented to the graduating senior with the highest cumulative GPA.

1980	Richard J. Ruh
1981	Gerald A. Niedzwiecki
1982	David J. Barnas
1983	Kevin C. McMahon
1984	Eugene J. Martin
1985	Ronald J. Granieri
1986	Vincent G. Roux
1987	Charles G. Chimera
1988	John P. Sutter
1989	Brian T. Piedad
1990	Nicholas F. Urbanski
1991	Brian C. Rider
1992	William J. Taylor, Jr.
1993	Michael R. Rausch
1994	Joseph A. Ippolito
1995	David T. Boyd
1996	Christopher L. Martin
1997	Jonathan J. Danner
1998	Marc V. Rugani
1999	Matthew J. Koss
2000	Craig R. Bucki
2001	Michael D. Bogdan
2002	John C. Williams
2003	Thomas Keenan
2004	John V. Ricotta
2005	Connor Matthew Oakley
2006	Michael T. Blake
2007	Brian E. Thomson
2008	Gregory Trietley
2009	Alexander Robert Chahin
2010	John Michael Cotter
2011	Geoffrey L. Fatin
2012	Nicholas T. Antoniadis
2013	Shane P. Fiust-Klink
2014	William J. Deuschle
2015	Anthony R. Taboni
2016	Tyler John Will
2017	Mark Michael Matthews
2018	Samuel L. Croce
2019	James F. Twist

Athletic Hall of Fame Members

This list is provided by the Alumni office. An updated list is maintained on the school website.

Michael Ahern '78

Vincent Amoia '81

Leonard Anthony, Jr. '81

Robert Austin '38 *

Keith Bakowski '81

Coach John Barnes, Sr. *

John Barnes, Jr. '76

Timothy Barrett '71

Chris Barry '99

Benjamin Batory '89

John Boehm '57

Christopher Bonn '73

John Brady 1908*

Patrick Brady '77

Martin Breen, Sr. '45*

Joseph Bremer '73

Michael Broderick '56

Arthur Buczkowski '54

Christopher Burns '70

John Buszka '72

David Butler '71

Mark Butler '76

Robert Campbell '22*

John Caulfield '68

Carl Chase '79

John Christ '95

Leo Coleman '64

Stephen Connelly '76

John Connelly, Jr. '44*

John Connolly '41

Alvah Connolly '44*

Michael Connolly '70

Dennis Conrad '70

Alan Cooper '60*

D. Steven Coppola '02

William Coppola '68

James Corcoran '59

Francis Cosgrove '67

Damian Courtin '73

Ryan Crawford '99

Stephen Creahan '69

Emmett Creahan '73

John Creahan, Jr. '77

Kenneth Crosta '83

Martin Crotty '94

Paul Cummings '67*

James Cunningham '54*

Brendan Curley '89

Kevin Curran '75

Peter Curtin '71

Edward D'Arata, Jr. '69

Victor Davis '83

Louis DePerro '31*

Richard Diebold '47

Paul Diehl '76

Joseph Dietrich III '87

Paul DiRosa '66

Richard Dobmeier '46*

Gary Douglas '66*

Elmo Drilling '42*

John Dunnigan '53*

George Ellis '42*

Carl Emerling '73

John Fahey '52*

Daniel Farley '63

William Farley '59*

Darren Fenn '97

William Fisher '68

Mark J. Fitzgerald '79

Raymond Flannery '86

Donald Fornes, Sr. '32*

Frank Fusco '98

L. Robert Gauchat '38*

Philip Gangi '90

Robert Glaser '64

Kevan Green '60

Paul Gregory '78

Peter Grimm '80

Nicholas Grunzweig '38*

Paul Guarnieri '57

Edward Haley '86

Martin Hanaka '67

Donald Harter '49

Frank Hartney '41 *

Brian Hennessy '93

Dale Hohl '53*

Kenneth Hohl '55

Lawrence Hokaj '81

Thomas Housler '66

Edward Howard, Jr., '75*

Jay Jakubowski '95

Mark Jay '71

John Jekielek '65

William Johnson '50*

John Kaminska '73

William Kaminska '76*

Timothy Kane '80

Thomas Keenan '96

Brian Keenan '99

William Knox '67

Ronald Koch '50*

William Koessler '74

Kenneth Komo '56

Jeffrey Korn '79*

Mark Kostrzewski '70

Joseph Krakowiak '63

Kraig Kurzanski '84

Salvatore LaDuca, III '87

Jon Lauria '84*

Michael Lawley '88

William Lawley, Jr. '81

Anthony Leone '69

Michael LoTurco '87

Gerard Lucas '68*

James MacKinnon '55

M. Kevin Maloney '69*

William Maloney, Jr. '80

Peter Mancuso '32*

Peter Mancuso, Jr. '59

Martin Mazzara '84

Michael Mazzara '88

Salvatore Mazzara '91

James McCarthy '53

John McCarthy, Jr. '84

Dennis McCleary '70

Philip McConkey '75

David McCracken '64

Cornelius McGillicuddy '39*

Vincent McNamara '26*

Kevin McNamara '75

Daniel McNaughton '67

Andrew Meaney, Jr., '43*

Anthony Merriweather '82

John Meyers '64

Joseph Michael '64

Lawrence Michael '65

Blue Doors

David Miller '80

Michael Muehlbauer '56*

Richard Myers '60

Paul Narduzzo '77

James Neil '86

Robert Nist '60

Brent Nowicki '97

Edward Odre '76*

Gary Pino '74

Thomas Pitz '63

Mark Pleto

Patrick Plunkett '77

Frank Polino '77

Gerald Pollock '74

B. William Ralyea '64*

Michael Regan, Jr. '52*

Mark Reger '69

John Restivo '94

Nathan Rewers '95

Timothy Rine '88

Marcus Romanowski '85

John Ruffino '72

Richard Saab '58

Donald Salva '53*

Michael Sansone '64*

Paul Sawicz '70

John Sawicz '75

Maynard Schaus '45*

Earl Scheelar '49

Aloysius Schmitt

James Schratz '65

Jeffrey Schratz '75

John Schratz '86

Robert Schuster '70

Kenneth Schoetz '74

Donald Seitz '77

Thomas Sherby '52

Barton Simonian '81

Peter Simonian '94

Sibby Sisti '38*

James Skipper

Paul Smaldone '60

John Stasio '61 *

Gerard State '46*

Rev. John Sturm, S.J., '35*

William Tatu '70

Bryan Tenney '76

Joseph Trimboli '42*

Istivan Tomoga '81

Francis Toomey '40*

John Turner '00

Jon Udwadia '88

Peter Vogt '77

Kevin Walter '73

Richard Watcher '62

Charles Weber '73

Rev. John Weimer '50*

Richard Werder '41*

Mark Werder '76

Kevin White '67

Brendan White '74

Martin White '84

Richard Willett, Sr. '38*

Richard Wnuk '85

Thaddeus Wojcinski '49

Jeffery Woeppel '64

George Zenger '50*

Charles Zernentsch '63

Gerald Zimmerman '13*

David Zygaj '81

* indicates deceased.

Athletic Hall of Fame Team Honorees

1950-51 Swim Team	1972-73 Varsity Football
1951 Varsity Football	1972-73 Varsity Hockey
1952 & 53 Basketball	1977-78 Varsity Wrestling
1961-63 Varsity Crew	1978-79 Varsity Cross Country
1962-63 Varsity Football	1980 Varsity Soccer Team
1963 Varsity Golf	1983 Varsity Hockey
1971 Mile Relay Team	1985-86 Heavyweight Crew
1971, 72, 73 Varsity Baseball	1986 Lightweight Crew
1972 - 1977 Varsity Football	1994-1997 Varsity Baseball

The undefeated 1963 Varsity Golf Team, inducted in 2015.

LEFT – RIGHT: (KNEELING) DANIEL LUCAS '63 AND PATRICK RIMAR '63; (STANDING) FR. JOHN G. STURM, S.J. '35, COACH, ANTHONY KAYE '63*, DAVID STEUERNAGEL '63, ROBERT GAUCHAT '63, AND TIMOTHY GALLAGHER '63*

Alumni Hall of Honor Members

This list is provided by the Alumni office. An updated list is maintained on the school website.

Mr. Ronald F. Ahrens '50

Mr. Joseph F. Basil, Sr. '50

Mr. Thomas R. Beecher, Jr. '52

Rev. Joseph A. Bissonette '50 *

Dr. Charles A. Brady '29 *

Mr. Erik L. Brady '72

Dr. John C. Brady '09 *

Mr. Robert T. Brady '58

Dr. John E. Breen '49

Mr. Norman E. Benz '43 *

Mr. William R. Brennan '38 *

The Honorable Carl L. Bucki '71

The Most Rev. Joseph A. Burke, D.D. '05*

Mr. James D. Burke '49

Rev. W. R. Burns, S.J., '28 *

Mr. Robert E. Campbell '22 *

Dr. Lawrence J. Casazza '56

The Honorable Frank J. Clark III '60

Mr. Paul T. Clark CPA '69

Rev. Monsignor John J. Conniff '42 *

Dr. James H. Cosgriff, Jr. '42 *

Mr. James W. Cunningham '54 *

Dr. Daniel E. Curtin '41 *

The Honorable John T. Curtin '39

The Honorable Charles Desmond '13 *

Mr. Richard J. Diebold '47

The Honorable Kevin M. Dillon '68 *

Mr. Anthony J. Domino '56 *

Mr. Paul P. Dommer '55 *

The Honorable Vincent E. Doyle, Jr. '50 *

Mr. Frank L. Eberl '63

Mr. George J. Eberl '63

Mr. George J. Evans '18 *

Mr. John P. Fahey '52 *

Mr. Lawrence J. Felser '51 *

Mr. Thomas M. Fontana '69

Mr. George Frauenheim '30 *

Dr. L. Robert Gauchat '38 *

Dr. Jerome J. Glauber '28 *

Mr. Eugene P. Grisanti '47

Mr. William D. Hassett, Jr. '53 *

Mr. Ronald J. Hastreiter '50 *

Rev. Franklin J. Heyden '24 *

Rev. Francis X. Hezel '56

Rev. James P. Higgins, S.J., '72 *

Mr. Patrick H. Hoak '68

Mr. Dale J. Hohl '53 *

Rev. Msgr. Sylvester Holbel '20 *

Mr. William Holcomb '52

Mr. Thomas J. Jones '19 *

Dr. Leo A. Kane '50 *

Mr. Bernard J. Kennedy '49 *

Mr. Nicholas H. Kessler '28 *

Rev. Donald L. Kirsch, S.J., '28 *

Mr. Kenneth L. Koessler '25 *

Mr. Paul J. Koessler '55 *

Mr. Robert J. Kresse '45

The Honorable John J. LaFalce '57

The Honorable William B. Lawless '40 *

Dr. Thomas J. Lawley '64

Mr. Raymond A. LeBlanc '48

Rev. Monsignor David M. Lee '60

Rev. Msgr. Eugene A. Loftus '16 *

Thomas A. Lombardo, Jr., MD '65

Mr. Alfred F. Luhr, III '64

Dr. John P. Luhr '39 *

Rev. Monsignor Robert A. Mack '49 *

Mr. Rocco J. Maggiotto '68

Mr. Peter J. Mancuso '32 *

Mr. Ray W. Manuszewski '42

Dr. Joseph M. Mattimore '45 *

The Honorable Edmund F. Maxwell '40 *

Mr. James A. McCarthy '53

Mr. Philip J. McConkey '75

Mr. Charles J. McDonough '20 *

Mr. Cornelius V. McGillicuddy '39 *

Mr. Thomas J. McHugh '27 *

Rev. William W. Meissner '48 *

Mr. Joseph P. Michael '64

Mr. Robert I. Millonzi '28 *

Rev. J. Donald Monan, S.J., '42

Mr. Carl J. Montante '60

Mr. Richard A. Neil '60

The Most Rev. Martin J. Neylon, S.J., '37 *

Mr. Joseph O'Connell, Jr. '39 *

Rev. William J. O'Malley, S.J., '49

Mr. Minot H. Ortolani '47 *

Mr. Norman S. Paolini, Jr. '65

Dr. Donald P. Pinkel '44

Mr. Lawlor F. Quinlan, Jr. '59

Rev. James J. Redmond, S.J., '18 *

Mr. Michael J. Regan, Jr. '52 *

Mr. Robert J. Reger '66

Dr. Edward C. Rozek '33 *

Mr. Mark Russell '50

Mr. Timothy J. Russert '68 *

Mr. Joseph M. Rutowski '52

Mr. Michael J. Ryan '60

Rev. Ronald W. Sams, S.J., '46

Mr. Carmelo A. Scaccia '47

Mr. Maynard C. Schaus '45 *

Mr. Aloysius J. Schmitt '20 *

Dr. George E. Schreiner '39 *

Mr. Francis G. Shinskey '48

Dr. Robert C. Sippel '47

Mr. Sibby D. Sisti '38 *

Mr. Paul J. Smaldone '60

Dr. Ralph Sperazza '64

Rev. John G. Sturm, S.J. '35 *

Mr. Michael F. Thompson '66

Mr. Francis L. Toomey '40 *

Mr. Carl J. Tripi '51 *

Sheriff B. John Tutuska '30 *

Mr. Lawrence J. Vilardo '73

Mr. Eugene P. Vukelic '48

Rev. Gustav A. Weigel, S.J., '22 *

Mr. Richard I. Werder '41

Mr. Charles J. Wick '28*

Mr. Robert D. Wischerath '48

Rev. Monsignor Robert C. Wurtz '50*

Mr. Anthony H. Yerkovich '68

Mr. George J. Zenger '50 *

Mr. Gerard M. Zimmermann '13 *

Rev. Eugene A Zimpfer, S.J., '49 *

Dr. John G. Zoll '30 *

* deceased

CHAPTER 17

Appendix B: Presidents and Principals

Presidents of Canisius High School

CHS has had 35 Presidents in 148 years (as of spring 2018). Notably, until the College moved to Main and Jefferson in 1912-1913, these men also presided over Canisius College, as the institutions were one on Washington Street.

	Name	Years in Office
1	Rev. William Becker, S.J., 1870-1872	2
2	Rev. Henry Behrens, S.J., 1872-1876	4
3	Rev. John B. Lessmann, S.J., 1876-1877	1
4	Rev. Martin Port, S.J., 1877-1883	6
5	Rev. Theodore Van Rossum, S.J., 1883-1888	5
6	Rev. Ulric J. Heinzle, S.J., 1888-1891	3
7	Rev. John I. Zahm, S.J., 1891-1896	5
8	Rev. James A. Rockliff, S.J., 1896-1898	2
9	Rev. John B. Theis, S.J., 1898-1901	3
10	Rev. Aloysius J. Pfeil, S.J., 1901-1905	4
11	Rev. Augustine A. Miller, S.J., 1905-1912	7
12	Rev. George J. Krim, S.J., 1912-1918	6
13	Rev. Michael J. Ahern, S.J., 1918-1919	1
14	Rev. Robert H. Johnson, S.J., 1919-1924	5
15	Rev. Bernard C. Cohausz, S.J., 1924-1930	6
16	Rev. Walter F. Cunningham, S.J., 1930-1936	6
17	Rev. Francis X. Dougherty, S.J., 1936-1939	3
18	Rev. Timothy J. Coughlin, S.J., 1939-1941	2
19	Rev. James J. Redmond, S.J., 1941-1948	7
20	Rev. James E. Barnett, S.J., 1948-1953	5
21	Rev. Gerald A. Quinn, S.J., 1953-1959	6
22	Rev. Donald L. Kirsch, S.J., 1959-1965	6
23	Rev. W. Robert Burns, S.J., 1965-1968	3
24	Rev. Vincent P. Mooney, S.J., 1968-1974	6
25	Rev. Robert G. Cregan, S.J., 1974-1981	7
26	Rev. Joseph E. Billotti, S.J., 1981-1989	8
27	Rev. Eugene A. Zimpfer, S.J., 1989-1989	½ (interim)
28	Rev. James F. Keenan, S.J., 1989-1994	5
29	Rev. Charles F. Kelley, S.J., 1994-1999	5
30	Rev. James F. Fox, S.J., 1999-2002	3
31	Rev. James P. Higgins, S.J., 2002-2008	6
32	Mr. John M. Knight 2008-2012	4
33	Mr. P. Joseph Kessler '81 2012-2013	1
34	Rev. Joseph S. Costantino, S.J., 2013-2015	2
35	Rev. David S. Ciancimino, S.J., 2015-current	4+

Principals of Canisius High School

CHS has had 24 Principals since 1912 (as of Spring 2018). Prior to this, there was no distinct Principal of the high school, as it was merged with the College on Washington Street.

Name	Years in Office
Rev. Michael J. Ahern, S.J., 1912-1918	6
Rev. George J. Krim, S.J., 1918-1919	1
Rev. Robert H. Johnson, S.J., 1919-1924	5
Rev. Bernard C. Cohausz, S.J., 1924-1929	5
Rev. Robert E. Holland, S.J., 1929-1932	3
Rev. Albert C. Roth, S.J., 1932-1935	3
Rev. Vincent J. Hart, S.J., 1935-1938	3
Rev. Walter A. Reilly, S.J., 1938-1940	2
Rev. Lorenzo K. Reed, S.J., 1940-1948	8
Rev. Michael Costello, S.J., 1948-1953	5
Rev. Donald L. Kirsch, S.J., 1953-1959	6
Rev. Edward I. Dolan, S.J., 1959-1963	4
Rev. Louis G. Mounteer, S.J., 1963-1970	7
Rev. Donald G. Divine, S.J., 1970-1973	3
Rev. Joseph J. Papaj, S.J., 1973-1980	7
Rev. Kenneth J. Boller, S.J., 1980-1986	6
Rev. Raymond M. Sweitzer, S.J., 1986-1989	3
Rev. John M. Costello, S.J., 1989-1992	3
Rev. David S. Ciancimino, S.J., 1992-1997	5
Rev. John J. Mattimore, S.J., 1997-2002	5
Mr. Frank D. Tudini 2002-2006	4
Mr. William Kopas 2006-2011	4
Mr. Timothy K. Fitzgerald 2011-2014	3
Ms. Andrea Tyrpak-Endres 2014-2015 (Acting)	1
Ms. Andrea Tyrpak-Endres 2015-current	4+

Bibliography

Arena – First a quarterly publication and eventually an annual yearbook of Canisius High School. Various iterations and editions dating to time of publication.

Arrupe, Pedro, S.J. "Men for Others." Accessed from the Internet March 31, 2017. http://onlineministries.creighton.edu/CollaborativeMinistry/men-for-others.html

The Citadel – The student newspaper of Canisius High School. Various iterations and editions dating to time of publication.

Ryan, Patrick, S.J., Introduction to *Thoughts of St. Ignatius for Every Day of the Year,* a translation of a translation of *Scintillae Ignatianae ("Ignatian Sparks"),* a collection of Ignatius's aphorisms first translated and assembled by Jesuit Fr. Gabriel Hevenesi, S.J., in 1712. Fordham University Press. 2006.

Russert, Tim. *Big Russ & Me – Father and Son: Lessons of Life.* Tenth Anniversary Edition. Weinstein Books. New York, NY. 2014

The Spiritual Exercises of St. Ignatius Loyola, quoted in *What Makes a Jesuit School Jesuit? The Relationship Between Jesuit Schools and the Society of Jesus. Distinguishing Criteria for Verifying the Jesuit Nature of Contemporary Schools.* A booklet published by the Jesuit Conference, Washington, D.C. 2007.

Index

Acknowledgments

THE JESUITS TAUGHT ME that all endeavors should begin and end with gratitude. With that in mind, I extend a most sincere thank you to several in the community without whom I could not have produced this book.

Foremost, I must thank the two deceased sons of Canisius to whom this work is dedicated, Mr. Nicholas Kessler '28 and Rev. Ronald Sams '46. Mr. Kessler's history was the starting point and the scaffold upon which this book is built. Father Sams offered a two-hour interview just a few months before his death. It provided much of the foundational knowledge and insight pertaining to the middle part of the 20th Century.

Miss Gretchen Kessler, in the course of preparing to write a history of Canisius in the early 1990s, compiled an invaluable trove of notes, articles, and archival material. Along with sharing many of her own labors to this end, she sat for an interview that offered deep insight about her father and his work.

Dr. Joseph F. Bieron, PhD., Professor Emeritus of Chemistry & Biochemistry at Canisius College, and Dr. Stephen Ochs, a friend and colleague from Georgetown Prep, both offered essential guidance at the outset of this project based on their experience authoring institutional histories.

Rev. Paul Naumann, S.J., Rev. Richard Zanoni, S.J., Mr. Donald Casciano, and Mr. Paul Zablocki '01 served as draft readers, fact-checkers, and advisors. They offered invaluable feedback.

Father Naumann also served as my editor. His expertise, precision, discretion, and capacity for nuance enabled the completion of this project in finer form that it would have otherwise taken.

Dr. Amy Kimmel of the English Department provided a fine-toothed proof read and valuable feedback near the end of the editing process.

Rev. Ronald Sams, S.J., '46, Rev. Richard Zanoni, S.J., Rev. David Ciancimino, S.J., Rev. James R. Van Dyke, S.J., '77, Rev. Frederick Betti, S.J., Mr. Tom Beecher '52, Dr. Thomas McPherson, Mr. Russell White, Mr. Joseph Lucenti '72, Mr. Robert Reger '66, Mr. Jeffrey Gemmer, Ms. Andrea Tyrpak-Endres, Mr. Dennis Beecher '86, Mr. Don Casciano, Mr. Paul Zablocki '01, and Mr. Jay Josker '01 all generously provided interviews. Seven members of the Class of 1950 offered interviews as well: Joseph Basil, Donald Seitz, Jack Quinn, Richard Griffin, Joseph Scully, Mark Russell, and Clarence Kregg.

I owe a debt of gratitude to my wife, Megan, who has always supported my work in Jesuit education, whether it be here in the classroom or in remote foreign villages where the roads don't have names. Likewise, to my three kids—Matt, Kate, and Ben—who right now are too little to appreciate the school's influence upon their father and his brothers.

To close, I will extend thanks to my own teachers, as well as my students and colleagues, past and present, who have made my time at Canisius tremendously rewarding in so many ways, for so many years. In a special way, I offer my gratitude to perhaps my most influential classroom teacher at Canisius, Mr. Frank Tudini, who coupled exacting standards and high expectations with intellectual inquiry and an obvious love of literature.

ABOUT THE AUTHOR

Paul Cumbo is a 1997 graduate of CHS. He began his career in Jesuit education in 2001 at Georgetown Prep, where he taught for three years while serving on the residential faculty. He has been back at Canisius since 2005, teaching English while serving in various program director roles. He co-founded the Companions/*Compañeros* service learning programs, the Alumni Volunteer Corps, and the Digital Citizenship initiative. He has facilitated national leadership seminars for the Jesuit Schools Network (JSN) and holds master's degrees in writing and educational leadership. He played an active role in designing and implementing the House System at Canisius, and was the first Head of Arrupe House.

Along with *Blue Doors*, Paul has authored two novels, a collection of short stories, and an assortment of essays and articles. He owns PJC Services, LLC, which offers editing, writing, training, and strategic consulting services to clients ranging from individuals, nonprofits, schools, and small businesses to multinational corporations and global nonprofits, including the World Economic Forum. He lives in Amherst with his wife, Megan, and their three children.

More information about Paul's other writing can be found at his author website, www.paulcumbo.com, while his editorial and consulting business is located at www.PJCServicesLLC.com.

He is on Twitter @PaulCumbo.

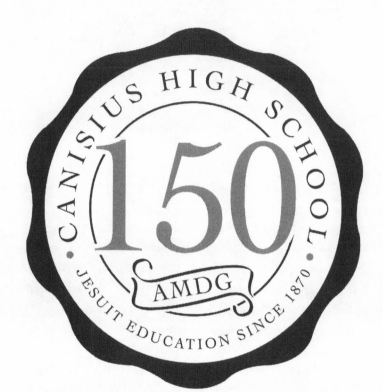